Children with Autism
2nd edition

of related interest

Autism – From Research to Individualized Practice
Edited by Robin L. Gabriels and Dina E. Hill
ISBN 1 84310 701 5

Autism: An Inside-Out Approach
An Innovative Look at the Mechanics of 'Autism'
and its Developmental 'Cousins'
Donna Williams
ISBN 1 85302 387 6

Asperger's Syndrome
A Guide for Parents and Professionals
Tony Attwood
ISBN 1 85302 577 1

Playing, Laughing and Learning with Children
on the Autism Spectrum
A Practical Resource of Play Ideas for Parents and Carers
Julia Moor
ISBN 1 84310 060 6

Music Therapy, Sensory Integration and the Autistic Child
Dorita S. Berger
ISBN 1 84310 700 7

Children with Autism
2nd edition

Diagnosis and Interventions to Meet Their Needs

Colwyn Trevarthen, Kenneth Aitken,
Despina Papoudi & Jacqueline Robarts

Jessica Kingsley Publishers
London and New York

The right of Colwyn Trevarthen, Kenneth Aitken, Despina Papoudi, Jacqueline Robarts to be identified as authors of this work has been asserted by them in accordance with the Copyright, Designs and Patents Act 1988.

First published in the United Kingdom in 1996 by
Jessica Kingsley Publishers Ltd
116 Pentonville Road
London N1 9JB, England
and
29 West 35th Street, 10th fl.
New York, NY 10001–2299, USA

Second impression 1997
Third impression 1998

www.jkp.com

Second edition 1998
Second impression 1999
Printed digitally since 2003

Copyright © 1998 Jessica Kingsley Publishers

Library of Congress Cataloging in Publication Data
A CIP catalogue record for this book is available from the Library of Congress

British Library Cataloguing in Publication Data
Children with autism : diagnosis and interventions to meet their needs. - 2nd ed.
1. Autism in children 2. Autistic children
3. Autism in children - Diagnosis
I. Trevarthen, Colwyn
618.9'2'8982

ISBN 1 85302 555 0

Printed and bound in Great Britain by
Marston Lindsay Ross International Ltd,
Oxfordshire

Contents

List of Tables

List of Figures

Preface to the Second Edition

We began the first edition of our book with the following story:

> A man looked under a lamp post for his lost keys. When asked where he thought he had lost them he said he wasn't sure, but he was looking under the light because it was much easier to see things there.

We said that we wrote our book because all the authors had come to the conclusion that lately autism research has been looking under one particular lamp post because the light there is bright. Interest in language and thinking in autism may have missed evidence that these aspects, which can be measured only in individuals whose mental abilities are functioning at a relatively high level, are facets of a disorder which begins to affect the human mind at a far more fundamental level. Underlying words and reasons, there are motives and emotions that make it possible for human beings to take interest in the world, and, above all, to be conscious of one another and communicate. We believe that language, and the processes of thought based on language, are affected in autistic individuals because these deeper and earlier developing attentional and intersubjective functions are disturbed.

In the second edition, we maintain the same focus on the disturbed motives underlying cognitive and linguistic disorders of children with autism, but add significantly to the evidence from the latest research, and we attempt to give a more comprehensive and unified presentation of a developmental approach to treatment. Every chapter has been rewritten with the addition of new material. We retain the conviction that the baffling complexity and fascination of autism mean that many kinds of information are valuable, and that an attitude that not merely tolerates, but expects to learn from many different methods of providing therapy or teaching for children with autism is needed. Thus we have added a final chapter on 'Putting the Pieces Together'.

There is new information on the findings of brain research, and we have preceded a summary of these by a simplified account of how the human brain develops, and, specifically, how this appears to affect communication in early childhood. We explain why we wish to encourage interest in what music therapy can offer, and why we think that a new attitude among many practitioners of psychoanalytic methods, one that takes note of findings in infant psychology, makes their work of interest for the light it throws on the motivational problems of children whose awareness of persons and feelings about them are compromised by the abnormal development of emotional and communicative functions due to autism. The chapter on educational provision for children with autism and Asperger's syndrome is greatly enlarged in this edition, with information on the latest methods for improving the learning of these children, to give them the best possible preparation for a life of greater autonomy and maximum self-satisfaction in the pleasure of human company.

The appendices summarise medical diagnostic systems, checklists and questionnaires for identifying autism, and give useful Internet addresses for obtaining information on autism.

In everyday life, awareness of others is taken for granted; it is so miraculously complex and efficient. Even toddlers seem to have the necessary psychological insight into what other people do and think, without being taught. Could it be that an autistic child is missing a key part of this set of talents? If so we need to know how an infant or a toddler perceives other people, and how communication is made with them. Developmental psychology can, indeed, lead to a more complete and coherent view of the experiences and feelings of an autistic child, and better interpretation of his or her behaviours and thinking. It can enable us understand better what his or her world is like, and what we might do to help. Rapid gains in knowledge of the developing human brain is also giving helpful information on how, and where, autism might begin and develop.

There continues to be a very active scientific interest in autism, both as a disorder of human psychology, and as a disorder of brain development and neurobiological function. While it is true that researchers in developmental psychology are led by beliefs they have about how cognitive processes develop, and by the tests they have devised to explore these beliefs, biases of interest also develop in research that is trying to identify what has gone wrong in the brains of autistic people, what makes them act the way they do. Time and again parts of the picture are illuminated by measurement of one kind of neurophysiological response, one change in concentration of a neurotransmitter, or one kind of anatomical change for which there is a handy detection technique. The story of the human brain is still very incomplete, like a newly discovered continent seen from a distance. But, there is great team work now among brain scientists and psychologists, with rapidly increasing technical power to see how brains work in regulating the inner and outer life of bodies in interaction with the world. Bit by bit the various patches of information reveal a larger picture. Above all, we are gradually realising that to understand autism, or any other kind of disorder in the human minds, we have to have a concept of how the brain grows, how its parts interact, and how the whole brain it interacts as a complex living system with the body and with stimuli from the world, from before birth until old age.

So, we have to make an effort to perceive the lie of the land, even the parts that are out of light, if we are to find what we are searching for. We will have to make some reconstruction of events that happened before the key was lost.

Most people reading this book will have ideas about autism, but few will have personal experience of living with or teaching an autistic person. Even the average British GP will see but a single autistic child in his or her working lifetime. For the rest of us knowledge might have come from seeing a film such as *Rainman*, in which an actor played an autistic person, or a TV documentary on an autistic individual, such as Stephen Wiltshire or the little girl called Nadia who have shown exceptional artistic gifts (Wiltshire, 1987, 1989; Selfe, 1983). Some will remember the marvellously articulate TV life story of Donna Williams, or the BBC's recent very moving QED programme documenting one family's experience of the Option approach to working with their son (Howarth, 1997). Donna Williams has written several books about her mind as a 'mono-' or 'one-track' processor of reality, trying to explain the often unhelpful responses of even the most well-meaning and 'expert' 'non-autistic' people to her condition (Williams, 1996). Temple Grandin (1995) writes enthrallingly about a different sense of being autistic, how she has learned to combat the anxieties and confusions of her life, and her incomprehension of other persons, to become a respected expert on animal welfare and a much sought after designer of elaborate treatment yards for cattle in abattoirs, designs that respect and reduce the animal's fear. She feels she has been able to make her autistic vision and spatial skills into an asset for a successful professional life.

The preconceptions or insight about autism that we pick up from even the best documentaries, or from books by articulate persons who live with their own autism or with an autistic child, will, inevitably, be incomplete. The fictional media presentations stress features that are judged to be the most 'media worthy', but these features are not necessarily the most important or disabling for those directly concerned. There is much that is mysterious about the problems autistic people have in sharing the world with us, even for the experts, and efforts to help them to realise the potential they all have for some development may seem like groping in the dark. Nevertheless, our review leads us to give an optimistic picture. Methods exist that bring improvements in the lives of autistic persons, and in the lives of those who care for them, or those who attempt to teach them. Autistic people do respond to other people in positive ways, and they learn.

Autism, by a strict definition, is a rare disorder. It affects only about 1 in 2500 people. But, less severe problems that resemble autism more or less closely, called 'autistic spectrum' disorders, affect around 1 in 400 people. There is always an association between cognitive problems (of awareness and thinking) and communication problems, and most children with autism have serious learning handicaps, related to peculiarities in the way they attend to experiences. Many, about 50 per cent, do not speak, though they may understand some of the speech of people they live with. Autism is a so-called 'pervasive' condition, affecting most aspects of a child's life.

Autistic children have problems of inner regulation in their brains that affect both their transactions with the outer world, including people, and the regulation of their bodily functions – digestion, resistance to disease, and so on.

To understand this disorder with all its symptoms we need a clear and balanced view of all aspects of human nature, and especially of its need for human relationships. A child is a kind of being that looks for companionship from parents, siblings, other family, playmates of all kinds, and from the adults who seek to teach meanings, manners, language, and the traditional awareness – of emotional and moral values, as well as beliefs and reasons.

We elaborate a model of autism that draws on developmental psychology and developmental brain science, and we situate the age-related changes in an autistic child's behaviour in relation to the way a normally developing infant gains understanding of the world, and of people, learning by sharing their aims, pleasures and discoveries – how he or she learns to speak and act as a knowledgeable member of society, skilled in culturally defined ways of knowing and doing. We find that recent accounts of the development and education of autistic children point towards agreement that this brings the clearest understanding and the best results (Jordan and Powell, 1995; Sigman and Capps, 1997).

Just about everyone has chatted to a small baby, or watched the wonderful mutual interest that sparks between a mother and her infant. As early as a few minutes after birth we were all capable of responding in that way. We sympathised, and the rhythms of our gestures and vocalisations interplayed with those of our affectionate partner to make a conversation, as shown in Figure 1. We sought for eye contact when our mother spoke to us, moved in time with the melody of her speech, and took our turn. These non-verbal responses and initiations are a part of a basic human repertoire carried in every 'neurologically typical' newborn baby's brain. As we live and learn about the world, and grow stronger and wiser, our innate sympathy for the feelings and interests of other persons remains as the guide to our consciousness and its increasing conventional sophistication. We shared what Margaret Donaldson (1978) called 'human sense' of the world, long before we went to school.

Autism is a condition that affects the development of this inborn prelinguistic interactive system, which serves as the teacher of social understanding. Present knowledge of the maturation of the complex and extensive brain systems involved in motivations for attending, acting and learning agrees with the evidence on emergence in the young autistic child of a pattern of increasingly abnormal behaviour. The time when autism begins, when parents and friends start to feel that something in a child's intelligence and sympathy for others' lives is starting to diverge from what is expected, gives us a vital clue. An autistic toddler's responses to people start to become strange about 18 months after birth, just at the age when language normally begins rapid development. Families have noted differences in some autistic children within the first year, but by the middle of the second year clear symptoms can be identified in nearly all cases, if there is sufficient understanding to recognise them.

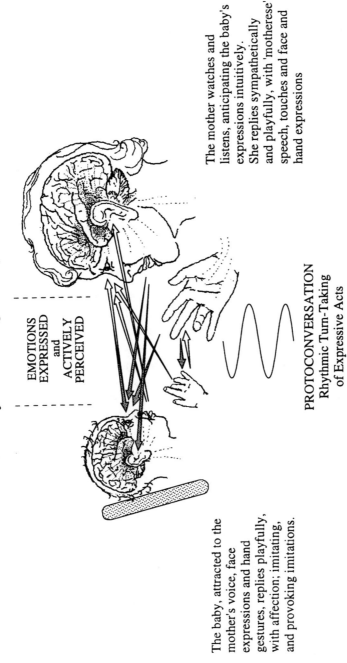

Figure 1: Early communication, between a mother and a two-month-old. This is the period of Primary Intersubjectivity, or direct person-to-person interaction. Rhythmic protoconversations set up the companionship on which the child's future learning in companionship will be built.

A clear picture of how autism begins has only come about by expert attention to age-related changes in infants and toddlers, and by engaging parents as informants in survey research. Ordinary medical attention to child disease missed the crucial signs. Classical theories of mental illness in adults have not provided an appropriate model. It is a major practical problem that in many places the first diagnosis for autism is often as late as six years of age, when a child begins formal schooling. Doctors and clinical psychologists even know of a significant number of persons with Asperger's syndrome for whom diagnosis was not arrived at until well into adult life, after they had experienced many difficulties. Some forms of autism may develop late in childhood, but late recognition is more likely due to inappropriate diagnostic criteria. On the basis of current evidence, it would be relatively easy to set up routine population screening for autism and autistic spectrum disorders as part of normal pre-school developmental monitoring at 18 months. There would be a high degree of specificity in diagnosis, and a fairly low false hit rate. We hope that our account will make it easier for this to be achieved, because we also know that the most effective treatment or special education begins while the child is young, and this is also the time when parents urgently need sympathetic support and informative advice.

We have shared the work as follows. Ken Aitken, the principal clinical neuropsychologist at the Sick Children's Hospital in Edinburgh, with experience of advising many parents in the care of children with autism and other disorders, has taken responsibility for the clinical and diagnostic review and for the explanation of methods of treatment. Despina Papoudi, who completed a PhD study of autistic children in the Psychology Department at the University of Edinburgh in 1993 and is now a lecturer in the Department of Psychology at the University of Rhodes, wrote the sections on play with autistic children and the development of communication and language, and contributed to writing on the discovery and definition of autism. Jacqueline Robarts is Research Fellow in Music Therapy, The City University, London, and works at The Nordoff-Robbins Music Therapy Centre, London and at the Guildhall School of Music and Drama. She helped to establish two music therapy departments in the NHS, where she worked for many years in Child and Adolescent Health and Mental Health services. She draws on her experience of work with autistic and emotionally disturbed children to explain improvisatory music therapy, with a case history to illustrate in detail the difficulties and progress of an autistic child drawn into communication by this non-verbal technique. Colwyn Trevarthen is Professor (Emeritus) of Child Psychology and Psychobiology at the University of Edinburgh. He has incorporated knowledge from 30 years of research on how infants and young children normally develop mastery of interpersonal and cultural understanding, and language, into an account of the ways the motives and learning of a child developing autism go astray. He, with the advice of Dr Aitken, is also responsible for our interpretation of autism as a developmental neuropsychological disorder that originates deep in the motive machinery of the brain from faulty genetic regulations that are probably expressed in the embryo stage, within two months of conception.

There is significant progress in our knowledge, and intense debate, concerning how brain systems are formed before and after birth, about what it all means for psychological growth. Autism is one of the most challenging disorders for developmental brain science, but also a richly informative one. It is helping to change the traditional view that a baby is born without psychological functions, with nervous reactions that serve only regulation of essential bodily needs, needing experience of reality to become conscious of the world and of people in it. Very human motives are shown by newborns, and the newborn brain is elaborately human, even if many structures are incomplete. Autism is a disorder of this innateness.

While we have strived to offer an up-to-date, and accurate, account of both neurobiological and psychological knowledge of autism, and information on the most reliable diagnoses and treatments, we have been conscious of an obligation to present a picture of the whole child, with all his or her motives, and in relation to those persons who have the greatest responsibility for the child's welfare and development. The authors feel that an original contribution of this text is that it appreciates the contributions that less orthodox interventions can give. It is true that some claims for treatment of autism are clearly the fruit of wishful thinking, and we have tried to indicated those, especially those who claim a cure, for which there appears to be no evidence or justification. But other attempts to engage with the motives and emotions of autistic children that do produce beneficial results have, we believe, not received adequate attention, and in some cases they have been treated as unacceptable by agencies who assume responsibility for giving advice to parents and teachers. We think it is time for a more inclusive approach.

However diagnostic or 'typical' the 'mentalising' cognitive deficiencies of children with autism turn out to be, they must, we believe, be consequences of some deeper problem in the development of a child's mind as it passes over the threshold of toddlerhood from infancy. Biological and psychological evidence exists of deficiencies in motivation, awareness and emotional response in relation to others at this age. Note that here 'psychological' is taken to mean more than the ability to form perceptions, to think out problems, to execute strategies of practical action. Most importantly, it includes the motives that impel a person to move while 'looking ahead' to what will happen, that is, that seek out experience prospectively, and that sympathetically relate to the motives and curiosities of others, not just conceiving their thoughts or beliefs (Hobson, 1993a,b).

As we focus on evidence for the emotional attunement of the normal mother–infant interaction, we also examine a variety of methods aimed to support similar intuitive patterns of emotion and interaction between adults and autistic children. Every autistic child retains a deep-seated human feeling for the rhythms and tones of musical and prosodic expression. Improvisational music therapy, as described by Jacqueline Robarts, can draw out and develop the talents of an autistic child to sympathise with the expressive impulses and awareness of other persons. Other techniques for facilitating communication and strengthening the sharing of attention and fragile linguistic skills use training of non-verbal expression and interpersonal contact with very positive results (von Tetzchner and Martinsen, 1992). Some computer generated displays and games that a child can interact with in the company of a teacher may be useful in this work (Heimann et al., 1995; Murray, 1997).

Dr. Olga Maratos, a developmental psychologist and psychoanalyst, who has made an important contribution to infant communication studies, gives us an account of her experience in helping autistic children and their parents in a small special school in Athens. In general, scientific psychologists and educators are sceptical, or outright dismissive, of any approach that seeks to interpret the unconscious motives and feelings of children, as psychoanalysts are trained to do. Interpretations of psychoanalysts, taken too far, have undoubtedly spread confusion and anxiety in the past for autistic children and their parents. The belief that autism is caused by emotional coldness of parents is both unjust and unfounded. But, on the other side, training in psychoanalysis of children has developed a tradition of close observation of the interpersonal reactions between child and therapist, and child and parent. Furthermore, contemporary psychoanalysts working with children have fundamentally revised their explanations in the light of new evidence on the innate powers of self-regulation and communication of infants (Alvarez, 1992, 1996). New understanding in developmental psychology that acknowledges the importance of inborn motives and their communication in the development of human consciousness, has led to a correction in the psychodynamic approach, facilitating the expression of useful insights into autistic experiences of a child, and how they may be assisted. Now this kind of work, provided it is not conceived in esoteric terms that only the initiated can understand, can be brought into effective collaboration with the techniques of management or skills training that have been developed to teach autistic children new habits of communication and learning, and new perceptual and motor strategies, or to eliminate self-injurious or socially unacceptable behaviours.

Finally, help for autistic children with their social, communicative and learning problems must be backed up by awareness of the medical disorders that may affect their health and feelings of well-being. While not pretending to make a comprehensive account of medical problems of children with autism or Asperger's syndrome, we have identified the commonest of these, and specified effective treatments.

CHAPTER 1

Introduction

A Rare and Baffling Difficulty in Communicating and Learning

Every year about 350 children in the United Kingdom develop a disorder of consciousness and feelings that will permanently affect their communication with other people and their ability to learn. For the first years the problem, which typically began many months before birth, is hidden in the emerging complexity of the brain. Parents sometimes remember that in the first year these children were undemanding and placid babies who did not seek to 'chat' in play. Perhaps they had rather weak muscles and restricted or unstable attention, but they did not appear significantly different from other babies at this stage, and raised no cause for concern. By about one to two years after birth, however, at a time when infants usually become acutely aware of other people and what they are doing, full of playful imagination and eager for new experiences, these babies became strangely self-contained or isolated in their own world and increasingly unresponsive or irritable, and difficult to understand; their vocalisations and movements often seemed repetitive and pointless, and their gestures and postures were also odd. Throughout their childhood they continued to express themselves in ways that made parents, teachers and other children feel unable to make contact.

As pre-schoolers, the children are not insensitive to others or unaffectionate, and they can show strong likes and dislikes for particular people. Sometimes they imitate or seek to interact, but never in a free and easy way, and sometimes with a peculiar ritualistic insistence, and remarkable inattention to their effects on other people. Strange postures and movements and a need for sameness, combined with obsessional interest in certain objects and experiences, cut them off from others. At times they seem to be in a trance, 'floating off', 'looking' or 'listening' when nothing is there, often with strange flapping of the hands, or an enigmatic smile, and they only make unintelligible baby-like vocalisations. They may get into inexplicable panics and seem very distressed, anxious or terrified, especially when forced to have close contact with people or in strange environments. In general they dislike, or fear, unfamiliar places or routines. They protest at irregularities in their world and repeat seemingly trivial actions for their own interest. Some, in panicky states or anger, may injure themselves. Most of the time, however, they seem content to amuse themselves, often performing favourite actions over and over. Their behaviours can be frightening and distressing to parents who need help to understand what is wrong and how to cope with a child who looks healthy enough, but won't respond.

About half of these children do not speak at all when they are older. Others who become fluent, or even exceptionally articulate, make inappropriate use of language – echoing what others say, including questions addressed to them, or repeating phrases automatically without obvious sense, mixing up personal pronouns and using pedantically rigid, 'concrete' language with 'odd', idiosyncratic and distracting expression or prosody, the 'music' of speech. Those who can speak and understand language find reversals and negatives particularly difficult. They tend to take utterances literally, missing the point of jokes or metaphors. Often they pick up fragments of sense in what is said to them, and respond to only a part of what was intended by the other person. They can be remarkable skilled at mimicry – reproducing utterances, advertising jingles and the like with startling precision, but irrelevantly, at the same time as they fail to respond to other persons with normal interest and expression in conversation.

Most have marked deficits in attention and intelligence. A few seem very bright and persistent in certain areas, especially in solving visual puzzles or working out and remembering series of events. In rare, but fascinating and theoretically intriguing instances, made famous by the film *Rainman*, a child with this condition may acquire an extraordinary highly specialised or focused ability to draw, to imitate musical performances or to calculate with huge numbers making seemingly miraculous deductions. An autistic girl called Nadia made brilliant perspective drawings from memory when she was four (Selfe, 1978, 1983), and Stephen Wiltshire has become famous for his ability to draw, often from memory, most difficult architectural subjects and cityscapes, capturing space and perspective with a freedom that is the envy of many a professional artist (Wiltshire, 1987, 1989). The memory of more gifted autistic people for intricate details of whatever interests them may, indeed, be astonishing, and difficult for them to live with (Luria, 1969). These, of course, are 'one in a million' cases, often benefiting from exceptionally sensitive support from carers or lucky opportunities to pursue their obsessions. A lucky and courageous few have become successful authors, notably Donna Williams (1996) and Temple Grandin (1995), who have 'broken the barrier' of communication to give some idea in text of what they have, and have not, experienced in community with other persons different from themselves.

In general autistic children are not aggressive, but they may fly into tantrums and struggle or scream if forced to do what they do not want to do. Sometimes they cry out for no apparent reason. Even though they are 'distant' and avoid intimate turn-taking and cooperation, they frequently show affectionate recognition of familiar people who are kind to them, and respond happily to cuddling and rough-and-tumble play. But, unless they are given special and patient encouragement, they do not 'mix in' and share with brothers and sisters, may imitate but do not try to join in play with other children at pre-school and are separate and uninvolved in classroom activities at school. Imitations tend to be automatic or delayed so they serve no communicative function, and attempts to join in play may be awkward and easily misunderstood by others. As adolescents, though sometimes more oriented to others than when they were younger, trying to make friends, they tend to be 'odd' and may act in quite inappropriate, sometimes over-familiar ways, careless of other persons' feelings or customs.

These are the children, known as a special group for 50 years, who are now described as 'autistic'. They are said to suffer from one kind of 'pervasive developmental disorder' – that is they have a disorder of development with many effects on cognition, emotions and behaviour. Though rare, they are well-recognised and distinct from other handicapped or emotionally disturbed children, but baffling to medical and psychological science, and they present very trying problems for their families. They need specialised education because they do not easily fit in with normal school work or keep up in class, but most do respond to carefully adjusted communication and teaching or therapy that fits their individual needs, and they can improve in their responses to people and in their learning. Their condition is not just a mental handicap or learning disability, and there are individuals with no apparent learning difficulties – their development cannot be simply described as 'delayed'. They all have very specific failure of responses to other people, and they need care that recognises and compensates for this.

These characteristics mean that parents and teachers need medical and psychological help to understand autistic children, and teachers need specialised training in the nature of autistic experience and behaviour, and how best to invite communication and motivate cooperative learning. Schools need professional support, and psychologists and teachers must be aware of the ways in which autistic children are unlike other children with special needs. Teaching autistic children needs dedication to intensely sustained procedures that attend to every idiosyncratic sign of response, and the learning environment has to be controlled and stabilised to reduce what the child may perceive as threats or distractions.

In level of cognitive ability or intelligence, perception, use of language, degree of withdrawal, excitability and self-injury and physical appearance autistic persons vary greatly. Nevertheless, the core of their motivation for relating to other persons is always characteristically 'absent' or inaccessible. How can we explain the baffling responses of the autistic child? The consensus now is that we should look at autism in comparison with normal development with careful attention to the changing motives for communication that normally lead children to learn from other persons, both adults and peers.

It seems that the primary cause of autism is related to the 'instructions' for brain development that control the way a child's mind grows and learns from experience, that is by investigating the world, especially the world of other people and their ideas. Autism is one of a much larger group of related disorders that affect the development of motivation and learning in the brains of approximately 1 child in 300. It is the most puzzling because it so obviously affects the basic human capacity for sympathetic thinking and feeling.

There is no known cure for autism, indeed a search for a cure may well be misguided because autism is not a sickness in any simple sense, but our knowledge of its causes in development and how to intervene to help the child and family to compensate for what is failing to function is growing in a period of unprecedented research activity and public interest. An important point is that autism, even for children at the same stage of development, is not a uniform condition with uniform prospects for improvement. In some subgroups of children there are effective treatments, and in a few cases a capacity to follow normal education is possible. A very few, probably with rare reversible states of autism, apparently come out of their confusion and withdrawal to live a rich and balanced life in the community (Kaufman and Kaufman, 1976). With very good community support and skilled specialist guidance, many others who, as adults, remain autistic have steady employment and are valued for their cooperative and conscientious skills (Howlin 1997; Schopler et al., 1984). Autistic children have much brighter prospects now than in the past. Years ago they were often given basic health care in a mental hospital or a home for severely retarded children and given little therapy or teaching, and indeed little opportunity for human life. Nevertheless, creation of adequate support services and education for autistic children from infancy to adolescence is a project that advances in very uneven ways in different parts of the world, and in different local communities within even the most well-resourced countries.

Commitment to methods that engage each child's investigative curiosity, and sense of pleasure, and his or her sensitivity to the behaviours of others, including other children, is essential, and to succeed any practice must involve parents in an organised way, responding to their difficulties and worries directly. Autistic children have very specific and multiple special needs which change with age. To meet their needs we have to develop the imagination and skill to step into their world, so they know we are there, with them.

CHAPTER 2

The 'Discovery' of Autism, and Many Definitions

First Description and Changing Explanations

The word 'autism' is a compound of two Greek words – 'aut-', which means 'self', and '-ism', which implies 'orientation or state'. So, autism could be defined as the condition of somebody who is unusually absorbed in him or her self (Reber, 1985). This captures how autistic children fail to act with interest in other persons, but misses many other features of their behaviour. It does not help us understand what the world of an autistic child is like.

The first accepted clinical paper presenting a clear picture of the psychological features of children called 'autistic' was published by an American psychiatrist, Leo Kanner (Kanner, 1943). The following year, a German psychiatrist, Asperger (1944), in a paper that remained obscure for many years, described a closely similar condition. Children with Asperger's syndrome (Wing, 1981) are similar to the least affected 'high-functioning' autistic children. They have obvious social awkwardness and lack of interpersonal understanding, exhibit a variety of patterns of cognitive and linguistic development, and are prone to clumsiness. This and other conditions with similarities to autism are discussed in Chapter 3.

Of course, there were autistic children before Kanner's paper, but they were generally thought of as psychotic or mentally deficient, and not recognised as a distinctive group. Many earlier reports of strange children – such as those of Victor, the 'Wild boy of Aveyron' who, at ten or eleven years old, was discovered and captured in 1799 in the remote woods of southern France, north-west of Montpellier, and then cared for and meticulously described by a young doctor, Itard (1801); and of Kaspar Hauser, reportedly discovered in 1828 (Tredgold and Soddy, 1956) – appear to identify the condition which Kanner so lucidly described (see Frith, 1989 for discussion and further examples).

Kanner, who called the condition he recognised 'early infantile autism', concluded that the essential characteristic is a 'biologically provided disturbance of affective contact'. This was a very important step, because it set the medical profession the task of understanding how the mind of a child becomes capable of establishing **emotional contact with other persons.** For many years before Kanner's paper, the term 'autistic' had been used to describe features of persons with schizophrenia (Parnas and Bovet, 1991). Bleuler (1913) employed it to mean actively withdrawn behaviour. He described the thinking of schizophrenics as autistic because it corresponds, not to reality and logic, but to fantasy. It is important to point out, however, that 'autistic thinking', in Bleuler's sense, is quite normal when people are being imaginative and creative. Thinking inwardly has an 'assimilatory' role, fitting reality to the fabrications of imagination and what has been retained in memory. Only if the balance between 'autism' and 'realism' is lost does a pathological form of behaviour emerge. Autistic children, however gifted a few of them may be, cannot be said to have normally creative imaginations. Autistic indifference to persons and their motives and feelings is not just the result of absorption in fantasy.

There is still belief that autism can be defined as a fault in **systematic reasoning.** In one 'microsociological' analysis of the logic of their thinking and interactions with others (Durig, 1996), autistic persons have been said to lack 'creative induction' (reasoning that moves from specific premises to general conclusions), while retaining 'deduction' (arriving at specific conclusions from specific premises) and 'abduction' (taking general premises to specific conclusions). But any features of autistic thinking corresponding to these very abstract or ideal rules of reasoning must be reflections of more fundamental disorders in the motives of individuals with autism for moving with purpose and for attending to the environment. After all, as we shall see, autism can be diagnosed in a child under the age of two, before language, when all thinking and imagining is involved with emotional expressiveness and social sharing of behaviours. Infants may be logical, but their system of reasoning must be more practical – directly involved in the movements of conscious interest in the world that is present, with special value given to what people offer in patterns of emotional response. Gradually they exercise more and more imagination, planning ahead and working out alternatives, predictively.

Kanner's and Bleuler's descriptions differed in the assumed innateness (or not) of the cause of social withdrawal in autism. This has been a point of contention all through the last 50 years, and Kanner himself changed his mind. Only now can we be sure that Kanner's first conception, that it is a 'biological' disorder of the mind, is essentially correct, and by far the most useful. Autism is the consequence in mental life of a complex disorder of brain development affecting many functions of perceiving, intending, imagining and feeling. As we come to understand this cerebral/mental disorder and its effects better, we will be more effective in assisting autistic children's development.

But the idea that an infant might have a mental illness was difficult to accept. In the decades following Kanner's accurate recognition of the features of autism in children under three, psychoanalytic preconceptions about the lack of psychic structure in the infant led to confused interpretations of the nature and probable cause of the condition. After all, if infants are born with no idea of other persons, with no conception of any 'object', they must also lack 'affective relating'. How could there be an innate disorder of a representation that does not exist at birth? The term 'infantile autism' was taken by Margaret Mahler to imply both an assumed normal phase prior to the development of self-awareness and a type of childhood psychosis (Mahler, 1952). During the phase of what Mahler calls 'normal autism', from birth until the second month of life, the infant is described as being unable to differentiate between him/herself and the outside reality, and therefore unable to relate to the mother as a separate 'object' distinct from the 'self'. Pathological autism (infantile autism) is then described as being caused by the fixation or the regression to the primary 'normal autistic stage'; the child who is stuck in this stage, or has slipped back into it, cannot orient to anything outside, so is restricted to his or her own self-centred world. Anthony (1958) also argued that autism occurs in infancy as a normal phase, and that the psychopathological form emerges only if the child is arrested in or returns to the 'normal autistic period'. Tustin (1981) took a similar approach, explaining autism as a normal phase in infancy in which the child cannot yet differentiate between the sensations of the 'self' and those of the 'not-self' (mother). Recently, however, she concluded (Tustin, 1991, 1994a) that this is manifestly an incorrect interpretation, because normal infants do not in fact behave at all like autistic children; '...there is not a normal infantile stage of primary autism to which the pathology of childhood autism could be a regression.' (Tustin, 1994a, p.3). Tustin reports that Mahler also changed her interpretation of the nature of autism, in response to the new information in Daniel Stern's book (Stern, 1985) on what young infants can normally do in communication (see Tustin, 1994a, p.5). Stern argues, from detailed observations of behavioural interactions and experiments with the discriminative reactions of infants to the stimuli from a person, that the infant is born with a self, and is immediately able to enter into an emotionally regulated engagement with the mother. Much evidence on these points was collected in the 1960s and 1970s (Trevarthen, Murray and Hubley, 1981)

As we shall describe, infants freely and sensitively seek to communicate from birth, and they need sympathetic company to develop their minds; they also exhibit rapid developments in motor and perceptive capacities, and in the regulation of both internal state and the awareness of their moving bodies. Tustin was led by her clinical observations, which we shall discuss more thoroughly later, to relate autistic hyper-sensitivity to bodily stimulation, with avoidance of others' 'intrusions', to the observation that a baby is often much involved with feelings of his/her own body and of its contact to the mother's body. She initially thought that if a serious emotional disturbance occurs in early life, the infant might react by developing pathological autism, in this sense as a 'shell' to protect an over-sensitive self. As we have said, she subsequently took evidence on the elaborateness of normal mother–infant communication in early months as evidence that autism must be a disturbance in the innate mechanism for relating to persons; that it relates to a *pathological* state of the infant, and is not a regression to any normal stage.

The more extreme psychoanalytic ideas of the recent past, about a normal autistic phase in infant development, based on inferences from behaviours of adult patients and older children with psychiatric illness, are now called seriously in question by the evidence from research on communication in very early infancy. Observations of babies' reactions to persons from a few hours after birth show that they are born, not only with the capacity to distinguish themselves from other persons, but also able to communicate by imitating expressive behaviours reciprocally, and with emotion (Kugiumutzakis, 1993; Meltzoff, 1985; Nagy and Molnár, 1994; Trevarthen, Kokkinaki and Fiamenghi, 1998). Newborns show purposeful orientations to the world, using inbuilt plans for moving to create useful experiences (Trevarthen, 1997a). Normally developing infants may be building new more ambitious motives and new cognitive abilities for communicating with persons and for manipulating objects, and they certainly gain new efficiency in physiological and psychological self-regulation, but they are not, at any age, like an autistic child (Trevarthen, 1993a). Nevertheless, the relation of autism to pathological conditions in adults where the self is poorly or inappropriately demarcated remains a significant problem (Hobson, 1990a, 1993a,b).[1]

The scientific psychology of infants has advanced greatly in the past 50 years, but there has been a bias towards considering the first steps of mental life as the making of a rudimentary philosopher-scientist, in the spirit of the seventeenth-century French philosopher René Descartes who explained his consciousness with the famous expression, 'I think therefore I am'. The infant has been viewed as an active explorer of sensations and objects, building, primarily on his or her own, images or concepts that can be used to make sense of the world. People are part of the 'objective' world to be understood. The Swiss child psychologist, Jean Piaget (1954, 1962), who was primarily interested in the intellectual development of children as active, problem-solving individuals, thought, like Sigmund Freud, that the infant and toddler had an undifferentiated 'egocentric' consciousness, that they could not take the view of any other person into account until an 'object concept' had developed which could 'represent' an outside object, event or cause. Some suggest that this supposed 'egocentricity' can also be interpreted as 'normal autism', but in Piaget's theory the emphasis is definitely on the mechanism of general knowing

---

1   In Chapter 12 Dr Olga Maratos explains how she uses a modified psychoanalytic approach to help autistic children and their parents.

(cognition), or perhaps on perception of objective or physical phenomena, and not on the interpersonal 'object relation' of the psychoanalysts, with its subjective and emotional regulation.

Piaget's theory, too, requires modification in the light of our present understanding of infant's early abilities for communication with the motives and feelings of other persons. The infant or young pre-school child can share in the everyday 'human sense' of the world with a purposeful and other-conscious enthusiasm (Donaldson, 1978). Infants learn about the sense of things by sharing them; children have a natural appetite for meanings in community (Bruner, 1996; Trevarthen, 1987a, 1992). We know more now about how communicating with companions of all ages contributes to a child's cognitive development, in collaboration with a different set of motives for private, investigative, problem-solving learning about the properties and uses of objects. This new understanding is discussed in relation to the peculiar difficulties of an autistic child in Chapter 8.

The Background to Medical Diagnosis of Autism

In the past 20 years, as psychological studies and theories of the nature of the disorder and its development have changed, medical definitions of autism have become more precise, moving away from concepts applied in adult psychiatry, and such diagnoses as 'mentally subnormal' and 'emotionally disturbed'. In the process, US and European diagnostic systems have differed considerably, and a succession of revised systems have appeared. Now differences on the clinical or medical side are resolved. Child psychiatrists use a uniform set of criteria everywhere to detect autism, and to compare it with other conditions treated as mental illnesses or as developmental disorders affecting behaviour.

Psychological assessment of children first used intelligence tests to measure their capacity to benefit from education. Gradually it became clear that, although it is possible to adapt testing procedures to get an IQ score for an autistic child, the peculiarities of their mental processes are so unusual and variable that this is an inappropriate way to approach children diagnosed as autistic. Observations were made on how autistic children behave in a wide range of situations, and tests devised to reveal how they differ from other children of their age in the way they attend to experiences and relate to other persons. Comparisons were made with normally developing children and those with other handicaps, often with an attempt to match for level of cognitive development (Mental Age score) or language proficiency so the features of awareness and thinking peculiar to autism could be revealed. Professionals continue to differ in their estimation of the extent to which the primary disorder is emotional, social, cognitive or 'meta-cognitive', but a great archive of information is now available in the literature on what children with different diagnoses, including autism, do with objects and with people in observational situations. These are supplemented by questions of parents concerning the development of the child they know at home and every day. It is evident that, as different models come in and out of favour, so what are accepted as scientifically valid measures of the condition also change.

Kanner's original idea was that the autistic child was born with an '...innate inability to form the usual biologically provided affective contact with people' (Kanner 1943) and, as we have said, he perceived autism to be 'a biological disorder of affective functioning'. This remains the central concept, and the basis for all psychiatric assessments. Gradually these assessments have moved from listing symptoms towards more coherent theory-based criteria that define autism in functional terms, separating learning difficulties of various kinds from disorders that impair social and interpersonal behaviours. The evidence is clear that there is no one, uniform condition; autism belongs to a family, continuum or spectrum of related disorders affecting cognition, affect and communication.

For many years after 1950, the psychogenic (psychoanalytic or psychodynamic) view that autism arises from cold emotionless parenting was predominant. Kanner, in later writings, when he was persuaded by this psychiatric theory, referred to this as 'refrigerator parenting' (Kanner and Eisenberg, 1956; Kanner, 1973). Bettelheim (1967), a child psychiatrist who specialised in psychodynamic treatment of abused and emotionally disturbed children, insisted on this interpretation of the cause of autism, although there was no more than circumstantial evidence to support it. Bettelheim undoubtedly knew a great deal about the behaviours of emotionally disturbed children, and is reputed to have been a sensitive clinician, but he has received opprobrium for his authoritarian recommendation that children with psychiatric disorders, including those diagnosed as autistic, should be separated from their parents and put in special institutions for therapeutic treatment.

With the advance of brain science and new concepts of how brain systems regulate psychological functions of perception, memory formation and thinking, there has been a major shift towards recognition that in virtually every case, even if there are other aggravating problems in the world of the child, there is evidence of an organic factor. That is, some abnormality in brain function and/or anatomy will be found if adequate examination can be carried out (Steffenberg, 1991) (see Chapter 5). But, even though Kanner's original view, that the primary cause is 'biological', is now generally accepted, it is obvious that there is no one local problem in the brain, and psychologists still offer many different views on how the functions of the child's mind are disturbed. These are usually divided into two main groups: those that consider the most significant problem to be a failure of awareness and thinking or **cognition**; and those that see self-regulation and control of interactions with other persons by motives and feelings, by **emotion**, to be the primary problem for the child with autism. More and more it becomes clear that this distinction is unnecessary and unhelpful. Autism is perceived most clearly, and responded to by therapeutic and educational methods most effectively, if the child's problems are seen to arise from the coordination of internally generated purposes and emotions with cognitions that process information from perception, and, most importantly, the child's state of mind and awareness is seen to be responsive in particular ways to the behaviours of other persons. It is not an 'either cognition or emotion' question.

In the UK, autism has been identified as a medical condition or neurological disorder requiring special educational treatment. Recognition of the problem was pioneered by Lorna Wing (1969). The English child psychiatrist Michael Rutter has applied an empirical approach in large epidemiological surveys and taken a leading role in defining criteria for discriminating and classifying varieties of psychotic disturbance in childhood (Rutter, 1966, 1978, 1983). His surveys have employed case notes from psychiatric examination and available standardised tests of children's intelligence, as well as evidence from parental interviews, and, more recently, notes made by clinicians in observation rooms where the child is in the presence of objects and examiners, as well as the results of psychological tests of children's problem solving and understanding of narratives about other persons' experiences and thoughts (Bailey, Phillips and Rutter, 1996). Lorna Wing (1976, 1988, 1996; Wing and Gould, 1979) has contributed a systematic analysis of the features of autism that has become the foundation for the clinical definitions.

In reaction to psychoanalytic theories of an environmentally induced emotional pathology, Rutter and Eric Schopler, the originator of the American TEACCH training system for autistic individuals, have firmly maintained the view that the only scientifically supported theory is thàt autism is primarily a disorder of 'cognitive processing' (Rutter and Schopler, 1978, 1987). However, in response to controlled psychological experiments that have measured autistic children's perceptions of persons and their distinguishing features (Hobson, 1983), Rutter has conceded that it is primarily social and emotional functioning that is affected. He expresses the turnabout in his thinking as follows:

> ...we are forced to the conclusion that autistic children's social abnormalities do stem from some kind of 'cognitive' deficit if by that one means a deficit in dealing with social and emotional cues...it appears that the stimuli that pose difficulties for autistic children are those that carry emotional or social 'meaning'. (Rutter 1983)

Subsequently, the view that autism is essentially a disorder of awareness and thinking that leads to losses in social functioning has been restated in more sophisticated form by psychologists Leslie, Baron-Cohen and Frith (Baron-Cohen, Leslie and Frith, 1985). Taking evidence from how speaking autistic youngsters fail to understand questions about other persons' knowledge and beliefs that normal five-year-olds find easy to grasp, they describe the condition as stemming from a primary disorder of 'meta-cognition' or 'interpersonal perspective taking' or 'thinking on thinking', especially **thinking on other persons' thinking.** The claim to have discovered a core deficit in the way all autistic children conceive the functioning of minds of other persons, and of their own minds. The idea comes from philosophical examination of how people might imagine other persons' beliefs, and especially from tests, inspired by this philosophy, of how children gain this ability (Baron-Cohen, Leslie and Frith, 1985, 1989; Leslie, 1987; Perner *et al.*, 1989). Papers reporting how autistic children, when interrogated, differ from normally developing age mates or much younger children in their interpretation of what characters in stories can imagine from their experiences, have given hope that a new understanding has been gained of the mechanisms by which personal attitudes and ideas are represented in the developing human brain. However, it is clear that this exciting analysis applies meaningfully only to 'high functioning' autistic children, the tests or demonstrations of 'theory of mind' failure being applicable only to individuals who understand language and speak. Theory of Mind theorists have, moreover, to find a way of explaining what the problem is for an autistic two-year-old who shows none of the normal willingness to share experience with others. No child of this age is old enough to have anything like what is identified as a theory of mind (Sigman and Capps, 1997). Evidently we need a theory of how human minds interact without any articulate theory about it, and why they are emotional about their interactions.

The cognitive view is to a large extent based on the assumption, traditional in modern medicine, as in the theory of educational instruction, that emotion must always be the lower-level output organised by some form of emotion-free higher cognitive-perceptual processing system that responds to information from both the environment and from the 'self' with its body. This premise, basic to the philosophy of rational individualism, has been under considerable scrutiny by developmental psychologists, and today it seems largely untenable. Emotions in a child are revealed to be organising principles of the mind that are communicated directly to other persons by facial, vocal and other expressions of activity in a coherent and intrinsically active conscious self. Emotions of young children do not depend upon the kind of culturally regulated cognitive or 'inner language' processes assumed to be essential for a person to possess 'meta-cognition', or a 'theory of mind' (Barnard and Teasdale 1991; Hobson, 1993a; Izard 1993; Schore, 1994; Trevarthen 1993b). There is support for a different view also from neuropsychology, the scientific examination of brain mechanisms of intelligence and their disorders in persons of all ages. Study of the effects of brain injury on adult thinking, personality and emotions shows that it is impossible to distinguish independent mechanisms for cognition and emotion, every significant psychological function, including reasoning and language, requiring both (Damasio, 1994). Now an 'Emotional Motor System' is identified with an intricate core system of the brain. This is able to influence activity in all other parts of the brain, and able to communicate its states by expressive movements, while reacting to the expressions of brain states in other individuals (Holstege, Bandler and Saper, 1997). (See Chapter 6 for information on brain mechanisms that show signs of abnormality in autistic individuals.)

A number of researchers and clinicians, while agreeing that the social deficits are central in autism, have argued that these are not to be seen as consequences of cognitive deficits that lead to problems in thinking about social and emotional information, but that they are primary deficits of an essentially non-cognitive (non-rational) nature (Fein, Pennington and Waterhouse, 1987; Rogers and Pennington, 1991):

> It is our contention that the social deficits in autism cannot be reasonably attributed to more primary cognitive deficits, but should be regarded as primary manifestations of the neurological disorder. (Fein, Pennington and Waterhouse, 1987)

Hobson has carried out tests of autistic children's perceptions of emotional expressions and their sense of the social significance of emotions. He concludes that they have an inability to relate to others as persons, or lack the capacity for 'intersubjective co-ordination with other people' (Hobson, 1993a). Similar difficulties in recognition of emotions in others have been reported by Macdonald and colleagues; however they interpret this deficit in cognitive terms as a 'deficit in recognition of emotional cues' (Macdonald et al., 1989). Sigman and Capps (1997) have demonstrated that, while autistic children are not insensitive, they fail to show the usual empathic reactions when their mothers demonstrate emotions of pleasure, fear or pain. As toddlers, they fail to understand the narrative connections in a story that are motivated by how people act and feel about what happens.

Thus 'autism', indeed a fascinating and confusing condition, remains enigmatic and provocative in spite of the advances made since it was first described some half a century ago. The developmental approach seems to offer the best prospects of a unified theory. Advances in developmental psychology help us relate the progressive isolation of the autistic child, and his or her failure to learn in communication, to normal stages of social or interpersonal development and learning (Sigman, 1989; Sigman and Capps, 1997; Rogers and Pennington, 1991; Nadel and Pezé, 1993). Especially significant are the changes that occur in late infancy and pre-school years, in eagerness to learn about meanings in the family culture and in games with child companions. The comparative-developmental view, and its origin in research on mother–infant communication, is discussed fully in Chapter 8 in relation to what fails to develop in autism.

Seeking a Standard Description

'Autistic infantile psychosis' (Mahler, 1952), 'childhood schizophrenia' (Creak, 1964; Wolff and Chess, 1964), 'early childhood autism' (Wing, 1966), 'autism' (Tustin, 1981), 'autistic disorder' (DSM-III-R, 1987) have been used as synonyms of the syndrome that Kanner first described as 'early infantile autism'. What is the whole child like whom these different terms are attempting to describe?

Kanner (1943) listed the main characteristics of an autistic child's behaviour as follows:

(1) an inability to establish social relatedness

(2) a failure to use language normally for the purpose of communication

(3) an obsessive desire for the maintenance of sameness

(4) a fascination for objects

(5) good cognitive potentialities

and

(6) these characteristics appear in the child before the age of 30 months.

Kanner's conclusion that autistic children generally have good cognitive potentialities appears to have been a result of his sample, which was composed of children of parents with above average intelligence, who were also high achievers, and possibly accidental inclusion of children with exceptional intellectual abilities. Children now classified as showing Kanner's autism generally have low IQ, and limited capacity for gaining in cognitive ability (Cohen and Volkmar, 1997). It is noteworthy that in subsequent descriptions Kanner reduced the main features of the autistic syndrome to two, less specific, which appear to identify qualities of *motivation* for relating to other persons and to the shared environment (Eisenberg and Kanner, 1956):

(1) aloneness, and

(2) obsessive desire for sameness.

Gradually, psychologists began to abandon attempts to assess autistic children with conventional intelligence tests, and especially those requiring verbal communication, in favour of more detailed examination of the abilities and behaviours of individual children (Mittler, 1966). Ornitz and Ritvo (1968), taking an approach influenced by conventional categories in laboratory psychology, which subdivides the functions of the subject in relation to discrete stimuli and the responses to them, classified the symptoms of early infantile autism into five subclusters, identifying disturbances of:

(1) perception

(2) motor behaviour

(3) relating

(4) language, and

(5) developmental rate and sequence.

Subcluster 1, the inability to maintain constancy or coherence of *perception*, was considered to determine all the others.

In the 1960s information was sought on autistic children's problems in cognition and language as symptoms of presumed neurological damage, to sharpen up distinctions between forms of childhood psychosis (Rutter, 1968). Rimland (1964) introduced a parental questionnaire to trace the onset of autism and the course of speech development and other symptoms, which has since (Rimland, 1971) been developed into the Diagnostic Checklist for Behaviour-Disturbed Children (Form E-2), widely used in analysis of medical conditions associated with autism and the effects of medical treatments (see below).

Rutter (1978) proposed the following diagnostic criteria:

(1) onset before 30 months

(2) impaired social development

(3) impaired language development, and

(4) insistence on sameness.

The last three criteria in this list became known as the 'triad of impairments' defining autism (Wing and Gould, 1979). They are the same as Kanner's first three characteristics of autism.

These diagnostic descriptions typify understanding of autism before the effort of the last 15 years to obtain a more subtle standard of diagnosis, one that can serve as a basis for research and treatment, and that will discriminate different types of autism and their relation to similar disorders of childhood. There is agreement about the social detachment and obsessional behaviour of autistic children. Level of language and of cognition or intelligence are generally lowered, but vary widely, with selective retention in many cases of certain types of intellectual ability (Shah and Frith, 1993). The ritualistic, stereotyped exploration of objects and insistence on sameness seem to be manifestations of an abnormal investigative or executive motivation, or they may be defensive, protecting from invasive experiences or novel situations that the child cannot understand or predict (Bishop, 1993; Jarrold, Boucher and Smith, 1994; Richer, 1978). They may point to a fault in regulation of motivation for attention and experience that should be addressed by those seeking to help the child, or to educate (Sigman and Capps, 1997; Jordan and Powell, 1995; Powell and Jordan, 1997; Peeters, 1997). They indicate the importance of sensitive, carefully adapted responses by any person who is attempting to gain the autistic child's confidence, affection and cooperation.

Varieties of Autism

> We may conclude that there is no doubt that autism constitutes a valid and meaningfully different psychiatric syndrome; indeed the evidence on its validity is stronger than for any other psychiatric condition in childhood. (Rutter and Schopler, 1987)

Despite acceptance that autism is a distinct and clearly recognisable medical condition, there is still considerable debate over the most useful diagnostic criteria (Aitken, 1991b). Autism remains a useful clinical entity, but evidently there is a range of autistic conditions that requires subdivision (Gillberg, 1991a). Classical Kanner's autism is but a part of this range. The refined definition, and, at the same time, a reduction in number of cases identified as autistic have come about as follows:

- There is increasing knowledge of a variety of biological causative factors, with clearer perception of different conditions that develop from them, some of which are not now accepted as 'autism'.

- There has been a significant reduction in the number of cases of autism caused by the genetic condition Phenylketonuria (PKU), which leads to abnormal accumulation of an amino acid that poisons the brain, or due to the infection of a mother with the viral disease rubella (German measles) in early stages of pregnancy.

- It is now accepted that Asperger's syndrome (Ghaziuddin *et al.*, 1992) and the mental retardation known as Rett's syndrome (Hagberg *et al.*, 1983; Hagberg, 1989) are distinct, but related, clinical conditions (see below). In the past, these were classified as 'autism'.

There are many different kinds of disorder in human psychological abilities and learning that can arise in childhood, either from a congenital change in the way the brain develops, or as a result of imposed damage to the brain, or from a mixture of genetic and environmental effects in the brain. Some of these factors affect intellect or language rather discretely. Autism comprises a subgroup that deeply affects intrinsic regulations of awareness and motor engagement with experience, that is it affects *motives*, and within autism there is a range of impairment, communication, thinking and learning being affected to differing degrees. Gillberg (1991a) has described this range as, 'a spectrum of disorders of empathy', identified in various ways, and the term 'autistic spectrum' is now widely adopted in accounts of the various manifestations of autism (Wing, 1996; Bailey, Phillips and Rutter, 1996).

Medical Diagnostic Systems: ICD-10 and DSM-IV

Two well-documented and internationally accepted diagnostic systems – the World Health Organisation's International Classification of Diseases (ICD), now in its tenth version (WHO, 1993), and the American Psychiatric Association's Diagnostic and Statistical Manual (DSM), currently in its fourth edition (DSM-IV; APA, 1994), are used to classify autistic children. Prior to the widespread medical acceptance of these systems there was a confusing variety of criteria, summarised in Appendix 1, Table 1.

Diagnostic systems developed since 1980, including ICD-10 and DSM-IV, incorporate the notion of a triad of impairments taken, as in Kanner's definition, to be characteristic of autistic individuals, affecting, in almost every case permanently, their **social relatedness** to other persons, their **communication** skills, and the richness of their **imagination** (Wing and Gould, 1979).

It should be noted that the above model does not incorporate recently gained insight into the innate motivating processes of the infant and pre-school child that, from the first year, regulate mental development, pre-verbally and emotionally, in interpersonal contacts (Rogers and Pennington, 1991; Sigman and Capps, 1997). We claim that these aspects of the intrinsic motivation for behaviour are more fundamental, more easily related to evidence on abnormalities of brain development, equally amenable to systematic assessment and a better guide to an integrated programme of treatments and educational management.

The condition of **childhood autism** (F84.0) is defined in ICD-10 as follows:

Impaired or abnormal development must be present before 3 years of age, manifesting the full triad of impairments:

(1) in reciprocal social interaction,

(2) in communication, and

(3) in restricted, stereotyped, repetitive behaviour.

When ICD-9 and ICD-10 are compared, the main differences are seen to follow from the introduction in ICD-10 of clear definitions for a number of conditions which previously had been grouped with 'infantile autism'. Most importantly, explicit criteria are given for distinguishing Rett's syndrome and Asperger's syndrome. This provides a more precise clinical definition of 'childhood autism', and one which corresponds well to the DSM-IV definition of criteria for 'autistic disorder'. (See Appendix 1, Table V)

The condition of **autistic disorder** is identified in DSM-IV (1994) as follows:

- Onset before three years of delayed or abnormal function in at least one of: social interaction, language for social communication, symbolic or imaginative play

- Qualitative impairment in social interaction (at least two of four criteria)

- Qualitative impairments in communication (at least one of four possible criteria)

- Restricted repetitive and stereotyped patterns of behaviour, interests and activities (at least one of four possible criteria).

Excluded are: Rett's syndrome; Childhood Disintegrative Disorder; Asperger's syndrome.

The different stages in the development of the DSM are summarised in Appendix 1.

The use of DSM-III-R after 1987 led to high rates of reported co-morbidity – that is, autism was often identified by this system as co-occurring with other diagnoses in the same person. Altogether, the period in which DSM-III-R was used represents a step back. Autism was not clearly defined, early diagnosis was unlikely, and high rates of occurrence were reported because the discrimination from other developmental disorders was poor. There has been such variation in the criteria used over the past half-century, especially since the introduction of DSM-III-R, that care needs to be taken in comparison of research studies which have used different systems. DSM-III-R classified twice as many children as autistic when compared to DSM-III (Hertzig et al., 1990) and described a much more heterogeneous and less severely impaired clinical population (Demb and Weintraub, 1989).

DSM-IV, summarised in Appendix 1, is the most rigorously constructed system to date (First et al., 1992). It has been validated against both previous versions of the DSM system and against the ICD-10, and has resulted in a return to the diagnostic stability that characterised the period prior to DSM-III-R. The major advance over previous versions is in its use of a three-phase empirical approach in its development and validation, incorporating a literature review, re-analysis of data from previous versions and, finally, field trials. DSM-IV has achieved its explicit goals of high compatibility with the European ICD-10 system, and low levels of co-morbidity between autism and other conditions.

In ICD-10 and DSM-IV, the term 'autism' now identifies a specific subgroup of individuals with empathy disorder and cognitive deficits, who will be likely to have the same characteristics throughout their life. In other words, they will have a moderately stable behavioural description or 'phenotype'. Both systems identify Asperger's syndrome, Rett's syndrome and Childhood Disintegrative Disorder (Heller's syndrome) as separate entities. Thus, for the first time, we now have closely comparable and concordant systems in use worldwide (Volkmar et al., 1994).

Questionnaires and Checklists for Behaviour and Psychological Functions

Identification of autism as a mental illness, a psychosis, results in a static description of abnormalities of behaviour as possible symptoms of neurological malfunction in the child. But the behaviours of a child with autism are not always the same. They are profoundly affected by the child's inner motivation, and by circumstances. Standard assessment of perception, reactions to stimuli, problem-solving intelligence or any behaviours with objects presented in an impersonal routine in a test room are not appropriate. Diagnosis of autism, as distinct from medical tests for specific problems in bodily function or sensory or motor handicap, if it is to be of use in guiding intervention to assist the child to emotional equilibrium in interaction with other people and to learn, must be made in a place where the child is free to make spontaneous choice of experience, and open to contact with persons who present themselves as attentive and responsive, but not intrusive. Furthermore, what an autistic child does with unfamiliar persons in a strange place is likely to give a poor indication of how the child behaves at home. Thus what parents observe and can remember will also be important.

Many checklists or questionnaires have been developed for psychological or behavioural assessment of autistic children diagnosed on the ICD or DSM criteria, and for further discrimination of autism from other developmental disorders. The aim of such further assessment may be to elucidate the specific nature of the problems for the individual case, or to provide a more discriminating diagnostic tool that can be used to track developments and the effects of interventions.

A review of questionnaires and checklists by Parks (1983) summarises the Rimland's Form E-2, the BRIAAC, the BOS, the CARS and the ABC, giving details on topics such as inter-rater reliability, internal consistency, test-retest reliability, content validity, concurrent validity and discriminant validity. The most recent review, covering reliability, validity and clinical applicability of th various diagnostic tools, is that of Lord (1997) in the *Handbook of Autism and Pervasive Developmental Disorders* (Cohen and Volkmar, 1997). The main checklists and questionnaires in use in the past 30 years are listed in Appendix 2, with brief descriptions.

The Earliest Appearance of Autistic Symptoms, and Their Development

The first attempt to describe the early development of autism was by Wing in 1969. Parents of children from 4 to 16 years of age completed, retrospectively, a schedule of questions about the children's development from birth until the time of the study. The schedule was divided into five main categories: 'auditory perception and speech'; 'execution of skilled movements'; 'visual perception and related phenomena'; 'social behaviour'; and 'non-verbal skills' and 'interests'. Each item was scored as having occurred 'always', 'sometimes', 'never', or 'don't know', and the age at which the particular behaviour first appeared and then disappeared was to be noted, as far as could be recollected.

Behaviours of autistic children were compared with children having congenital receptive aphasia (poor hearing of speech), congenital performative aphasia (poor production of speech), congenital partial blindness combined with partial deafness, or Down's syndrome and with a group of normal children. Her conclusions were as follows:

> The comparison showed that autistic children are multiply handicapped, combining problems of comprehension and use of speech, and right-left, up-down, back-front disorientation similar to those found in the congenital aphasic syndromes, with abnormalities in the use of vision, difficulty in understanding gestures, abnormal bodily movements and preference for the proximal senses as in congenitally partially blind/deaf children. (Wing, 1969, p.21)

Ornitz, Guthrie and Farley (1977) created an inventory for parents of children less than four years old to complete from memory, seeking information about their children's motor and perceptual development, speech and language in their first and second year of life. The results showed that young autistic children, compared to a group of normal children of comparable age, had already been delayed in motor and communication skills, and to a minor degree also in perceptual responses, by two years, at least as far as the parents could recall. The fact that the parents of the autistic group knew of their children's disorder may have affected their recall of the period of infancy.

In another retrospective study (Dahlgren and Gillberg, 1989), a control group of mentally retarded individuals was included. Questionnaires of 130 items were completed by mothers, seeking information about the early development and the typical symptoms of autism. Autistic, mentally retarded and normal individuals were matched on sex, chronological age (CA) and measured intelligence (IQ). However, the groups' ages at the time the questionnaire was completed ranged from 7 to 22 years and doubts are raised about the reliability of the study because of the time elapsed since the child was an infant, and in view of the mother's knowledge of the child's diagnosis. The results showed that the following 18 of the 130 items discriminated autistics from other non-autistic mentally retarded individuals (we have grouped the items according to their relationship with communication and language, sensory functions, play, and self-regulation):

Table I Items which discriminated autistics from other non-autistic mentally retarded individuals (from Dahlgren and Gillberg 1989)

Communication and language	Sensory functions
• difficulties with imitating movements • lack of attempts to attract adult's attention • lack of smile when one expected • lack of play with other children • content when alone • over-excitement when tickled	• strange reactions to sound • isolation from surroundings • suspicion of a hearing deficit or deafness • empty gaze
Play	**Self-regulation**
• play only with hard objects • odd attachments to odd objects • bizarre visual inspection of objects, patterns and movements	• severe problems with sleep • variability of behaviour • no reaction to cold • dislikes to be disturbed, in own world • occupation with self when left alone

The same questionnaire was used in a prospective study (Gillberg et al., 1990) of 28 children, 8 to 35 months of age, who were identified as probably autistic. The aims of the study were to find symptoms specific to autism, to relate these to underlying causes, and to follow up children for confirmation of the diagnosis. It was confirmed that the crucial characteristics of the autistic disorder in young children are abnormalities of play, aloneness and peculiarities of gaze and hearing.

'The clinical picture is usually such that a diagnosis can be made on the basis of interview with the mother and observation of the child in the 1–3 year old age range,' (Gillberg et al., 1990, p.933). The CHAT questionnaire, described in Appendix 2, has successfully screened for autism from a high risk group at 18 months. The key items discriminating infants who developed autism from those who did not were pretend play, proto-declarative pointing, joint attention, social interest, and social play (Baron-Cohen, Allen and Gillberg, 1992; Baron-Cohen et al., 1996).

Adrien and colleagues (Adrien et al., 1993) have published the results of retrospective studies of home movies. Films of 12 infants under two years of age who had later developed autism were rated by two diagnosis-blind psychiatrists in comparison with films of 12 normal infants taken at the same ages in similar everyday circumstances, birthdays, etc., using the Infant Behavioural Summarised Evaluation (IBSE) scale. Pathological behaviours were found in the first year relating to socialisation, communication, motility and attention and these same behaviour problems were present and more intense in the second year. They conclude that poor social response, lack of smiling, absence of appropriate facial expression, hypotonia (muscle weakness) and unstable, easily distracted attention can, occasionally, be indicative of autism in the first year, but that all these become more marked in the second year, with excessive calmness and inactivity, unusual postures and absence of emotional expression, appropriate gestures and eye-contact with other persons. This supports the view that autism first becomes a serious failing in development in the second year. Degree of mental retardation and developmental delay varied, but were not controlled.

The above studies agree. All confirm that early recognition of autism and its discrimination from other developmental problems requires attention to a number of subtle indications. It is not easy to detect autism in a routine medical examination, and, indeed, most cases are first picked up by psychologists or teachers who possess knowledge of the important social features. The signs of reduced motivation for interpersonal contact are particularly important, and these may escape medical attention. Parents are usually the first to be aware that something is wrong. Clinical assessment may lead to the child being pronounced *not* autistic after a hospital visit, with the risk of reducing the parents' confidence in their own judgement. Instruments of observation that collate results over a number of sessions and in a number of settings are most reliable.

As we shall see, the manifestations of autism in early pre-school years, and responses to interventions, give strong indication that early diagnosis and early remedial education are highly desirable. Social interaction, imitation, play and non-verbal communication, to all of which parents are normally very sensitive, are more reliable indicators of a positive diagnosis before four years than an insistence on sameness and preference for fixed routines (Sigman and Capps, 1997; Stone *et al.*, 1994). Frustration brought on by difficulties in social understanding, and common, if occasional, problems in the behaviour of all infants, such as displays of irritability, temper tantrums and self-injury, tend to be seen as abnormally intense and persistent by around 2.5 years in children who later develop unmistakable autism.

Ways in Which Autistic Infants and Toddlers May Behave Like Other Children

While recent research has made some progress in defining early behavioural indicators that a child is likely to be developing autism, it is important to add that many of the preconceptions concerning the pathogenesis of autism and what its first manifestations will be have been cast into doubt by more systematic study of early development. The practice of focusing on one or two aspects of early behaviour previously assumed to be strongly suggestive of autism, such as abnormalities of early attachment and absence of joint attention, is now being systematically questioned. Autistic children do not lack emotions, or sensitivity to other persons' emotions. They can recognise themselves in a mirror, and indeed may enjoy exploring the experience of the mirror, much as infants may do. The sensitivities that the children retain are extremely important as elements on which interventions to help their learning and development can be built.

Much of the literature to date has made the assumption that autistic pre-school children will be likely to show weak emotional attachment. An autistic one-year-old has been expected to be indifferent to the mother's presence and free of distress in her absence. However, in a recent study (Capps, Sigman and Mundy, 1994) in which **security of attachment** was examined in 19 autistic children aged 3–6 years, it was found that the affectionate relationship was not always weak. Fifteen of the children proved classifiable in the Ainsworth Strange Situation (see Glossary), and of these some 40 per cent were rated as securely attached. The same group has looked at the relationship between assessed IQ, developmental level, and **joint attention** in autistic pre-schoolers, mental aged matched normal controls and IQ matched developmentally delayed controls (Mundy, Sigman and Kasari, 1994). In contrast to the expectations of current cognitive models of autism (e.g. Baron-Cohen, Tager-Flusberg and Cohen, 1993), the joint attention differences seen in the autistic subjects proved to be largely accounted for on the basis of differences in IQ and/or developmental level. Absence of joint attention, as it was defined in this study, could not be used to discriminate the children with autism (Sigman and Capps, 1997).

Towards a Synthesis – Current Concepts of Autism and an Up-to-Date Description

Autism is now more difficult to understand than it is to recognise. We know consistent features that are peculiar to the condition. However, autism is both complex and rare, and presumably this explains why it was not identified until much later than the classical mental illnesses of adults.

Kanner's description captured the characteristics now accepted to describe a coherent abnormality of behaviour due to abnormal brain development. Autism directly affects the way the expressions and actions of other persons are perceived. This is associated with problems in expressive communication, in understanding other persons' thoughts, and in comprehending the ordinary use of language and the meanings others give by convention to actions and objects.

The probable causal brain fault also affects basic functions of sensation, perception, motor coordination, thinking and learning to varying degrees. In addition, autistic children often have other medical problems (Gillberg and Coleman, 1992).

One difficulty, in the past, was the reluctance of psychiatrists and psychologists to believe that a very young child could develop a disorder comparable with the mental disturbances of some adults. Babies were thought not capable of coordinated representational mental activity and un-differentiated in their emotions. On the other hand, autism is different from any psychiatric illness that develops in an adult. It can only be perceived clearly as a disorder that emerges in development of a young brain as it passes through a critical phase in mental growth.

This is not to say that any stage of normal development is autistic, or that a normal child will develop autism if it does not receive an adequately 'constructive' mothering that builds a boundary for the infant's ego or self-awareness. There is, as we have explained, no 'normal autistic phase'. The view of some psychoanalysts that autism is a failure of differentiation of self due to unresponsive, cold and emotionless mothering in early infancy misread the direction of the emotional effects between mother and child. There is a principle motivational fault **in the developing child,** and this will distress and confuse parents and may make them lose hope and confidence.

Nevertheless, there are points in which the confused interpersonal relating of an autistic child and the symptoms of isolation and lack of contact in a mentally ill adult may bear important similarities. To understand these we need to conceive of the emotional system as regulating relationships and contacts, in childhood and at all later stages of life – we have to be able to conceive both behaviours and their origin in brain processes (Holstege et al., 1997; Schore, 1994; Stern, 1985; Trevarthen and Aitken, 1994). If we cannot imagine the inner processes of human consciousness and natural sympathetic responses between people, we will not understand what has gone wrong in autism. Giving support to the ill-defined self-and-other awareness of an autistic child requires special, well-informed, dedication. When appropriate support is found, it can significantly improve communication and learning (see Chapter 10).

The diagnostic or descriptive systems that we have reviewed affirm that autistic children have **a primary inability to perceive others as people** and to conceive what they may communicate. This is easiest to understand in the perspective of normal development, because children normally have such explicit and demanding motivations to communicate with and learn from others. Again, the most informative and reliable diagnostic instruments are those that examine the ways the child uses objects in the context of communication with familiar others. They record both object use and interpersonal behaviours.

Recent attempts to identify autism at younger ages have tended to confirm that the abnormalities are usually absent, or fragmentary or subtle and difficult to detect, before one year. As we shall see, in Chapter 8, nine to twelve months is a stage in development when a baby is normally changing rapidly: in alertness of investigative intelligence and in systematic, purposeful, constructive handling of objects, in memory, and in willingness to share experiences and actions with companions with the help of early language-like behaviour, combining vocalisations and gestures. There are new demands on selective attention, memory and coordination of action, as well as a much greater involvement with other people and their interests and purposes. A further step in the direction of imaginative understanding with other people occurs at the middle of the second year, and this is when most autistic children begin to show clear abnormalities that lead to a confident diagnosis.

Individual autistic children **differ in their intelligence, capacity for learning and use of language,** but **all are abnormal in the ways they relate to other persons.** It is significant that their insensitivity to other persons' feelings, purposes and experiences appears before the child is three years old and after an early infancy that was apparently almost normal. That is, the development of the child's mind fails at the time when most children begin to be extremely sensitive to and interested in other people's ideas and actions, and when speech is beginning (see Chapter 8). This is normally a time of the most intense communication and sharing of imaginations and habitual ways of doing things, when children are expected to be insatiably curious and full of fantasy about meanings in their play, and wanting to put these ideas into language.

Autistic children, as was mentioned above, **do respond to others' emotions** and they **are able to form affectionate attachments** (Capps, Sigman and Mundy, 1994; Sigman and Capps, 1997), but they do not show an intense eagerness to share and in play they do not pretend to act like other people, except in a ritual, echolalic kind of way. Autistic children may imitate, but they do so self-centredly or like an echo, without the creativity, humour and companionship that is so remarkable in ordinary toddlers' play, and they often seem not to be aware of what language is for – how one normally negotiates meanings, intentions and beliefs with it. They do not readily seek adults' attentions and respond badly when efforts are made to force them to attend to others' interests and purposes. Communication with an autistic child requires patience, with attention to how the child's interests and feelings change.

Close observation of autistic children and many tests of their reactions to stimuli have shown that they have **characteristic problems with experience,** and that they explore objects differently. They show peculiarities of looking and listening. In some respects they are hypersensitive or easily overwhelmed and unable to shut out adverse experiences by attending elsewhere, but they also show strangely blunted reactions to stimuli and are likely to not notice things that one would expect to be of great interest or concern to a child. They develop meaningless habits of repeating self-stimulation, and they tend to fear novelty and change, apparently being easily panicked by complex new situations. These features indicate that there are problems with the way their brains admit or select stimuli – **the investigative intelligence is incoherent or distorted** in autistic children compared to unaffected age-mates. Abnormalities of perception, attention and exploration undoubtedly handicap the learning and thinking of autistic children, leading to an accumulation of disability. Those that appear to develop high intelligence usually do so in narrow or specialised areas that seem to be practised through the child's unusual capacity to become absorbed, over and over again, in a preferred activity, in isolation from other people (Sigman and Capps, 1997; Treffert, 1989).

The perceptual, attentional and cognitive difficulties of autistic children, and their tendency to protect themselves by repeating familiar actions and forming odd attachments to objects, are of great significance to parents and teachers who are seeking to make contact and to help the child's learning, but these features cannot be viewed as the heart of the problem, and they may not be the aspects that will respond best to remedial education.

There are clearly also **problems with the generation of movements,** especially those that a normal child would use efficiently to communicate feelings. Autistic children make strange gestures, hand-flapping, blinking, fiddling with things, repeatedly tapping. They may be hyperactive and often have ritualistic activities that make no sense. Many have some degree of motor weakness and are delayed in motor milestones (Gillberg and Coleman, 1992). They do not use pointing communicatively and may not understand the gestures others use to direct their attention. Like the peculiarities of perception, the abnormal spontaneous movements of autistic children indicate something about abnormal brain processes, but they are not individually peculiar to autism. Many disorders of the young brain are likely to be associated with an excess of repetitive involuntary movements (Lees, 1985; Comings, 1990).

Autistic children **do not lack emotions.** They **can show strong and disturbing reactions** to difficult, frustrating or frightening situations and are inclined to become restless and have sleep problems. On the other hand they **often have an empty gaze** and tend to **smile to themselves** and not in reaction to others' greetings. They often appear to lack curiosity and initiative. Affectionate responses are shown to familiar persons and responsive enjoyment can be gained with body or contact play. Autism seems to combine an unbalanced motivation for learning the conventional meanings of objects with defence against complexity and change. The imagination is hemmed in by desire for sameness and obsessional exploratory behaviour.

The fascinating studies of the ways older, 'high-functioning' or verbally fluent children fail to understand **other persons' beliefs,** and what others can imagine about what other people think and know, seem to be clarifying disorders of later development that may follow from the deeper failing in the younger child, without language or with distorted awareness of language, to relate directly to other people. Clever autistic children who may read exceptionally well do not understand original jokes or metaphors and cannot create new evolving narratives with adjustment of the dialogue to different characters' 'voices'. Their occasional very fluent and expressive 'readings' of characters' performances will most often be echolalic reproductions of what they have seen and heard others perform, and they may be often repeated with little variation. The majority of autistic children cannot be examined for verbally mediated 'theories of mind' as they have a level of language expression and/or comprehension insufficient for such material to be administered with them (Fay, 1993).

CHAPTER 3

Similar Disorders
and Important Distinctions

Correct identification of autism that pays close attention to how it develops is important for a number of reasons. Some conditions that are easily mistaken for autism in a young child will develop quite differently. They will require different therapy or care and will have different implications for education. For example, although all children with autism have problems with language, and about 50 per cent never develop functional speech, they are different in their interpersonal and social behaviour from children who have specific disorders of language and communication (Donaldson, 1995), and they need a different kind of help to improve their communication. Other disorders of psychological development in young children, such as Rett's syndrome and Childhood Disintegrative Disorder, show sudden deterioration in aspects of behaviour and consciousness that are not typically affected in autism. The withdrawn and depressed behaviour of abused children is also different form autism, and has very different implications for care.

Autistic behaviour is significantly more common in both the visually and hearing impaired than among children with normal senses (Ellis, 1986; Hobson, 1993a,b). However, children who are blind or deaf are likely to respond immediately to aids that reduce the child's sensory isolation, while a child with autism may show no change in communication and social orientation after receiving a sensory aid or compensatory communication. Autism affects the child's motivation for contact with the world and people in it, and these difficulties remain even when all the child's senses are responsive. Indeed, the children with autism are often hyper-responsive to simple sounds and sights, such as sirens or vacuum cleaners, or bright reflections, while apparently not perceiving more complex patterns. Some react strongly to contact with clothing, or to being touched.

If loss of vision or hearing, or both, is not the cause of a child's autistic-like learning difficulties and social withdrawal, several alternative possibilities need to be considered. The following descriptions identify the chief differences between Kanner's autism and other forms of autism, and closely related disorders of brain development and behaviour or other psychological disorders of childhood that can be confused with autism in some of its manifestations.

Asperger's Syndrome and 'High-Functioning' Autists

One year after Kanner's description of autism was published, Asperger (1944) defined a new and very similar condition, which, however, because Asperger was isolated in occupied Austria during the war, did not receive wide attention until Wing's clinical analysis of the disorder in 1981.

The main diagnostic systems have only recently, with the DSM-IV and ICD-10 revisions, defined Asperger's syndrome as distinct from autism. A variety of diagnostic criteria have been proposed (Ghaziuddin *et al.*, 1992). In general, Asperger's discrimination of the key features has been upheld (Table II).

Table II Diagnostic Criteria for Asperger's Syndrome

	Autistic Social Impairment	All-Absorbing Interests	Pedantic Speech	Clumsiness	Speech Delay	Cognitive Delay
(1) Asperger (1944)	YES	YES	YES	YES	NO	NO
(2) Wing (1981)	YES	YES	YES	YES	Possible	Possible
(3) Gillberg (1989)	YES	YES	YES	YES	Possible	Possible
(4) Szatmari *et al.* (1989)	YES	YES	YES	Clumsy Gestures	Not stated	Not stated
(5) Tantam (1988)	YES	YES	YES	YES	Possible	Possible
(6) ICD-10 (1993)	YES	USUAL	Not Stated	USUAL	NO	NO
(7) DSM-IV (1994)	YES	YES	Not Stated	Not Stated	NO	NO

In summary, the most widely accepted features of the population of persons with Asperger's syndrome are:

- Autistic social impairment

- Clumsiness (usual, but not necessarily present)

- 'Concrete' or pedantic speech

- All-absorbing circumscribed interests (usual)

- Lack of appreciation for humour (commonly described)

There is disagreement about delay in language development, or in cognitive development. Both ICD-10 and DSM-IV state that individuals with Asperger's syndrome do *not* have delays in language or cognitive development, while three of the leading clinical authorities, Wing (1981), Gillberg (1989) and Tantam (1988), claim that language and cognition can be delayed. These different conclusions about how to define the disorder, besides generating disagreements over diagnosis in individual cases, lead to widely different estimates of the likely numbers of children, adolescents or adults with Asperger's syndrome in any given population (Ghaziuddin *et al.*, 1992; Gillberg and Gillberg, 1989).

While most autistic individuals have below normal intelligence scores, those with Asperger's syndrome usually function in the normal range of intellectual ability (Baron-Cohen and Bolton, 1993), some showing evidence of exceptional savant skills. Likewise, in Asperger's syndrome early language milestones are usually not delayed, and speaking may even be precocious. Even so, once language is fluent, it is used in a characteristically stilted and stereotyped manner scarcely to be distinguished from that of the high-functioning autistic child (Jordan and Powell, 1995; Sigman and Capps, 1997).

According to the DSM-IV criteria Asperger's syndrome, in contrast to autistic disorder, cannot be coded as co-morbid with schizophrenia. This, too, is a surprising conclusion, in view of the psychotic symptoms described in the early literature in a significant proportion of subjects with Asperger's syndrome (Tantam, 1991). It is admitted in the ICD-10 that psychotic episodes may occur in the early adult life of a person with Asperger's syndrome. Emotional stress at this stage of life is a natural consequence of the social and interpersonal difficulties that an adolescent with Asperger's syndrome is likely to experience with family and with peers (Attwood, 1997; Sigman and Capps, 1997), but a susceptibility to a psychiatric condition allied to schizophrenia may well be a part of the condition that causes Asperger's syndrome.

Debate continues among developmental psychologists over whether persons with Asperger's syndrome should be differentiated from those with autism who are identified as 'high-functioning' or not mentally retarded (Bishop, 1993; Ozonoff, Rogers and Pennington 1991; Happé, 1994). School-age children with Asperger's syndrome are, unlike those with autism, commonly able to perform well on 'Model of Mind' tests (Ozonoff *et al.*, 1991).

The former show more subtle socio-linguistic deficits, such as failure to modify pronunciation to express context-specific meaning, and, indeed, a generally poor attention to subtleties of the interpersonal context for communication (Attwood, 1997; Jordan and Powell, 1995; Sigman and Capps, 1997). Children and young persons with Asperger's syndrome are more likely to show clumsiness and less likely to be delayed in their language development than autistic individuals who are not mentally retarded.

By all definitions, including the original clinical descriptions, Asperger's syndrome shares many features with Kanner's autism, and we conclude that the distinctions between them are matters of degree. Diagnostic systems, such as DSM-IV and ICD-10, force categorisation into named disorders by artificially simplified criteria. In reality both conditions seriously affect motives for interpersonal life in characteristic and similar ways. Asperger's syndrome is best understood, for all practical purposes, as part of a range of autistic disorders known as the 'autistic continuum' or the 'autistic spectrum' (Gillberg, 1991a; Wing, 1996). Differences in the developmental course of the two conditions suggest that they affect the process of development in differing degrees, and at different stages.

Szatmari and his colleagues (Szatmari et al., 1990) found that a group of individuals with Asperger's syndrome showed more affectionate behaviour in early childhood, enjoyment of others and sharing of interests, when compared to a group of individuals with autism whose IQ was at the same level. Those with Asperger's syndrome also exhibited fewer abnormalities of language use, fewer automatic movements or stereotypic behaviours, and had fewer bizarre obsessions. In other areas of functioning – in gaze avoidance, reluctance to initiate communication and insistence on routines and rituals – the two groups were alike.

Klin, Volkmar, Sparrow, Cicchetti and Rourke (1995) made a comparison of two groups: 19 high-functioning autistics and 21 with Asperger's syndrome, similar in IQ, age and sex distribution, and all diagnosed on ICD-10 criteria. In cognitive tests, the Asperger's group had a pattern of scores consistent with their non-verbal learning disability, but this was not the case for the high-functioning autistics. This study helps define subtle differences between the two syndromes, and, furthermore, it appears to indicate that Asperger's syndrome has more impact on functions of the right hemisphere, which, in comparison with the left hemisphere, is known to be more adept at non-verbal intellectual functions.

There are fewer neurological abnormalities in individuals with Asperger's syndrome when they are compared, as a group, to those who are diagnosed as autistic (Gillberg, 1989); but, some in both groups show defects in neural migration, which suggests a similar pathophysiology (Berthier, Starkstein and Leiguarda, 1990).

Parents of individuals with Asperger's syndrome have been found to show a significant similarity to affected individuals in certain cognitive strengths and weaknesses (Baron-Cohen and Hammer, 1997). On an Embedded Figures Task (where a target shape had to be identified within a more complex stimulus) they performed better than expected while on a task where mental states had to be inferred from facial photographs, they had more difficulty. This fits the hypothesis that both parents and their children who develop Asperger's syndrome show different degrees of a genetic fault in socio-affective or interpersonal functions that leaves visuo-spatial skills and interest in technical objects relatively intact.

Altogether, there is still confusion between medical and psychological experts as to whether Asperger's syndrome and autism should be viewed as part of a continuously varying condition or two different conditions. As the diagnosis of Asperger's has only recently been accepted into the ICD-10 and DSM-IV systems, insufficient systematic research has yet been done to resolve the problem. If we use performance on intelligence tests as the variable on which groups with the two diagnoses are to be matched, differences can be shown. But this may not be the best yardstick by which to gauge what is affecting these individuals' psychological functions, development and potentiality for learning.

Autism and Asperger's syndrome occur together in the same family groups at much greater than chance levels, and given the increasing evidence for broader behavioural patterns or 'phenotypes' in the families of autistic individuals (Le Couteur et al., 1996) and those with Asperger's syndrome (Baron-Cohen and Hammer, 1997), it seems most likely that the two conditions constitute parts of one broad continuum of motivational disorders of affective contact and social understanding due to different degrees of abnormal function in core regulatory systems of the developing brain.

Other Childhood Psychoses and Mental Handicap

Childhood Schizophrenia

Some children, after the age of six or seven or in the early teens, begin to show bizarre detached behaviour with evidence of hallucinations. These are the early manifestations of schizophrenia. A diagnosis of schizophrenia can rarely be made before this age, and the condition normally becomes more serious in adolescence. Nevertheless, there is some evidence from analyses of home video recordings of earlier abnormality of psychological function in children who later become schizophrenic (Walker et al. 1993).

Delusions and hallucinations, the main features of childhood schizophrenia, are not common in autism. They were explicitly excluded for the diagnosis of autism in DSM-III-R, but now co-morbidity of schizophrenia and autism is accepted as possible in DSM-IV. The obsessional and ritualistic behaviours of children with autism, and their strange self-stimulatory behaviours, are not seen in childhood schizophrenia, and the schizophrenic children usually develop speech and may not be mentally retarded. Current models of psychopathology treat autism and schizophrenia as mutually exclusive conditions that are due to different defects in brain development, and surveys of family pedigrees and population studies indicate that the two conditions do not share a cause, but that a child can, by chance, suffer from the two conditions together (Volkmar and Cohen, 1991a).

A family history of schizophrenia is common in childhood schizophrenia but is uncommon in autism. Moreover, with the exception of occasional cases who show sudden loss of early language, autism does not typically show a fluctuating course. Childhood schizophrenia can fluctuate wildly in its presentation. Finally, epileptic seizures are common in autism, affecting 25–35 per cent of cases, but they are rarely a feature in childhood schizophrenia (Gillberg and Steffenburg, 1987; Wing and Gould, 1979).

Mental Retardation: William's and Down's Syndromes

A wide range of biological causes of developmental delay in intelligence has been identified. In certain of these, there is a clear behavioural description, or phenotype, which includes, in some cases, 'autistic' features, of behaviour, speech and affective engagement. Children with cognitive handicap due to genetic disorders such as William's syndrome (WS) and Down's syndrome (DS) also have various impairments or differences in their social reactions, joint attention and communication about objects (Berger, 1990; Wang and Bellugi, 1993; Franco and Wishart, 1994).

When retarded autistic children are matched for Mental Age with non-autistic children, by appropriate standardised tests of intelligence, the non-autistic group, including those with DS who are not also autistic, are different in their associated illnesses and in their communication. We now know that a child with Down's syndrome can also be autistic, and that the two conditions do occur together at considerably higher frequencies than would be expected by chance (Howlin, Wing and Gould, 1995). The children with autism show a characteristic pattern in cognitive problems, with relatively poor abilities in language and abstract thought. By definition, they have a special difficulty with interpersonal understanding, and they also show characteristic deficits on 'Model of Mind' tests of interpersonal perspective taking. Even those with a relatively high or normal Mental Age on standard intelligence tests show these features (Bartak and Rutter, 1976; Hobson, 1986a,b; Hobson, Ouston and Lee, 1988a; Yirmiya et al., 1989; Baron-Cohen, 1990; Capps et al., 1992).

Down's syndrome, with a very distinct chromosomal abnormality (trisomy or triplication of chromosome 21), is easily identified at birth by the characteristic appearance of the face and hands. Older DS children are typically defective in ability to represent objects and events in the environment, and they have impaired spatial representation. Cognitive abilities remain those of a young child, with little progress beyond the second decade. Motor control of hands, tongue, lips and respiration has problems, and vision and audition may be affected. Language development is slow, speech production being most affected, and usually remains at about the level of a three-year-old, though there is a considerable range. Early vocalisations and 'universal phonemes' develop normally, but both babbling and hand banging are delayed by about three months. Learning of reading, by-passing auditory sequencing requirements of speech perception, may assist development of language. Responses to speaking and touching are much more positive than in autism, but vocal activity and vocal turn-taking are slow, and use of referential gaze in communication is retarded, which causes clashes with the mother, who may become too intrusive. Unlike autistic children, DS children show similar preferences to normal children of the same level of development for nursery rhymes and for their mother's voice when she is addressing them. However, they are less expressive vocally in the Ainsworth Strange Situation Test (see Glossary), and less overtly affective, their emotional reactions being reduced and flat, with less laughter for interpersonal jokes.

Infants with DS develop essentially normal expressions in communication (Franco and Wishart, 1994), but there emerge differences in the effectiveness of their signals (Cicchetti and Sroufe, 1978), often exacerbated by the emotional responses of parents in face of the child's slow development, especially in language (Berger, 1990). Infants with DS are slow to develop a cooperative combination of interest in a partner's communication and use of objects. They show less interest in the object world and, as their attention is easily overtaxed, they fail to switch between the partner's motives and the object's uses (Wishart, 1991). Thus at 12 months infants with DS have marked difficulty in maintaining joint attention to their caregivers and objects. It is often true that play becomes more difficult for a handicapped child if a parent tries to join in, possibly because of the way the parent enters the play or invites cooperation. A lack of referential eye contact and a poverty in initiatives to play leads mothers to have difficulty interpreting the handicapped child's intentions. Many of these features of behaviour can resemble those of children with autism, but children with DS are more attentive to people and they show more positive emotional responses directed to other people.

Epileptic seizures appear earlier on average in mentally handicapped children. In autistic children fits commonly begin in late childhood or adolescence. The sex distribution is different in the two groups: the male/female ratio is 4:1 in the autistic population and 1:1 in the non-autistic handicapped. However, as intellectual level reduces in the autistic group, so does the preponderance of male cases.

The recently discovered William's syndrome is a condition in which language may be well developed while other aspects of cognition are considerably impaired. Both DS and WS children are delayed in vocabulary acquisition and motor milestones as pre-schoolers, but adolescents with WS have correct, complex if somewhat echoic grammar, a large vocabulary with uncommon words and are reported to be strong in discourse abilities such as narrative cohesion and conversational turn-taking (Wang and Bellugi, 1993). Prosody has not been systematically studied, but it appears to be preserved, though possibly 'over-rich' in affect tone. Children with DS, in contrast, have poor, simple grammar, a smaller vocabulary and reduced linguistic affective expression. There are interesting differences in visuo-motor ability. Drawings of children with WS are poor and fragmented, retaining local detail but losing the Gestalt; those of children with DS are simple but cohesive, representing the overall shape without detail (Wang and Bellugi, 1993). When compared to effects of brain lesions in adults who were normal before the injury, these findings would suggest that while children with WS are impaired in parietal cortex of the right hemisphere, those with DS have left hemisphere deficiency. Children with WS are proficient at face recognition, but this could be based on a left hemisphere strategy of feature listing.

Non-verbal interpersonal communication, joint attention with sharing of spatial reference and affective exchange are, as we discuss below, critical in the early development of both language and cognition (Adamson and Bakeman, 1985; Bates, 1979; Bruner, 1983; Dore, 1983; Rheingold, Hay and West, 1976; Stern, 1985; Tomasello and Farrar, 1986; Trevarthen and Hubley, 1978). Deficiencies in non-verbal communication (Mundy, Kasari and Sigman, 1992) distinguish not only empathic disorders such as autism (Mundy *et al.*, 1986), but also, as described above, varieties of mental handicap (Kasari *et al.*, 1990). Reasoned or intentional response to a clinically identified deficit in the non-verbal communication of the child, in other words, an intellectual response to an expert diagnosis, may be the cause of maladaptive or unsupportive communication from the carer that makes the child's problem worse (Berger, 1990; Mahoney, Fors and Wood, 1990).

As with autistic children, the difficulties of attention and coordination of even profoundly mentally handicapped children can be reduced by communication with a partner who adapts stimulation and response to the child's ability to share feelings and actions (Burford, 1992). Conversely, children classified as suffering from emotional or empathic disorders fail in cognitive tests, and this is taken to show they are mentally handicapped in some degree. That is why Kanner's autism was not specifically recognised by the DSM III-R diagnostic system, which conceived the intersubjective processes of such a 'pervasive developmental disorder' to be consequences of general deficiencies in behaviour and cognition (Aitken, 1991c).

Rett's syndrome

This syndrome was first described by Rett in 1966 in a paper describing a link between a consistent constellation of behavioural and physical features and elevated levels of ammonia in the blood. It was seen only in girls. The association with blood ammonia has since been shown to be atypical, but the physical and behavioural phenotype that Rett and, later, Hagberg described is now accepted as a distinctive syndrome (Hagberg, 1989, 1993; Hagberg, *et al.*, 1983; Rett, 1966). Rett's syndrome is rare, but, with its variants at a prevalence rate of 1 in 10,000, it is second only to Down's syndrome as cause of severe mental retardation in girls (Hagberg, 1993). Rett's syndrome is usually reported to occur only in females, but some males appear to have a condition with the same features (Philippart, 1990). It has been suggested that Rett's syndrome is an X-chromosome disorder fatal to males in the embryo (Comings, 1986), but this explanation of the high preponderance of females with the condition has not, to date, received empirical support.

Developmental studies show that the early stages of Rett's syndrome may resemble those of autism. At around nine months, a baby, who at six months was thought to be normal, shows distracted attention, weak posture, and poor coordination of limb movements (Kerr, 1995; Witt-Engerström, 1990). The girl may advance through protolanguage and learn a few words, but by 18 months, she will be retarded and deeply disturbed in motivation and emotions. She will show autistic withdrawal and fits of agitation, will lose voluntary use of her mouth, arms and hands, and make stereotyped licking and tonguing and patting or stroking movements, rubbing the hands together and bringing them, with athetoid twisting, to the mouth. These hand movements are very distinctive. Object prehension will cease, as will all deliberate gestures of communication and speech. By age two, the autistic and agitated emotional features pass, leaving a profound and permanent mental handicap.

The girls, who utter only undifferentiated cries and laughter, with primitive babbling, seek eye contact and smile or laugh in response to an approaching face accompanied by friendly cheerful speech and encouraging hand contact. There is little evidence of learning, no voluntary hand use, and no comprehension of language, but they can be assisted to indicate their preferences by eye pointing (von Tetzchner and Martinsen, 1992). Measures of head circumference are subnormal by 6 to 12 months, and below the 2 per cent level of the normal population by two to four years, when brain growth ceases. Available evidence points to a non-Mendelian gene fault expressed in the core of the brain in the mid embryo stage, possibly first in the *substantia nigra* and *locus ceruleus*, whose activity in producing and distributing biogenic amines is essential to the formation of effective cortical networks (Armstrong, 1992; Hagberg, Naidu and Percy, 1992; Nomura, Segawa and Higurashi, 1985; Segawa, 1992; Trevarthen and Aitken, 1994). Girls with Rett's syndrome have reduced blood circulation in the midbrain and upper brainstem from early in development as well as in the frontal lobes and may have failure of left fronto-temporal function. It has been proposed that the frontal lobe remains immature (Nielsen *et al.*, 1990).

Childhood Disintegrative Disorder: Heller's Syndrome

In 1908, Heller described a group of children who, after a period of normal development, typically between three and four years, showed changes in mood and character followed quickly by loss of speech and ultimately by extreme regression in development (Hulse, 1954). Heller called this condition 'dementia infantilis'. More recently it has been called either 'disintegrative psychosis' or Heller's syndrome. Until recently, this group of children were considered to have an atypical form of autism. They show marked deterioration in many areas of psychological functioning after at least the first two years of generally normal development. The timing of onset often leads to a suspicion of brain damage following vaccination. Seizure problems are frequent, there is often loss of functional language, and males are more commonly affected than females (Volkmar and Cohen, 1989; Volkmar *et al.*, 1994). Heller's syndrome has only recently been defined on the DSM-IV and ICD-10 systems, and we know little about children with this condition.

Language Disorders

Receptive Developmental Dysphasia (Poor Comprehension of Speech)

Disorders in the perception and comprehension of language affect boys and girls equally. Autism is the only disorder that impairs receptive language which is significantly more common in males. The prognosis for social adjustment is, at least in the short-term studies to date, significantly poorer in the autistic population compared to children diagnosed as receptive dysphasic. Autism leads to a pervasive failure of orientation towards messages of all kinds from other persons.

Children with receptive language disorders, though they often fail to understand language properly, are usually attentive and responsive to other persons (Donaldson, 1995). In a detailed appraisal of studies comparing children with autism and those with receptive dysphasia, von Tetzchner and Martinsen (1981) find that both conditions vary greatly in all parameters measured, and these authors suggest that autistic subjects were found to be different in their social functions simply because that was the basis on which they were diagnosed. The autistic group did do worse in use of gestures, while dysphasics had more problems with speech articulation, and, though they read the text better, they were not as proficient as the autists in mechanical reading skills requiring good rote memory. After language disability has been taken into account, autistic children as a population also have a broader range of cognitive problems and lower IQ than children diagnosed as having a 'pure' receptive dysphasia (Bartak *et al.*, 1975).

Semantic-Pragmatic Disorder and Specific Language Impairment (SLI)

Semantic-Pragmatic disorder was first described by Rapin as a distinct clinical entity characterised by unusual language use and differentiated from autism (Rapin and Allen, 1983). More recently, Rapin has suggested that the distinction between autism and 'semantic-pragmatic disorder' is not as clear as she had originally drawn it. She now believes there to be a high degree of co-morbidity, a significant proportion of high-functioning autistic children having semantic and pragmatic disorders in their language (Allen and Rapin, 1992).

Whether a semantic-pragmatic disorder is a clinically significant entity has still to be determined, but the term is in widespread use by speech and language therapists. Many children so diagnosed may, in fact, be autistic by all accepted criteria. However, while many children who misunderstand the meanings of words or who make grammatical errors may make mistakes like those of autistic children, and these problems may make communication with them difficult, they may not avoid all communication like autistic children do, and they are not likely to have difficulties with non-verbal communication (Bishop, 1989; Donaldson, 1995; Jordan, 1993; von Tetzchner and Martinsen, 1981, 1992).

Most children show transitory deficiencies in phonology and grammar at the stage just before fluent speaking, and many with language deficits or delay in pre-school lose their problems in primary school. With Specific Language Impairment (Bishop, 1992), or Developmental Language Disorder, these idiosyncratic and undifferentiated elements persist in the absence of mental or physical handicap, hearing loss, emotional disorder or emotional deprivation. It is not clear that a specific language process is impaired in SLI, and the common auditory processing difficulty may be a consequence of loss in 'speed of processing' that impairs sequential auditory information more than persisting visual patterns. Language-disordered children experience general difficulties with combining skills, as in doing two tasks at once, and they perform below age expectations in a wide range of tests of knowledge, symbolic and non-symbolic activities, and non-verbal skills. The cognitive deficits and 'social immaturity' of children with SLI may be secondary to language losses, or the interpersonal aspects may be more fundamental. Some children with SLI can have difficulty with prosody including stress segmentation rules, and with comprehension of other paralinguistic cues, such as the eye movements of people with whom they are communicating, and, for these reasons, fail to perceive the communicative context of language use. This is more likely in the subgroup with 'semantic-pragmatic disorder', who are more similar to children with autism.

There is increasing recognition of a need to broaden the concept of autism, both in terms of the expectation of a higher rate of associated conditions in members of the extended family (Le Couteur et al., 1996), and to recognise a continuum model for severity of expression (Gillberg, 1991a; Wing, 1996).

This means that it will not always be possible to distinguish autism sharply from either receptive or productive language disorders. Furthermore, methods for ameliorating temporal processing and rhythmic patterning of expression that are applied to help children with language learning difficulties, or training in use of hand signs to substitute for or support speech, may also benefit some autistic children (Merzenich *et al.*, 1996; von Tetzchner and Martinsen, 1992).

CHAPTER 4

How Many Autistic Children?

The Prevalence of Autism

A number of studies, using a variety of diagnostic criteria, have attempted to determine how many children have autism at any one time in a population of given size – that is, to find the *prevalence* or 'rate' at which the disorder appears. Earlier studies, most of which used DSM-III or ICD-9 diagnostic systems, gave estimates of approximately 4.5 to 6 cases per 10,000 population. More recent studies, using DSM-III-R, gave higher rates, in the region of 10 to 14 cases per 10,000 population (Table III).

As we have explained, the DSM-III-R description includes, more so called 'non-nuclear autistic' children, that is, boys and girls with difficulties in language development who do not show the deficits in interpersonal relating that were considered specific to the condition, called 'nuclear autistic', that was described by Kanner. When compared to earlier systems, the DSM-III-R appears to classify approximately twice as many children as autistic. With a return, in DSM-IV, to stricter criteria essentially the same as those by which the condition was originally defined, the numbers diagnosed have fallen back to the pre-1987 levels.

Over the past 30 years, rates appear, in fact, to have been rather constant. Moreover, there is little evidence for an increase in the numbers of children who fulfil any particular set of diagnostic criteria over time, except where environmental factors, such as epidemics of rubella, are known to have caused geographical and temporal variations in disorders attributable to early brain damage.

The Predicted Incidence of Autism in Given Populations

The incidence of autism in a population of known size is estimated from the prevalence data, assuming the latter identifies all cases fitting the definition of autism, and that few false positive identifications are made.

In reality, the number of children who are diagnosed to have autism will be somewhat less than the incidence figures predict because no cases will be found

Table III A Selection of Population Studies

Author	Place	Prevalence Number in 10,000	Age Group Studied	Population
Rutter, 1966	Scotland	4.4 ('psychotic')	?	?
Lotter, 1966; 1967	England	4.5	8–10 years	78,000
Brask, 1970	Denmark	4.3	?	?
Wing et al., 1976	England	4.8 mild to moderate; 2.0 severe	5–14 years	25,000
Wing and Gould, 1979	England	4.9	?	?
Hoshino et al., 1982	Japan	4.96 2.33	5–11 years 0–18 years	217,000 609,848
Bohman et al., 1983	Sweden	6.1	?	?
Gillberg, 1984	Sweden	3.9	4–18 years	128,584
Steffenberg and Gillberg, 1986	Sweden	7.5	?	?
Bryson et al., 1988	Canada	**10.1**	6–14 years	20,800
Tanoue et al., 1988	Japan	**13.8**	?	?
Sugiymama and Abe, 1989	Japan	**13.0**	?	?
Ritvo et al., 1990	USA	4.0 (estimated)	3–25 years	1,461,037
Cialdella and Mamelle, 1989	France	4.5	3–9 years	135,180
Gillberg et al., 1991a	Sweden	11.6	?	?

* In this table the numbers, expressed per 10,000 of population, record children classified as having either 'nuclear' (Kanner's) or 'non-nuclear' autism, unless stated otherwise. Figures in bold type reflect the more inclusive criteria of DSM-III-R.

? Information not given

Table IV Incidence of Autism and Related Disorders for the UK
(Estimates, derived from 1993 Census Data CSO Annual Abstract of
Statistics, 1995, which gives the population to the nearest thousand)

	Total Population	Autism Proper At 4.5 per 10,000; to nearest 100	Other Autistic Spectrum At 26 per 10,000; to nearest 100
UK			
All Ages	58,191,000	26,200	151,300
0–4	3,888,000	1,800	10,100
5–19	10,847,000	4,900	28,200
19+	43,454,000	19,600	113,000
England			
All Ages	48,533,000	21,800	126,200
0–4	3,244,000	1,500	8,400
5–19	8,950,000	4,000	23,300
19+	39,264,000	17,700	102,100
Scotland			
All Ages	5,120,000	2,300	13,300
0–4	324,000	c.150	800
5–19	960,000	400	2,500
19+	3,836,000	1,700	10,000
Ireland			
All Ages	1,632,000	700	4,200
0–4	130,000	c.60	300
5–19	385,000	c.170	1,000
19+	1,117,000	500	2,900
Wales			
All Ages	2,906,000	1,300	7,600
0–4	189,000	c.90	500
5–19	552,000	c.250	1,400
19+	2,115,000	1,000	5,500

until the second year or later, and some will escape recognition altogether because they are not presented for medical or psychological attention, or because they have been misdiagnosed as belonging to some other condition (e.g. they are identified as 'language-delayed' because only their language was assessed). Nevertheless, the following figures can serve as a guide for an adequate educational provision that meets the special needs of autistic children in the UK.

The estimates of children with autism shown in Tables III and IV are based on the more conservative prevalence rate of 4.5/10,000 and a sex ratio of four males to one female. Numbers are rounded to the nearest ten. On the most recent Swedish estimates, there will be many more cases of related 'autism spectrum' disorders, in addition to autism, who also require specialist help and provision. Gillberg and Gillberg (1989) found a prevalence rate of 26/10,000 for Asperger's syndrome, which is by far the most numerous of the autistic spectrum disorders.

Table V International Comparisons for Estimated Incidence of Autism
Cumulative total population data only: Statistical Yearbook (39th Edn)
(1994) New York: UN.

These figures are based on the unlikely assumption that children with autism and related conditions will have the same life expectancy as the general population. In countries where, for example, medical management is less advanced, the above figures will considerably overestimate the numbers actually surviving with autism.

	Total Population	Autism Proper At 4.5 per 10,000; to nearest 100	Other Autistic Spectrum At 26 per 10,000; to nearest 100
New Zealand	3,307,000	1,500	8,600
Republic of Ireland	3,541,000	1,600	9,200
Switzerland	6,366,000	2,900	16,600
Sweden	8,360,000	3,800	21,700
Greece	10,269,000	4,600	26,700
Sri Lanka	14,847,000	6,700	38,600
Nepal	15,023,000	6,800	39,100
Australia	15,602,000	7,000	40,600
Morocco	20,500,000	9,200	53,300
Sudan	20,594,000	9,300	53,500

Table V International Comparisons
for Estimated Incidence of Autism (*continued*)

Kenya	21,000,000	9,600	55,600
Algeria	23,039,000	10,400	59,900
South Africa	23,386,000	10,500	60,800
Canada	25,309,000	11,400	65,800
Colombia	27,838,000	12,500	72,400
Zaire	29,917,000	13,500	77,800
Argentina	32,609,000	14,700	84,800
Spain	37,746,000	17,000	98,100
Republic of Korea	40,488,000	18,200	105,300
Ethiopia	42,169,000	19,000	109,600
Egypt	48,254,000	21,700	125,500
Turkey	50,664,000	22,800	131,700
Ukraine	52,000,000	23,300	134,300
Thailand	54,533,000	24,500	141,300
France	57,000,000	25,500	147,000
Italy	56,557,000	25,500	147,100
Vietnam	64,411,000	29,000	167,500
Germany	77,781,000	35,000	202,200
Pakistan	84,254,000	37,900	219,100
Bangladesh	87,120,000	39,200	226,500
Nigeria	88,515,000	39,800	230,100
Brazil	121,149,000	54,500	315,000
Japan	123,611,000	55,600	321,400
Russian Federation	147,022,000	66,200	382,300
USA	248,710,000	111,900	646,600
India	844,324,000	379,900	2,195,200

The Age Distribution of Autism

The total number of children recognised as having autism will depend on the age at which the condition can be recognised. As we explained in Chapter 2, it is still unclear how early it is possible to diagnose autism from the behaviour of a child.

Autism probably originates in the genes or from a pathogenic influence that affects brain organisation in early embryo or foetal development long before birth (see Chapter 6), but the behavioural effects do not appear until the brain has attained a certain level of maturity – until certain psychological functions emerge. This results in different estimates of the beginning of the condition, depending on what behaviours are taken to be the best indicators. For example, it is not possible to identify a language disorder before a normally developing child can be expected to speak and understand words.

Nevertheless, there is agreement that most autistic children show a number of characteristic abnormalities in the second year, and secure diagnosis of Kanner's autism is usually possible before the child is four. Late diagnosis results from an understandable professional reluctance to attribute delays in communication and language development to such an incurable condition. It is also the case that a focus on language or intelligence may lead to important and reliable signs of early failure in awareness of persons and their feelings and purposes being overlooked. Psychological rating systems frequently assume that language and intelligence are more measurable and therefore more 'reliable'. This is largely an artificial effect created by the tests themselves. It is also the case that standardised tests of early mental development require high levels of psychological training in their use and interpretation.

With the greatly improved understanding of the early stages of autism that we now possess, and recognition that motivation and expressive behaviour, for example, those indicative of joint attention, can be measured with appropriate techniques, it will become possible to identify more autistic children in pre-school stages, when they are most receptive to intervention. This will be a key element in an effective educational provision.

Efforts to trace features of the disorder down to the first nine months of infancy are, however, less likely to succeed. No behaviours have been reported in retrospective accounts that could serve reliably to separate an autistic child from the wide variation that is usually seen in the behaviour of infants at this stage (Adrien et al., 1993). The limited data we have at present come from retrospective parental accounts, which have uncertain validity, and from analyses of a limited number of home video recordings. The findings are suggestive, but they need systematic, prospective validation. Current research on behaviours of infants in high risk families may identify important marker behaviours leading to more efficient diagnosis in the second and third years (see CHAT, Appendix II).

The brain structures that are believed to be most affected in autism, and most involved in the manifestations of the disorder (see Chapter 7), include the prefrontal cortices, which, though they are first laid down in very early foetal stages, only begin to take on their primary functional roles around 12–18 months after birth (Dawson and Fischer, 1994).

Sex Differences

As in many other developmental disorders, there are more males than females in the autistic population, most studies reporting around four males to one female (see Rutter, 1985, for review). Higher male/female sex ratios appear for the classical Kanner autism, which describes a population that have comparatively high intelligence. Ratios as high as 13:1 (Gillberg, Steffenberg and Schaumann, 1991) and 16:1 (Wing and Gould, 1979) have been reported. In autistic individuals with lower IQ, however, the ratio has been reported to be much closer to 1:1.

Wing (1980b) found a ratio of 1:1.1 in the lowest IQ range of 0–19, of 1.3:1 for IQ = 20–49 and 4.2:1 for IQ > 50. At the time of this study, Rett's syndrome, a progressive disorder leading to profound mental handicap that affects only girls (Hagberg et al., 1983; Hagberg, 1989) was not recognised as a different condition. If the Rett's syndrome girls were removed from the very low IQ group in this analysis, the remaining group of autistic children would have many more males than females, not approximately equal numbers of the two sexes, as shown above.

Social Class or Level of Education of Parents

A once commonly held view was that autism occurs more frequently among the children of families in higher, more educated social classes. This impression is probably related to the surprising focused intelligence of some autistic children in families with a high level of education where such concentrated interest is valued and encouraged. Furthermore, better educated, well-off parents will be more likely to come forward for professional help. In an extensive research literature, only one study (Lotter, 1967) has found evidence for a slight effect in this direction. Other publications (Wing, 1980a; Gillberg and Schaumann, 1982; Cialdella and Mamelle, 1989; Gillberg et al., 1991) find no effect of social class. This finding remains of interest, however, because developmental disorders in general, like other health problems, occur more frequently in lower social classes. Autism is, therefore, exceptional if there is no bias of this kind. This can be taken as further evidence for a genetic rather than an environmental cause.

Handedness and Autism

Considerable attention has been given to reports that handedness, the preference for using the left or right hand in more skilled actions and for gestures of communication, and therefore cerebral dominance or asymmetry of brain function, may be anomalous in the autistic population (Dawson, 1988). This interest has been fuelled by the predictions of the Geschwind and Galaburda hypothesis (Geschwind and Galaburda, 1985), described below (see

Chapter 7), that ascribes variations in asymmetries of brain development, behaviour and cognitive functioning to the influence of the male sex hormone, testosterone.

Several studies (Boucher, 1977; Tsai, 1982; Fein et al., 1985) have failed to demonstrate an increased rate of familial left-handedness in relatives of left or right-handed autistic individuals, which suggests that any increased rate of anomalous hand dominance has a pathological and not a genetic basis. The currently favoured explanation is expressed by Dorothy Bishop, who describes what is found as follows:

> ...increased non-right handedness in autism arising as a consequence of generally poor motor functioning which results in a failure to learn the types of motor skills for which hand preference is normally shown. (Bishop, 1990)

It should be noted, however, that mechanisms of the brain that have been hypothesised to be the sites of primary defects that cause autism, that is, limbic and midline interneuronal systems, have asymmetric organisation from early in brain development (Chapter 7; Trevarthen, 1990, 1996). Anomalies of handedness, in addition to disorders of motivation affecting social responses, attention and cognitive functioning (Dawson, 1988), could be initiated by abnormal pre-natal developments in these systems, and then lead to aberrant post-natal motor learning.

Seasonal Variations

A number of studies have found that children who develop autism are more likely to have been born at certain times of the year.

The first study reported an excess of March and August births and a relative shortfall in October and November (Bartlik, 1981). Data on 179 Canadian (DSM-III) autistic subjects also showed an excess of spring and summer births (March to August with a winter shortfall), the effect being evident primarily in non-verbal, developmentally delayed subjects (Konstantareas et al., 1986). In 80 Japanese autistic (DSM-III) children, an increase in spring births was again reported (April–June) with a high level of annual fluctuation correlating (with a coefficient of 0.92) with rates of admission for bronchiolitis and pneumonia (Tanoue et al., 1988). A series of 100 Swedish children with autistic disorder of uncertain origin showed a significantly higher than expected incidence of March births (Gillberg, 1990). The largest study to date is a national UK survey. Data were collected on 1435 autistic individuals by questionnaire along with a clinic sample of 196 cases with 121 sibling controls, and normal population data (Bolton et al., 1992). This study has thrown up major inconsistencies between the clinic and survey data, and it failed to replicate the earlier findings on seasonal variation in birth of autistic individuals. Nevertheless, significant deviations from normal expected seasonal birth patterns in certain times of year, but not in March, were identified for the autistic individuals.

One possible explanation for any seasonal birth effect, which is also observed in other anomalies of brain development, is that environmental stress on the mother at a particular stage of pregnancy may contribute to abnormal development of the brain, early foetal stages being more vulnerable. Infants born in spring or summer would be early foetuses in winter when the mother's health may be most likely to suffer from stress or infection. This could increase the effects of a genetic factor that weakens brain development in early stages. Aspects of such a model have been discussed in a series of papers by Geschwind and Galaburda (1985).

CHAPTER 5

What Causes Autism?
What Are the First Effects?

Concepts of the Psychology of Autism, and of Biological Causes

There are many ways to an understanding of how human minds work and how they develop. Inevitably, there are many ways of explaining how a complex psychological disorder like autism begins. Even if we know accurately what autism is like on the outside, how to describe and recognise it, can we imagine what it is like to be autistic, and what the world might be like for a child who is becoming autistic? Trying to match autistic behaviour to our own experiences and feelings seems hazardous. A parent or a teacher of an autistic child can be forgiven for feeling lost. It is easiest to perceive the child just in terms of the faults that are most disturbing to ourselves. The child has autism and that means he or she cannot communicate or understand, and is unreasonably preoccupied with a private world and prone to emotional storms.

Is there any way to get inside? Some believe they have found a way by testing how autistic children answer questions about what goes on in other persons' minds, and that the discovery helps explain much about any human mind. This can be a circle of reasoning, but the quest has proved rewarding, and it has certainly stimulated interest in autism among psychologists, teachers and brain scientists. More experiments have been made with the behaviour and thinking of autistic children in the past 15 years than ever before. In a sense we know more. But different ideas of what autism is lead to rival claims for therapeutic or educational intervention, and confusing information for parents and teachers. It is important to try to reconcile the different viewpoints. Can we get the pieces of the puzzle to fit together?

Psychologists, educators, psychiatrists, brain scientists, geneticists have different ways of looking at, describing and explaining human behaviour, and the behaviour of children with autism is no exception. An interesting new hypothesis identifies the cause of reduced social sensitivity and interpersonal communication in autism, often combined, and especially in Asperger's syndrome, with well-developed visuo-spatial abilities and interest in technical objects and problems, with an abnormal gene expression in an X chromosome from the mother (Skuse *et al.*, 1997). The fact that autistic disorders are much more common in males than in females fits this idea. However, there are many processes between the expression of genes on the sex chromosomes and the formation of brain mechanisms that mediate psychological abilities or disabilities, and the causal link will not be simple.

Unravelling causes is difficult because autism, like psychological life itself, is a condition that has many and varied manifestations, and these manifestations change with age. Some will pay more attention to signs of abnormal coordination of movements, or sensations, or thinking, or emotions; some will attempt to measure problem-solving activities of the children, using experiments that have proved useful in the study of psychological developments and special educational needs; others begin more interested in the children's interpersonal or social responses, and the techniques of child psychotherapy. A number of psychologists have come to the conclusion that the best basis for understanding the disorder of autism is to see how it fits with the whole pattern of normal development (Rogers and Pennington, 1991; Sigman and Capps, 1997). Many remarkable discoveries have been made in developmental psychology in recent decades, and the new awareness of children's minds has benefited research on autism and other disorders of mental growth.

Brain science has come of age in the same period. New methods for studying the anatomy, chemistry, and development of brains have led many to pin their hopes for understanding, and perhaps for improved methods of treating autism, on research into neuronal systems in the brain, hunting for features that turn out to be consistently different in autistic individuals. New genetic and molecular-biological theories that seem to explain how inherited factors control normal and abnormal building of the tissues and organs of the brain, and the balance of the brain's chemical communication systems, obviously promise a more fundamental explanation of the source of trouble. There are others who feel that autism might be triggered by faulty chemical communication between the brain and the body, due to abnormal hormones, by products of digestion, abnormal diet, or failure to process food in the normal way. Factors of the environment, or infections, may cause effects that mimic the effects of altered genes.

Whatever approach is taken, it is always necessary to remember that autism is a condition that develops. All developments in brain function are the consequence of interacting factors, some from inside the genetic growth programme that controls steps in the formation of different cell populations and networks in the brain, some coming from the environment that stimulates and transforms the brain as it is growing. Stimulation affects how nerve connections are sorted out, some cell-to-cell contacts being confirmed and many others lost.

Most of the arguments about rival concepts have, in the past half-century, revolved around this problem: is autism caused 'genetically' and 'inherited', or is it caused by an abnormal environment of the brain, either in the body chemistry, or coming from stimuli from the outside world, and especially from experience of the social world of people? The preferred answers have been important, because they have influenced how autistic children are perceived and the attempts that are made to help them develop with less handicap.

Autism is not a disease, like measles or AIDS, that any person can catch, if infection occurs in the right conditions – that can be treated, and possibly cured, if treatment eliminates the cause and reverses at least a significant part of the damage done. Nor is it like a consequence of accidental injury, like the loss of a limb, or the effects of a car accident on the head or internal organs. It is better likened to unusual body height, such as dwarfism or exceptionally large size, which is a feature of an individual – inherited but affected by conditions of development.

Evolving Ideas About the Nature and Causes of Autism

At first autism was perceived as a 'mental' or 'emotional' illness. As we have seen, Leo Kanner (1943) first suggested that all symptoms of autism, which he described with such skill, stem from an **innate inability for interpersonal contact,** implying that a disturbance in the growth of brain is responsible. He did not think it was an emotional reaction to stress in early childhood. Later he considered that experiential factors combined with innate ones produce the clinical picture of autism (Eisenberg and Kanner, 1956). Having first presented autism as an intrinsic disorder of affective contact, he was persuaded that the emotional characteristics of the mother, with a possible link to high intelligence and upper social class of the parents, could be a cause. This is now known to be a misconception. It receives no support from later population studies, as has been mentioned.

A more cautious opinion of the early days, when the newly recognised syndrome was being investigated as an important medical condition, was that parental coldness can support the development of autism in a child with a constitutional weakness in brain development (Eisenberg and Kanner, 1956), or that a combination of unresponsive child and unresponsive mother exists where autism appears (Anthony, 1958). Now experience of a great variety of methods developed in special schools and clinics for helping autistic children in collaboration with parents has identified the need to advise or train parents how to respond perceptively to their children in ways that reduce distress and avoidance, and that promote positive enjoyment of shared interest and communication (see Chapter 10).

Hobson (1989, 1990c,d, 1993a,b) claims that the observed social impairment in autism is created by a fundamental **inability to respond emotionally** to others. He explains cognitive and language deficits in autistic children as developmental consequences of failures in interpersonal relatedness, and he draws evidence from comparison with the autistic-like behaviour of some children born blind and consequently cut off from contact with other persons' feelings (Hobson, 1993b). Tests prove that autistic children do have problems in recognising and interpreting or understanding emotions (Capps *et al.*, 1992; Hobson 1986a,b; Hobson *et al.*, 1988b), and in expressing emotional states (Ricks, 1975; Snow *et al.*, 1987; Yirmiya *et al.*, 1989). This disability directly interferes with all their communications with other persons, and it must affect their development in all psychological areas. Hobson's approach is one that recognises that a child develops understanding and skills through 'mediated learning' with the aid of confident and trusting communication with companions of various ages, and he believes that emotional responsiveness and self-awareness in relationships, or 'intersubjectivity', is the bridge that makes such companionship possible.

Now the evidence is overwhelming, from neuropathology (Bauman and Kemper, 1994), from imaging of CNS structure and activity (Aitken, 1991b), and from neurochemistry (Barthélémy *et al.*, 1988), that a pre-natal fault in brain development can cause autism, and that this, and not parental behaviour, is the root cause of the affective and motivational disorder in most cases of infantile autism, as well as the associated motoric, sensory, cognitive, rational and linguistic abnormalities that emerge in early childhood.

Nevertheless, respecting the clinical insights of psychodynamic therapists and the attachment theorists who have studied development of the mother–infant bond and its intuitive regulations (Schore, 1994), we would add that it is important to acknowledge that a child developing autistic behaviour, whatever the prior cause, will be a strain and worry for parents and the rest of the family, will certainly affect their emotions, and may threaten their emotional health and the integrity of the family. Parental anxiety can aggravate an autistic child's problem of development, reducing his or her ability to cope, leading to ineffective attempts to control the child. This point is considered later when we compare successful treatments and educational interventions that work with the autistic child and the parents together.

These issues, which are still highly controversial for theorists of psychological functions and their development, assume great practical importance, as we shall see, when one has to plan intervention to help the autistic child and to advise the parents in their demanding task.

The quality and consistency of affectionate care an infant receives from the mother or other principal caregiver, and the kind of emotional attachment that the child develops for that person, is important in normal development. The emotional quality of maternal care can affect, or be correlated with, the immediate emotional development and future social responsiveness and self-confidence of the child (Main and Goldwyn, 1984; Murray, 1988, 1992; Schore, 1994; Stern, 1985). However, even if some behaviours may be similar, the psychological disturbances of temperament, social responsiveness and learning attributable to this disordered or unsupportive kind of experience are not the same, nor as resistant to changes in human relationships, as those seen in autistic children.

Autistic children, unlike, for example, abused children, and in spite of their avoidant or unresponsive behaviours in communication, are emotionally attached to their carers (Rogers and Pennington, 1991; Sigman, 1989). What they lack is flexibility in interpersonal responsiveness, and they are often unable to learn through ordinary communication, or are very limited in what they can learn from other persons' guidance. This is evidence that autism must have a primary cause within the child's systems that regulate interactive learning or **companionship,** and not in the presumably more primitive systems that maintain emotional attachment to a caregiver (Aitken and Trevarthen, 1997; Reddy *et al.*, 1997; Trevarthen and Aitken, 1994).

Even though it may be decided that there is an innate cause of autism in the way the child's brain has grown, we are left by the above diversity of theories with a fundamental question about the psychology of the child. Is autism primarily caused by an affective failure specific for relating to persons, as Kanner's clinical intuition strongly suggested, or is it a more general cognitive deficit, a loss of 'information-processing' capacity? Is it at base an emotional illness, or is it the result of faulty perceptions or reasoning? Is the primary factor to do with the purposeful initiation of behaviour, or with strategies for attending to the world, selecting what deserves the focus of interest and concern?

Measuring Physiological Signs

Psychiatrists attempting to find an objective or biological cause in abnormalities of brain physiology, studied by measuring signs of electrical activity in nerves, found evidence that **sensory functions and attention** are abnormal in autistic children. Ornitz and Ritvo (1968) postulated that autistic children's inability to maintain constancy of perception stems from a pathologic mechanism with a neurophysiologic basis. They identified the fault in the input pathways from receptors of touch, hearing, vision, etc.

Recent evidence, reviewed in Chapter 6, indicates that a primary disorder, not in the sensory pathways, but in the functioning of neurons in the core of the brain that distributes and focuses attention and learning, aiming the receptors so they will pick up stimuli in the appropriate direction and with appropriate sensitivity, also leads to faults in brain growth before birth, and in the emotions that serve to regulate learning through communication with other persons in early childhood (Rogers and Pennington, 1991; Schore, 1994; Trevarthen, 1989; Trevarthen and Aitken, 1994). The central reticular formation and associated limbic system make up the **core regulator of brain activity** and brain sensitivity; this system is involved in the patterning of selective attention, coordination of perception with action, and in memory. It also determines the levels of activity and efficiency of transmission in sensory pathways.

Innate Behaviour Patterns and Motivation

No amount of information on brain anatomy or basic physiological functions can replace the insight into the nature of psychological functions that can be obtained by careful examination of how behaviour adapts in different circumstances. From the point of view of ethologists, specialists in accurate description of how animals communicate and how they set up their social relationships, **motivation for approach or withdrawal** from social contact with other individuals, and for picking up the signals that regulate communication, is critical in parent–child relationships (Tinbergen and Tinbergen, 1983). Autism is seen by the Tinbergens as an imbalance of this motivation and emotion leading to a confused state dominated by **anxiety,** and they, with the psychoanalysts and attachment theorists, think the intrusiveness of the human environment toward the child must be a key factor in its cause. Anxiety causes social withdrawal and consequent failure to learn and benefit from social interaction.

Holding therapy, described below, has been developed as an application of the Tinbergens' theory, to overcome anxious avoidance by restricting its expression (Grandin, 1992; Richer, 1983; Richer and Nicoll, 1972; Zappella *et al.*, 1991). It must be emphasised, however, that autistic avoidance is often not accompanied by any signs of agitation or anxiety. Cognitive problems with selective attention in autism are unrelated to emotional evaluation and affective self-regulation.

The Search for a Primary Cognitive Disorder, or Fault in Planning Thought

On the assumption that the disorder stems from a **cognitive or intelligence** deficit that interferes with the pick-up of every kind of information, its remembering and recall, Hermelin and O'Connor (1970) claimed that the autistic children's inability to recode all kinds of stimuli meaningfully underlies the apparent social impairment. Tilton and Ottinger (1964) suggested that autistic children's inability to perceive relationships between objects might contribute to their failure to develop social skills, relations between the child and things, or between things and things, being conceived in the same way as relations with persons. Rutter (1983) proposed that a cognitive deficit is the basis of autism. He noted that autism is always accompanied by a measurable loss in intelligence. In her autobiographical account of the experience of being autistic, Donna Williams (1996) claims that her sensory processing problems generate a need to protect herself from the barrage of meaningless excitation she receives, from objects or places and from people.

Recently, deficits found in autistic children's cognitive **'executive function'**, defined as:

...the ability to maintain an appropriate problem-solving set for attainment of a future goal...[which]...includes behaviours such as planning, impulse control, inhibition of prepotent but irrelevant responses, set maintenance, organized search, and flexibility of thought and action (Ozonoff, Pennington and Rogers, 1991, p.1083)

have been taken to be fundamental. It has been found that all autistic individuals perform poorly on 'executive function' tasks, and this, taken with neuropsychological evidence (of the effects of abnormal or damaged anatomy or brain chemistry in different brain areas), indicates that all share a loss of function in the prefrontal part of the brain (Bishop, 1993; Dawson and Fischer, 1994). This explanation brings in the notion of an active investigative motivation in the brain that directs cognitive functions such as perceiving, knowing, remembering and thinking. In Chapter 7 we review evidence that the brain systems linked to this function are indeed not functioning normally in autistic persons.

Deficiencies in Symbolic Thinking, and Language

Autistic children are often diagnosed when they fail to develop speech, and all have problems with language. Autistic people appear to perceive the world 'literally' or imitatively, without accepting conventional interpretations.

Taking symbols to be cognitive representations or codes for concepts, psychologists suggested that the central problem is an impairment of the **comprehension and use, or formation of symbols** (Hammes and Langdell, 1981; Ricks and Wing, 1975). Studies on the acquisition of language and on the functional and symbolic play in autistic children have been cited to support the idea that a major impairment is in symbol formation (Sigman and Ungerer, 1984a; Ungerer and Sigman, 1981). However, autism is not simply accounted for as a defect in language or symbolic communication. Indeed, the level of speech function varies from total muteness to a prolific, if abnormal, fluency (Donaldson, 1995; von Tetzchner and Martinsen, 1981). Nor is language simply the acquired store of semantic elements and grammatical rules; its development and use involve motivation for sharing interests and feelings with other persons, as we shall describe.

The 'Theory of Mind' Hypothesis and Joint Attending

A new kind of cognitive theory has become popular in the last ten years, which identifies the fundamental cause of social deficits in autism with failure in a 'meta-cognitive' mechanism of the mind, one that models 'thinking about thinking'. This approach has been driven by philosophy of mind and it is, in consequence, both intellectually sophisticated and seductive. Its success has been due to the development of clever narrative tests for determining what children believe about other persons' thoughts as these are represented in a little story. The autistic child is described as lacking a normally developed **theory of mind,** that is, of other persons' minds. The main feature of the disorder is said to be an inability to attribute beliefs to others. The child does not form a mental image of what can go on in other people's heads and this stems from a failure in thinking about his or her own mental states, as well as the mental states of others (Baron-Cohen, 1989b; 1990, 1995; Baron-Cohen, Tager-Flusberg and Cohen, 1993; Leslie and Frith, 1988).

Experiments on theory of mind tasks use a test situation in which dolls are shown performing different roles and experiencing different parts of the story. The child is asked to say what a particular doll who missed an essential part of the drama will think, or know, or do. These experiments have proved that, within the definition of the test, autistic children do have a deficit in 'theory of mind'; autistic children of five or older make judgements like those of young toddlers, under four, who have not yet developed the required imaginative representation of other persons' experiences. Autistic children have been described as having problems in understanding other persons' 'false beliefs' (Baron-Cohen et al., 1985; Perner et al., 1989), 'true beliefs' (Leslie and Frith, 1988), and 'desires' (Harris, 1989), and, correspondingly, they make aberrant interpretations of event sequences in psychological-intentional terms (Baron-Cohen et al., 1986), of emotion caused by beliefs (Baron-Cohen, 1991b) and of deception (Baron-Cohen, 1992). They have difficulties in distinguishing mental from physical entities and appearance from reality (Baron-Cohen, 1989c).

The normal 'theory of mind' is hypothesised to be an innate cognitive capacity first appearing in the second year of life, which, besides conferring the abilities just described, accounts for the remarkable development of children's **symbolic pretend play** at that age (Baron-Cohen et al., 1985; Leslie, 1987). The same cognitive capacity is also manifested in 'ostensive communication' by which interests and meanings are demonstrated and shared, '…something broader than just pointing and showing: namely, any act in which one person places a stimulus in the environment of another person for purposes of communication and which achieves communication by directing attention' (Leslie and Happé, 1989, p.206). This kind of behaviour is a key component of intentional communication (Leslie, 1991). It includes gestures, such as pointing to draw someone's attention to an object (Baron-Cohen, 1989a) and joint attention, the converging of interest with another on an item or task (Baron-Cohen, 1991a). According to Leslie (1987), infants and toddlers have 'first-order representations' of other persons and objects, and then they form 'second-order representations', imagining that other people have minds like their own. Autistic children are thought to pass through the first stage of this process but to fail in the second step, and that is why they exhibit deficits in symbolic play (Baron-Cohen, 1989b; Baron-Cohen *et al.*, 1985; Leslie and Frith, 1988).

There are a number of reasons for scepticism as to the practical utility of this explanatory framework for autism (Frith and Happé, 1994), and 'Model of Mind' deficits are not confined to autism. They are found in Down's syndrome (Zelazo *et al.*, 1996) and children with 'Semantic-Pragmatic' language problems (Shields *et al.*, 1996). Furthermore, mentalising difficulties are not the only kind of cognitive disorder in autism, and they appear in association with other problems in other disorders as well. They correlate with lowered levels of performance in tests of 'executive function' (Zelazo *et al.*, 1996), and with reduced receptive language ability (Happé, 1995). Executive function deficits, while characteristic of the autistic child, are also seen across a broad range of other clinical disorders, such as Attention-Deficit Hyperactivity Disorder (Pennington and Ozonoff, 1996), temporal lobe epilepsy (Hermann and Seidenberg, 1995), pituitary tumours (Peace *et al.*, 1997), schizophrenia (Liddle and Morris, 1991), and in the survivors of acute lymphoblastic leukaemia (Cieselski *et al.*, 1997).

The theories of meta-cognition and executive functioning are manifestly explanations of rational processes. They separate the cognitive capacities of the mind from the body. They do not seek evidence on bodily expressions of emotion – vocalisations, facial expressions, gestures and body movements – that mediate communication about psychological states. Such movements are crucial to the management of self–other awareness (Aitken and Trevarthen, 1997), and central to the emergence of a child's companionship with others from infancy (Reddy *et al.*, 1997).

This is the principal point of contention between Hobson and the proponents of the 'theory of mind' theory. According to Hobson, who has a psychoanalytic orientation interested in the emotional dynamics and self-regulation of infants and young children, '...children do not develop, nor do they need, a 'theory' about the mental life of others. What children acquire is knowledge that other people have minds' (Hobson, 1990b, p.199). For the acquisition of this knowledge there is, according to Hobson, a path of three stages that one must follow: first, a person acquires a concept of self; second, the individual establishes relatedness between himself and the others by means of observing others' bodily expressions; and third, he develops a relation based on analogy between his subjective experiences and the others' bodily appearances (Hobson, 1990b). Hobson (1990c) does not agree that autistic children are able to form first-order representations for the perception and expression of emotions, and for normal social-affective responsiveness. He suggests that autistic individuals '...from an early age...should be impaired in those primary representations that are relevant for socioemotional and especially affective interpersonal relations' (Hobson, 1990c, p.118). Indeed, evidence on the development of infants that later develop autism does indicate that emotional responses may not be normal from the first year, long before a normal child will develop a 'theory of mind' (Baron-Cohen, 1995; Sigman and Capps, 1997). Studies with autistic adults have shown that the difficulty of recognising emotional states remains in adult life (Harris, 1989).

Object Concepts or Person Concepts? Evidence from Imitation

The problem of what the consciousness of an autistic child is like has been considered in comparison with supposed stages in the development of **object awareness** (Piaget, 1954). It is not clear to what extent a 'general purpose' visual or spatial concept of an object is needed to account for the differentiation between the child's 'self' and another person. Evidence that infants only minutes old can imitate various kinds of expressions of a partner, including the expressions of many emotions, shows that some representation or reflection of the other person who is in front of the infant is normally present from birth. Furthermore, imitations of young infants are manifestly not reflex automatisms – they serve in the purposeful regulation of reciprocal communicative interactions (Kugiumutzakis, 1993; Nagy and Molnár, 1994). The ability to respond communicatively clearly does not wait on the development of rational thinking.

In a study formulated in terms of Piagetian cognitive theory, autistic children were not found to be impaired in their ability for self-recognition (Dawson and McKissick, 1984) and Hobson (1984) showed they could appreciate others' points of view in a visuo-spatial setting as well as non-autistic children of matching IQ. These studies suggest that autistic children are, in fact, able to differentiate between self and other as separate objects, and that they can imagine themselves to take the position of another subject relative to an object at a given location. Their failure in 'theory of mind' tests must be due to a different component of understanding about the other persons.

Piagetian theory is concerned with the development of logical operations that allow inferences to be made about the consequences of the subject's act on objects and about the interactions that may occur between objects. Durig (1996) has proposed a 'microsociological theory', that is a theory of conversational interactions and social learning of a self-description, that would explain autistic thinking and behaviour as due to a limitation in inductive logic. Where 'deductions' seek specific conclusions from specific premises, keeping fixed in real and certain entities and relationships, and 'abductions' attempt to make, creatively, specific conclusions from general premises, 'inductions' move from specific premises to general conclusions about the likely principles of life and experience. Durig collects evidence that a lack of inductive reasoning makes it impossible for autistic individuals to gain, as normal persons do, from social negotiations with others, and achieve a self-and-other awareness of roles, interpretations, etc. that is readily shared. He explains the pronominal errors, echolalia and other faults in language use by autistic children as due to the breakdown of their understanding of other persons' views of persons. They can focus on tasks that yield to deduction and they abduct from memory of personas they have experienced, but cannot project the expectations of others and gauge their own actions accordingly in live transactions. This theory, though it attempts to explain the detailed symptoms of autism, is abstract, like those attributing autistic behaviours to faults in 'meta-cognition' or 'theory of mind'.

It now seems likely that autistic children's varied impairment in **imitation,** which correlates with the degree of impairment in social relating (Dawson and Adams, 1984; Nadel, 1992; Nadel and Fontaine, 1989; Nadel and Pezé, 1993; Rogers and Pennington, 1991), is part of a fundamental intersubjective deficit, an aspect of an overall impairment in reciprocal communication, and not that both these interpersonal problems result from a deficiency in meta-cognition or any other general aspect of 'thinking'. It seems likely that a fundamental inability to form a responsive internal image of the other who can then be a partner in truly reciprocal interaction, with whom the child can explore how to share orientations to objects, exchange feelings about actions, objects and events and cooperate in performance of tasks, would undermine consciousness of persons and impair all kinds of social learning. The latest theories of the key psychological deficit in autism are considered further in Chapter 9.

Innate Intersubjectivity, Representation of a 'Virtual Other', and Regulation of Self-with-Other

On the basis of observations from micro-analysis of video of communication between mothers and young infants at a non-verbal level, the 'Theory of Innate Intersubjectivity' was proposed (Trevarthen, 1979; 1997d). The claim was made that the efficiency of sympathetic engagement between an infant and the adult signals the ability of each to 'model' or 'mirror' the motivations and purposes of the partner, immediately.

The performance observed in mother–infant interactions, which we discuss more fully later, requires a 'virtual other' representation of the kind that Bråten (1988) has postulated in an elegant formal theory of how humans engage in conversational intimacy. In his 'Theory of the Virtual Other', Bråten describes the mutual assimilation of two subjects in intersubjective communion as 'dialogic closure' in 'the mode of felt immediacy'. The efficiency of the processes of human sympathy is explained in terms of how the mind's innate organisation with a virtual companion perspective includes actual others in 'companion space', permitting 'co-enactment' of self with other, each in 'alter-centred' agency. He hypothesises that autism involves a failure of this mechanism, and that evidence for this is found in the errors of body-to-body mapping made when autistic children are asked to reproduce the orientation of gestures that others make in front of them (Bråten, 1998; Ohta, 1987).

Perceiving other persons' emotions cannot be divorced from the generation of expressive forms of acting because every person's communicative signals are made by highly specific forms of movement that are adapted to fit human perceivers' sensitivities (Trevarthen, 1993a,b). A smile *is* happy, as is walking with a fast, tripping step; tears *are* sad, as is a slow dragging way of walking and a downcast look, and emotions expressed by one person can lead to instantaneous sympathetic mimicry in an other. Expressions of the self 'invade' the mind of the other, making the moving body of the Self resonant with impulses that can move the Other's body too.

Infants are born with dependency on affectionate responses from caregivers who are ready to share motives and feelings, and this fundamental Self–Other system can suffer breakdown in different ways. We have proposed an analysis of the regulations involved when an autistic child is with a parent who is trying to understand (Aitken and Trevarthen, 1997). This analysis is based upon the theory, discussed in Chapter 6, that the brain of an infant is equipped with an Intrinsic Motive Formation (IMF) that develops in the brain of the embryo and foetus, before birth (Trevarthen and Aitken, 1994). We propose that autism is a condition in which the affected individual, lacking effective motive representations for the 'virtual other', interprets the actions of other persons as if they are not clearly distinct from those of the autistic individual himself or herself. In circumstances where the actions of the other correspond to the motives attributed by the autistic child, this can prove an adequate frame for successful interaction.

There will, however, be many situations where such expectations will result in collapse of all satisfying mutuality, and the partner will 'give up'. We think that development of this effective absence in the child of a 'virtual other' in 'companion space' (Bråten, 1988), would be likely to be preceded by early interactional difficulties, which would, however, not become clearly manifest before the stage in development known as 'secondary intersubjectivity', typically beginning at around nine months of age. At this age there are large transformations in behavioural evidence of motives for joint awareness, self-presentation, and cooperative task performance (Sigman and Capps, 1997), as well as in neurobiological evidence for significant developments in the brain, especially in the frontal lobes (Dawson, 1994).

Based on understanding of developments in the first two years (Trevarthen, Murray and Hubley, 1981), we believe that the autistic infant has a latent disorder of intersubjectivity and narrative organisation of thinking that becomes critical around the middle of the second year, following mastery of joint awareness and cooperative task performance at around one year. Where children that become autistic are abnormal in their attention and responsiveness in early infancy, in the first six months, this appears to be an indication of a broader neurological disorder. Such signs will not be diagnostic – they appear in other developmental abnormalities on the 'continuum of empathy disorders'

(Gillberg, 1991), and evidently also in conditions leading to mental handicap, such as Rett's syndrome (Witt-Engerström, 1990).

CHAPTER 6

Brain Development and Autism

Autism is now understood to be a neuro-developmental disorder – a disorder of the way the brain develops. To understand how such a baffling condition of mind and behaviour as autism could be the result of faulty brain development, we have to imagine how brain tissues might gain the organisation to regulate perceiving and acting, learning and feeling, as well as vital functions inside the body. All these can be abnormal in autism.

Here we summarise the evidence that a brain scientist would use to conceive how an autistic child's problems might arise. We present a simplified overview of brain development in an attempt to explain how development may become deviant in autism. The account has enough detail for a student of psychology, with key references to recent research. It might seem overwhelming to the uninitiated. If the reader feels such a mass of new facts and terms is unnecessary to his or her understanding of autism, please turn to the paragraph at the end of the chapter. This draws out essential conclusions and their practical implications.

Every human brain is made up of astronomical numbers of interconnected nerve cells, organised in systems, each of which performs some part of the job of initiating, directing, guiding, elaborating and coordinating consciousness, emotions and behaviour. Moreover, the brain is not only in control of how a person acts in an awareness of the world outside the body. It is also a key regulator for vital body functions, having direct nervous and/or hormonal contact with all the internal organs. None of this regulating and integrating of behaviour would be possible if the brain was an incoherent chaos of nerve impulses going off at random. Its staggeringly complex activity must be integrated in space and tightly orchestrated in time to represent the form and functions of all the parts of the body at once. Cells in different brain parts are linked by nerve fibre connections that synchronise activity in clusters or sheets of cells that are far apart in the body, from low down in the back to the top of the head. And while this activity in nerve circuits responds to stimulation from outside the body, it is not wholly dependent on it. There is much spontaneous and organised activity generated inside the brain.

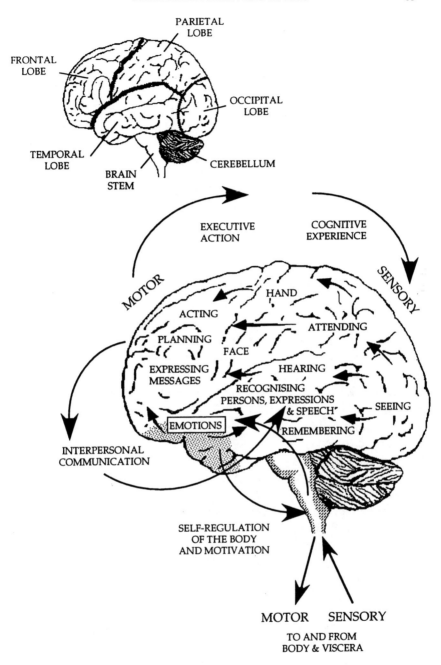

Figure 2: Adult human brain from the left side, to show the main anatomical regions. Also shown is the approximate distribution of functional systems for dealing with the physical environment, communication with other persons, and regulation of body functions.

We all know that a person's intelligence and emotional stability depends on internal motives as well as on information from outside his or her brain and body. Autistic people have intelligent brains that represent their world and that regulate their bodily health, but they have more or less serious problems with awareness, learning and investigative acting, and they also suffer from many kinds of internal, self-regulatory, problems. As we have seen, they are most handicapped in their perception and responsiveness to what is going on inside other people – how they feel, what they are conscious of and how they wish to act. While sensitive to emotions and aware of people, they reciprocate poorly with the expressions and experiences of even those they know well. To understand this characteristic feature of the psychology of autism we have to extend brain theory further, to take account of how brains might map other persons' bodies and their behaviours – how they might tap into what is going on in the brains hidden in their heads.

Basic Brain Design, and Representing Persons (see Figure 2)

Intelligent behaviour requires 'prospective awareness', a conscious anticipation of what might be done in the world, both in the immediate solid present and in preparation for imagined future events. Such consciousness and its imagination is enriched by learning. We take in new ideas and skills from experience of the effects of what we do. Thus our understanding becomes more comprehensive and more efficient, linking effects inside the mind, its emotions and feelings of confidence or fear, to the real possibilities.

The human brain in a person has a unique power to do all these things in sympathetic communication with the bodies and minds of other individuals, picking up the patterns and rhythms in their brains by sensing and interpreting their movements. As we shall see, this ability to sympathise brain-to-brain with others via their expressions is an inborn talent in every baby (see Figure 1). This is an important clue when we are trying to understand why an autistic three-year-old has become so unaware and so unimaginative in reactions to people, and so turbulent in emotions and many vital self-regulations, in comparison with an unaffected, normally developing age-mate.

Motor systems of the 'central nervous system' (CNS) generate patterned output to muscles, moving the body and aiming and focusing sense organs, and also modulating spontaneous activity of the visceral muscles of the gut, heart, glands and so forth (see Figure 2). Sensory mechanisms receive and process input from the receptors of all kinds, including those inside the limbs and trunk of the body and in the internal organs, not just those that pick up visual, auditory, tactile or chemical information about the world outside the body. Intermediate neuronal systems, those that are neither sensory nor motor, perform a wide range of coordinative and motivating functions, from local adjustment between reflexes to the genesis of coordinated motivations for the whole subject, and they fix or erase memory traces, producing predictive cognitive representations that guide the choices and adjustments of goal-directed behaviours (Nauta and Feirtag, 1979).

Cells that perform more automatic functions at a low, unconscious level are concentrated in organised groups or nuclei. Some nerve fibre bundles are compacted into distinct tracts. Between the motor nuclei in the 'core' of the CNS and the tracts that tend to accumulate near its surface, is the 'reticular system', a network of less compact populations of cells and intermingled axons that receive sensory input and serve in regulation of the balance of activity in the whole nervous system, and the changes of physiological and psychological states. This we have called the Intrinsic Motive Formation (IMF), because it has its own organised anatomy and physiology and because it is the generator of initiatives and flexible responses of the body in its awareness of the world (Trevarthen and Aitken, 1997). The motor, muscle activating, mechanisms, including a pre-programmed system in which instinctive behaviour patterns are represented, lie within the lower 'ventral' or 'basal' half of the central nervous system. In the sensory mechanisms of the upper 'dorsal' half of the CNS very large populations of cells are arranged in layered sheets or cortices that may be greatly expanded for specialised perceptual and cognitive functions and therefore bulging or folded.

Mechanisms that control autonomic and 'visceral' functions, including basic appetites and aversions for biological regulation of the whole individual, are concentrated around the cavities of the CNS. The coordinated 'overseeing' functions of intelligence and learning are mediated in the anterior enlarged brain stem, and the highest cognitive and learning systems, with the most future sense and the greatest capacity for storing experience, are developed in two vast additions in which all lower functions are re-represented many times – the forebrain hemispheres, each with a huge folded 'rind' of cells called the 'cerebral cortex', and an outgrowth of the hind brain, the cerebellum with millions of cells in its cortex. At all levels, from the spinal cord to the cerebral cortex, the brain centres and the connecting tracts between them are ordered in maps that are linked to the parts of the body in anatomical order, though with distortions depending on the relative density with which different parts require neural representation. Those regions that pull the whole together in integrated states are the most diffusely or intricately designed, but body-maps are the common code of brain communication (Trevarthen, 1985b).

The cerebral cortex and cerebellum of the human brain are proportionately much larger than in other animals, and they are reciprocally interconnected with each other by great fibre systems, as well as with ascending and descending subcortical systems of the brainstem and spinal cord. But these two great components of the human brain, with their advanced features and interconnections, are only partly formed in a newborn baby and they develop slowly throughout childhood (Rakic, 1991; Sticker, et al., 1990). An infant's

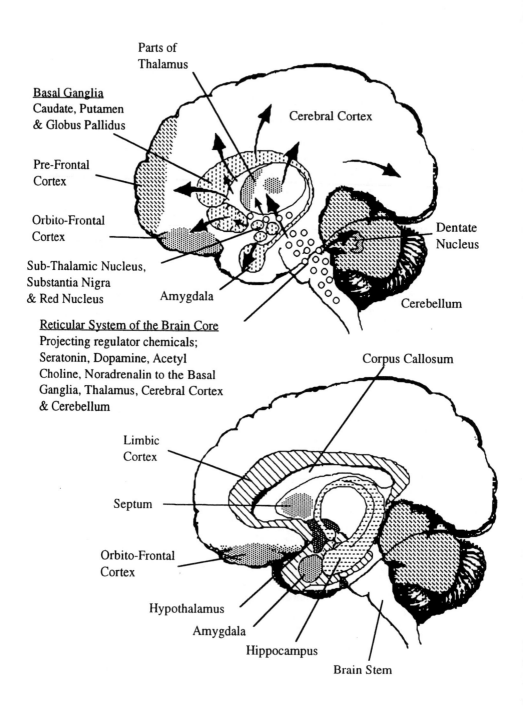

Figure 3: Motive and emotion systems of the human brain

psychological functions must be largely subcortical or limbic, and the later developing cortices must play a limited part. The cerebral neocortex and the cerebellar cortex are essential to the resolving power and versatility of our consciousness, but the human brain stem still retains the more automatic regulators of the whole subject, including the sensory-motor mechanisms for selectively orienting to locations in the environment, for patterning adaptive behaviour routines and for controlling the relationship between brain-directed behaviour in engagement with the external environment and the changing internal physiological requirements of the whole body. This is the heart of the developing mind, and the roots of its highly complex organisation are laid down long before birth, in direct chemical communication with the rest of the body, but without the benefit of input from the world and without free behaviour or learning (see Figure 2).

Although a newborn baby has learned almost nothing, has never had the benefit of imagining things far outside the body or actively experimenting with experience of objects, and has never used vision before, this baby can recognise the mother as a person (Bushnell, Sai and Mullin, 1989; Johnson, 1993), and can move in rhythmic sympathy with her (Condon and Sander, 1974), imitating expressions, exchanging well-defined emotions (Field *et al.*, 1982), provoking affectionate responses. How the brain in a baby grows this power to reflect and communicate with another person's body and mind is the greatest challenge to brain science, more wonderful than the astonishing powers of learning that will bring the child into full participation with the meanings and language of the parents' culture. It would seem that having one's own motives and emotions, and being able to recognise them in another, are vital starting components of this very human learning ability (Schore, 1994).

Anatomy and Chemistry of Motives: Regulators of Development and Learning

The changes of brain activity that move us to do particular things, with certain intensities and in particular directions, that cause us to seek for particular goals or pleasures, are determined in the core of the brainstem by an intricate set of counteracting neuro-chemical systems (see Figure 3). Motives arise among a population of specialised nerve cells in the 'reticular formation', the IMF, inside the stem of the brain (Trevarthen and Aitken, 1994). Their output in dynamic displays of emotion and changing moods involves a great Emotional Motor System (EMS) (Holstege, Bandler and Saper, 1996), reaching from the spinal cord to the relatively ancient 'limbic' regions of the cerebral cortex (MacLean, 1992). Two regions are crucial nodes of interplay between the reality-sensing and act-initiating intelligence mediated in the cerebral cortex and the motivating and coordinating functions that involve the brainstem core and hypothalamus: the subcortical 'amygdala nucleus' at the tip of the 'temporal lobe' (Aggleton, 1992, 1993), and the 'orbito-frontal cortex' in the lower mid portions of the frontal lobe, and the septum and cingulate cortex in the inner face of the frontal lobes. We shall find that these regions are important for analysis of what goes wrong in the brain of a young child developing autism (Holstege, Bandler and Saper, 1997; Vogt and Gabriel, 1993).

The brainstem cells of motives and emotions convey their excitatory or inhibitory molecules down to spinal circuits and up to the cerebral cortex. The key reticular neurons are a few per cent of the population in the whole brain, but their fibres reach to contact cell bodies and their branches throughout the brain. Projections of differing chemical type act collaboratively and are complemented by local circuit neurons that may focus their effects. The chemicals that they release at the surfaces of the target cells have the capacity to change the excitatory or inhibitory effects of junctions between nerve cells and thus to change the integrative functions of nerve pathways (Trevarthen and Aitken, 1994). These include the 'neuropeptides' (NP) and the classical monoamine transmitters, 'serotonin' (5-HT), 'dopamine' (DA), 'norepinephrine' (NE) and 'epinephrine' or 'adrenalin'. Chemicals that mimic these natural transmitters have been developed into psychoactive drugs that may give rise to good, alive states of mind, but that can seduce human feelings, making serious problems in modern societies, ultimately destroying brains. Hormones circulating in the blood also affect nerve cell activity, and hormone production by glands outside the brain (digestive glands, the thyroid, the reproductive glands, the adrenals and so on) is regulated by the brain, principally from the cluster of nuclei that serves as the 'head ganglion of the visceral system', the hypothalamus. The hypothalamus is the centre of regulations of appetites and aversions, including the reproductive impulses of sex, and the chemistry of human attachments (Morgane and Panksepp, 1981).

Reticular neurons, through release of their chemical products to appropriately responsive receptors on the surfaces of other nerve cells at all levels of the brain, perform or influence a great variety of essential functions: suppressing responses to touch or pain stimuli; organising rhythmic oculomotor (eye muscle) control and visual tracking, and performing analogous functions for hearing, tasting and the sense of smell; sharpening resolution of sensory cortex responses in moments of attention; setting the gain in all senses; activating and directing alertness and learning; regulating cortical habituation and conditioning; activating or suppressing instinctual motor patterns.

The NE system projects from the 'locus ceruleus' and other hindbrain reticular cell groups throughout the brainstem, down into the hindbrain and spinal cord and widely to the cerebral and cerebellar cortices (Barnes and Pompeiano, 1991). It is primarily concerned with alertness, defence and attack. In animals it patterns fear and rage and threat-aggression, and possibly submission. A small ensemble of cells in the 'substantia nigra' and parts of the 'mid-brain floor' (tegmentum), with very widespread effects, are the source of the DA rich nigrostriatal pathway, projecting up to the basal ganglia, limbic cortex and neocortex via the median forebrain bundle. They control the strength of elicited motor activity and involuntary motor patterns. Serotonin-rich cells are found in the hindbrain and through the midbrain in and about the midline. They project from the hind portion of midbrain to the limbic forebrain, neocortex and hypothalamus, stimulating calmness and sleep. The 'neuropeptides', including the opioid peptides ('endorphins' and 'enkephalins'), are the largest group of central transmitters. They are found in the dorsal half of the spinal cord and hindbrain visceral region, the grey matter round the cavity of the midbrain (the 'peri-aqueductal grey'), some nuclei in the hypothalamus, and in the 'central amygdala nuclei'. Some are found in cortical interneurons. NP secretions act as neuromodulators, with the monoamines, in pleasure versus pain sensations, and in the regulation of body temperature, drinking, sexual behaviour and locomotion (Holstege, Bandler and Saper, 1996; Panksepp, Nelson and Sivy, 1994).

In sum, the aminergic systems of the IMF contribute state-control-modulation of sensory-motor mechanisms and the outputs of the EMS, establishing patterns of motivation and affect and emotional expressions. Their connections to brainstem nuclei mediate balance and hearing and visual scanning, maintaining meaningful contacts of the organism with the environment while gating and selecting inputs to the cerebral cortex. The hypothalamus and reticular systems are reciprocally linked to the orbito-frontal cortex and temporal lobe cortex, both of which are very much enlarged in the human brain, and with the amygdala, also part of a system much elaborated in humans. As we shall see, all these mechanisms are thought to have a crucial role in the production of the characteristic abnormalities of behaviour and mental activity in autistic persons.

A new form of intelligence has evolved in humans and this has required the inheritance of changes in the brain at all levels, not just the addition of a large new cognitive and learning capacity in the cerebral cortex. The internal motives for being intelligent have also been transformed. Traces of this massive evolutionary creation can be found very early in the formation of a human brain, many months before birth, and even before the cells of the cortex exist.

Evolution and Development of Expressions of Self-Regulation and Social Attachment

In fish, absorption of oxygen into the blood, and the secretion of waste substances from blood to water, depends on the swimming movements of the whole animal, and upon movements of the mouth and gills. Nuclei in the brainstem, the cranial nuclei, contain cells of the special visceral motor system that control the heart and the gill arches, regulating the vital functions of respiration and blood circulation, principally by action of one cranial nerve, the

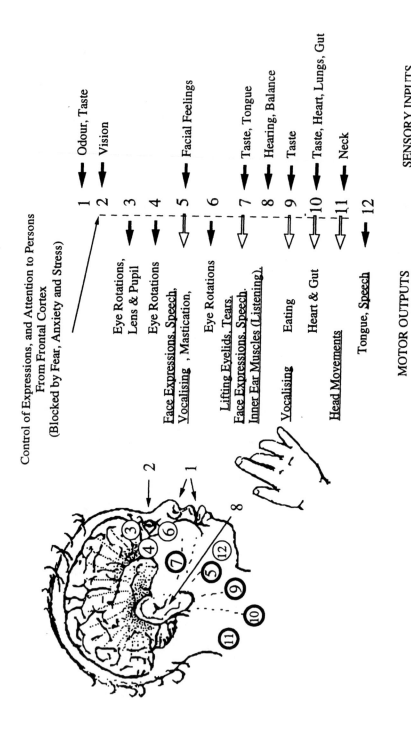

Figure 4: Special sensory and motor organs of the head, with their cranial nerves and brainstem nuclei. These are developed pre-natally and are functional from birth. (Gestures of the hand are regulated by motor nerves from nerves of the neck region of the spinal cord, under control of many levels of the brain.) White arrows = special visceral efferent nerves.

vagus (cranial nerve number 10). In humans the muscles of locomotion, and of the throat and face, have evolved to be important in both emotional self-regulation social life. When we look at the parts of the nervous system that control the expressions of the eyes and mouth, the vocal apparatus and the inner ear, we find that regulation of the action of key muscle activating nerves has evolved from the special visceral motor system of less evolved forms of animal (Figure 4). Brainstem nuclei are coordinated with the neuroendocrine system that controls states of behavioural excitation and emotion in collaboration with the hypothalamus and other components of the Emotional Motor System (Holstege *et al.*, 1997). Thus communication of emotions between human beings, such as between a mother and child, has come from mechanisms that controlled vital functions in each individual (Carter, Lederhender and Kirkpatrick, 1997; Schore, 1994). Self–other regulations have evolved out of self-regulations. Porges (1995, 1997, 1998b) has presented a theory of the evolution of vagal function that explains how the automatic self-regulations of the brainstem come under the control of the cerebral cortex in the evolution of emotional expression and speech, thus enormously increasing the capacities of individuals to cooperate in behaviour and thinking. Special visceral motor nerves regulate the lifting of the eyelids to look, the tensing of middle ear muscles to listen to a human voice and filter out the low frequencies that are irrelevant to verbal communication, the facial expressions used in gesturing, the vocalisations used to communicate, and the tilting of the head and neck to signal communication. Porges believes that autism (as well as other disorders of social engagement) is a problem in the regulation of both the sensory and motor elements of the ancient system for self-regulation, and, as we explain in Chapter 10, he has applied this hypothesis in a technique for improving filtration of sounds in the inner ear of people with autism, to help them listen to speech.

Human Brain Development Before and After Birth (O'Rahilly and Müller, 1994; Trevarthen, 1985a)

A fertilised human egg has a structured interior and surface and it is situated in a patterned cellular and molecular environment. It is possible that the future polarity and mapping of tissues and organs of the body have already been determined, invisibly, before there are any divisions of this cell. However, organisation of the body and its nervous system becomes definite only after two weeks, when the embryo is about one millimetre long. Then what will be the brain (the 'neural plate') can be located in the upper surface of the embryo. Forebrain, midbrain and hindbrain can then be distinguished, but the brain is still just a sheet of quite undifferentiated cells.

In Week 4 of gestation the central nervous system rolls into a tube and cells multiplying in the 'germinal layer' around the central cavity migrate outwards in the wall to form rudimentary neural masses in the 'mantle layer' of the ventral spinal cord, hindbrain and midbrain. Nerve fibres will spread through the outer 'marginal layer'. Motor nerves grow from the spinal cord at the same time as the limb buds and primordia of the special senses (eyes, vestibular organs and cochlear, olfactory and gustatory organs) and the first afferent tracts appear. Rudimentary nuclear masses form in the 'basal (motor) plate' of the brain, extending from the ventral horns of the spinal cord through the ventral hindbrain, midbrain tegmentum, ventral thalamus and subthalamus in the diencephalon, to the lamina terminalis and commissural plate in the forebrain. The dorsal 'alar (sensory) plate' is less developed. In the hindbrain the important reticular nucleus, the 'locus ceruleus', appears.

In the second half of the embryo period, Weeks 5 to 8, all the main components of the brain are formed, and the body takes the appearance of a miniature human with a disproportionately large head. The 'special sense organs' (eyes, vestibular canals and cochlear, hands, nose and mouth) are rapidly differentiating their dedicated forms. The cerebral hemispheres and cerebellum are in very rudimentary condition, but the brainstem regulatory and motivating structures are remarkably well-formed. And yet, at this stage the nervous system is inactive – it generates no behaviour. In Week 5 the brain almost doubles in size and the first monoamine transmission pathways grow from the brainstem into the cerebral hemispheres in which cells are completely undeveloped. The nuclei in the base of the forebrain, called 'basal ganglia', are relatively large. They will be important in patterning unconscious 'instinctive' movements, including expressive gestures. That important link between the emotional mechanisms and the future cerebral cortex, the 'amygdala', begins to differentiate from the basal ganglia, and integrating tracts appear in the midbrain and hypothalamus. Thus the mechanisms of emotional expression, the Emotional Motor System (EMS), defined earlier, are formed in outline when a human being is still an embryo just a few millimetres long.

The reticular formation and the pituitary gland under the hypothalamus develop conspicuously in the sixth week, as does the cerebellar ridge, which receives its first input fibres. Cells in the basal ganglia multiply producing bulges into the cavity of the hemispheres, the cortical and anterior nuclei of the amygdala develop and important subcortical centres – the hippocampus, red nucleus, subthalamic nucleus and mamillary body – appear, as does a generative region of the cerebral hemispheres, the 'insula', from which, in evolution, tissues of the higher mental functions have emerged. All these structures in the brain will be important later, in motivation and learning, and in communication. Tracts continue to develop throughout the brainstem, for example, connecting the hypothalamus and thalamus. The 'median forebrain bundle' carries descending fibres from the amygdala and ascending fibres from the locus ceruleus. The hormonal functions of the hypothalamus plus pituitary appear to begin at this time as well.

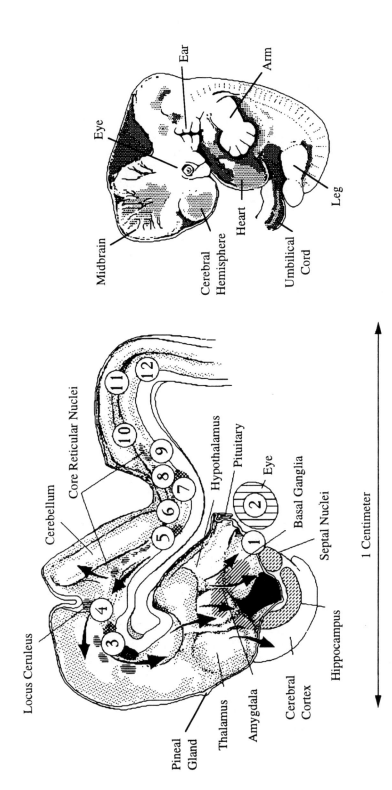

Figure 5: Right: Human embryo at seven weeks gestational age. Left: The brain of a seven-week embryo showing the location of the special sensory organs and cranial nerve nuclei in the brainstem, and the nerve pathways from the reticular formation in the core of the brainstem that carry nerve activity and regulatory chemicals into the developing cerebral hemispheres. The basal ganglia, septal nuclei hippocampus and amygdala are well developed, but the cerebral neocortex is just beginning to form. Cranial nerve nuclei numbered as in Figure 4.

In the cerebral hemispheres the first synapses or intercellular connections are seen at about six weeks, and then the first radially migrating neurons appear, starting the formation of the elaborately layered cortex (Rakic, 1991). The characteristic cell columns of the neocortex arise from precursor stem cells in the proliferative zone next to the cavity of the hemispheres. All cells in a column come from one germinal cell. The size of each functional cortical area depends on the number of proliferative units, which form a 'proto-map' of the whole cortex in the zone round the hemisphere cavity. The total number of columns is about 200 million, with large individual variation. The neocortex seems to have expanded in evolution by adding proliferative units, finally resulting in a revolutionary transformation that produced human cultural intelligence (Rakic, 1995). Pathological brain organisation appears to come about in the same way, under deviant genetic instructions, missing out components or producing distorted cell arrangements. Neuron cell type in the cortex is determined before cells reach their final position in the cortex. Nerve fibre growing up to the cortex from sensory systems are guided by 'position specific molecules' or 'body-mapping factors' which are in place on the surfaces of cerebral cells before they arrive. Clearly regulatory inputs from the brainstem reticular formation, the IMF, can impose their influence right from the beginning of the development of the cognitive mechanisms of the forebrain.

In Weeks 7 and 8 neurogenesis (nerve cell multiplication) in the cerebral cortex proceeds apace, and it continues until Week 18. Cells produced in the generative zone migrate radially into the columns along glial strands and come to lie in a layer in which most recently arrived cells move to the outer surface, through those already present. This inside-out migration is thought to enable communication between cells of instructions for differentiation. Differentiation of the migrating cortical cells is also influenced by their passage, before they reach the plate, through a dense cellular lattice and 'sub-plate' of early neurons, axons, dendrites and glia fibres (projections from non-neural glia cells which are abundant in the CNS, between the neurons). The sub-plate is larger in humans than in other primates and contains waiting input fibres generated ahead of their neuronal targets in sequence from the brainstem, basal forebrain, thalamus and ipse- and contra-lateral cortex. This structure can be regarded as a mechanism for establishing integrative regulation over the initial steps in morphogenesis of what will be the cognitive machinery of the hemispheres. Influences from the foetal IMF in subcortical regions will decide the distribution and laminar structure of the neocortex, including asymmetries of function in left and right hemispheres (Trevarthen, 1996).

Genes new to humans may trigger the formation of additional cortex that makes possible important innovations in culture-related learning of the adult human brain, including the learning of language. These added territories, in the parietal, temporal and frontal lobes of each hemisphere, are particularly rich in connections with other more narrowly specialised cortical areas, those representing separately the special senses and movements of parts of the body, and they are in close reciprocal relation with limbic or emotional and motivational cortex. Two major motivating mechanisms, the amygdala and hippocampus begin rapid differentiation in the seventh week, with fibre connections through the lateral forebrain bundle, and the septum develops acetylcholine producing nuclei that become of fundamental importance in the regulation of behavioural and cognitive functions. The basal ganglia, substantia nigra and globus pallidus appear, establishing the basic EMS mechanisms for instinctive motor functions. The eye-movement nucleus also shows important differentiations. The rudiments of the cerebellum, which begins complex new developments, and the cochlear (hearing) nucleus grow as the sensory nuclei of the hindbrain develop. The cerebellum, like the cerebral hemispheres, has two lives – part of its organisation develops and becomes functional before birth, but the enormous cerebellar cortex, like the forebrain neocortex, develops after birth.

The eighth week marks the end of the embryo and the beginning of the foetus. The first fibres grow down from neocortical cells *en route* to lower regions, and the hippocampus, which will be a key element in the mechanism that builds up memories of the environment after birth, enlarges. The roof of the midbrain swells, indicating a significant advance in primitive visual and auditory centres. Tracts linking the cerebral cortex and the cerebellum appear. The cortical plate has now three to five layers of cells. Integration of functions within the cortex is achieved by means of a vast number of cortico-cortical connections, which are also important in moulding the folds of the cortex. Long axons grow within and between the hemispheres from about the tenth week.

Cortical nerve cells stop appearing almost halfway through gestation, in the eighteenth week, and cell death starts, eliminating cells that are out of place or left out of the competition for connections with the rest of the brain. Cell numbers are essentially stable from the twentieth week, but there is some further cell loss later in development, indicating that basic brain-sculpting is still going on. Rapid growth in the cerebral wall and buckling of the cortical mantle is due to nerve cell enlargement and separation of cell bodies as their branching outgrowths, 'dendrites', grow. Anatomical asymmetries in the neocortex are evident at this stage, notably on the size of the dorsal surface of the temporal lobe and in the shape of the Sylvian sulcus. Experiments with monkeys prove that, while differentiation of cortical areas is self-regulated, relative size of areas depends on input from subcortical centres before there is any environmental stimulation. Basic structures and biochemical characteristics of the cortex develop with no sensory input.

Brain development is linked with differentiation of the gonads and the appearance of secondary sexual features of the body in the late embryo, and male/female differences in both brain anatomy and in the gonads appear to stem from differences in the organisation of neuro-hormonal systems of the brainstem. Hormonal control of sexual differentiation in behaviour is related to the biochemical mechanism by which gene expression is controlled in the central nervous system itself. There is a feedback loop between neurons of the hypothalamus and medioventral reticular formation, and the endocrine system of gonads and adrenals that regulate reproductive activities and development of the body and its secondary sexual features. This connection, which is of importance in the post-natal growth of the mental abilities in children, and especially in adolescence, is first evident in the early foetal stages (Geschwind and Galaburda, 1985, 1987; MacKinnon and Greenstein 1985).

Cortical cell layers are well-delimited in the newborn human brain, but this is just the beginning of a great development of new functional connections that continues through early childhood. There is a vast post-natal production of cell contact points or 'synapses', then a process of selective elimination or stabilisation of synapses that responds to environmental influences. Functional systems are formed by a sorting process involving loss of many components. Cell death is important in embryo brains, and then nerve fibres (axons), their branches (dendrites), fine extensions (dendritic spines), and functional contact points (synapses) show competitive selective elimination through to post-natal stages (Cowan et al., 1984). The initial cell proliferation, neural migration, outgrowth of axons and distribution of receptors generates patterned arrays without nerve impulses. Then elimination of neurons, axons and synapses and shaping of final circuits of topographical maps is regulated by electrical activity via effects on neurotransmitters, hormones and gene expression.

Connections within the cerebral cortex develop throughout life, and relative rates of development can be charted (Thatcher, 1994; Thatcher, Walker and Giudice, 1987). Late maturing axons include both the long reach 'association fibres' inside each hemisphere, and the inter-hemispheric fibres of the giant bridge known as the 'corpus callosum'. Short associative links in the non-specific 'association' cortices (intracortical neuropil) mature their insulating sheaths of a substance called 'myelin' (i. e. they 'myelinate') slowest of all the neocortical systems (Trevarthen, 1985b). Axons of the reticular formation of the human brain core also mature for decades. Developments of electrical linking between cortical points, charted from birth to adolescence, show asymmetries in the maturation of the cortex, left and right hemispheres showing 'growth spurts' at different times. For example, there is a significant growth spurt in connections of the left hemisphere between two and four years of age that co-occurs with development of speech and the expansion of vocabulary. Regional differences in the extent and timing of cortical development relate to gender, handedness, educational level, deafness, or blindness, and other differences between individuals, including the acquisition of different forms of language. Intrinsic regulations of post-natal brain growth, and of hemispheric plasticity of function, have relationship to the education of children in socially desired skills in which motivation for social engagement and learning mediated by communication has a key part.

Maturation of Neurochemical Regulation in the Brain

The widespread axons of the first reticular nucleus to appear, the locus ceruleus, develop in the mid embryo period at the end of the fourth week of gestation (Barnes and Pompeiano, 1991). This centre of the EMS in the hindbrain reticular formation will have a key role in early brain development, as well as in the coordination of emotions post-natally.

The precocious appearance of monoamine neuron systems in the cortex before development of the network of dendrites and establishment of normal cell-to-cell contacts suggests that cortical cells may be responding to the neurotransmitters flowing into the watery medium between cells before they are connected. However, selective growth into nuclei and cortices by transmitter-secreting axons that do make close contacts with them has the greatest potential for selective control of nerve net development and function.

Cortical neuron assemblies are built up cooperatively, by effects transmitted from different active nerve fibre endings to post synaptic cells, according to how action potentials and secreted transmitter chemicals become distributed in space and time within the nerve network and interact (Hebb, 1949; von der Malsburg and Singer, 1988). In the epigenetics or 'education' of the developing nervous system, components of all kinds are produced in excess and more refined functional cell groups and cell-to-cell transmission lines are selected by eliminating the great majority of elements, or closing off contacts (Changeux, 1985). Quantitative matching of cell systems is achieved by death of cells that fail to gain access to growth substances (Oppenheim, 1984). The selection processes driven by impulse activity of the cells and exchange of messenger substances begin *in utero*, without excitation from stimuli of environmental origin. After birth environmental stimuli enter an already active and highly structured nervous system in which the values of experience can be specified in advance.

Learning in the cortex requires change in nerve circuits, and this process is regulated by biogenic amines, the chemical messengers projected from the brainstem. The brainstem reticular formation of the IMF 'gates' the responses of cortical neurons, both by these chemical effects and by aiming receptors, the eyes, ears, hands, in relation to objects round the body. The process is driven, not only by stimuli, but also by the coordinated, internally generated, interest and attention of the subject, by the activity of the EMS, and these investigative activities can be seen in a newborn baby immediately after birth, though they are still rudimentary at this stage. Later the same core regulations selectively enhance, and retain, discriminatory or 'semantic' memories in category-defining cell assemblies. The internally generated 'interest', with affective evaluations transmitted in communication with other members of the social group, effectively 'rewards' or 'punishes' the receptive networks.

In infants, very important developments occur in the frontal cortices of the cerebral hemispheres and in the temporal lobes, in both of which limbic or emotional activity joins with cognitive information distributed from the rest of the neocortex (Dawson and Fischer, 1994; Schore, 1994). Recognition and recall memory for recognition of, and affectionate response to, a caretaking individual (a cortical-limbic-brainstem system) and species specific habits (a cortical-basal ganglia system) are both involved in attachment (Goldman-Rakic, 1987; Mishkin and Appenzeller, 1987; Squire, 1986). Affectionate contact between an infant and a mother involves activity in limbic and mesofrontal regions which undergo developmental changes for years after birth (Schore, 1994). The focal regions of the amygdala, orbito-frontal cortex and cingulate provide the necessary integration between feelings, impulses to act and experiences of the world, including experiences of people and their actions and emotions.

Nerve fibres from monoamine systems are intensely active in the early post-natal period, when there is most rapid selection of cortical circuits. This is certainly related to the regulation of early brain development with the aid of affective support from an affectionate caretaker (Kraemer, 1992). The DA system, associated with tuning of attention and response to stressors, reinforcement, circadian rhythms and neuronal plasticity, which develops postnatally, is especially sensitive to breakdown of attachment. In normally developing babies NE, DA and 5-HT output is stable and correlated, but this balance is disturbed in social isolation, which also produces reductions in cortical and cerebellar dendritic branching as well as altered limbic and cerebellar activity, as for a neural lesion. This is believed to give rise to denervation supersensitivity (Prescott, 1971), such as occurs in certain developmental disorders, including autism, that interfere with emotions and communication. Social deprivation seems to produce depression followed by 'supersensitivity' to both biogenic amines and novel situations.

Genetics of Brain Development and its Disorders

A range of genetic mechanisms are emerging as crucial to the integrated development of the embryo and foetus. These factors determine a coherent individual with body-form, internal organs and central nervous system adapted to maintain and direct an active life and intelligent behaviour (Gardner and Stern, 1993). Presumably they establish first steps in the embryology of motive systems in the brain. Of particular interest are the so-called 'homeotic' genes, 'hedgehog' and 'homeobox' sequences, which show a high degree of conservation across animal phyla, from insects to mammals (Duboule, 1994). Evidently solutions to the problem of mapping programs in brain circuits that are adapted to guiding behaviour of a motile body were found early and kept in evolution.

Homeotic gene products (morphogens) can be detected in very early stages of the embryo and appear to be crucial to the regulation of whole CNS polarity, with effects on cell division and axon growth at subsequent stages (Echelard *et al.*, 1993). Homeobox genes expressed in the CNS are important in imposing a segmental organisation on the nervous system. Integrated activity of the nervous system depends upon the establishment of somatotopic (body mapping) arrays of nerve cells in which axes of body symmetry and polarity are represented and that define matching connective affinities between cells in different parts of the brain, its receptors and the muscles (Sperry, 1963; Trevarthen, 1985b) Apparently hedgehog and homeobox genes control the induction and polarisation of these maps in the early embryo brain.

It is likely that anomalies of development in the motivating and emotional systems that originate in the embryo brain are mainly of genetic origin (Lyon and Gadisseux, 1991). The neuro-developmental effects of certain gene abnormalities are beginning to be elucidated. For example, examination of FMR-1 (the gene locus for the CGG repeat sequence responsible for Fragile-X syndrome) in the human foetus shows FMR-1 messenger RNA to be expressed in proliferating and migrating neuroblasts at least by 8–9 weeks post-conception and to be in most of the differentiated CNS structures by 25 weeks (Abvitbol *et al.*, 1993).

There is now evidence for genetic bases to many disorders which have core affective components (Plomin *et al.*, 1997), and this includes 'autistic spectrum disorders' (Gillberg and Coleman 1992). Autism occurs in populations with Fra-X (Brown *et al.*, 1982, 1986; Blomquist *et al.*, 1985; Fisch *et al.*, 1986; Hagerman *et al.*, 1986a,b; Rutter, 1991). Tuberous sclerosis (TSC), a condition in which nerve cells fail to migrate and develop correctly, is another genetic condition linked with autism. Autism is variable in its manifestations, so its genetic and epigenetic regulation are certainly not simple. Family histories show that it has associations with other genetic disorders known to affect brain development. Fra-X cases exhibit different neuropsychological signs in males and females, and autism, Tourette syndrome and dyslexia are more common in males.

It has recently been found that girls with Turner's syndrome, who are of small size and with unusual features of the head and face, have psychological makeup of two kinds, depending on the condition of the single X chromosome they have received from their mother. In most females there are two sex chromosomes of the X type, but Turner's syndrome individuals have only one. They have female bodies and most are feminine in behaviour, but some have difficulties with interpersonal life, while others are poor at spatial reasoning. This appears to depend upon the condition of the X chromosome inherited from the mother (Skuse *et al.*, 1997). Some young women with Turner's syndrome resemble males with autism or Asperger's syndrome in their cognitive functions and interests, and it has been suggested that a similar condition of the genes on the X chromosome of males may be responsible for changes in the brain that cause autisic disturbances of interpersonal relating. Maleness is determined by a small Y chromosome, which is absent in females.

Evidence is emerging of a strong link between autistic disorder and abnormal activity of genes affecting the neurotransmitter serotonin (Cook *et al.*, 1997). These findings are of interest in view of the evidence that children with autism show differences in serotonin levels and turnover (Chugani *et al.*, 1997).

Conclusion

It now seems certain that the brains of persons who become autistic in their early childhood already had microscopic faults in their development in early intra-uterine life, probably first expressed among cells of the early embryo, in the first month. It is likely that the differences between autism and related pervasive disorders of children's mental development, and between these and mental handicap on the one hand, or disorders of higher cognitive processes such as specific language impairment or dyslexia on the other, depend on when and where gene faults become expressed.

We have suggested that the core regulators of the brain, in the motive-generating and emotional systems of the brainstem, are to be conceived as an Intrinsic Motive Formation (IMF) (Trevarthen and Aitken, 1994). We propose that regulator genes act through the IMF in shaping the thinking and remembering systems of later developing higher centres of the brain, in the cerebral hemispheres and cerebellum. If follows that the first error may be in the generation of particular species of reticular cell in this core motive formation, leading to a confusion in the neurochemistry and in intercellular communications of the embryo brain, before there are any cortical neurons.

Another possibility, which is certainly not a conflicting one, is that the time at which an error of this kind is transmitted to the intra-cortical regulatory mechanism may be critical. When the multiplication and/or migration of nerve cells or selective cell death occurs in brain systems may decide the fate of the cognitive machinery of the child after birth. Different cortical tissue sectors mature and become functional at different ages. The earlier they are disorganised the deeper the abnormality. The profound mental handicap of Rett's syndrome is an example of a genetic disorder in which the development of the whole cerebral cortex has been compromised, leading to a small cortex and a small head. In autism it appears that the prefrontal and temporal regions, with their important limbic connections, may be critical, along with parts of the cerebellum that also mature after birth. In dyslexia a restricted part of the cortical machinery in the junction of temporal and parietal lobes, which is important in the seeing and recognition of written words, appears to show abnormalities due to disturbed neural migration at a late stage of cortical neurogenesis. These are examples of disorders that probably originate before birth, but which affect development and learning drastically some time after birth – in autism at the end of infancy, and in dyslexia, years afterward, when a child is at school.

We have to see these various developmental disorganisations of the brain's growth regulators in relation to the overall strategy of human brain form and function through childhood, a strategy that is so dependent on interpersonal transmission of motives and feelings, and intersubjective collaboration of awareness and understanding (Aitken and Trevarthen, 1997).

CHAPTER 7

Brain Abnormalities in Autism

In nearly every case of autism, when appropriate techniques are available, some abnormality in the brain can be found (Gillberg, 1988a, 1991a; Steffenberg, 1991). Recent observations on the brains of autistic individuals, comparisons of the psychological deficits produced in human beings and in animals with damage to the parts of the emotional system in the cerebral hemispheres, and better understanding of the complexity of the core regulatory systems of brains and their importance in emotional communication, maturation of the cerebral cortex and learning, all support the hypothesis that autism may originate as a defect in these core systems (Aitken, 1991a; Schore, 1994; Trevarthen and Aitken, 1994).

A clear distinction between pure or primary autism, and other recognised neurological illnesses that result in mental retardation with autistic features, may lead to identification of brain systems in which damage by a gene fault or specific noxious agent can cause autism when other parts of the brain are intact. On the other hand, there may be no such 'pure' condition, and no single source of malfunction, in the range of conditions diagnosed as autistic, and any one type of autism may have a variety of causes.

Neurologists are familiar with conditions in children that can be attributed to gross malfunction in the neocortex, basal ganglia or other structures. Autism, while it may have manifestations like these conditions, is not associated with such massive neurological abnormalities. The defects that seem to be characteristic of autism are increasingly perceived as deep-seated, subtle and widespread in the brain.

We have seen how brain development depends on an unfolding succession of structure-building processes that begin with the formation of the embryo brain. A fault in pre-natal brain formation can lead to defects in higher functions that only emerge long afterwards in childhood. Autism appears to be such a condition. From this perspective the cognitive and linguistic features of the disorder are not primary, but secondary to dysfunction of more fundamental mechanisms of motive regulation (Trevarthen and Aitken, 1994).

Here we summarise the various ways that brain scientists have obtained information about the brains of persons with autism, and present a summary of their findings. Recent reviews that detail the findings of a wide range of studies show that many and variable changes in brain anatomy and function occur in autism – no simple interpretation of the cause of the disorder can yet be made, and there a number of rival models (Belmonte and Carper, 1997; Courchesne, 1997; Dawson and Fischer, 1994).

Evidence from Brain Scans

Anatomical abnormalities of major regions in the brains of autistic individuals have been sought in images made of the intact brain with the aid of X-radiography or magnetic resonance imaging. More recently, functional brain scan techniques, which detect transitory concentrations of nerve activity when subjects are involved in particular psychological tasks, emotional reactions or cognitive activities, have made it possible to visualise abnormal features on a much finer scale. Both the anatomical and the temporal resolution of brain scan techniques is rapidly improving.

In the earliest studies, radio-images were obtained by **Pneumo-encephalography (PEG)** showing the fluid-filled cavities of the brain (the ventricles) after injection of air into the fluid surrounding it. It is a distressing procedure no longer in use, which has been superseded by superior non-invasive methods. Nevertheless, a considerable body of research did use this method to investigate the brain in autistic individuals. One report claimed that the cavity of the left temporal lobe (the left ventricle) was dilated in 13 of 18 cases of autism studied (Hauser, DeLong and Rosman, 1975). The increase in the size of the ventricle indicates a loss of tissue in the cortex of the left temporal lobe, which might explain severe deficits in language in some autistic children, though the central features of autism cannot be explained either as a language deficit or as a consequence of left hemisphere atrophy (Fein *et al.*, 1984).

Numerous **Computerised Axial Tomography (CAT)** studies have been useful for imaging defects in the cerebral cortex, but this technique has limited ability for showing up abnormalities in the structures that are now seen as likely to be involved in the abnormal motivations characteristic of autistic children. More recent reports (Campbell *et al.*, 1982; Damasio *et al.*, 1980; Tsai *et al.*, 1982) have failed to replicate studies which suggested there were atypical patterns of cerebral asymmetry or dilated ventricles in autistic cases. Some reports from CAT scans claim a wide variety of abnormalities but there is little evidence of consistent features across the autistic population from this technique (Ballotin *et al.*, 1989).

The 1980s saw the introduction of a new technique, **Magnetic Resonance Imaging (MRI)**, previously known as Nuclear Magnetic Resonance Imaging

(NMR), that, for the first time, allowed clear imaging of deep midbrain and cerebellar structures. This has yielded quite unexpected findings on the structure of brains of autistic individuals.

The seminal single-case report described a previously unknown pattern of **reduced development in cerebellar tissue** in the brain of a high-functioning (IQ 112), 21-year-old right-handed male (Courchesne *et al.*, 1987). The mid portion of both cerebellar hemispheres were under developed. This individual also showed a reversed structural asymmetry of the cerebral hemispheres and a dilated ventricular system. Subsequent papers from the same group claimed that the findings could be replicated in a series of 18 subjects and was, therefore, not a scan artefact caused by the way the first brain had been positioned (Courchesne *et al.*, 1988, Murakami *et al.*, 1989). This work has been reviewed by Courchesne, and a model of autism based on the cerebellar abnormality has been proposed (Courchesne, 1989, 1995a,b).

Although cerebellar malformations are relatively common in developmental disorders of the brain, this particular type of fault seems to be associated with autism while the other forms are not. It could imply a far more complex functional role for the cerebellum in humans than had been previously imagined, implicating it in communication and/or cognition. Such a 'high level' function is also suggested by evidence of strong correlations between metabolic rates of cerebellar and frontal cortical areas, indicating that these structures may be involved together in thinking and communicating (Junck *et al.*, 1988), and by cognitive planning deficits found in patients with 'pure' cerebellar atrophy (Grafman *et al.*, 1992).

Evidence for conspicuous central cerebellar abnormalities has been found to apply primarily in individuals with particular gene faults (Joubert's and Fragile-X syndromes) who also fulfil diagnostic criteria for autism (Reiss, 1988; Reiss *et al.*, 1991; Holroyd, Reiss and Bryan, 1991).

Piven and colleagues have demonstrated significantly smaller cerebellar lobules VI and VII and significantly enlarged mid-saggital brain areas in 15 autistic adults who were compared to controls matched for age and parental socio-economic status, but not matched for IQ (Piven *et al.*, 1990). There have been negative findings in other investigations. Garber and Ritvo (1992) could not demonstrate any significant cerebellar abnormalities in 12 autistic adults with DSM-III defined autism, or in a matched group of 12 normal controls. Kleiman and colleagues also found no differences on a range of cerebellar parameters when 13 autistic children were compared to a non-specific control group of 28 children (Kleiman, Neff and Rosman, 1990). Nowell, Hackney, Muraki and Coleman (1990), who also failed to replicate the Courchesne group's findings, used a patient group who were shown to be free of Fragile-X chromosome abnormalities. This study appears to identify one group for whom the gross structural cerebellar abnormalities are not seen.

Recently cases have been reported of selective central cerebellar hypoplasia without autism (Schaefer *et al.*, 1996). It seems likely that more systematic analysis of other groups will show this type of cell migration failure to be more general than was previously thought. At present, abnormal development of the central cerebellum can be best viewed as a signpost for the probable timing of developmental problems in autism, rather than a core physical feature that can serve to identify the clinical disorder.

MRI and CAT scans have demonstrated a range of non-specific differences between brain structure in autistic and control populations which are neither necessary nor specific to autism. They provide limited aid in diagnosis. The same gross abnormalities of the brain anatomy occur in children who are not autistic.

Positron Emission Tomography (PET) records the relative physiological activity in brain regions. It is increasingly applied in developmental brain research and for the early identification of developmental brain disorders of all kinds (Chugani and Phelps, 1986). However, the few published studies on PET findings in autism lead to varied interpretations. US studies seem to show metabolic differences from controls, with **abnormally high levels of cell activity** overall (Rumsey *et al.*, 1985) and lower correlations between metabolism in frontal and parietal areas of the cortex than in controls and between these structures and brainstem nuclei and basal ganglia (thalamus, caudate, lenticular nucleus and insula) (Horowitz *et al.*, 1988). A UK study (Herold *et al.*, 1988) did not replicate these findings in six cases.

Single Photon Emission Computerised Axial Tomography (SPECT) is a simpler and more widely available technique than the very costly PET technique, requiring less sophisticated apparatus, and it is increasingly used with autistic subjects. The major limitations in comparison with PET are a lower resolution, and an inability to provide real-time imaging of task-related brain function.

Zilbovicius and colleagues in France using SPECT found no evidence for abnormal areas of cerebral cortex in 21 children who met DSM-III-R criteria for autistic disorder compared against an age matched group of 14 children with language disorders (Zilbovicius *et al.*, 1992). This study was restricted to measurement of cortical blood flow, and did not examine cerebellar or midbrain function. Furthermore, since DSM-III-R criteria were used, many of the children diagnosed as autistic would have slight and mixed symptoms. A second study of four young adult subjects (George *et al.*, 1992), again diagnosed by DSM-III-R criteria, demonstrated a significant reduction in total brain perfusion (58–72% of control values), and **reduction in blood flow in frontal and right lateral temporal lobes.**

Research reports using both PET and SPECT have two shortcomings. Appropriate standardised psychological or pharmacological activation procedures have not been used, and the studies compare major diagnostic groups rather than subgroups with similar symptomatology. Interesting and consistent results are being achieved in adult schizophrenia research when these issues are addressed and patients are grouped by symptomatology not by diagnosis (see Liddle, 1992).

In summary, then, there is a wide variation in the abnormalities reported from structural and functional CNS imaging tests. This variation may, in part, reflect current limitations in diagnostic systems and activation procedures, but it seems likely that it is an accurate reflection of differences in underlying pathology that result from differences in causative mechanism. The relationship found between Fragile-X, autism and cerebellar hypoplasia may point the way to more accurate interpretation of the discrepancies. The current status of information about the

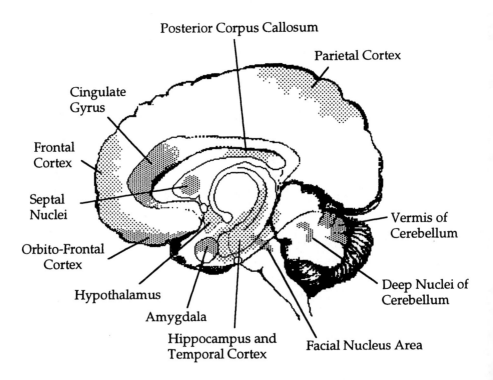

Figure 6: Abnormalities, shown as stippled areas, of anatomy or function, that have been reported for individuals with autism. Based upon data from various techniques described in the text.

brains of subjects with primary autism appears as follows: no consistent abnormalities appear in CAT scan (Prior *et al.*, 1984), but recent MRI research (Courchesne *et al.*, 1987, 1988) confirms histo-anatomic findings (see Figure 6) that parts of the neocerebellar cortex are underdeveloped.

Abnormal Brain Cells and Tissues

There have been few detailed investigations of the tissues of brains obtained after death from autistic individuals.

Bauman and Kemper (1985) found abnormal anatomy in many parts of the brain of a 29-year-old autistic man. All were **structures linked with emotional functions** (the hippocampus, subiculum, entorhinal cortex, septal nuclei, mamillary body, central and medial nuclei of the amygdala, and, surprisingly for this time, before the brain scan results discussed above, they also found changes in the **neocerebellar cortex,** the roof nuclei of the cerebellum and the inferior olivary nucleus. Autopsies of four autistic/retarded boys 10 to 22 years of age demonstrated reduced numbers of the integrative Purkinje cells in the cerebellum (Ritvo *et al.*, 1986). These findings have led to a search for evidence and to the confirmation by several methods that the cerebellum is involved in many functions other than those traditionally ascribed to this structure, including functions implicated in cognition and communication. It is certainly involved in attentional processes, and in the coordination of body movements, including those by which states of motivation are communicated, but there remain considerable differences of opinion concerning the role of the cerebellum in 'higher' mental functions and communicative expression (Belmonte and Carper, 1997; Leiner, Leiner and Dow, 1993).

It has been suggested by Ritvo *et al.* (1986) that the Purkinje cell deficits lead to failure of inhibition and the brain becomes flooded with stimuli – hence the withdrawal and self-stimulating behaviours of autistic children. Such an interpretation may be premature until more is known about how patterned inhibition from the cerebellum regulates experience in relation to action. It could be vitally involved, for example, in the timing of communicative engagements, as well as in organisation of exploratory behaviour, and it is certainly important for learning precise motor skills.

There has been remarkable consistency in certain tissue abnormalities reported in the brains of autistic subjects. The ascending fibber tracts from the olivary nucleus in the midbrain to the Purkinje cell baskets in the cerebellum appear absent in all subjects. This finding, if substantiated, would seem to identify a narrow temporal window in brain development, in the last half of the embryo period, about one or two months of gestation, in which that particular step in neural development takes place. It may also reveal the particular form of structural abnormality that makes this temporal window critical.

Recent work has demonstrated other features in the autistic brain that point to a very early failure of the mechanism regulating brain formation. Abnormal structure in the facial nucleus are consistent with a fault in the late embryo or very early foetal stage (Rodier, 1996; Rodier *et al.*, 1996). A recent epidemiological study in Sweden of thalidomide deformity found that only the few cases that were affected in the late embryo (mid third trimester of gestation) were autistic (Miller and Strömland 1993).

Hormonal and Neurochemical Abnormalities in Autism

Evidence for neurochemical abnormalities comes primarily from studies on the effects of a number of forms of medication on the behaviour and status of affected children.

Raised levels of urinary **serotonin** has been observed consistently in some 30 per cent of autistic cases. This finding has resulted in clinical trials of the drug fenfluramine which tends to normalise serotonin levels.

Recent work from two controlled clinical trials in the Netherlands (Buitelaar *et al.*, 1990; Buitelaar *et al.*, 1992) demonstrates clinical improvement in autistic children administered an **adreno-cortico-trophic hormone** (ACTH analogue, suggesting an abnormality in this neurotransmitter system.

The Geschwind and Galaburda Model

To many parents who meet together in local support groups, at schools or specialist units, or at national meetings, surprising similarities begin to emerge across their children which on first sight seem difficult to explain. Most autistic people are male (around four to one). Many (up to a third) suffer from epilepsy. Many have immune problems (migraine, food allergies, hay fever...) or gastrointestinal difficulties (many parents, for example, comment on their child's unusually large or foul-smelling bowel motions). Significantly more have larger than average heads and have had from as early as they were being measured. In many groups, unusual birth peaks are reported, and more of these individuals are pale-skinned, light-haired and light-eyed than might be expected. To attribute the above associations to chance seems unacceptable. Is there any way in which such associations might be explained?

One model which has attempted to bring these strange findings under one theoretical umbrella has been proposed by Norman Geschwind and Albert Galaburda from Boston. They built up an intricate model to account for a diverse collection of developmental disorders, including autism (Geschwind and Galaburda, 1985; 1987). Their central claim was that differences in sex ratio, handedness, epilepsy, immune function and learning problems can be consequences of exposure of the foetus to higher levels of the male sex hormone, **testosterone**, which is produced both by the mother and by the gonads of the male foetus. This, Geschwind and Galaburda argue, results in poor development of the thymus gland and hence immune difficulties, and an increase in the rate of growth of the right hemisphere. There is interference with the normal patterns of cortical nerve cell migration and development, which, in turn, gives rise to abnormal structures in the cerebral cortex, an increased frequency of epilepsy, and anomalous cerebral dominance in psychological functions.

This model provides a very attractive general theory linking hormones with brain development, and it does appear to explain common features in a very broad range of psychological disorders, including dyslexia, mixed dominance and autism. Its main shortcoming, however, is that it gives no explanation for the features of autism that distinguish it from the other developmental disorders (Johnson and Morton, 1991).

Other Medical Conditions Linked with Autism

Many medical problems, identified problems in function of parts of the body, have been reported in the autistic population, and there are several comprehensive reviews of this area (Cohen, Donellan and Paul, 1987; Dawson, 1989; Gillberg, 1989b; Gillberg and Coleman, 1992; Schopler and Mesibov, 1987).

Genetic Faults in the Brain

The idea that autism could be caused by a fault in the genes that changes the brain, as is the case for Down's syndrome, may be increasingly attractive as more is learned about brain genetics, but there is no reason to expect that a single gene change can account for such a complex disorder of brain development and function. If it is caused by inherited factors, there will probably be several different genes responsible.

Autism is associated at a greater than expected level with a variety of inherited disorders, including Down's syndrome, Neurofibromatosis and Tuberous sclerosis (see Gillberg and Coleman 1992), and, indeed, a number of genetic factors implicated in autism have now been identified (see e.g. Cook et al., 1997). Furthermore, it is clear that close family members are at higher risk of exhibiting similar problems. Twins of individuals with autism have higher than chance rates of communication problems, and rates are higher in identical than non-identical twin pairs. It is much more likely that both twins will be autistic where they are genetically identical (Le Couteur et al., 1996). A specific gene abnormality associated with regulation of the brain chemical serotonin, which has a major role in regulation of emotions in communication and learning, as described in Chapter 6, has recently been found in a significant number of children with autism (Cook et al., 1997).

The most commonly reported genetic feature associated with autism is **Fragile-X syndrome**, an abnormality in the DNA molecules of the sex chromosome. This fault in the gene code, the result of a massive over-replication of a sequence of nucleic acids (a CGG repeat) near the tip of the X chromosome, is apparently a frequent cause of mental retardation (5–7% in males), and approximately 26 per cent of these retarded individuals also fulfil diagnostic criteria for autism. Conversely, analysis of 20 studies of autistic individuals tested for Fragile-X found 8.1 per cent to have this chromosome condition (i.e. they are **'autistic with Fragile-X' or AFRAX**). Autistic behaviour is now well-documented in Fragile-X children (Gillberg, Persson and Wahlström, 1986; Cohen *et al.*, 1989). The most obvious correlate of the Fragile-X condition in behaviour is an extreme avoidance on being greeted, by turning head and eyes away (Wolff *et al.*, 1989).

It has been suggested recently that the diagnosis of autism should be divided on the basis of the presence or absence of certain genetic markers, such as the Fragile-X condition, which are coupled to distinct forms of behaviour (Gillberg, 1992), or by discrimination of groups with differing cognitive or behavioural features, on the supposition that these differences are due to different, as yet unknown, genetic conditions (Fein *et al.*, 1985; Volkmar, 1992). A natural subclassification may give valuable pointers to different ways in which autism can come about, and also assist in finding more effective forms of intervention.

A wide range of other genetic abnormalities have been reported in autistic individuals at what are thought to be higher than chance levels. The ways these gene conditions affect brain development are not known. For a detailed review consult Gillberg and Coleman (1992, pp.179–202).

Tuberous Sclerosis (TSC)

Between 17 and 58 per cent of individuals with this condition, in which neurons of the cerebral cortex form amorphous tuber-like clumps indicative of disturbance of the biochemical processes that normally regulate cell migration and formation of cell-surface material, are autistic. They constitute a small but significant proportion of the total autistic group (between 0.4 and 3%). Within the TSC population as a whole the sex ratio is close to one, but those with autism are more likely to be male. Those with autism also have more seizures and are more retarded (Smalley *et al.*, 1992). A further interesting finding is that mothers of those TSC cases with autism are significantly more likely to have experienced a depressive episode before the conception of the index child (Smalley, personal communication, 1992).

Abnormalities of Melanin

Abnormal skin pigmentation resulting from unusual levels of melanin in discrete areas visible when the skin is examined under ultraviolet light appear to be common in autistic individuals. This finding may help to unravel the abnormalities of neural migration which give rise to autistic behaviour. In addition to tuberous sclerosis, described above, two conditions in particular, neurofibromatosis (Gaffney *et al.*, 1989) and hypomelanosis of Ito (Akefeldt and Gillberg, 1991; Zappella, 1992) have been well-documented, each of which account for between 3 and 5 per cent of autistic cases.

Phenylketonuria (PKU)

This disorder results from an abnormal accumulation of the chemicals phenylalanine and phenylpyruvic acid in the urine, and is associated with extreme mental defect. Untreated PKU is a well-documented cause of autism (see Friedman, 1969 for a review); however, with routine neonatal screening for PKU throughout the UK in recent decades, this is now a rare factor here. Autism consequent on PKU is still reported in countries where such early detection is less common.

Purine Autism

Abnormalities of purine metabolism resulting in autistic behaviour are well-documented in the literature (see Gillberg and Coleman, 1992 for review) and are important in that they are, in many instances, potentially treatable. As severe self-mutilation is a concomitant of an extremely rare purine abnormality (Lesch and Nyhan, 1969) this is to be noted as a horrifying cause of autism in a very few cases.

Measles in Pregnancy

Chess's study of the New York rubella epidemic of 1964 (Chess, Korn and Fernandez, 1971; Chess, 1977) showed that if a mother contracted measles during pregnancy this will increase the chances of her child developing autism. Seventeen of the eighteen children described as autistic also had significant sensory impairments which may have contributed to their autistic symptoms. As with PKU, greater awareness of the disorder and widespread inoculation have virtually eradicated rubella as a significant cause of autism.

Epilepsy

Some 20 to 35 per cent of autistic individuals develop epilepsy. Reports vary as to the most likely age of onset. A recent study of 192 autistic individuals (Volkmar and Nelson, 1990) found 21 per cent to have developed a seizure disorder. The likelihood increased with lower IQ and risk of seizure onset was highest during early childhood with a second less pronounced peak in early adolescence. Overall this represented an increase of between 3- and 22-fold over normal population rates. It is possible that the concurrence of autism and epilepsy is the result of a common causal mechanism interfering with neural migration, migration abnormalities being significantly more common in the epileptic population in general (Brodtkorb *et al.*, 1992).

Conclusion: Autism is a Brain Growth Disorder Affecting Motive Regulations

All of the evidence now available from studies of the brains of autistic people supports the conclusion that Kanner's autism is caused by abnormal development that begins before birth but shows its effects in behaviour only at the end of infancy, when the child should be beginning to develop language.

The parts of the brain that have been found to be abnormal in some or all of autistic people appear to belong to a very large set of systems (see Figure 6). These link emotions with cognitions, attentional regulation of perception with motor patterning and learning, eye movements with gestures and speech, imitation of other persons' actions and expressions with the acquisition of language. The emerging picture is summarised in Figures 3 and 4.

The findings of several decades of accelerating research on autistic brains indicate that whatever goes wrong in brain formation is related to the functions which emerge at the stage of childhood when the cortex of the brain is growing very rapidly and the brain as a whole is motivating the individual to seek stimulation from the environment to support that growth. Figures 6, 7 and 8 give a synopsis of the psychological and neuro-developmental events of this eventful period of human life.

As we shall see in Chapter 8, observations of the normal course of psychological maturation and learning in the last year of infancy and through pre-school years confirms that this is a time when emotionally regulated human communication is vitally important for cognitive growth. Thus it is not surprising that the parts that appear to show abnormality in the brains of autistic people are motivating ones that are involved in patterning of emotions and their communication, as well as in the control of attention and perceptual guidance of action (Aitken and Trevarthen, 1997). There is a great deal of supportive evidence from brain science for this view of the disorder (Trevarthen and Aitken, 1994).

CHAPTER 8

Where Development of the Communicating Mind Goes Astray

Conversations in Early Infancy, and the Emotions that Regulate Them

The common-sense belief of parents that even very young infants recognise people and enjoy chatting with them is abundantly confirmed by recent research using microanalysis of film and television. It has been shown that infants are born able to communicate with the feelings, interests and purposes of other persons, and that it is by development of these innate abilities to communicate that they learn how to share ideas, identify them with symbols and explain them in the language of the 'mother tongue' (Bruner, 1983; Bullowa, 1979; Halliday, 1975, 1979; Locke, 1993; Stern, 1985; Trevarthen, 1979, 1980, 1987a, 1997a, 1998b,c; Trevarthen and Hubley, 1978; Trevarthen, Kokkinaki and Fiamenghi, 1997; Trevarthen and Logotheti, 1987; Trevarthen, Murray and Hubley, 1981). Many experimental studies prove infants to be critically aware of their surroundings and capable of remarkable discriminations among the signals from people, especially those giving information about states of mind (Bremner, Slater and Butterworth, 1997; Field and Fox, 1985; Mehler and Fox, 1985; Reddy *et al.*, 1997; Stern, 1985; Trevarthen, 1985b, 1993a).

A newborn may show complex responses when greeted by a person, picking up information on their feelings through many senses and showing emotions by expressions of face, voice and hands. They can imitate expressions of face, voice or hands in a communicative way (Kugiumutzakis, 1993; Meltzoff, 1985) or enter into a 'proto-conversational' exchange (see Figure 1). Some of the infant's signals, like crying and smiles, serve to solicit human aid, for protection or comfort and for feeding. These, obviously, are important for the infant's physiological well-being and survival. But information from people about their emotions when they offer face-to-face play has a special extra interest for the infant.

From very early in life infants reveal their ability to recognise the special nature of a person in the way they move their hands. And even newborns move their own hands in more complex rhythmic patterns when they see a person, and differently from the way they reach out or point at an object that is not alive and not capable of communicating (Rönnqvist and von Hofsten, 1992; Trevarthen, 1986, 1996). Infants, indeed, move their whole bodies in dance-like enthusiasm when excited in chat. These movements, and the vocalisations that accompany them, are remarkably sensitive, not only to the rhythms of human speech and song, but to recorded music.

A baby learns quickly to identify who is his or her most constant caretaker. A mother's voice can be learned by the foetus *in utero* (DeCasper and Fifer, 1980). Very soon after birth her individual odour may be preferred, and there is rapid learning of her face.

By analysing the timing of the infant's sounds in their interactions with the vocalisations of the mother (Beebe *et al.*, 1985; Stern and Gibbon, 1980; Trevarthen, Kokkinaki and Fiamenghi, 1997), as well as by describing the special kind of affectionate speech of a person who is trying to get a response from the baby (a form of speaking called 'intuitive motherese'), it has been possible to show that infant and mother share the same feelings about expressions (Fernald, 1985; Papousek *et al.*, 1985; Stern *et al.*, 1982; Trevarthen and Marwick, 1986). Thus they can share in a mutual regulation of feelings. Motherese has unconsciously regulated features of pitch variation, duration and spacing of utterances, and these features appear to be the same in all languages (Grieser and Kuhl, 1988). Not surprisingly, the universal, intuitive features of motherese, transcending differences between languages, are found to be the features that the infants prefer to hear. They are part of the baby's inborn 'sketch' of the 'ideal mother' (Trevarthen, 1993b).

Six weeks after birth a baby has more sharply focused sight of a familiar person's eyes and mouth and a greater readiness to greet a friendly face and voice with a smile and a coo. Cyclic 'proto-conversations' now develop, in which the baby replies to evenly spaced invitations of motherese, taking turns with a pattern of imitations and invitations that links focused attention, smiling, cooing, 'pre-speech' movements of lips and tongue and gestures of the hands (Trevarthen, 1979, 1990b, 1993a,b; Trevarthen and Marwick, 1986).

The complex emotions that regulate these exchanges are further revealed when the infant's conversational partner does not fulfil the infant's needs for companionship. In experimental studies, various awkward situations are contrived; either a stranger attempts communication with the two-month-old, or the mother behaves with inappropriate timing or withholds her normal responses. Artificial interference of this kind causes infants to make signals of distress mixed with withdrawal or protest (Murray and Trevarthen, 1985; Reddy *et al.*, 1997; Trevarthen, Murray and Hubley, 1981; Tronick *et al.*, 1978). Evidently the infant's pleasure in normal chat with a loved caretaker needs the response of the affectionate, joyful and 'considerate' partner, supported by recognition of a familiar face and voice.

Double Television Intercom recordings made at Edinburgh for this research also prove that proto-conversations can be well-sustained between baby and mother by two-dimensional TV images with accompanying voice from a loud speaker, that is, transmitted by sight and sound alone (Murray and Trevarthen, 1985; Trevarthen, 1985, 1993a,b; Trevarthen, Murray and Hubley, 1981). The two-month-old can communicate with a mother who is out of range of touch or body contact, even if she is in another room. Touch and odour may be more effective ways for the infant to perceive the mother immediately after birth, but they are soon superseded by seeing and hearing her, channels of human contact that have vast potential for carrying specific information, both about mercurial states of mind and, with the aid of pointing and looking, and especially with the addition of language, about an infinity of significant elements of the shared world.

In our attempt to understand autism, it is important to note that when the contact of a two-month-old with the mother has been cut off by her assuming a still face, the baby's signs of distress may show 'autistic' features, such as avoidance of eye-to-eye contact, compulsive fingering of clothes, cessation of smiling and a complaining kind of vocalisation (Murray and Trevarthen, 1985; Trevarthen, Murray and Hubley, 1981; Weinberg and Tronick, 1994). An avoidant or unresponsive state of this kind may persist for a minute or two after the mother resumes normal behaviour and tries to get the infant to communicate warmly with her again. This is not to say that it is autism that is produced, or that autism could be caused by a mother's lack of response, but there is an important similarity. The autistic child's older brain evidently finds it peculiarly difficult to use the efforts of other people to be friendly and intimate at a distance. The child effectively suffers from being cut off for some inside reason from the other person's feelings for communication, like the infant is in the still-face situation – and comparable expressive movements of a disordered, distressed, detached or avoidant kind are released as a result. There may be important implications for the facilitation of one-to-one teaching approaches to help autistic children who may have to be supported or encouraged somewhat like an avoidant infant, with measured, responsive and unintrusive approaches. This does seem to be borne out by the experiences of therapists and teachers who use child-focused methods of intervention to help autistic youngsters come into contact, as we report in later chapters.

The elaborate dependence of the two-month-old on a particular patterning and emotional quality of sensitive and instantaneously-reactive face-to-face communication with the mother, capable of generating a specific mutuality of active emotion, changes within a few weeks. Perturbation experiments with infants over three months of age give different results. When the mother withholds her responses, the older baby's attention usually becomes side-tracked into an exploration of the environment, interrupted by periodic glances at the unresponsive mother and by calls for her attention. The baby has less distress than at two months, along with an increased curiosity and autonomy. This, too, may have important implications for understanding an autistic child's tendency to turn aside from people, to become preoccupied with inspecting and manipulating things, or simply repeating some stereotyped movement.

With a stranger, a three to four-month-old may exhibit a rapidly changing array of reactions, varying between timid withdrawal and an expression of fear or crying, coquettish or bold smiles of short duration, and self-conscious avoidance with self-touching, exploration of clothes, or studious examination of hands or nearby objects (Reddy et al., 1997; Trevarthen, 1984b, 1986a, 1990b). The intricate, sometimes conflicting, relationship between the motives

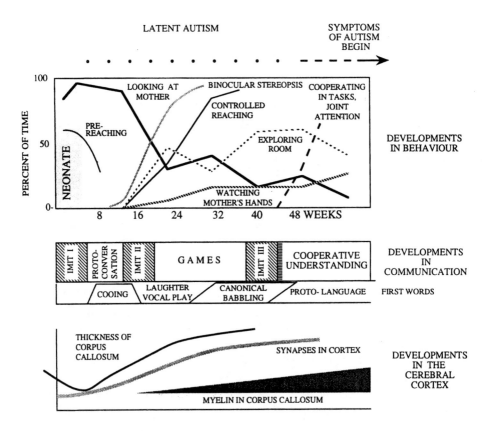

Figure 7: Some important developments in the behaviour and communication of infants in the first year that reveal changing motives in the infant brain. IMIT = imitation

for attention to and exploration of the environment, and those for getting into communication with people who are familiar and whose affections can be counted on, is already clear (Reddy, 1991).

Growing Awareness of Objects, and a New Playfulness with People

From birth, infants can certainly pay attention to and begin to explore the evidence they get from their senses about the existence and nature of objects and events in the physical, impersonal world. They orient to auditory and visual stimuli, and they even make 'prereaching' attempts, as yet unsuccessfully, to get hold of nearby objects. They learn to recognise familiar things and to forget those things that turn out to have no special interest or usefulness. Such attentions, explorations and learning are, however, relatively weak and undeveloped compared to the behaviours described above of communication addressed to people.

Infants have few effective object-related behaviours before three months, at which age a baby begins rapid development of a strong body capable of lifting itself against gravitation to give the head stable and mobile support and to stretch out the arms and hold the hands close to nearby objects so that they can be explored by the fingers or grasped and picked up. This development of body-action and orientation to surroundings is associated with a fall in readiness to engage in face-to-face proto-conversation (Trevarthen and Marwick, 1986). Curiosity about the environment of things to be watched, grasped, sucked, rattled, etc. evidently competes with, or takes motivation away from, the desire for direct engagement with a person at this age.

At the same age, however, communication, too, advances to a new level. The infant gains in speed and elaborateness of moves with another person in body play, becoming humorously combative and laughing when teased (Reddy, 1991; Trevarthen, 1986, 1990b). Play with people is not abandoned while cognitive mastery of objects is sought. A familiar partner, who is affectionately attached to the baby, reacts to this change towards playfulness and a more complex attentiveness to the world by presenting more animated and complex patterns of communication, which may take the form of a culture-specific repertoire of ritual nursery songs or action games (Trevarthen, 1987). In many of these games, objects are presented in a way that amuses the baby.

Baby songs, rhyming chants and action games that are played with infants about the middle of the first year have recently been found to be similar in different languages and cultures. They have predictable features of beat, rhythm, melody and use of rhyme that suggest innate foundations in brain activity for what turn out to be universals in the timing and prosody of music and poetry (Trevarthen, Kokkinaki and Fiamenghi, 1997). By six months, a normal infant in a happy family will most likely have learned several favourite routines of play with familiar people, adults or older children, at the same time as he or she has been gaining efficiency in tracking, recognising, grasping and manipulating objects. At this age, the vocalisations of infants may imitate musical forms (Papousek and Papousek, 1981).

After three months, infants characteristically begin to show systematic 'problem solving' behaviours, and thus they become good cooperative subjects of experimental psychologists' tests of their powers of perception, object awareness and instrumental activity. Some 20 years ago Papousek made the important observation, in an experiment in which he also made films of his subjects' faces, that such problem solving behaviour was normally accompanied not only by a studious, serious concentration or tracking on the patterns of test stimuli, which were made contingent on the baby's movements, but by smiles and coos of pleasure when a right choice was made, or a pout of disappointment at being wrong (Papousek, 1967). He called this a 'human kind of response' to consequences of attempts at cognitive mastery and prediction of events. The baby's expressions are obviously useful for communication. We see that developments in curiosity and affectivity, taken together, show how cognitive processes and active exploration of objects grow in close, partially competitive, relation with the precociously manifested special abilities for communication. It appears, moreover, that rational or object-directed, practical abilities may be given motivation to develop by the expressions of feeling, interest and purpose of other people, through communication.

In the middle six months of the first year, an infant's intelligence (awareness, memory, prediction of events, adaptive guidance of movements) clearly advances greatly. With the growing skill of manipulation, occasions for discrimination and exploration of objects automatically increase in frequency and variety, because the baby has better controlled movements and stronger exploratory awareness. Six-month-olds are curious and alert observers of and 'tinkerers' with the nearby world. This is the time in which the 'clinical' tests of Piaget, and the more elaborately systematic experiments of contemporary cognitive psychologists, have revealed the baby to be developing the 'object concept' – that is the concept that a thing in the present and nearby space may persist in various properties beyond its instantaneous perceptual presence; that it may survive occlusion or concealment by something else; that it has a collection of features that distinguish it as different from other things (Wishart and Bower, 1984). Younger infants follow and identify things with eyes and ears and hands, keeping track of what things are (Johnson et al., 1991; Trevarthen, 1984b). Manipulative 'tests' are used by the older baby to uncover new properties or 'affordances' of objects. The curiosity that infants demonstrate from soon after birth for novel experiences; their declining interest in often repeated events (habituation); their appreciation of 'interesting' transformations that violate expected natural manifestations or motions of objects, especially those that may indicate an animate object, allow for experimental demonstrations that they can perceive critical differences and similarities between events in the space around their bodies, demonstrations that increase in variety as the infants gain in acuity of perception and versatility and power of motor action (Bremner, Slater and Butterworth, 1997).

The engrossing exploration by psychologists of what infants can perceive, what problems of information pick-up they will try to solve, has led a majority to place cognitive developments first – to see a rational process as the necessary basis for every advance in behaviour. But this approach should not be permitted to explain away person awareness, that selective precocity which infants show for getting into active and effective relation as a person with another person, and with their emotions, their changing interests and their constantly redirected purposes. The one-sided analysis of object awareness has helped to make autism incomprehensible. Clearly autism is a disorder of the dynamic balance of two kinds of motives adapted, respectively, to dealing with objects and communicating with people – a balance for combining cognition of things in general with sympathetic, expressive communicating. Emotions are essential in relating to people.

'Self-Awareness'

The personality of an infant, it is true, develops markedly after six months (Stern, 1985; Trevarthen, 1984a, 1986, 1990b; Trevarthen, Murray and Hubley, 1981). The often noted increase in 'self-awareness' at this age is a change in the infant's people-sensitive responses and actions. The self-awareness, not entirely a new faculty, is a manifestation of a development in sensitivity to the way others attend to the infant's person; it has important feedback effects on this attention from others, changing the way adults communicate to the child, and it makes the child imitate in new ways. It is a 'self–other awareness' (Aitken and Trevarthen, 1997; Fiamenghi, 1997; Reddy, 1991; Reddy et al., 1997; Trevarthen, Kokkinaki and Fiamenghi, 1998).

With strangers, the infant becomes less trusting and playful and more watchful or fearful, and may cry (Trevarthen, 1986, 1990b; Trevarthen, Murray and Hubley, 1981). Absence of the mother leads more quickly to distress and efforts to find her, and this is evidence that 'attachment' to her is developing a new intensity (Schore, 1994; Sroufe, 1996). In play, the baby starts to act with well-marked orientation and timing in relation to the awareness and behaviour of familiar partners: 'showing off' to amuse; seeking applause; trying to attract them into play; or, if they are oriented elsewhere, calling to get help with objects or protection from threats. Confronted with a mirror, the baby, who, before five months, would have been disinterested or avoidant, is now observant, coy or demonstrative, and can be seen to be aware of the communication-limiting tension that exists between his or her expressive and demonstrative self and the instantaneously imitative image (Reddy *et al.*, 1997; Trevarthen, Kokkinaki and Fiamenghi, 1998).

The infant is also now ready to imitate simple actions of other people on objects, as well as their expressions and gestures. Indeed, about one month before starting to experiment with his or her own syllabic babbling at six months, the baby may imitate well the pitch and prosody of other persons' vocalisations, and may also copy hand movements that resemble gestures of communication (Locke, 1994; Trevarthen, 1986, 1990b). The six-month-old is beginning to be aware of other persons' line of sight and hand gestures, and tries to understand what they mean when they point to things (Scaife and Bruner, 1975; Butterworth and Grover, 1988; Bruner, 1983, 1990; Butterworth, 1991). Indeed, before mastering efficient picking up and manipulation of objects, a baby of three to four months can be interested in what a mother is doing with her hands when she presents a toy (Trevarthen and Marwick, 1986). 'Other awareness', and even a capacity for 'observational learning', may be present from the earliest stage of these developments.

After a baby has become six months old, people like to present objects in games and to accompany their actions, or the actions of the infant, with synchronised vocalisations and expressive gestures, giving emotional gloss or 'attunement' to the engagement (Stern, 1985; Stern *et al.*, 1985). They are excited to do this by the eager way the baby responds. The forms of these emotional and dramatic expressions in play give further evidence that the baby is adapted for, and responsive to, particular patterns of signalling from others, and is becoming more critical of the patterning, more aware of its finer points. Mother and baby join in elaborate displays that extend the principles of 'intersubjective' (two-mind) control which were seen operating in a simpler, more restrained way in proto-conversations at two months (Trevarthen, Murray and Hubley, 1981; Hubley and Trevarthen, 1979; Trevarthen and Hubley, 1978).

The rationalist/cognitivist school of psychology explains all such changes in temperament as consequences of changes in awareness, memory or thinking of the baby individual: because tests of orientation to and manipulation of objects with infant subjects show them to have gained new cognitive capacities for all kinds of experiences of 'objects' of interest and goals for action; people, too, are treated in a new way. The baby, they say, *consequently* recognises strangers as different, knows the mother is temporarily absent and can be expected to return, differentiates effects of self-action from the actions of others (Kagan, 1982; Sroufe, 1996). Recently meta-cognitivists attribute such changes in self-awareness to first signs of emergence of a 'theory of mind' – the baby starts to act as if attributing consciousness, that is, awareness and thinking, to others (Baron-Cohen, 1987; Leslie, 1987). But the facts of the early communication, at a stage when exploration and manipulation of objects has not developed, indicate that emotional or motivational reactions to others, and reciprocal engagement with them and with the direction of their interests, do not require the postulated cognitive development; or, that the cognitive development must be occurring very much earlier than the cognitivist-constructivist theory claims is possible, and without the help of thought in words (Aitken and Trevarthen, 1997; Reddy et al., 1997).

A more parsimonious explanation, more in line with both common sense and the facts of development from birth, is that the self-presenting and self-expressing, and imitative, behaviours of the six to nine-month-old represent a new state of communication – a transformation of motivations present at birth that are specially adapted to regulate contacts with other people and to engage with their purposes and feelings.

Emergence of Protolanguage, Joint Perspective Taking and Cooperative, Meaningful Use of Objects

At six to nine months infants often concentrate self-centeredly on exploration of objects, and on developing their own manipulative activity. They tend to become 'absorbed' in the task; that is, they are for a time mentally isolated and resistant to any overtures from another person to share the object or task.

After nine months there is a crucial transformation in this balance between, on the one hand, exploratory and performatory motives involved in mastery of impersonal objects, and, on the other, the motives for contact and communication with people (Bakeman and Adamson, 1984; Bretherton and Bates, 1979; Bruner, 1983, 1990; Hubley and Trevarthen, 1979; Tomasello, 1993; Trevarthen and Hubley, 1978). The change is manifested in many new kinds of behaviour that open the child's mind to learning about how other people view the world and how they use the objects in it (Trevarthen, 1992).

First, the child orients to and follows expressions and actions, for example pointing, by which others present objects for sharing and use them in ways that invite cooperation (Butterworth and Grover, 1988; Scaife and Bruner, 1975). Conversely, when trying to deal with a task in the presence of the other and encountering a difficulty or a surprising change, the baby tends now to turn to the other for support or help, preferring the mother over the stranger in this, as in all social transactions. When offered instructions, approval or help, the child waits to observe the 'intrusive' gesture or utterance, and then attempts to react to it in a complementary, cooperational way. When attempting to 'perform'; when 'deliberately' teasing or being 'naughty' or 'funny'; when repeating a 'joke' or a forbidden action, such as is usually received with praise or laughter even when the parent is somewhat annoyed – the child observes the partner to see the effect (Reddy, 1991).

In short, the expressivity of the child is contrived to make well-timed and well-oriented 'acts of meaning' (Halliday, 1975), acts that refer to some event or

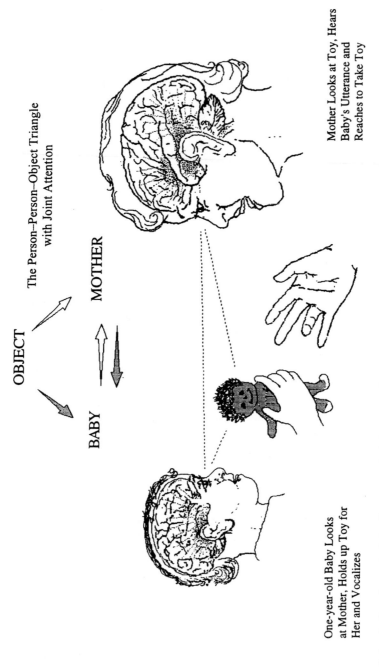

Secondary Intersubjectivity

The Person–Person–Object Triangle
with Joint Attention

OBJECT

MOTHER

BABY

One-year-old Baby Looks
at Mother, Holds up Toy for
Her and Vocalizes

Mother Looks at Toy, Hears
Baby's Utterance and
Reaches to Take Toy

Figure 8: Just before the end of the first year, a baby starts to show interest in sharing purposes and interests with familiar companions. Here we show how this cooperative awareness requires the ability to shift attention between an object and a person, while paying attention to their emotions, signs of interest and readiness to act. This is the time an infant will being to vocalise 'comments' with gestures, to make 'acts of meaning'.

object in a shared consciousness and that allow for infusion of a sharable emotional appraisal of reality.

In protolanguage, vocalisations are combined with gestures to make declarations, indications, observations, orientations, etc., sharing interest in events and combining them with signs of where and when the events are occurring (Bretherton and Bates, 1979). This is what is meant by 'protodeclarative pointing', absence of which is one indicator of autism in a one-year-old. Clear invitations, questions, refusals and denials are made by the 9 to 12-month-old, with appropriately different intonation and gestural form. The combined effect of these behaviours is that the infant becomes a partner in a new level of communication and negotiation of purposes that has been called 'secondary intersubjectivity' (person–person–object interaction (Trevarthen and Hubley, 1978)) or 'protolanguage' (Halliday, 1975). Its essential feature is the elevation of the shared topic to meaningfulness in joint awareness (Bruner, 1975, 1990, 1996; Tomasello, 1993).

When the development of this remarkable and very human level of communication, which has language-like aspects but which precedes language by several months, is traced in detail, it becomes clear that it is caused by changes in the motivations and awareness inside the child. True, this growth of mind requires support by complementary behaviours of adult partners – they must provide the occasions for a shared perspective on the world and transfusion of knowledge and skill into the infant. But, in an important sense, the initiative is with the child. The older partner enters into a role that has been made active, attractive and satisfying for him or her by the child's new feelings and expressions, alertness and vitality. That this initiative from a child is not developing normally is often the first sign that autism has affected developments in the child's brain, and is beginning to interfere with consciousness and learning.

The mother's emotions are used by the one-year-old increasingly to evaluate experiences of the world. The attention an infant gives to how a mother feels about some happening in their common world is called 'emotional referencing' (Klinnert et al., 1983; Stern et al., 1985); and it plays a central role in the child's learning from then on. The partner generously uses praise, shared enthusiasm and 'naming with approval' to expand the infant's interest in reality. Again, we can relate this to effective forms of intervention, ones that will help a child combat autism, as is explained in subsequent chapters.

By treating objects and events as having more properties than can be tested by his or her own efforts alone, the toddler opens the way to conventional and symbolic awareness of a social or cultural reality – one that has been built up by people comparing feelings, interests and actions in relation to their different experiences (Tomasello et al., 1993). Thus the one-year-old embarks on a uniquely human quest with its own psychological motives – a quest for knowledge or meaning of a kind that is essentially shareable. This is the first step in what becomes a rapid development towards symbolic and cultural life and towards both the need for, and mastery of, language (Halliday, 1975; Trevarthen, 1987a, 1992; Trevarthen and Logotheti, 1987). This is, also, the beginning of systematic education of the child for life in the culture (Bruner, 1996). It is about this time that a child developing autism becomes markedly 'different' – both less aware and less cooperative.

It is important to emphasise that the motivation for acquiring symbolic means of expression is not confined to a speech and hearing system. Understanding of symbols is organised at a deeper level and can be attached to different senses and expressed by different parts of the body. For example, besides permitting the dawning of recognition of the conventional nature of simple artefacts, rituals, manners, and roles by which people share cultural awareness, it gives the toddler a capacity to acquire the beginnings of languages that are independent of speech, languages that are felt and seen, instead of heard. In a deaf family that uses hand sign language for daily communication, a deaf or hearing baby can begin to pick up and use signs before one year of age (Bellugi *et al.*, 1988; Newport and Meier, 1985; Volterra, 1981). Given appropriate affectionate encouragement through use of written words in cooperative games, a one-year-old can begin to read whole words. There is even evidence that instruction of a deaf toddler in reading can enable the child to acquire fluent reading before the age of entry to primary school, and thus keep up with the reading ability of hearing-speaking peers (Söderbergh, 1986).

These variants of normal education for language prove that the foundations for learning symbols are not confined to the cognitive system that processes sounds of speech or that coordinates the oral motor apparatus to produce speech. Further support for this conclusion is to be found in the gestures that all people make unconsciously when they speak (McNeill, 1992). These hand movements may not be conventionalised in a language, but they do convey thoughts being put into speech, and they do so at the same time, or even a moment before, the utterance of words. They take over and strive to convey clarity when speaking becomes difficult. The use of signs and 'augmented communication' of various kinds for an autistic pre-school child is relying upon activation of the innate, but developmentally weakened, motives to communicate by any and all means possible (von Tetzchner and Martinsen, 1992).

An interesting manifestation of the brain's organisation for communication by symbols lies in the fact that speech in the brain, and both spontaneous gestures and the signs of hand sign languages, are typically asymmetric (Corballis, 1991). The majority of people, of all ages, make more explicit other-directed moves of their hand with their right hands. Most infants, too, start to exhibit a consistent handedness for skilled actions, usually preferring the right hand at the same time as they acquire proficiency in language, in the second and third year (Trevarthen, 1986, 1996). Toddlers show hand

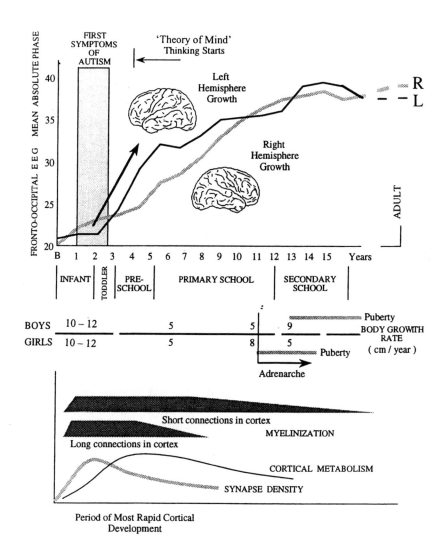

Figure 9: Asymmetric development of the cerebral hemispheres. There is a large 'growth surge' in the left hemisphere between two and five years, when language normally undergoes its most rapid phase of development. Important developments in the brain are summarised below. Girls develop a little ahead of boys, notably in the period of puberty, when a second development of the left hemisphere is seen. Autism appears before the left hemisphere is developing new nerve connections most actively. (Fronto-occipital EEG Mean Absolute Phase is a measure of the synchronicity of brain waves. Adrenarche is a physiological change in the adrenal gland causing increase in some sex and growth hormones.)

preference in many kinds of expressive and purposeful movements – for imitated gestures, for pointing, greeting and many other acts of meaning, and for meaningful manipulation of such cultural objects, or tools, as feeding utensils, pencils, brushes, combs, etc. A majority appear to be right-handed, and left-brained, for all such 'other-directed' and meaningful behaviours. A minority are firmly left-handed. Others are slower to show consistent handedness and may remain 'mixed' in hand preferences. These one-sidednesses of expression appear to be triggered by left–right differences in the chemical regulatory mechanisms of the core of the brain, which direct developments in the cognitive parts of the two cerebral hemispheres, and set conscious interests, intentions and emotional evaluations in behaviour, as has been explained in Chapter 6. We have seen that autistic children tend to have less clear handedness (Dawson, 1988). This is further evidence that the core regulators of their brain have not operated correctly in early stages of the development of their brains, and/or are disorganised in the control of current behaviours (Trevarthen, 1996; Aitken and Trevarthen, 1997).

Toddlers' Role Play: Imitating to Communicate and Pretending to Know

By the middle of the second year a toddler is starting to pick up many conventional, meaningful ways of behaving and ways of using artefacts. Learning by observing others and imitating fuels the development of creative play in socially recognised roles, and leads to acting out of performances such as having a cup of tea, talking on the 'phone, preparing a meal, driving a car, vacuuming, pretending conversations and attitudes in encounters or purposeful actions with puppets or dolls, and so on (Fein, 1981; Leslie, 1987; Lowe, 1975; Matthews, 1977; Nadel and Pezé, 1993; Rogoff, 1990; Rosenblatt, 1977; Trevarthen, 1990a). Such meaningful tasks or roles are often closely observed and performed with accurate imitation in the second year, before the child has any clearly recognisable words. Thus, some skills of culture start to be picked up, at least as ways of acting, before language, or while language is in its most rudimentary 'protolanguage' phase. The conventional meanings of actions and tools or instruments can be assimilated by observing others before the words as labels for these things are understood (Trevarthen, 1990b).

Of course, cognitive powers are needed to perceive what the meaningful objects are like, to apprehend their spatio-temporal coordinates, to identify and compare them, to solve practical or physical problems of how they may be combined and transformed. The child has also to be able to discriminate the communicative signs of other people and to perceive how they are combined. But the crucial factor that makes reality meaningful for a toddler is the special orientation the child takes towards other people and their way of intruding on and evaluating reality. A child with severe sensory or motor deficit can master communication well, if given a way to meet other people's ideas and respond to their expressions. An autistic child with no defect of senses or movements fails to communicate, because the impulse to find companionship in experience has been weakened.

The first two years of life are a period of observation, instruction and practice in detecting and negotiating with the wills and emotions of other persons, an apprenticeship supported in a relationship of trust through affectionate individualised attachments (Rogoff, 1990; Bruner, 1996). However, the intimacy and mutual confidence of a good relationship largely conceals these motivations and how they are realised. They can be brought out by comparison with the behaviour of the same child with strangers or with peers, neither of whom can support the toddler in as high a level of imaginative and cooperative play as can the mother.

Peers stimulate a child below two to convergent and imitative patterns of action, in which pursuit of meaning tends to repetition with little progress. Thus two-year-olds find it difficult to cooperate with one another in a creative task, but they may greatly enjoy creating symmetry of play that involves much mimicry, and that may generate conflict if interest of two children focuses on one goal (Nadel, 1986; Nadel-Brulfert and Baudonnière, 1982). What they can achieve depends on how well they know and like each other (Dunn, 1988; Rubin, 1980). Non-friends do not play with as much mutual interest and pleasure. Simple acts of giving and taking can go on between friends, they can even express feelings about the rightness or wrongness of actions, but the performance of 'tasks' is limited, in comparison with the asymmetrical play of the same child in the presence of a trusted adult. The adult playmate will automatically supply props in an appropriately considerate and cooperative way, or at least will assure the potential availability of such a supply, and will make approving noises, joining with appreciative comments in the child's efforts at meaningful action (Rogoff, 1990). The behaviours of normal two-year-olds show they are passing through a major change in their ability to imagine meaning and to share in social conventions. This development goes beyond the acquisition of language, and beyond cognitive functions that might be called 'self-awareness'.

As language floods the mind of the child, imagination and communication are enriched and extend away from the 'here and now'. Most children speak clear words in short telegraphic sentences by two, and this is the beginning of a phase of accelerating vocabulary learning (Brown 1973; Bruner, 1983). By 30 months a child and mother playing together may make almost equal verbal contributions (Stewart-Clarke and Hevey, 1981). Toddlers chatter to themselves about what they are doing and discuss their experiences and plans, demonstrating a considerable repertoire of socially and culturally defined ideas and skills.

INFANCY: With Mother or Other Caregiver

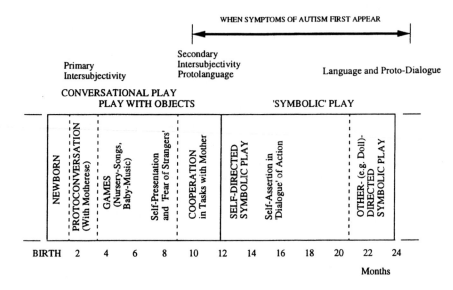

PRE-SCHOOL: With Adults or Peers

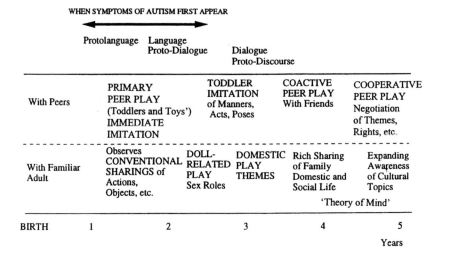

Figure 10: Developments in communication and play with different companions through infancy and in the pre-school period, and an indication of the time at which the symptoms of autism usually become apparent

Entering Narratives of a Meaningful World

Studies of the way children play with meaningful objects and with dolls reveal that after one year they gain rapidly in representational or symbolic awareness. They are also more and more interested in how their ideas are perceived by others. By 18 months, mere 'sensory-motor' play, taking objects for their obvious 'physical' appearances and uses, has become a minor component, the child preferring to take up things as objects that have a defined use in the culture, seeing spoons, cups, brushes, telephones, baskets, pots, knives, cars and so on as attractive because they can be used 'properly' in 'routine representational schemas' (Rosenblatt, 1977). When dolls are available play becomes, after 18 months, increasingly doll-directed. This seems to be another manifestation of a spontaneous opening out of self-related imitative consciousness towards more cooperative other-directed understanding – towards identifying sympathetically with other person's lives (Leslie, 1987; Hobson, 1993a,b).

By the end of the second year pretend play exhibits more complex ideas, requiring more elaborate combinations of objects and sequences of action (Lowe, 1975; Nicholich, 1977). The child is beginning to make substitutions of meaning or 'metaphorical' uses of objects, taking the act of communication and meaning-creation to transform an object and to have it named as something else (Leslie, 1987; Lowe, 1975; Matthews, 1977). At the same time, the two to three-year-old is taking up socially approved and co-operatively motivated roles, boys and girls beginning to choose different play themes (Fein, 1981).

With the use of language that most children have gained by three years, absent things become topics for conversation. This allows anyone who speaks the same 'mother tongue' to meet and satisfy the child's growing imagination and curiosity about the shared world and its meanings and roles, whether the ideas are about things that are actually present in the 'here and now' or not. Sharing stories about people and places – real or imaginary; past, present or yet to come – becomes a favourite game (Sigman and Capps, 1997).

Three-year-olds with strong friendships may exhibit clear discriminations about the age and sex of other children, knowing well who is a 'big' child, and who is 'little'. Especially among friends, pretend play is increasingly absorbed in elaborated socio-dramatic themes with the children taking complementary, rather than imitative, roles and often demonstrating elaborate knowledge of real family and social life. This play is sustained and rapidly extended by the increasing fluency in language.

The evidence we have from studies of toddlers and nursery school children, briefly sketched here, shows clearly that growing cultural understanding is in good strong life before formal schooling begins. The reasoning of the pre-school child takes place in awareness of everyday things that are shared and evaluated with friends. Adjustments are made to the age and familiarity of companions which reflect the confidence and ability the children have with symbolic awareness. The child learns with what Margaret Donaldson (1978) calls 'human sense'.

This learning by cooperating is seen in all cultures, whatever their forms of language or technology. Studies of cultures that differ widely in family and social organisation, in manners, beliefs and technology support the idea that young children everywhere, in spite of being viewed by adults in different ways, are making the same kind of active entry into their society and its culture well before the age of five (Rogoff, 1990; Trevarthen, 1992). In this learning they receive support from elders that is matched to the child's interests and abilities. In some cultures, three-year-olds can perform useful 'work', this being but slightly different from the preferred play of children of other cultures who are not given responsibility so young.

Developmental Psychologists' Models of Autism and its Development

Many recent attempts to explain autism have been influenced by theories about mental processes derived from cognitive science and computer logic, by the findings of more naturalistic observations of the psychological development of children and by new discoveries about brain development and about abnormalities in the brains of autistic individuals. There is a greater willingness in recent reviews of the now very large literature on autistic children to take all kinds of evidence into account.

In an effort to establish a scientific, objective and well-measured set of procedures for assessing cognitive or linguistic attainments of autistic children and for administering treatment, Schopler and Rutter, two highly influential authorities, were led to reject ideas that the disease involves a basic abnormality of emotion, or of emotional communication (Rutter, 1968, 1978, 1983, 1985; Rutter et al., 1971; Rutter and Schopler, 1978; Schopler, 1983; Schopler, Reichler, De Vellis and Kock, 1980). Dismissing the psychoanalytic assumption that such a pattern of emotional stiffness or coldness and unapproachability could only be the result of an environmental stress or deprivation (Mahler, 1952; Bettelheim, 1967), they overlooked the simpler interpretation that an autistic child's brain has an intrinsic defect in the generation of communicative and emotional responses because of disorganisation in a system specifically adapted for regulating contact with people.

In consequence, careful observations on the behaviours of autistic children when they are interacting with people, with accurate information on their reactions to other persons' responses, were for a time neglected. It was claimed that they were based on ideas that are illogical or too intuitive. However, observations confirm that the orienting and expressive responses of autistic children tend to cut them off from emotional and communicative transactions with those around them (Hobson, 1983, 1987; Hutt and Ounsted, 1966;

Kanner 1943; Richer, 1976, 1983; Sigman and Capps, 1997; Tinbergen and Tinbergen, 1983). This evidently is related to (and may produce, rather than reflect mis-timing of expressive behaviours of autistic individuals and breakdown of the patterns that normally sustain efficient reciprocity or turn-taking in communication (Beebe et al., 1985; Condon, 1975; Feldstein et al., 1982). Experiments show that autistic children have difficulty in perceiving the differences between emotional expressions and in judging other personal attributes of people (Hobson, 1983, 1986a,b; Hobson et al., 1988a,b). At the same time, the affected child is abnormally sensitive and distorted in awareness of and attention to many sorts of environmental stimuli, unable to solve cognitive problems that should be simple for a child of that age, and, when not mute, bizarre in social use of speech. But these features of the disorder in no way contradict the view that a specific deficit in person-perception and in motivation toward persons is the root of the problem. Indeed, it is the rule for attentional and cognitive processes to be close-coupled to motivation for communication. Attention, cognition and memory are typically defective or abnormal in emotional illness.

How Awareness of Others Becomes Derailed

The course of normal development, outlined above, demonstrates that children are dependent on learning by way of sensitive identification and cooperation with people and that they are naturally interested in what other people experience, feel and intend. Autistic children are severely deficient in these vital responses (Sigman, 1989; Sigman and Capps, 1987).

Mundy and Sigman (1989a, b) review evidence on the social responses of autistic children and conclude that they show impairment first in affective responses and non-verbal communication. Hobson presents a theoretical interpretation of data on interpersonal relations and intentional communications, which he summarises as follows:

> Autistic children have a biologically based impairment of affective-conative relatedness with the environment, which has especially far reaching implications for their social relations. The defining characteristic of autism is a uniquely severe disruption in the children's personal relatedness with others. (Hobson, 1989)

Hobson is drawing attention to the changes in purposiveness and drive for experience of the autistic child, as well as to the differences in emotionality in their reactions to persons. In a recent review of the psychological characteristics of autistic children and a discussion of rival models of the disorder and its causes in development, Rogers and Pennington (1991) conclude that autistic children retain affectionate reactions to persons they know well because this kind of learning emerges early in development, in the first nine months. As we have mentioned, affectionate attachment to the mother may, in fact, begin before birth by auditory learning, and preferences in relationships are clear from early infancy. On the other hand, as Rogers and Pennington point out, reciprocal imitation and joint perspective taking, at a level where they contribute crucially to cultural learning (Tomasello *et al.*, 1993), are selectively impaired in autism. These are behaviours that develop after nine months and that become elaborated in the second and third years (Trevarthen, 1992).

The philosophical 'Theory of Mind' theory of Leslie, Baron-Cohen and Frith (Baron-Cohen, Leslie and Frith, 1985; Leslie, 1987), which emphasises developments in general representational cognition that are hypothesised to generate awareness of other persons' awareness, and also pretence in the form of imagination about what might be, and to permit emergence of awareness of other persons' knowledge and beliefs, is set aside by Rogers and Pennington. They also give qualified acceptance to Hobson's theory that the main defect is in emotional relating to other persons in favour of a model based on Stern (1985), who describes stages by which the infant constructs a 'self' in interpersonal relations and through communication. They concur with Sigman (1989) that examination of the deficits of autism within the framework of normal development has both theoretical importance and pragmatic utility. This position, with the evidence for it, is fully explored by Sigman and Capps (1997).

Bringing In Evidence from Brain Science

In Chapters 6 and 7 we summarised the evidence that autism is caused by a fault in brain development. There would seem to be very secure anatomico-functional grounds for regarding autism as primarily developmental disorders in the *regulation* of the post-natal formation of cognitive and learning systems, with, at the same time, a central disturbance of the socio-emotional interpersonal signalling processes that are essential to communication and the transmission of learning by human instruction (see Aitken and Trevarthen, 1997; Fein *et al.*, 1986). This kind of learning, through sympathetic involvement in other persons' lives, be they other children or adults, is the key process by which a child learns to understand, and talk about, the world like the older members of his or her community.

Thus it now seems likely, for example, that slowly maturing cortical systems of cells and interconnections that result in different cognitive activities in the two cerebral hemispheres, or in development of different sections of the cognitive mechanism in the brain such as may be tapped by different kinds of intelligence test, or by tests for language function, owe their initial differentiation to the projection into them of different influences from the brainstem during pre-natal hemispheric growth (Trevarthen, 1987b, 1989b, 1990b, 1996).

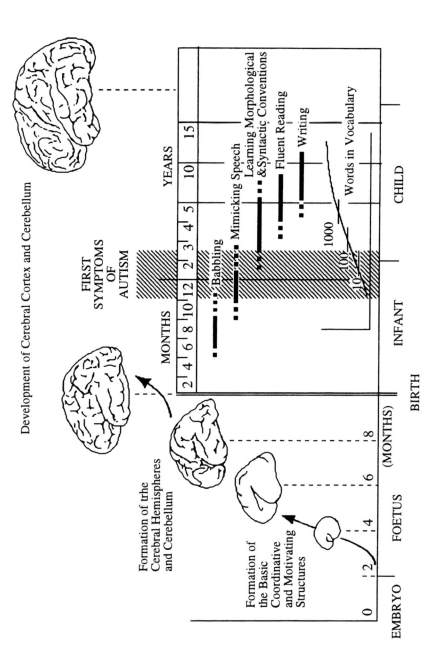

Figure 11: Hemisphere development and language learning. The left hemispheres of the brain are shown to the same scale, illustrating how they expand in the foetal period, before birth, and then go on elaborating after birth. Autism appears at the critical stage shown in Figure 9, as language begins.

Increasing evidence that growth and differentiation of the cerebral cortex may be directed by reticular and limbic influences, that is, by chemicals transmitted from cells in the brain stem and more ancient and earlier developing parts of the hemispheres, cells that can become organised in some independence of input to the special senses both before and after birth, gives new perspectives for theories of learning. It also opens the way for a theory that would give emotional states, which are sustained by patterns of activity in the same reticular and limbic systems, a role in regulation of brain development (Trevarthen, 1987b, 1989b, 1996). These new ideas tend to reverse the traditional concept that emotions are by-products of rational processes, and they are compatible with the theory that autism is a disorder in the internal regulation of brain growth that has its effect at a particular stage of development, beginning about the end of the first year of infancy (Trevarthen, 1989a). Recent studies of human psychological development compared with developments in the behaviours of monkeys that relate to known steps in the development of the monkey's brain give support to the idea that the symptoms of autism appear when parts of the frontal lobes of the human brain are rapidly developing. The evidence for this 'frontal hypothesis' is reviewed by Rogers and Pennington (1991).

Neuropathological and neurophysiological findings summarised in Chapter 7 supported the idea that autism is a disorder of the same regulatory core system of the brain that is found to control the patterning of normal brain maturation and to motivate learning in the adult. If this is so, cognitive and linguistic disabilities that autistic children commonly come to have are probably consequences of abnormal neocortical development *produced by* the core systems, rather than causes of the disease in its emotional facets. It seems justified to conclude that emotional abnormality and consequent deficits in social communication are expressions of an essential starting feature of the abnormal path of brain maturation, not a by-product of general information-handling cognitive or learning deficits.

A different approach to understanding autism, as well as related developmental diseases of the brain that reduce intelligence, such as Rett's syndrome, promises to assist our comprehension of genetic regulation of growth and differentiation of neural systems in the brain (Trevarthen and Aitken, 1996). It may also lead to improved methods for mitigating the effects of autism and related diseases, by helping us understand how best to manage the abnormal child's emotions in communication, and so to assist improved motivation for engagement with the environment, especially the 'human environment', and more efficient retention of experiences that favour positive mental growth.

Conclusion: Developing Humanness is Essentially Interpersonal

We can summarise the argument of this chapter as follows:

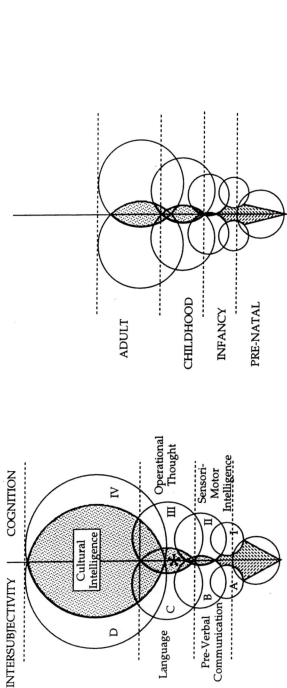

Figure 12: Diagram to illustrate the concept of development of two fundamental motive systems in the human mind: one is concerned with individual cognition, or rational awareness of objects; the other is adapted to sympathetic engagement with the motives of other human beings. Precursors of the two systems are laid down in the embryo and foetal brain before birth, and both are essential for the development of cooperative understanding, and for learning the symbols and other conventions of a culture. The main stages can be summarised as follows: A = Primary Intersubjectivity; B = Secondary Intersubjectivity; C = Emergence of language in toddlers and school children; D = Maturation of understanding for a fully responsible life in a community with its culture. The asterisk (*) indicates the approximate point of development of 'Theory of Mind' thinking. In autism abnormal developments in the embryo lead to failure of both systems. Secondary intersubjectivity fails and a toddler show both cognitive and intersubjective problems. Cultural learning is severely compromised. (Aitken and Trevarthen, 1997; Trevarthen and Aitken, 1994)

(1) Infants are ready from birth to establish communication with their caretakers by means of emotional or motivational expressions and sensitivities, imitating and making utterance-like messages. With appropriate support from an identified and affectionate caretaker, they communicate at this proto-conversational level elaborately and efficiently before they begin manipulative testing of 'object concepts'. Indeed, reactions to a mother's vocalisations, and learning to identify her by voice, starts before birth. Subsequently, the child's cognitive development and 'processing' of experience, which advances rapidly after the development of strong head support and effective reaching and grasping at four months, are regulated by emotions in play with other people, whose interests and actions are complemented and imitated by the child. After infancy, toddlers develop representations, conventional and role-based play as they learn language. They also develop cooperative skills with peers, copying gestures and tasks and sharing lively and imaginative communication.

(2) Of these developments, the ones that develop after the end of the first year, which normally lead a child towards proficiency in the culture's meanings and its 'mother tongue', are impaired in autism. It would appear, therefore, that this developmental disorder originates in failure of cerebral systems that regulate a child's motivation for learning meanings in communication.

(3) Present knowledge of brain abnormalities that accompany autism, or that produce autism-like disorders in monkeys and in adult human beings, which we have presented in Chapter 7, is compatible with the above interpretation. Brain research does not support the view that the emotional and interpersonal aspects of autism are consequences of primary failure in sensory, motor or linguistic processes. Nor do they support the hypothesis that the central deficit in autism is the lack of a cognitive capacity to 'represent mental states', although such a deficit does appear to follow from the primary fault in awareness of changing relationships to other persons and their feelings, and how to cooperate with them through communication. However, we cannot hope to localise a single mechanism in the brain for this functional disorder, because the whole of the human brain has been transformed in the evolution of a mind that has the need to develop by learning a culture – by education.

CHAPTER 9

Communicating and Playing with an Autistic Child

Given that an infant, even one only a month or two old, can join in a 'conversation' of feelings with a caregiver – an imitative meeting of rhythmic motives for expression that is driven by contributions from both that person and the baby – it follows that the communication can break down by defect in the person-recognising 'conversation regulator' of either party. Part of the problem with understanding autism is that we have to perceive the infant, any infant, as a person with feelings and interpersonal needs, and active ways of expressing these. Human interaction in relationships is a two-way business from the start of life.

First, there can be disorders of the infant's playful communication – either faulty sensitivity for the mother's feelings, or abnormal expression or timing in reaction to what she does. Alternatively, a mother's support of her infant's readiness for affectionate and playful contact can fail. Stress, or an emotional illness can interfere with free signalling of feelings and reduce responses to other persons' emotions, including those a baby expresses to a mother or father. Post-natal depression, for example, may make it impossible for a mother to support proto-conversational play, and there is evidence that this is disturbing for the infant, and can have lasting effects (Cohn and Tronick, 1983; Fraiberg, 1980; Murray and Cooper, 1997; Tronick and Field, 1986). Psychiatrists, particularly the psychoanalysts whose theories have traditionally portrayed the infant as emotionally dependent on the mother, and needing comfort and 'holding', have seen this as an explanation for the appearance of autistic symptoms in infancy. They confuse the different effects of parental mental illness, or a caregiver's inability to relate sympathetically with the baby, from the withdrawal and confusion of expressive motives in the child that characterises autism from its early stages. They fail to recognise that these symptoms appear even when maternal, and paternal, care is warm and intensely sympathetic to the child's needs.

Infantile autism can be differentiated from the emotional problems resulting from maternal emotional withdrawal. It is a disorder originating in the child. It results from abnormality in the child's capacity for perception of emotions and for interpersonal recognition in all kinds of interaction (Hobson, 1989, 1993a,b; Rogers and Pennington, 1991; Sigman and Capps, 1997). This abnormality is not apparent at first. It emerges around the end of the first year of infancy. That is why it is called a developmental disorder. It always affects communication and play in ways that are confusing and distressing for parents. We can learn what the child needs to recover happier regulation of emotions and interests and better understanding of the world by careful study of how communication and play go wrong.

The abilities of very young infants for communication while learning about their bodies, about the environment of usable objects, and above all about other people and the special experiences that can be shared with them, prove that a human being is born wanting to investigate the patterns and possibilities of acting in various ways, and is seeking to form companionable relationship to others. **Autistic children, even the most incapacitated, retain at least some of this early basis for relating to the world, and to people.** They can sense other persons' emotions, and express emotions. They show sensitivity to, and can imitate, rhythmic and prosodic features of other persons' gestures and vocalisations, and, for example, the elaborations of these in music. They develop attachment to familiar and affectionate others, and they can enjoy kinds of play that explore the effects of moving with others, or sharing gentle teasing. They take an interest in objects, and, although their interests may become odd, they have favourite comforting objects like other children, and they develop interest in exploring objects and deriving excitement from 'studying' them. This is the positive basis on which the fragile and distorted motives that appear in an autistic toddler can be encouraged and given order with help from other people, making it possible for the child to learn habits and adjustments to compensate for the developmental motives that have been weakened or lost, or that tend to become trapped in sterile repetitive activities. It is important not to let the obvious and puzzling failures of playful imagination and of initiative to communicate obscure the human sensibility that remains, and that can be strengthened and used to help the child develop and learn.

How Autism Changes Imagination and Its Sharing

Autism appears at an age when a toddler is expected to be developing motivation to attempt more elaborate partnership of mental life with companions, in the early stages of language. To explain the characteristic cognitive disorders and peculiarities of language development in autistic children we must, therefore, consider how development of an infant's knowledge of the world, problem solving and use of words all depend on narrated and inventive sharing of communication about things with others, and on the emotional regulation of this sharing of meaning in companionship with identified persons. The early failure affects all future learning and relations with society, although to differing degrees in different individuals.

Information on this critical phase of early child development, information that emphasises both the interpersonal and the cognitive aspects, must be an essential component in training for teachers who are destined to work with autistic pupils of whatever age, in pre-school, primary and secondary levels (Jordan and Powell, 1995; Powell and Jordan, 1997; Kaufman, 1994; Schopler and Olley, 1982).

We have described how normally developing infants are eager to engage in interactions with their mothers and other adults, and as they grow older we see them become increasingly adept at mimicking the creative acts and roles of others. Then, in the second and third years, they rapidly become competent in the comprehension and expression of meaningful acts, and the shared values and conventional uses of objects. They also become fluent in use of spoken language. After apparently normal developments in the first year, it is the second set of developmental milestones that appear deviant in autistic children (Sigman and Capps, 1997). Evidence on how, and when, development fails can be found in retrospective studies of infants later diagnosed as autistic, in empirical studies of autistic children's verbal and non-verbal communication, and in the analysis of playful interactions between young autistic children and their mothers or with peers.

The Earliest Stages

We want to begin helping an autistic child as early as possible, preferably in infancy. But first it is necessary to identify who are the infants that have this rare condition. All successful therapeutic and educational interventions work best if they begin early, in the pre-school period.

As we have explained in Chapter 2, it appears unlikely that it will ever be possible to diagnose autism in a newborn baby. There is anecdotal evidence about the behaviour of autistic children in early infancy taken from retrospective parental accounts and video data. Some mothers report that there was something abnormal with their child since he/she was born, but most say that they recognised a problem in the second year that became more worrying as the child progressed into the third and fourth years. The most reliable information comes from family videos where one can see the baby reacting to people and objects in the home. There is such variety in the personality or liveliness and eagerness to communicate of different young infants, all of whom will develop normally, that discriminating the first signs of abnormal withdrawal or disorientation to people and things is bound to be difficult.

It is sometimes reported that infants who later developed autism did not cry in the first year, and rarely demanded any attention. However, others cry often, they even scream, and they have feeding and sleeping problems. A lack of interest in social contact and in the human voice is reported. The babies smile, but not in response to social approaches. In the final part of their first year the autistic babies do not show exploratory behaviour with curiosity about their environment, and they do not seek to engage in shared activities with their parents. They are self-content, manipulating one object over and over, fascinated with certain sensory experiences (Wing, 1976). Eriksson and DeChateau (1992) analysed videotapes of an autistic girl filmed from birth and observed that, after developing normally during the first year, she later showed these symptoms of withdrawal. A number of such studies have recorded a sudden change toward very peculiar behaviour early in the second year, around 14 to 18 months after birth. This is too young for a lack of language development to be securely determined, but it is often the time that parents become aware that a change has occurred in the concentration, exploration and social responsiveness, and perhaps in emotional stability, of a child who later has autism.

The few studies that purport to find features of the autistic syndrome very early in infancy also detect effects of the children's behaviour on their mothers. Massie claimed, in the period when the 'psychogenic' hypothesis was strong, that mothers of 'psychotic' (that is 'autistic') children were relatively insensitive to their child's smiles and eye contact in the period from birth to six months (Massie, 1978a). In analysis of interactions in the first six months, mothers and babies showed lower frequencies for holding, and mothers showed lower ratings for touching and eye gaze compared with normal mother–infant interaction (Massie, 1978b). It is likely that such features of mothers' behaviour result from the strange behaviour of the babies. Sparling (1991) reported, in analysis of a prospective case study, that abnormalities in expressive and receptive communication, and in eye contact during interaction with the mother, could be observed at three months, even though the mother's interactive style was characterised as of high 'quality' and 'appropriateness'. Kubicek (1980), taking advantage of a remarkably fortunate source of information, described the organisation of a mother's interactions with two infants: a normal boy and his fraternal twin brother, Twin A, who was later diagnosed as autistic. These recordings were made when the infants were between 3 and 16 weeks of age. She reported that:

> ...[the] system of mutual exchange, based on subtle differences in facial expression and body movement, never occurred in the interaction between the mother and Twin A. Twin A failed to provide his mother with positive feedback, which is considered essential for establishing a 'normal' mother–infant interaction... Furthermore, he did not respond

differentially to subtle changes in maternal behaviours, making it difficult for her to respond appropriately... (Kubicek, 1980, p.109).

Other studies give more reliable information about the development of autistic disorder later in infancy. Adrien, Faure, Perrot, Hameury, Garreau, Barthélémy, and Sauvage (Adrien et al., 1991a) analysed home movies of children later diagnosed as autistic. They observed that in the first two years, problems with social interaction, emotional disorders, abnormal visual and auditory behaviours, atypical behaviour and disorders of muscular tone or strength and motor behaviour appeared. In another study of ten cases in the same age range, the same behaviours were again identified as differentiating autistic from normally developing children. These behaviours were described as poor social interaction and poor communication (no social smile, lack of appropriate facial expressions and gestures), restricted adaptation to environmental situations (hypoactivity), reduced motility (calmness and hypotonia), depressed emotional reactions (no expression of emotions) and abnormal attention (poor concentration) (Adrien et al., 1991b).

By selecting a high-risk group from families with incidence of autism, Baron-Cohen and colleagues have shown, with the CHAT questionnaire, that 18-month-olds can be identified as developing autism when they show abnormalities in pretend play, proto-declarative pointing, joint attention, social interest, and social play (Baron-Cohen, Allen and Gillberg, 1992; Baron-Cohen et al., 1996), and Gillberg concludes that diagnosis can be made on the basis of interview with the mother and observation of the child between one and three years (Gillberg et al., 1990).

The above studies argue that the interaction which takes place between autistic infants and their mothers may not follow the pathway of the reciprocal, rhythmically-timed and synchronised communication that is typical of the normally developing baby, but none of the abnormalities reported for the first year are of a kind that suggest an irreversible deterioration. Later, as the infant grows older and the acquisition of skills for verbal and non-verbal communication is expected, much clearer impairments emerge in the autistic population. All diagnostic descriptions specify impairments in communication – verbal and non-verbal, receptive and expressive – and in sharable imaginative play. They also specify that these signs will appear in late infancy, and that they will be definitive by the time a child is three years old.

Development of Communication and Language in Toddlers with Autism

Many autistic children do not speak, and others develop speech late and abnormally. But autism affects all communicative behaviours from early stages (Jordan, 1993). Ricks (1979) investigated the way in which pre-verbal autistic children, between their third and sixth birthday, and normally developing infants in their first two years of life, conveyed emotional meaning in four different types of sounds, to express: 'request', 'frustration', 'greeting' and 'pleasant surprise'. He found that parents of an autistic child were able to recognise messages of their own child and of normally developing children from their sounds, but they were not able to identify the sounds of other autistic children. Thus, the signals given by pre-verbal autistic children were perceived as idiosyncratic. They lacked the universal communicatively effective prosodic features observed in the normal infants and toddlers.

Autistic children also have problems understanding other persons' language. The severity of their problems is influenced by the content of language and the context in which a concept is expressed (Garfin and Lord, 1986; Jordan, 1993; Jordan and Powell, 1995). Expressive language is both deviant and delayed (Cunningham, 1968). Typical peculiarities include both immediate and delayed echoing of speech, reversing the person ('I' or 'me' vs. 'you') that pronouns refer to (Kanner, 1943; Rutter, 1978; Jordan, 1989), stereotypic utterances, often repeated with no discernible meaning (Rutter, 1978), abnormal prosodic patterns (Tager-Flusberg, 1989) and inappropriate metaphors (Kanner, 1946). If speech is present, it is often not used spontaneously and functionally in conversation (Rutter, 1978).

On the other hand, those autistic children who do speak usually do not have severe problems in the phonological and syntactic development of the language; they pronounce correctly and make grammatical constructions. It is the semantic and functional use of words, in appropriate relation to the pragmatic or social context, that constitutes the basic deficit (Jordan, 1993; Tager-Flusberg, 1981). In other words, the well-articulated and grammatically correct speech is not used to share meaning and information in ways other people find easy to understand. Delayed language production is manifested in the ways autistic youngsters use speech spontaneously in conversation (Rutter, 1978) and in the ways they use language to serve purposes of clear communication (Cunningham, 1968). Autistic individuals have difficulties in giving or requesting or sharing information (Hurtig et al., 1982; Cunningham, 1968), in conversational turn-taking (Prizant and Schuler, 1987), and in speaker–hearer relationships (Baltaxe, 1977).

Clearly the problem goes beyond language in the limited sense of using words. Non-verbal communication is also affected (Jordan, 1993; Kanner, 1943; Ricks and Wing, 1975). Autistic children do not anticipate by reaching out when they are to be picked up (Ricks and Wing, 1975) and they show abnormalities in eye-to-eye contact (Hutt and Ounsted, 1966; Rutter, 1978), in imitation (Rogers and Pennington, 1991), in comprehension and expression of facial expressions (Hobson, 1983, 1986a,b; Sigman and Capps, 1997; Snow et al., 1987; Yirmiya et al., 1989) and gestures, including pointing (Attwood et al., 1988; Curcio, 1978; Ohta, 1987). The autistic child's 'path to language' (Locke, 1993) is deviant and difficult.

These general problems of communicative expression are addressed by methods of teaching that employ a wide variety of gestures and expressions in addition to speech to help autistic children understand other people and be understood by them, as explained in Chapter 10 (Davies, 1997; von Tetzchner and Martinsen, 1992). Rhythmic games, group play, music, dance and dramatic play can engage the interest and pleasure of autistic children, and this can, in some cases, greatly aid language learning and the efficacy of speech therapy (Davies, 1997; Lord, 1997; Wimpory *et al.*, 1995). In Chapter 11, Jacqueline Robarts explains the experience of music therapists in giving aid to development of autistic children's communication and self-expression.

Getting at the Essential Problem in Autistic Intersubjectivity

Human life depends on rich cooperation between the mental activities of conscious, feeling and intending persons, who share interest in a world interpreted as having meaning; that is on 'intersubjectivity' (Hobson, 1993a; Trevarthen, 1993a, 1998b).

There are many ways to begin an analysis of how far children cooperate socially, depending on how mental life is conceived. McHale (1983) defined communication in terms of mere physical proximity or aggregation; children were considered to be part of a group if they were within five feet of one another. On this criterion, autistic children in a school may communicate much less than other children, but it is not evidence that while keeping a distance they do not have communicative interest. In terms of Speech Act Theory (Austin, 1962, which analyses the **communicative intentions** of language users), autistic children can, again, be viewed as interactive to some degree, since they do use verbal and non-verbal communication intentionally to reach certain goals with other persons' aid (Wetherby, 1986; Wetherby and Prutting, 1984). For example, an autistic child can often be seen to pull a person by hand toward a desired object the child cannot reach, without making signs of interest in what that person feels or attends to. In the framework of the theory of **pragmatics in language,** defining the effects of utterances or gestures between people, what they do to each other with language, the abnormal language of autistic children can still be seen to have a functional role, though a limited one (Jordan, 1993). For example, a single apparently meaningless repeated utterance of a four-year-old boy was found to be used effectively as a tool to engage his conversational partner in interaction (Coggins and Frederickson, 1988).

The deficiencies in Speech Acts and pragmatics of high-functioning autistic individuals are subtle (Loveland *et al.*, 1988). On the other hand, when communication is studied in terms of the use of **'joint attention'** or **'shared focus'** (Mundy *et al.*, 1986; Sigman *et al.*, 1986; Sigman and Capps, 1997), autistic children appear characteristically impaired. They often fail to engage with and direct another's attention, and they do not use postures or gestures such as pointing to help other people share what they are experiencing or thinking about (Jordan, 1993). Moreover, those individuals who do share attention more are also more advanced in their use and understanding of language (Loveland and Landry, 1986; Mundy *et al.*, 1990). Thus it would appear that the central problem in communication of autistic children has to do with the autistic child's recognition of the 'interpersonal' functions of language, those that are normally very strong and effective from the time a child begins to speak (Lyons, 1977; Locke, 1993), rather than with the cognitive and rational systems involved in the comprehension or expression of words and the formulation of grammatical constructions. The problem concerns the child's interest and concern for communicating. Loss of language is apparently a secondary effect.

The difficulty that autistic children have in understanding others and in interpersonal motives for **cultural learning** (Bruner, 1996; Bruner and Feldman, 1993; Hobson, 1993a,b; Sigman and Capps, 1997; Tomasello, Kruger and Ratner, 1993) does not mean that they are insensitive to others and unaffected by who other persons are – they, like other children, need to form attachments. Autistic children change the form or content of their communications depending on who they are with. Freitag (1970) observed that an autistic child may show less positive response to an encouraging or supportive adult than normally developing children, but McHale *et al.* (1980) found a higher level of communicative behaviour among autistic children when their teacher was present. Another study (Bernard-Opitz, 1982) revealed that an autistic boy communicated verbally more frequently with his mother and a clinician than with a stranger, and the level of the communication was higher when the mother or the stranger responded to the child's initiations. These observations would not be difficult for any parent or teacher of an autistic child to confirm.

Autistic children **imitate,** and they are also often highly sensitive to other persons' imitations of what they do. In a study of play, Tiegerman and Primavera (1981) found that the frequency and duration of object manipulation was higher when the experimenter imitated the child's behaviour. Nadel's work (Nadel and Pezé, 1993) confirms that autistic children, though they are abnormal in the give-and-take of imitative behaviours, do imitate, and an autistic child can become more communicative when their partner imitates them. One can develop communicative exchange through imitation (Tiegerman and Primavera, 1984). Nadel and Fontaine (1989) emphasise the special role of imitative behaviour in the development of communicative understanding in infants and toddlers, and Nadel (1992) and Nadel and Pezé (1993) show that the same developmental sequence can be seen, but at later ages, in autistic children, who, while they cannot communicate well, do show social interest and do watch others.

Richer (1978), who accepts an ethological approach based on research into the instinctive controls of animal communication and the theory of motivational conflict, observed that autistic children's avoidance is often followed by, and may seek, an adult's approach. Avoidance may be a communicative signal waiting for a reaction. Clark and Rutter (1981), seeking to better understand the conditions that favour teaching of autistic children, investigated the way certain types of social approach, involving a high degree of structure combined with low interpersonal demands, facilitate interaction of autistic children with others. A more recent study (Landry and Loveland, 1989) reports that autistic children did not, in fact, show more attention-seeking behaviour when in a situation that was directed and structured by an adult. However, teachers find that brighter autistic children who like to work on a computer benefit from the predictable and restricted effects that they can control, and can enjoy sharing these experiences with a teacher who avoids intrusive encouragement, but remains ready to share (Murray, 1997).

Thus, the social impairment in autism appears not to reside mainly in a lack of social and emotional responsiveness of the child, or in imitative tendency, but to reflect a specific failure in comprehension of how to **reciprocate** with other people (Sigman and Capps, 1997; Sigman and Mundy, 1989). This interpretation of autistic children's behaviour with others, which draws a distinction between the sensitivity of the autistic child to other known persons and the difficulty that the child has in exchanging interests and point of view, is supported by studies that examined the **attachment behaviour** in autism in more detail. It was shown that autistic children exhibit social responses to separation from and reunion with their caregivers like other children, and that they direct more social responses to their mothers than to strangers (Sigman and Ungerer, 1984b; Shapiro, Sherman, Calamari and Kock, 1987; Sigman and Mundy, 1989). In a comprehensive theoretical review, Rogers and Pennington (1991) find that autistic children demonstrate the same level of attachment to their mother or carer as mental age matched Down's syndrome children, but are typically unable to join in reciprocal imitation.

We may conclude, from the characteristically mixed ways in which autistic children react to other persons, that teachers and parents should both be encouraged to believe that even a grossly avoidant autistic child may feel an affectionate attachment and may be sensitive to the feelings and attitudes of other known persons. They should not be led to treat an apparently indifferent autistic child as if he or she cannot feel emotional about human contact, or sense the messages in behaviour or speech. In their account of effective teaching practices for autistic children, Jordan and Powell (1995), though they consider the essential problem to be a cognitive one, emphasise the importance of emotions, and sensitivity to interpersonal concerns.

As we have explained, it has been proposed, as a consequence of recent psychological research on children's thinking and understanding, that communication in autism depends on the exercise and development of cognitive skills. This approach has some affinity with the theory of Piaget (1954, 1962), in which development of the child's **sensorimotor mental schemes** for understanding objects of any kind is considered to be a necessary precursor for the acquisition of social skills and language. Curcio (1978) examined the sensorimotor development of mute autistic children and its relationship with the level of non-verbal communication. Those children with relatively complete sensorimotor functioning in **'object permanence'**, gestural imitation, means used for obtaining environmental benefits and **'causality'**, were claimed to be more inclined to exhibit spontaneous gestures of pointing or showing. However another study (Sigman and Ungerer, 1981) found that autistic children with good sensorimotor skills, in particular good 'object permanence', may, nevertheless, be impaired in communication and language. A different interpretation of the significance of objects to normal and autistic children is provided by studies of children's choice of favorite toys, discussed below.

Play of Children with Autism

The study of how autistic children play, and why they play abnormally, has been bedevilled by the same complexity of approaches and responses as has the study of their communication. As with communication, play of children with autism is best understood by comparison with the normal course of development, which reveals how the motives for play and fantasy involve the child in increasingly complex levels of communication, interpersonal attachments and cooperation (Sigman and Capps, 1997).

Research with infants has shown that two to three-month-olds can communicate with their mothers with refined synchrony, reciprocity and complementarity of expressions and older babies gain increasingly elaborate capacities and appetites for play (see Chapter 8). By one year a baby is capable of cooperation in simple arbitrary tasks and has a well-developed sense of a performing social 'Me' who proudly knows certain games routines or tricks that have been the source of fun in the family. It seems clear that the development of the 'representational' or meaning-carrying capacity, which accelerates in symbolic play during the second year, has its origins in the affective and cooperative pattern of communication with familiar persons that grows in the first year (Bruner, 1983, 1990; Winnicott, 1971).

In autism, interpersonal responses and cooperation are impaired about the end of the first year or during the second year. The current literature supports the conclusion that this describes the heart of the disorder, but additional specific problems exist in the playful imagination of autistic children, and these correlate with the difficulties the children have in communicating and learning meanings in joint interest and by instruction from other people.

A Bewildering Array of Theories and Measures of Play

Many terms have been used to describe play in studies of autistic children, as with normally developing children. The many terms do not help comparative study of how autistic children, at any particular developmental level, play. Some commonly used categories are overlapping (e.g. 'simple manipulation' and 'sensorimotor' play), others are employed with different meanings (e.g. 'symbolic' play and 'pretend' play) and still others are defined in an idiosyncratic way and used by few studies. It seems that this variation in usage reflects the differing aims and theoretical backgrounds of the projects. The concept of play objects is different again for psychotherapists who accept the very fertile thinking of Winnicott about 'transitional objects', that serve to represent attachment figures and give self-assurance while also stimulating creative invention (Winnicott, 1953, 1971).

Earlier studies looked for deficits in play of autistic children, describing, for example, their abnormally repetitive activities, but the latest studies are comparative, seeking to understand what autistic children lack in motivation or cognitive sophistication by applying descriptions of play developed for understanding normal development (Sigman and Capps, 1997). An increasing logical focus on representational or 'symbolic' play has generated redefinition of 'symbolic', 'pretend', 'imaginative', 'representational', 'make-believe' or 'fantasy' play. Here we briefly discuss the most commonly quoted studies to illustrate multiple classifications of play. They divide into two broad categories: those that can be called 'cognitive' (or 'meta-cognitive'), and those that focus more on the 'emotions' that accompany different kinds of play with objects.

Cognitive Theories of Early Play

(1) Wing, Gould, Yeates and Brierly (1977) classified play into three classes; **'non-symbolic'** play includes repetitive manipulation of objects; **'stereotyped'** play is symbolic play that is characterised by stereotypies, that is, repetitive acts lacking innovation; **'symbolic'** play or other relevant activity includes activities that recreate the impression of some absent thing or event in a conventional way, such as eating imaginary food with elaborate gestures, making airplane noises, pretending to drive a piece of soap into a garage, and functional activities such as brushing a doll's hair with a toy brush.

(2) Ungerer and Sigman (1981) and Sigman and Ungerer (1984a) developed an extensive coding system for recording play in autistic children based on play behaviours they observed in normal development. Their coding scheme comprises four categories, as follows:

(a) **Simple manipulation** is described as each separate instance of mouthing, waving, banging, fingering or throwing of a toy.

(b) **Relational play** includes combinations of objects, stacking objects and using an object as a container to hold another.

(c) **Functional play** refers to self-directed acts (e.g. brushing one's own hair), doll-directed acts (e.g. brushing a doll's hair), other-directed acts (e.g. brushing the mother's hair) and object-directed acts (e.g. placing the cup on the plate).

(d) **Symbolic play** incorporates **substitution play**, as in the use of one object as if it were a different object (e.g. using a banana as a telephone receiver), **agent play**, as in the use of a doll as an independent agent of action (e.g. propping a bottle in a doll's arm as if it could feed itself) and **imaginary play**, as in the creation of objects or people having no physical representation in the immediate environment (e.g. making the phone ring).

(3) Baron-Cohen (1987), influenced by Leslie's (1987) theory of 'pretense', introduced the notion of 'pretend' play as an equivalent for 'symbolic' play. He defined **'sensorimotor'** play as the use of objects with no attention paid to their function (e.g. throwing a toy animal), and **'ordering'** play, as in the imposing of some pattern in disregard of the meaning of the objects (e.g. piling animals up). More advanced forms of play are: **'functional'** play in which the child uses objects imitatively, according to their usual function, and **'pretend'** play in which the child uses an object as if it were another object (e.g. using a banana as a telephone receiver), or attributes relevant properties to an object which it does not actually have (e.g. attributing heat to a cooker), gives animate properties to toys, or refers to absent objects as if they were present.

(4) Lewis and Boucher (1988) defined **'manipulative'**, **'functional'** and **'symbolic'** play much as in Baron-Cohen's definitions of 'sensorimotor', 'functional' and **'pretend'** play, respectively. In addition, Lewis and Boucher used the term 'pretend' play to refer to both 'functional' and 'symbolic' forms of imaginative play. They introduced the use of unconventional toys, and they added two new categories: **'no play'** to indicate absence of play, and **'intermediate'** play to record instances of play falling between the categories of 'functional' and 'symbolic'.

Theories of the Emotional Significance of Forms of Infant and Toddler Play

Psychoanalytic studies with children often use play with objects that might excite emotional recollections of persons, places or things, or the recall of emotionally charged events, to gain information about what disturbs or confuses their young, often unspeaking clients. A most fruitful theory of the subjective and emotional significance of play objects is that of Winnicott who defined 'transitional objects', such as self-soothing blankets, or soft dolls, as substitutes for the mother's holding. These tend to be cast aside as the child develops a clear enough representation (or 'working model') of her, and other 'evoked companions', in memory, a development which makes such a substitute unnecessary (Stern, 1985). Attachment objects can be defined to cover the range of things children choose to hold or keep in their possession: **pre-transitional objects, primary and secondary transitional objects,** and **favourite toys** (Busch, 1977). Toys have many functions in supporting the child's development of experience, skill and cultural awareness (Sutton-Smith, 1986). Jonsson, Reimbladh-Taube and Sjöswärd (1993) studied favourite objects (FOs) as objects that both occupied and absorbed children. Their findings show that children distinguish pacifiers and pieces of soft textile, which are not played with, but are held close to the body or mouth, as one kind of object, from things with shape and form (most commonly toy animals, rather than soft dolls) and non-cuddly objects, which are often used in simple functional play. There is a developmental trend through pre-school to school-age children for the soft comforting toys to be replaced by the second more representational kind, and school children are less interested in FOs than the pre-school children. The animal toys are probably used as 'social companions'.

In a second study the FOs of autistic 4 to 11-year-olds, mentally handicapped 7 to 11-year-olds, healthy pre-school children (1.5 to 3 years old) and primary school children (7 to 10 years old) were compared (Jonsson and Sjöswärd, 1993). The first two, abnormally developing, groups also had a fourth group of **deviant objects** picked up idiosyncratically from the household environment. Pacifiers and soft textile objects, as the first transitional objects and their forerunners, were used in a similar way by pre-school, mentally handicapped and autistic children. Soft toy animals, as secondary transitional objects, held for self-soothing close to the body and touched, were also used in simple functional play by pre-school children and a few primary school children; they were not very popular with either deviant group. Hard, non-cuddly toys, such as plastic animals, cars, houses etc., were common in functional play of primary children, and in simpler functional play by mentally handicapped and autistic children. Manufactured objects and household tools were very popular 'deviant' FOs with some mentally handicapped and autistic children who were dependent upon the objects for excitement but not soothing. Several autistic children had a peculiar liking for electrical gadgets. One girl collected hair ribbons; she looked hard at the edges, shook them and beat her teeth with them, which seemed to be both calming and exciting. This kind of obsessional play in a young autistic child can, in more able children, develop into a highly practised island of exceptional ability or 'idiot savant' skill (Happé, 1995a).

It is important to keep in mind the somewhat chaotic variation in the categorical analysis of play behaviours when we discuss the findings from the various experimental or comparative studies with autistic children. Careful observations have often come to the conclusion that many kinds of play are less affected in autistic children than was expected. Obviously, when attempting to identify what autism affects most, it will be necessary to distinguish the various possible motives for playful behaviour unambiguously.

Problems in Interpreting Autistic Children's Play

Some features of the odd way autistic children investigate and imagine appear to be easily defined. Their play is typically dominated by fascination with the mere presence of objects and their immediate sensory features, or what they offer for manipulation, rather than their cultural or symbolic meaning (Eisenberg and Kanner, 1956; Hobson, 1993a,b; Sigman and Capps, 1997). This peculiarity of autistic awareness is vividly portrayed by Donna Williams in her description of herself as a 'mono'-track processor (Williams, 1992, 1996), and in her video biography, in which she recreates her experience of a bewildering world of distracting sensory effects and disconnected events (Williams, 1995). Temple Grandin, too, describes herself as someone who is attracted to the immediate appearances of things, or parts of things, despite her highly developed scientific and technical intelligence, and she also comments on the difficulty she has in comprehending the 'plot' or meaning of romantic drama (Grandin, 1984, 1992).

Autistic youngsters also engage in many repetitive activities (DeMyer *et al.*, 1967; Eisenberg and Kanner, 1956; Kanner, 1943; Rutter, 1978; Tilton and Ottinger, 1964), do not make up combinatorial uses for objects (DeMyer *et al.*, 1967; Tilton and Ottinger, 1964). Even relatively able autistic children play in peculiar ways (Lewis and Boucher, 1988) and symbolic or meaningful fantasy play appears to be poor or absent (Baron-Cohen, 1987; Kanner, 1943; Rutter, 1978; Wing *et al.*, 1977; Wulff, 1985). Every kind of play that implicates sharing of imagination in free communication with others is limited by the cognitive processes of the autistic individual (Hobson, 1993a,b). All would agree on these descriptions. However, further quantitative analysis of these apparently abnormal features has proved difficult.

Autistic children's 'sensorimotor' or 'manipulative' play has been found to be unimpaired in several studies (Baron-Cohen, 1987; Lewis and Boucher, 1988; Sigman and Ungerer, 1984a; Stone *et al.*, 1990; Ungerer and Sigman,

1981; Wetherby and Prutting, 1984). On the other hand, it has been reported that, with toys that would be expected to elicit varied exploratory behaviour, they prefer to repeat stereotypical behaviours (Hutt *et al.*, 1964). Only one study has reported a relative absence of combinatorial use of objects for autistic children, when they were compared with developmentally delayed and non-delayed children matched for chronological age (Tilton and Ottinger, 1964). A number of other studies that employed stricter matching procedures did not find that autistic children's 'combinatorial' or 'relational' play was particularly impaired in comparison with unaffected children of approximately the same cognitive level (Baron-Cohen, 1987; Riguet *et al.*, 1981; Sigman and Ungerer, 1984a; Stone *et al.*, 1990; Ungerer and Sigman, 1981; Wetherby and Prutting, 1984).

Surprisingly, the 'functional' play of autistic children has also been found to be unimpaired in both observational studies (Baron-Cohen, 1987; Ungerer and Sigman, 1981) and those employing experimental situations to elicit such play (Lewis and Boucher, 1988). However, other studies report that, in spontaneous or free play sessions, the amount of 'functional' play of autistic children is lower than in control groups (Lewis and Boucher, 1988; Sigman and Ungerer, 1984a; Stone *et al.*, 1990). Probably, the capacity of autistic children for accurately imitating use of objects, as in echoing of speech or expressive gestures without attention to context, can give the impression that their functional understanding is higher than, in fact, it is.

The findings on 'symbolic' play are even more contradictory. In free or spontaneous situations, some studies claim that 'symbolic' play is impaired in autism (Baron-Cohen, 1987; Lewis and Boucher, 1988; Sigman and Ungerer, 1984a) and others that it is unimpaired (Stone *et al.*, 1990). Autistic children have been reported to lack 'symbolic' play in structured, eliciting or modelling situations (Mundy *et al.*, 1986; Riguet *et al.*, 1981; Sigman and Capps, 1997; Sigman and Ungerer, 1984a). Others cannot support this claim (Lewis and Boucher, 1988).

It is doubtful that the descriptive studies, especially the earlier ones, garnered sufficiently unambiguous or detailed data about the development of play in children who were also properly identified as 'autistic'. They drew their conclusions from clinical impressions (Kanner, 1943; Wing *et al.*, 1977), from observations of the play of children diagnosed variably as 'childhood schizophrenic', 'autistic type' or 'autistic with symbiotic features' (Tilton and Ottinger, 1964), or from maternal questionnaires (DeMyer *et al.*, 1967). Studies carried out in experimental settings have measured autistic children's play in the form of imitations of acts modelled by the researcher (Mundy *et al.*, 1987; Riguet *et al.*, 1981; Ungerer and Sigman, 1981).

Recent studies have tried to tackle questions about the autistic children's deficits in 'symbolic' play by employing tasks designed to measure their ability for comprehension of 'pretence' (Jarrold, Boucher and Smith, 1994), or 'executive function' – the children's ability to plan thoughts systematically (Jarrold, Smith, Boucher and Harris, 1994). Bishop (1993) reports that *all* autistic individuals perform poorly on 'executive function' tasks, while only a proportion of individuals fail 'meta-cognitive' tasks. She concludes that executive function problems, which are known to detect abnormality in prefrontal activity of the brain, are more central to autism. However, none of the experimental strategies or measurements of performance on specific tests can be expected to reflect the more investigative functions of play, which is typically flexible, spontaneous and socially interactive in pre-school age children. In only one study, by Baron-Cohen (1987), has the spontaneous play of solitary autistic children been examined in detail.

Interactive or interpersonal play, which is so characteristic of toddlers or pre-school children, has not been described in any of the above studies. Other methodological problems concern diagnosis, the chronological age of the children and matching procedures. In the recent studies of play, children are most commonly diagnosed as autistic if they meet Rutter's criteria (e.g. Baron-Cohen, 1987; Lewis and Boucher, 1988), or DSM-III criteria (as in Mundy *et al.*, 1987; Sigman and Ungerer, 1984a; Stone *et al.*, 1990; Ungerer and Sigman, 1981). Findings in different studies might differ because the children do not have the same profile of autism. Furthermore, autistic children who have been examined for their participation in imaginative play were, in some cases, too old for this kind of play to be expected on normal developmental criteria, and, moreover, these 'too old' children were compared with much younger normal children (Baron-Cohen, 1987; Riguet *et al.*, 1981). In other studies young autistic children were observed without comparison to any control group (Mundy *et al.*, 1987; Ungerer and Sigman, 1981).

Procedures for matching autistic children with developmentally delayed and/or normally developing children in the various studies have not been uniform and in many cases they are not adequate for clear conclusions to be drawn. Some studies have compared autistic children's play with that of children with developmental disorders, making no attempt to match the groups on other characteristics (Wing *et al.*, 1977). Still others matched subjects for chronological age only (DeMyer *et al.*, 1967; Stone *et al.*, 1990; Tilton and Ottinger, 1964). In other studies, autistic and non-autistic groups were equated only on tests measuring general intelligence (Sigman and Ungerer, 1984a). The autistic children are matched with comparison groups according to their intellectual abilities to control for the effects of mental retardation. Ideally, this procedure allows the behaviour differences observed in the autistic children to be attributed to autism, and not to mental retardation. However, it is more appropriate to match the autistic and comparison groups on language ability, because language loss is often the most profound of their cognitive impairments, and language functioning correlates closely with the level of play. The importance of language as an index has been accepted in some studies, in which autistic children and other groups of children were matched on tests measuring verbal abilities (Baron-Cohen, 1987; Riguet *et al.*, 1981), but in these problems remain concerning the particular verbal test that was used.

A persistent problem in studies of autistic children's play arises from the varied definition of the term 'symbol'. A symbol is usually conceived as a representation in the mind, part of the mind work in one head, and the interpersonal emotions and the communication or cooperation normally involved in the creation and use of symbols, especially important for a young child, is overlooked. Thus a symbol is taken as, 'something that stands for, represents, or denotes something else, not by exact resemblance, but by vague suggestion or by some accidental or conventional relation' (Ricks and Wing, 1975, p.192); or, 'as a representation of a representation, or as a "second-order" representation' (Baron-Cohen, 1987, p.146). It is worth mentioning here that recent research on the relationship of 'pretend' play and children's performance on 'theory of mind' tests brought evidence that 'pretend' play does not require competence for understanding second-order mental representations (Lillard, 1993). On the other hand, an autistic child's deficit in social negotiation, which requires reciprocity of feelings and ideas in communication with other people, may be expected to impair the process of symbol formation, and thus the development of language. In an analysis of this learning of meaning, symbols are more usefully viewed as, 'experiences and actions with interest and usefulness given to them by the motives for cooperative awareness' (Trevarthen and Logotheti, 1987, p.4). It is important to recall that symbols have an emotive power, and they are strongly associated with subtle emotional values (Hobson, 1993; Trevarthen, 1994). Symbols are created by sharing and for sharing, as are all cultural meanings (Rogoff, 1990).

An Attempt to Resolve Confusions about Autistic Play

The level of verbal ability of a child is obviously one important component of the motivation and intelligence that makes advanced kinds of play possible. Does this level depend on motivations for sharing all kinds of experience, verbal and non-verbal?

In a study set up to directly examine interpersonal factors in children's symbolic play with their mothers (Papoudi, 1993), verbal or less affected autistic children of pre-school age were matched with developmentally delayed and non-developmentally delayed children on the Reynell Developmental Language Scales. The mean verbal age of all the children was 27 months. 'Symbolic' play, involving pretence, occurred during moments of communication in all three groups with no significant differences between them. However, when these verbally expressive autistic children were compared with a group of autistic children who were less able verbally, significant differences were revealed. The significant factor was the level of verbal ability, and this correlated with other aspects of readiness for communication.

The latter group, with poor language skills, were not just unspeaking, they were usually out-of-contact with their mothers. They failed to initiate gestures or symbolic acts that were directed to their mothers and failed to share objects with them. It may be concluded that general motives for cooperative awareness are affected to a varying degree in autism, and that the severity of this basic impairment in capacity for sympathetic interaction, by whatever means, is related to, or part of, the level of linguistic and interpersonal skills that a child can reach. These findings support a theory which suggests that a minimum of interpersonal skills for communication by non-verbal means are essential motivation for learning verbal communication, as well as for the development of representational play and other symbolic processes. This is true for normally developing toddlers, as well as for autistic children.

How Mother's React to Autistic Children's Limited Sharing

Study of mother–infant communication leads to the hypothesis that the origins of symbolic play are normally to be found in affective and cooperative communication for which an infant has innate motivation. Some studies of autistic children and their mothers support this idea of how play develops.

A conspicuous feature of autistic children's behaviour is infrequent initiative in 'sharing of attention'; they rarely point to an object, hold an object up for the mother to see, or bring an object to her (Sigman *et al.*, 1986). They also do not readily share emotion (Dawson *et al.*, 1990; Hobson, 1993a,b; Kasari *et al.*, 1990; Mundy *et al.*, 1986; Sigman and Capps, 1997; Snow, Hertzig and Shapiro, 1987; Yirmiya *et al.*, 1989). In a natural reaction to this unusual and disturbing 'unavailability' or remoteness, mothers of autistic children may physically hold their children on task (Sigman *et al.*, 1986), and they are directive in their speech, attempting to initiate cooperation even when the child is unresponsive, a strategy which is often counterproductive (Papoudi, 1993). Children with different degrees of autistic impairment and language ability have different patterns of communication with their mothers (Mundy *et al.*, 1987; Nadel, 1992; Nadel and Pezé, 1993; Papoudi, 1993). Mothers will therefore encounter differing degrees of difficulty when they attempt to share play, and some will be more patient than others.

It seems likely that mothers behave as they do in response to the puzzling ways their autistic children behave. They may automatically behave in ways that do not give the child the specially responsive and directed kind of response and example that is needed to help development. The more impaired the child is in 'sharing of attention', the more likely is the mother to be directive (Kasari *et al.*, 1988). Mothers also adjust their speech down to the child's language level, for example, using 'baby talk' or speaking as would normally be appropriate for a one-year-old when addressing a much older child. The less well children do, the more mothers use directives and short utterances and the more they reinforce motoric rather than spoken behaviour (Konstantareas *et al.*, 1988). On the other hand, the fact that mothers often appear 'asynchronous' in their responses to the acts and expressions of their autistic children, and are unable to set up 'dialogues' or maintain 'joint attention' with them (Shapiro, Frosch and Arnold, 1987), indicates that they may not be as sensitive to the capacities that their children do have, or as ready to make appropriate adjustments of their communicative behaviour, as they could be.

This interpretation, which would apply not only to mothers, but to all adults seeking to interact with autistic children, including clinicians and teachers, leads to a philosophy of intervention that encourages a more accepting kind of approach, one that deliberately tries to make contact with, and accept, whatever signs of interpersonal interest or play the child can show. There is much experience in the practice of therapy or teaching with autistic children that endorses this conclusion (see Chapter 10).

It is important to note that the medical diagnosis of autism may, in itself, cause a mother to feel like 'giving up' in communication with her difficult child (Eikeseth and Lovaas, 1992), which further indicates the need mothers have for helpful information on the nature of the disorder in communication, and how best to cope with it to obtain positive and encouraging results. There are many possibilities for applying forms of play systematically to improve the communication of autistic children: in groups, with pairs of children and with individual children interacting with an adult; at school and in the home. A child who appears to have little imagination or enterprise in fanciful play, and who seems unable to join in role play or invention of pretended meanings with normal age-mates, may nevertheless gain great pleasure from sharing playful interactions that make less demands on creativity and shared meaning. Treatments which attempt to use playful and imitative behaviours to encourage autistic children to be more responsive and cooperative are described in the next chapter. Musical improvisation therapy is a special level of communication in which an autistic child can discover forms of interaction with emotions and forms of play (Chapter 11).

CHAPTER 10

What Can Be Done?

Specialists start with different ideas about what is wrong with an autistic child, with different views of how it might be changed by treatments, and different conceptions of how difficulties might be overcome by changing, not the child, but the environment – including the way other people behave toward the child. Those that see autism as a health condition seek medication or drugs that will effectively alleviate symptoms or improve psychological functioning, without unwanted side-effects. Few believe that a cure is possible by medical treatment, even when targeted on known abnormalities in chemical regulation of brain activity. By a different approach, many autistic persons have gained a richer, more rewarding life after receiving sympathetic and well-informed therapy or education early in life. Specialists adhering to the older medical tradition, who perceive autism as an emotional illness, may advocate psychodynamic therapy, or some related course of treatment that brings the emotional responses of the child into positive and productive communication with the therapist. Psychologists who research or measure behaviour, problem-solving intelligence, social responses or language believe that an autistic child can be aided to happier, more autonomous and more socially appropriate behaviour, and discouraged from unacceptable or self-damaging behaviour, by an organised regime of training. They may set goals in behaviour and apply differential reinforcements in the form of rewards and negative communications to increase or decrease the frequency of target behaviours, or to change the way behaviours are performed, or their dependence on environmental cues. Changes in behaviour can certainly be made this way, at least for a short time. A rather different approach is taken by practices that seek to identify the child's motives and feelings, especially those for interpersonal relations and cooperative learning, before attempting to make the environment more acceptable and supportive to the child.

There is, indeed, a great variety of attitudes, culturally or professionally defined, to the inner motives and consciousness of autistic children. Those taking a 'child-centred' approach attempt to engage with the desires and purposes of the child, hoping to make the tasks of interacting with people and the world easier and more satisfying, convinced that, in the long term, this produces the best results. Others point to the cognitive handicaps of the autistic child, and conclude that no gains in communication or learning can be achieved unless the home and school environment is made highly predictable and organised so that it is easily understood and the child is not overwhelmed. Recent educational practices emphasise the way autistic thinking, with its insensitivity to other person's states of mind and the meaning of speech, interferes with understanding, and thence with communication and learning – approaches to the child are recommended that deliberately simplify the child's cognitive tasks in dealing with other persons, their interests and their language.

In this chapter we review the most reputable and successful of the many and varied approaches, while pointing out others that have proved of little worth, or are untested and of doubtful value. We summarise this information in preparation for a review and interpretation, in Chapter 13, of how education has been provided for autistic children, and for a final chapter that considers the advantages of a tolerant multidisciplinary theory and that advocates a combination of methods that can be relied upon to give autistic children, their parents and siblings, their teachers and the community, a good chance for active and happy relationships that last.

Over the years, medical and educational authorities have assumed responsibility for handicapped children with greater or lesser regard for the role of parents. In the past it was deemed by clinical or educational authorities that parents should not be left in charge of psychologically disturbed children. Such children were taken into custodial care and given little or no treatment or education. Now that is seen to be unacceptable in a humane society. In the United States and European countries parents, especially well-educated and more affluent parents, have assumed a major role in deciding what their affected children should have in the way of care and education. New laws have transformed the responsibility of states for provision of education for all children with special needs, and the concept of individual rights, as well as parental rights, has influenced the way medical, educational and social services are provided. Great disparities exist in the provision of medical and educational services for autistic children everywhere, not least in the US and the UK. Parents, depending on their knowledge, beliefs and the advice they receive, and on their resources and access to information, seek different kinds of care or treatment for their autistic sons and daughters. National Autistic Societies, animated by parental concerns, attempt to give reliable advice, influenced by a great variety of academic, scientific and political interests.

Treatment for a Medical Condition, Therapy for an Emotional Disorder or Special Education for a Mental Handicap?

Ever since child psychiatrists identified the mentally handicapping and socially isolating condition now called autism, there has been disagreement about the causes and best treatment. The modern history of this form of mental disorder, and the controversies about its nature, begins in France.

In a new book, Jacques Hochmann (1997), Professor of Child Psychiatry at the University Claude-Bernard in Lyon, who heads a service for diagnosis and treatment of autistic children in collaboration with parents and schools, describes the arguments between the medical experts and educators of France that began in the early years of last century when the 'wild boy of Aveyron' was found, a century and a half before Kanner's famous paper (Kanner, 1943). In those days, long before Freud began to study the psychology of hysteria with Charcot in Paris, French psychiatrists, or 'alienists' as they were called, were world leaders in efforts to understand and help mentally ill persons. The sadly disturbed children, who could not communicate or control their withdrawn and obsessional behaviours, became the subject of disputes between those who regarded them as errors of nature beyond treatment, and those with more idealistic and humanistic convictions – including the young military doctor who, working in an institution for deaf-mutes, took the 'wild boy' in charge. Itard (1801), refusing to accept absurd tests that made the child appear blind and unable to make the simplest sensory judgements, believed him to be retarded by lack of human company, and began a course of stimulation in interactions with the child, expecting this could lead the boy to language and civilised behaviour. Itard's failure was followed by the efforts of a teacher Éduard Seguin (1846), who made an accurate description of the condition of autism in individuals he called 'idiots', meaning those excluded from society, and he undertook a process of 'physiological education' – a systematic stimulation of the senses, motor functions, memory and imagination.

Seguin was driven from France to the United States by controversy around his views that medical treatment of idiots was useless, and that they could be educated. The same view was later taken up by Bourneville, and again it was contested by doctors and by administrators who wanted to avoid wasting money on the ineducable. The mental condition that Seguin and Bourneville wished to educate was considered an inherited 'degeneration' that would increase through the generations, and idiots were left without care to pass their lives in asylums. A teacher or 'psychopedagogue', Binet, and a doctor, Simon, developed the idea, at the beginning of this century, that intelligence could be measured with scientific precision (Binet and Simon, 1905). They presumed that below a certain mental level no further development was possible, and no money should be spent attempting education. Binet and Simon, in whose laboratory Piaget began his psychological training, developed formal intelligence tests and the concept of an Intelligence Quotient, which measured a 'mental age' compared to the subject's real age, as a percentage. Those with an IQ below 100 but above a certain level were deemed worth education. 'Idiots', which would include the majority of autistic children, were left without instruction in their family, or in an institution.

In the 50 years since Kanner's paper, the arguments have continued. Kanner's clear view was that the autistic child's pervasive aloneness and incapacity to share interests and plans with other persons through any medium of communication (and especially in language) was due to a condition born in the child. He thought that improvement would require some treatment of the faulty brain, or some radical modification of the human environment that would make a bridge over which the child's disturbed motivation could be supported to serve in effective learning. Soon, however, Kanner's clinical insight was drawn to the psychoanalytic way of thinking, the dominant scientific position in US psychiatry in the 1950s. The aim of treatment was directed to removal of the supposed cause of what was perceived as an adaptive withdrawal of a child from a cold and intrusive parenting, a regression to a supposed earlier stage of development, or a fixation in an incomplete state of self-differentiation. The medical advice, shared by the educator Bettelheim, was to separate the child from the parents, and to give an affectionate therapeutic attention in a foster home where people trained in psychodynamic therapy could direct the reconstruction of the child's damaged emotions, self-image and consciousness of reality. Asperger, who identified higher functioning children with features very similar to those Kanner had described simultaneously in the US, was isolated in Austria under the Nazis, and the war prevented communication between the two doctors (Asperger, 1944). Asperger insisted that the constitutional change in personality he had identified was different from other mental disorders, and he put stress on the sometimes exceptional abilities of his patients, which he felt could be useful to society. It is important to note that Asperger was practising under a political regime that put psychotics to death. He was trying to save the lives of affected persons.

In recent decades, with the evident failure of psychodynamic therapy to produce reliable improvements, plus the development of a behaviouristic science that would explain the motives for development in less complex terms, allied to growing expression of resentment by parents who knew they were not the primary cause of their child's aberrant behaviour, there occurred a sharp change of view. The fault, now back in the child, was perceived as a defect in sensations, in perception, in intelligence, in cognition or in ability to analyse objective situations rationally. Intensive behaviour modification techniques, systematically controlling the way stimuli are presented in contingent relation to target behaviours, gave positive results, reducing undesirable behaviours and progressively developing some useful skills, including improvements in communication. It was decided that the autistic child could be taught, provided a way could be found to give inducements in a form acceptable to the child and related to the child's motives for action, expression or communication. Increasingly, it has been recognised that successful behaviour modification requires intensive, sustained and often one-to-one procedures that give attention to the particular habits and reactions of the individual child, and parents have become allies in this effort.

Autistic children show peculiar sensivities to environmental features that would be given little attention by normal children, and they tend to become overwhelmed and may be very distressed in new surroundings, with strange people, or in circumstances where they feel lost. A policy of schooling in which the environment is managed in every detail to take account of the need that every autistic child has for a consistent structure in the world, and stability in time and space of conditions for learning as well as relationships, has proved effective both in helping the child to attend and learn, and in giving encouragement and relief for parents. It became generally accepted that the primary condition in the child was not just an emotional illness as the psychoanalytically-trained psychiatrists thought, but there was still confusion.

Through the 1970s and 1980s an academic battle was joined between those who said the disorder was social or interpersonal, and those who thought it was one of cognition or intelligence and not specially concerned with social 'objects'. We now see that this dichotomy or choice is artificial and profoundly confusing. Motivation for learning in children, for their cognitive development, is necessarily affected by, indeed regulated and directed by, motives for communication with other persons, and therefore by the 'social environment'. Learning involves communication with people, and communication involves emotions. Thinking and understanding are generated by motives that also produce emotions, and emotional states affect consciousness, reasoning and remembering.

A seeming breakthrough in understanding cognitive development came in the 1980s with the demonstration that 'high-functioning' (i.e. the verbally and rationally most competent autistic children) had a peculiar and marked inability to imagine and adjust to states of mind in others, or to pretend in play. They could not understand stories or fictional dramas in which they had to get into the heads of the protagonists to decide what, given the described circumstances, they, the characters and not the child onlooker, would believe, know, want etc. Apparently the autistic consciousness has a weakened comprehension of other persons' thoughts, beliefs and feelings. Indeed, an autistic person, child or adult, has a matching lack of self-awareness of their own thinking and believing. This is coupled to a peculiar rigidity of imagination, a lack of flexible or creative pretence, and an impoverished comprehension of meaningful narrative.

This theory is a 'cognitive' one because it recognises the internal mental functions that are responsible for conscious representations and interpretations of meaning. It encourages attention to the processes that cause autistic withdrawal and stimulus-seeking behaviour, but does so largely in terms of *verbal* expression of states of mind. It cannot explain the behaviours of the majority of autistic children who are either too young or too 'low-functioning' to participate in the subtle linguistic and rational problems of 'theory of mind' tests. Nevertheless, the 'theory of mind' approach, emphasising as it does how, in everyday life, at home, at school, or in play with peers, a child must be able to imagine how other persons imagine and intend, appears to be a real help to parents and teachers, helping them to conceive the difficulties the child faces, and why autistic individuals often find all other persons' behaviour incomprehensible and threatening.

With increasing evidence from research on autistic persons' universal shortcomings in tests of perception of persons and their feelings and motives, a majority of those who work successfully with autistic children would now accept the following:

- Person perception is affected in all its aspects, leading to difficulties in all social contacts and relationships, but in varying ways that lead to recognition of types of autism.

- Emotional and affective reactions to persons are not absent, and attachments do form.

- There are specific deficiencies in imitation and in sharing of purpose or point of view which greatly handicap negotiated learning.

- 'Non-verbal' expressions, of eye contact, voice quality, hand gestures, body attitude and approach to other persons are reduced and deviant, leading immediately to difficulties in communication and social adjustment.

- Failure to share attention and follow pointing are among the earliest signs of developing autism in infancy.

- The disorder is not just a defect in language, which varies from total absence of speech to a fluency that is superficial in meaning or poorly related to the responses of other persons. There are always peculiarities in the way language is used to engage with other persons' wishes and beliefs, to express human interests and purposes, or to describe human relationships.

- There are often signs of abnormal sensitivity to sounds, light or touch, and obsession with sensory effects.

- Exploration and use of objects tends to be stereotyped, repetitive and unimaginative.

- Movements, especially expressive ones, may be awkward, with sometimes bizarre automatic gestures repeated for self-stimulation, and even high-functioning autistic children or those with Asperger's syndrome are often clumsy.

- General cognitive faults, in perception of any objects or events, or in reasoning cannot alone explain the disorder.

- IQs are usually below normal, but are different in different individuals and generally higher in non-verbal components, which are in some cases above the normal range while language-related intelligence is clearly reduced. Some individuals develop exceptional skills in computation, art or music, but depend largely on imitative or rote learning, and on obsessional practice.

- Changes occur with age which tend to increase the orientation of the child to others, without loss of oddness and incomprehension of ideas, feelings, purposes, etc. Social gaucheness persists even in remarkably gifted 'high-functioning' autistic adolescents or adults, including those with Asperger's syndrome.

- Many different approaches to intervention can bring improvements in 'availability' of an autistic child to other persons, and autistic children can be taught in a variety of ways.

- Non-linguistic and para-linguistic forms of communication, including special forms of game-playing and controlled musical improvisation therapy/training offer highly effective means of transforming the autistic child's 'availability' to human companionship and shared experience.

- It is not possible to understand the interlocking problems of an autistic child and their difficulties in educational settings without comparisons with normal development and with other kinds of developmental disorder.

It is generally accepted that, in all its varieties, autism is to be distinguished from other psychological disabilities by a full 'triad' of abnormalities, that is, autistic individuals are affected in all three areas of 'social interaction', 'linguistic and other forms of communication', and 'flexibility of cognitive functions' (Kanner, 1943; Wing and Gould, 1979). This division of abnormal features of autistic behaviour has been taken as the basis for medical diagnosis (DSM-IV, 1994; ICD-10, 1993). However, other developmental disorders may be very similar to autism in one or two of these kinds of function. The three areas identified do not necessarily occupy the same plane of complexity, and they may have different developmental origins. Moreover, they require interpretation in terms of more fundamental characteristics that might reveal primary intrinsic failures in the developing autistic mind.

In the following we have grouped treatments, therapies and training regimes in a sequence that progressively accepts more complex psychological explanations, and that moves from focus on the behaviours and experiences of the individual autistic child, to his or her relationships and communications with other persons, and motives for developing these relationships and communications. Treatments that address cognitive problems of autistic children are favoured now, but these need to be understood in relation to the interpersonal relations in which all parenting, teaching and therapy must take place.

Medical Treatments

Digestive and Dietary Problems

There has been considerable interest in the possibility that diet problems might be important, both as symptoms and as possible cause of autism (e.g. Williams, 1996). Children with autism often have strong eating aversions or preferences, and they may develop digestive disorders. There are indications that the amount of the amino acid **tryptophan** in the diet can have effects on both metabolism of the important neurotransmitter serotonin and on behaviour (Cook and Leventhal, 1996),

It has been claimed that autistic children have difficulties in metabolising **casein** (cow's milk protein) and **gluten** (starch) and that this might be a factor that causes autism. Abnormal substances consistent with this hypothesis have been found in the urine of autistic patients, but it has not been ruled out that these are due to an unusual diet in these individuals.

Finally, there is evidence that supplementary vitamins in the diet, particularly B6 (in combination with a magnesium supplement to avoid peripheral nerve damage) can be helpful in some cases (see below under Megavitamin Therapies).

Attempts to Counteract Chemical Abnormalities in the Brain

Drugs, vitamins and other biologically active substances have been administered in attempts to treat the brain condition of autism directly. Initially, interventions were prompted more by the availability of substances than by any clear rationale. Various medications were applied because they had proven effective or popular in treatment of adult psychiatric conditions. Phenothiazines, used successfully in the treatment of schizophrenia (Fish, Shapiro and Campbell, 1966), lithium, for bipolar emotional disorder (Gram and Rafaelsen, 1972), and haemodialysis, used with no apparent benefit in the treatment of schizophrenia (Varley *et al.*, 1980), have all been tried with autistic children. Neither phenothiazines nor haemodialysis were of any demonstrable help, while lithium proved to benefit the small subgroup who show autism coupled with bipolar affective disorder. For detailed reviews of this largely unproductive era of drug research, the reader is referred to Campbell (1975, 1989).

More recently, pharmacotherapies have been implemented and evaluated with more rigour and more thorough theoretical rationale. Treatments have been adopted with one of two justifications – either they are based on a research-based model of the underlying pathophysiology of autism, with the hope that an intervention targeting the cause will improve the overall condition of the child, or they have been focused to relieve a specific symptom, such as hyperactivity, sleep disorders, mood swings, self-injury or aggression. They should not be presented as treatments for autism as such. The discovery of identified neurochemical abnormalities in autistic individuals, such as abnormal levels in the blood of the neurohormone endorphin (Gillberg, Hagberg, Witt-Engerström and Eriksson, 1990), raised urinary homovanillic acid (HVA) (Garreau *et al*, 1988) and raised blood levels of the neurotransmitter serotonin (Schain and Freedman 1961; Piven *et al.*, 1991), has led to a number of drug studies being conducted on the basis of a more sound clinical reasoning. Some doubt that there is any value in using drug therapies with the autistic population (Sloman 1991). However, research on psychoactive drugs is very intense, and will certainly bring advances in the identification and manufacture of new drugs that have both more specific beneficial effects and fewer undesirable side-effects.

THE OPIATE HYPOTHESIS

Panksepp was the first to propose that abnormalities in the systems activated by the natural opium-like substance **endorphin** may be implicated in autistic behaviour (Panksepp, 1979). This was based on observations of opiate-addicted young animals of a variety of species, which often showed signs that Panksepp felt were directly analogous to autistic behaviour in children. In particular, the animals showed decreased pain sensitivity, reduction in crying, poor clinging to the mother, low desire for social companionship, and extreme persistence in certain behaviours in the absence of external rewards. Subsequent theoretical papers have argued for the use of opiate antagonists as part of the treatment for the 'subpopulation of autistic children having elevated brain opioids' (Deutsch, 1986; Panksepp and Sahley, 1987). Gillberg and his colleagues have reported significantly raised levels of endorphins in the brain fluids in approximately half of autistic individuals, but in none of their normal or neurological controls (Gillberg, 1988b; Gillberg, Terenius and Lonnerholm, 1985). Those autistic children with higher levels of endorphin were more likely to be self-injurious, and they had more motor stereotypies and significantly decreased sensitivity to pain.

There is some evidence that **naloxone,** a short-acting intra-muscularly administered drug that blocks the action of the natural endorphin system, can reduce abnormal movements and self-injurious behaviour (Barron and Sandman, 1983; Richardson and Zaleski, 1983), and that it can also result in improved interpersonal functions (Sandman *et al.*, 1983). The varied results reported with naloxone may have been due, in part, to the need to inject it several times each day to achieve therapeutic levels. Subsequent research has used **naltrexone**, which has the considerable advantages of being long-acting and orally administered. Campbell, Adams, Small, Tesch and Curren (1988) have carried out a well-designed study of the effects of naltrexone on autistic children. Eight boys, 3.75 to 6.5 years of age with moderate to profound levels of mental retardation, took part. A low dose (0.5 mg/kg/day) reduced fidgeting and uncooperativeness; a higher dose (2.0 mg/kg/day) markedly reduced stereotypies and increased relatedness to people. Six of the eight subjects were judged to respond well.

It is clear that more detailed evaluation of endorphin antagonists such as naltrexone is required before their use should be widely adopted in clinical management. For the present, all such treatments should be closely monitored using single case research methods.

FENFLURAMINE TO REDUCE SEROTONIN LEVELS

One of the earliest and clearest neurochemical abnormalities reported in autistic patients has been raised urinary **serotonin,** a neurotransmitter with important functions in motivation and mood (see Chapter 6). This was first reported by Schain and Freedman (1961), and has been consistently replicated in approximately 30 per cent of cases in subsequent studies. The recent discovery of a gene change linked to abnormal serotonin activity (Cook *et al.*, 1997) adds interest to the theory that this transmitter has a key place in the genesis of autism. If serotonin levels are abnormally high in autism, a chemical that would reduce serotonin effects might be beneficial.

Fenfluramine is a weight-reducing medication that lowers levels of serotonin in the blood. Some improvements in autism have been observed after treatment with this drug (Campbell, 1988; Sloman, 1991), including improved social behaviour, better attention span and reductions in motor restlessness. There are, however, many undesirable side-effects, including weight loss, lethargy, sleeping problems and gastro-intestinal upset. In open trials, most patients have been discontinued from longer-term use because of developing problems with appetite, weight loss or drug intolerance. Several recent studies have found that there is often little change in autistic symptoms despite normalisation of urinary serotonin. It is not, therefore, the promising treatment it was expected to be.

SELECTIVE SEROTONIN RE-UPTAKE INHIBITORS (SSRIS)

Drugs have been produced that selectively prevent the reabsorption of serotonin by the nerve cell which has released it, thus making more of the transmitter available to be effective on the next cell in the chain. Tests show that these drugs, which include **fluvoxamine** (McDougle *et al.*, 1996), **fluoxetine** (Cook *et al.*, 1992) and **sertraline** (see McDougle, 1997), have beneficial effects in some cases. Recent functional imaging research adds support to the clinical impression that there are abnormalities of serotonin metabolism in persons with autism (Chugani *et al.*, 1997).

HALOPERIDOL AND DOPAMINE ACTIVITY

The **dopamine** neurotransmitter system of the brain is involved in regulating levels of motor activity and other functions (see Chapter 6). A number of early studies had suggested that **haloperidol,** which reduces the activity of dopamine, could help the autistic child. The first well-controlled, randomised, double-blind trial (Campbell *et al.*, 1978) claimed significant reductions in autistic withdrawal and motor stereotypy in 40 cases. Subsequent work by the same group has demonstrated that treatment with haloperidol can improve cognitive functioning, as well as reducing motor restlessness. Detailed double-blind, placebo-controlled studies have shown consistent improvements in activity level, involuntary movements and aggression (Cohen *et al.*, 1980). Unfortunately, approximately a fifth of cases developed a drug-related movement problem, even with low doses. Because of this side-effect, haloperidol is not recommended as a medical treatment for autism.

Epilepsy

Many autistic children have epileptic seizures, especially those in whom autism is the consequence of one of the known medical causes such as tuberous sclerosis, and they may be prescribed anti-epileptic medication. Current prevalence data suggest that around one third of autistic persons will have a seizure disorder, and some are unusual among epileptics in having seizures beginning late in development, at puberty. Epileptic aphasias (Landau-Kleffner disorders of language processing) are also more common among autistic individuals than in other groups.

Close medical attention will be needed for a child with epilepsy, and parents and teachers will need to be trained to recognise fits and in their treatment (e. g. by the use of Paraldehyde or rectal Valium). Autistic children require close monitoring if epileptic seizures are to be detected and appropriately treated.

Epilepsy is caused by irregular electrical activity in the brain, and is controlled by drugs that depress neural activity, particularly in the cerebral cortex. It is inevitable that any medication for epilepsy will interact with the actions of chemical systems of the brain that regulate motivation and emotional states, as described above and in Chapter 6. New anti-epileptic drugs have been developed and more will come on the market in the near future (Brodie, 1996a).

Treating Sleep Problems with Oral Melatonin

Many young autistic children have sleep problems, and wakefulness can be very trying for parents (Richdale and Pryor, 1995). A substance called **melatonin,** produced by the pineal gland in the brain, has a major role in regulating the sleep–wake cycle. It has been used extensively in the treatment of jet lag in adults (Claustrat *et al.*, 1992). If there is abnormal production of melatonin, particularly if this leads to a flattening out of the normal daily fluctuations in its concentration, or a reduction in night-time melatonin levels, this might prevent a child finding rest at night. Both kinds of abnormality have been reported in autistic children (Nir *et al.*, 1995; Ritvo *et al.*, 1993), but studies with larger numbers are needed to confirm these preliminary results. Studies of the effects of administering oral melatonin have been published demonstrating reasonable success with sleep problems in children, including some autistic subjects (Jan, Espezel and Appleton 1994; Jan and O'Donnell 1996), but no treatment trial has been published that examines the efficacy of melatonin specifically for autistic children.

Megavitamin Therapies

There is evidence that **vitamin B6** can be of help in the treatment of autism. The idea that this might work stems from the discovery that the common factor across families who claimed improvement in children on vitamin supplements was the inclusion of B6 in the supplement. A number of trials have been conducted in France (LeLord *et al.*, 1981; Barthélémy *et al.*, 1988), and there is clear evidence of benefit in a significant proportion of cases. Children who are younger, of higher IQ, with better initial language and with raised pre-trial urinary HVA (Homovanillic Acid) levels seem to derive particular benefit from vitamin B6.

Attempts to Correct Sensory Problems

High sensitivity to certain stimuli, or abnormal sensory responses, are characteristic of autism. Autistic children often act to avoid lights or sharp sounds. On the other hand, an autistic child may have a favourite toy, or ritual behaviour, that is used to create repeated visual, auditory or tactile stimulation. The child may become very excited or obsessed by self-produced stimulation. Autistic authors Donna Williams (1996) and Temple Grandin (1997) give clear accounts of the often painful experiences they have had in everyday situations, and difficulties in 'shutting out' what distresses them.

Therapies for Abnormal Hearing

Autistic children often seem to have either abnormally high sensitivity to sounds (hyperacusis) or difficulty recognising or hearing sounds (hypoacusis). They sometimes seem to find speech difficult to listen to, as if it were just an unpleasant noise. Donna Williams (1996) is quite clear about her experience of talk as irritating 'blah-blah-blah', and Temple Grandin (1997) reports on her problems with hearing. Theories have been proposed that this may, in some cases, be a primary problem (Goldfarb, 1961; Porges, 1997), or at least a serious impediment to comprehension of other persons' expressions. Attempts have been made to help reduce distortions of sensitivity to sound by training hearing so the autistic child will experience less pain and confusion.

Bérard Auditory Therapy, popularised through Annabel Stehli's description of work with her autistic daughter Georgiana (Stehli, 1991), employs systematic desensitisation or habituation of the child to particular frequencies of sound that have been causing the child distress and interfering with everyday life in the family. It relies on the finding that selective auditory attending with heightened sensitivity to certain kinds of sound is common in autistic children. There has, however, been no systematic assessment of its efficacy. A recent double-blind controlled study of 17 autistic subjects produced promising results (Rimland and Edelson, 1995), but none responded as dramatically as in Stehli's description.

This, and the other approaches which attempt to correct for auditory abnormalities in the autistic child, drew their theoretical rationale from a model developed by Goldfarb (1961) to explain such abnormal behaviours as the spinning, rocking, motor stereotypy, selective attention and hyperacusis, all seen in autistics. Goldfarb hypothesised a primary abnormality of vestibular (inner ear) balance-control function. More recently, Porges proposes that many disorders of social engagement, including autism, express a failure in the special visceral motor nerves of the head that control the linkage between eyelid lifting and the tensing of the middle ear muscles when a person looks up and listens to another person's speech, shutting out distracting environmental sounds (Porges, 1997, 1998). By 'exercising' and stimulating middle ear function to dynamically extract human voice sounds, he reports success in increasing range of facial expressiveness, flexibility of intonation, and social behaviour in several children, and has demonstrated this phenomenon in a 42-year-old autistic adult (Porges, personal communication). Under conditions of stress or anxiety the inner ear muscles are poorly regulated and interpersonal attention is degraded. As we have explained in Chapter 6, the brainstem systems that regulate cranial nerve outputs to the special sense organs, including the ears, are at the heart of the mechanism for control of interpersonal communication of emotions, and there is direct evidence that these parts of the brain may be affected in autism (Rodier, 1996; Rodier *et al.*, 1996).

Filtering Visual Stimulation

Donna Williams (1996) describes her visual experiences as confusing and explains the relief she finds from wearing tinted Erling glasses that cut down the glare and glitter of well-lit environments, helping her to focus on useful information and control her tendency to 'one-track' cognition. She gives information on how specialist advice can be obtained, and on suppliers of the glasses. Most parents and teachers find that visual problems of autistic children can be controlled by simplifying the environment, eliminating harsh contrasts and insistent stimulation.

Dealing with Abnormal Body Feelings, and Avoidance of Contact

Autistic children often react with protest to clothes, as if they are uncomfortable, and show other signs of seeking relief from irritations of the skin. They also act as if they experience deep pain in the body. Temple Grandin (1992, 1995) developed an apparatus, a squeeze machine, by which she subjected her body to controlled pressure to obtain relief from feelings of restlessness and anxiety.

Firm restraint of the body is used in a treatment intended to combat autistic avoidance of interpersonal contact. **Holding Therapy**, also called 'ethologically based' therapy, was developed by Martha Welsh (1983) on the theoretical foundations of the Tinbergens' identification of autism with a motivational conflict behaviour (Tinbergen and Tinbergen, 1983). The parent is encouraged to take the child on their lap, surrounded with their arms and to use positive affective expressions combined with eye contact to overcome the child's avoidance of an affectionate approach. If the child struggles and protests or becomes enraged, even this is praised. Inappropriate behaviours, such as echolalia, are ignored. It is claimed that holding can lead to a reduction of avoidance and promote positive orientation and gentle affectionate touching (Richer and Nicoll, 1972; Richer, 1983; Zappella et al., 1991). Zappella et al. (1991) identified 10 children as autistic by DSM-III criteria and showed they had no neurological or biochemical abnormalities on routine testing. Assessments were made by analysis of videos of each child with the parents, with the therapist and alone. Following treatment as described, two improved rapidly with the disappearance of autistic behaviour, six improved to various degrees, and two showed no change.

Holding Therapy, in which parents are the main agents in attempts to change the child's behaviour, has the following aims:

- to reduce motivational conflict and increase affiliation, attachment behaviour, exploration and play

- to obtain rich, extensive, emotionally directed communication

- to increase cooperative interactions

- to give parents a direct control of their child.

It appears likely that the children can gain a calming effect from firm restraint, in addition to any benefits from enforced contact with a person. Holding is not likely to be more beneficial than less coercive techniques for overcoming avoidance, such as those employed in the Option approach described below, but may aid development of communication with some children.

Stimulation By Intensive Motor Training, or Guided Moving

The Doman-Delacato Method (Delacato, 1974) is conceived as a treatment for any developmentally disordered population. The rather simplistic assumption is made that ontogeny (development of an individual) recapitulates phylogeny (evolution of the race). Working methods have to reflect a supposed evolutionary order of behaviours, hence an emphasis on practising supposedly ancestral locomotor patterns, such as swimming or swinging from the arms (brachiation). There has been no systematic appraisal of Doman-Delacato Methods with autistic children, and the method has been extensively criticised (see Cummins 1988 for a comprehensive review).

Facilitated Communication, another movement training approach, is also based on a single supposed fault in autism, and is, likewise, highly controversial. An adult therapist or 'facilitator' supports the hand and arm of the handicapped individual in the hope of eliciting the execution of messages by means of typing, or of other ways of producing symbols. Its developers claim that autism is, in every case, primarily a form of communicative apraxia, or inability to make movements as intended. They believe that the communicative purposes and thoughts of autistic individuals can be revealed if sensitive support is given to attempts at execution of directed hand movements. This claim has received widespread interest from media and from parents. However, the only controlled evaluation of this method indicates that the effect may only be demonstrated when the facilitator knows what the individual is being asked and what the answer should be. It disappears when he or she is wearing headphones and a blindfold that prevent this knowledge (Prior and Cummins, 1992). Schopler (1992) in an editorial of the *Journal of Autism and Developmental Disorders* summarises his conclusions as follows:

> As of now it appears that 'Facilitated Communication' has the potential for becoming a useful though not new technique for some people with autism most likely found in the group known to be precocious readers, good with computers, signs, and other forms of communication. Current promoters of this technique have been unwilling to differentiate those clients for whom a facilitator is useful from those who can learn spontaneous communication on their own.

Von Tetzchner (1996) reviews work in Denmark, where a form of facilitation has been promoted for many years, and concludes that the field is very unsatisfactory, with little basis for distinction between true facilitation of a handicapped child's intended expressions, and well-meaning but false attribution of the facilitators wished-for results to the child – a kind of 'automatic writing'.

This method for aiding a child to express communication is not to be confused with a variety of ways of adapting or augmenting communication, discussed below.

Behavioural Training

A structured regime of behaviour training, or 'conditioning', can improve communication, social adaptation and learning of autistic children, especially if it is introduced early in development (Harris *et al.*, 1991). Early detection of autism has only recently been feasible, and it may transpire that the critical factor in the success of behavioural intervention is the age of the child when it is begun. With older autistic children or adolescents behavioural approaches prove to be less successful in changing long-term outcomes, but they can be helpful in management of specific problems.

The Lovaas technique attempts a comprehensive transformation in the child's learning in all areas, shaping the necessary skills step by step. Others use behaviour shaping in conjunction with less directive educational methods, taking limited goals addressed to the reduction of elimination of specific problem behaviours, such as self-injury, aggression, stereotypies, tantrums and obsessive preoccupations (Clements, 1987; Marchant *et al.*, 1974; Murphy and Wilson, 1985). There are many reports from parents of significant successes, but there is a problem with generalisation of skills-teaching to other persons, and to other behaviours and situations.

Less rigorous behaviour modification regimes are widely used in schools, or parent-help programmes to improve acquisition of specified skills and in curricular teaching, as part of a child-centred approach that admits that the children may have more complex motivations (Clements, 1987; Jordan and Powell, 1993a; Repp, 1983; Schreibman, 1988), and in the systematic teaching of social and language skills, usually in combination with methods for encouraging motivation and orientation to persons (Carr, 1982; Howlin and Rutter, 1987; Howlin, 1989; Jordan, 1993).

The emphasis in behaviour therapy is on the development of a consistent, responsive environment which minimises the apparent benefits of solitary activity and of 'problem' behaviour, and maximises the benefit from the child's perspective for cooperative activity. This goal is often achieved through the use of external, non-social rewards, with the social development arising as a consequence of the child's interest in a particular reinforcement that is a tangible object or an activity desired by the child. Preferably, the child will be included in a peer group, and a consistency of responsive adult supervisors or teachers is essential. Negative reinforcement in the form of punishment is not now accepted, on the grounds that it is inhumane, unnecessary, and likely to be damaging to the child's need for affectionate attachment to a parent or teacher.

It is unclear at this point whether any of the effects of the behavioural methods that have been developed are best suited to the special needs of autistic children. Functional analysis and a single-case, client-centred approach are fundamental requirements for any effective behaviour modification technique, and autistic children always present unique problems in a teaching situation.

Some workers using behavioural training methods have successfully pioneered recruitment of the family and peers as co-trainers of the autistic child (Charlop and Walsh, 1986; Jenson and Young, 1985; Strain, Jamieson and Hoyson, 1986; Strain, 1987; Simmeonson, Olley and Rosenthal, 1987). Supervised involvement of the family is certainly important, both to increase the regularity and hence the effectiveness of therapy, and to help reduce family anxiety. Training methods instituted by experts, and kept entirely in their control, run the risk of disempowering the child's principal companions and caregivers.

The Lovaas Method of Applied Behaviour Analysis

This is the most coercive of behaviour modification methods, relying on a systematic, logical, intensive and prolonged programme of skills training by the 'discrete trial' method, individually tailored for each child and led by a detailed and continuing inventory, or 'behavioural analysis', of the child's habits and responses to stimuli (Lovaas, 1978, 1987; Lovaas and Smith, 1988). It is based on the theory of conditioning by contingent reinforcement, introduced by Watson more than 75 years ago and developed by Skinner a generation later, and attempts to eliminate autism by controlling stimuli linked to specific actions of the child, systematically rewarding desirable actions and discouraging undesirable ones. It is claimed (McEachin, Smith, and Lovaas, 1993) that a high proportion of young autistic children can be successfully integrated in mainstream schools if such approaches are adopted in an intensive and long-sustained programme. The critical discussion that follows the report by McEachin *et al.* (1993) grants guarded acceptance to the authors' conclusion, but advises independent replication of this small-scale study to prove that the method is indeed as successful as is claimed. Those children who improved may have been an exceptional, less affected group. It is also possible that this form of training may prepare children better for more formal kinds of school practice, and be quite inappropriate for other schools where consistent flexible relations with teachers and classmates have high priority. Spontaneity of behaviours, and, indeed, flexibility of thinking, are not well supported by a strict regime of behaviour modification. Nevertheless, versions of the Lovaas approach are widely practised in many countries, and it does enable teachers and parents to have an intended and augmenting influence on the behaviour of autistic children. Applied with skill and sensitivity it can strengthen and enrich the life of an autistic child and transform relations with family and peers.

In beginning a course of training, both antecedent 'trigger' events and consequent stimuli after the subject has responded are noted. Then identified behaviours of the child are strengthened or reduced, and new skills formed, by regulating stimuli and immediate reinforcements. This is the ABC Model, describing 'antecedents–behaviour–consequences' sequences. Each discrete trial or 'drill' consists of a verbal 'discriminative stimulus', the child's response, and a reinforcer – positive (such as food or a favourite game or toy, always emphasised by smiling and emphatic vocal praise), if the response is judged 'correct'; negative if the response is 'incorrect'. Negative reinforcements take the form of a sharp 'No!' with discouraging tone of voice, temporary isolation, or loss of privileges, marked by avoidance of the child by the teacher. Now, in most centres, physical punishment or unpleasant stimulation is *not* used. Prompts are minimised, to prevent the child becoming dependent on them, and reduced until the child acts in the desired way without them, and then the stimulus is repeated a number of times until the child responds on most trials. Generalisation is tested, and strengthened, by using a variety of potentially distracting situations. Skills are taught along a presumed scale of difficulty, and by successive approximation, or 'shaping', to the desired form of response, with the criterion that compliant behaviour should increase to a level above 60 per cent correct. Well-shaped behaviours enable the 'therapist' to identify when the child does not understand.

Examples of desired skills that can be taught this way include: looking in response to name, giving age, learning prepositions and pronouns, naming objects or their colours, thinking about missing items, imitation skills, recognition of facial expressions and gestures, appropriate times for behaviours, socially appropriate attitudes and gestures, and so on. With more able pupils, the training programme builds to academic skills, such as numbers and reading. Token reinforcers are used to help the child wait for reward, and to achieve more independence from reinforcement. Lovaas training is very intensive and prolonged, requiring dedicated efforts by parents and the help of volunteers or paid assistants who must be fully conversant with the method.

Functional analysis works on the assumption that many aberrant behaviours, such as screaming or banging, are actually attempts at communication, or provocations to get a reaction, and therefore open to shaping into a more acceptable form by contingent reinforcement. A controversial aspect is the severe concentration on desirable outcomes and 'success as reward', even when the child is expressing upset, or exhibiting a tantrum. Each trial *must* end on a positive note. The child is not allowed to get the idea that the tantrum was instrumental in having the session ended. Such an attitude towards the child's motivation, and how it should be supported, accompanied or guided to expand its efficacy, is in contrast to that adopted, for example, by the Gentle Teaching method, or the Option (Son-Rise) programme, described below, and quite different from any form of therapy where the child's working through negative emotions is given sympathetic mirroring, explored and redirected.

The Lovaas approach has been adopted in a number of well-supported privately funded schools and parent-support centres in the United States, including the following, all in New Jersey: The Douglass Disability Center, Douglass College, Rutgers University, New Brunswick; The Princeton Child

Development Institute (PCDI), Princeton; Eden Family of Services, Princeton; Bancroft Rehabilitation Services, Haddonfield.[1] The Groden Institute in Providence, Rhode Island, also offers a 'full-service, real-life' provision for autistic children and their families structured on behavioural lines. The methods and interdisciplinary collaboration in the Institute are described by Groden and Baron (1988). Carr's group at Stony Brook, New York State also employs a behaviour modification regime that has success in improving communication (Carr and Durand, 1985).

Daily Life Therapy (The Higashi Approach): Training in a Group

This method of collective education, for which considerable success has been claimed, was developed in the 1960s by Dr Kiyo Higashi, at the Musashino Higashi Gakuen School in Tokyo, for autistic children or those with pervasive developmental disabilities (Kitahara, 1983/1984). It is based on the conviction that these children can best be helped to achieve their full potential near their families and in a community of children with similar cultural experience. A holistic approach aims to reduce the child's autism by developing close bonds in the family, with the teachers and between the children in a group who are kept in intense activity together. These bonds enable the children to identify with 'the rhythm of life' in the group, taking the pace from the slowest member, and from this to mutually responsive life in the community.

Strenuous exercise programmes directed by firm and enthusiastic verbal encouragement from a well-regimented staff aim to build physical strength, coordination and balance, stability of emotions and elimination of obsessions, to the benefit of more normal intellectual interests. With the opening in 1987 of the International Boston Higashi school, which caters for over 100 children from many countries, the Higashi method has received a high press profile. As yet, however, it awaits systematic investigation (Quill, Gurry and Larkin, 1989). The principal difference between the Japanese and US schools is in the limited integration and lack of parental participation in the latter because many of the parents live far from the school. Residential support is provided where this is needed. There is also a large cultural difference in regard to cooperative versus individualistic values, which affects educational orientations and what parents or society accept as desirable. Some of the methods of Daily Life Therapy have been considered or adopted in Britain (Hardy, 1991; Rigg, Gould and Bignell, 1991), but the complete programme does not fit well with the philosophy of

1   The methods of these centres and others in the US (TEACCH, Boston Higashi School, and the Option Institute) are reviewed and compared with UK methods in a useful report by Fiona Knott (1995). Jordan and Jones (1997) review adaptations of various therapies and techniques for teaching in a report on provision for autistic children in Scotland.

most schools or special education units where individual skills development and scholastic attainment is given more importance than group participation (Jordan and Powell, 1995; Jordan and Jones, 1997).

The Daily Life Therapy approach concentrates on a few basic methods, simplifying what the child is expected to do. Activities are group-oriented and highly structured with an emphasis on learning transmitted from child to child through synchronisation and imitation. Assessments of individual attainments do not form the basis of practice. There is considerable emphasis on physical activity in groups – running three times per day for 20 minutes, gym for one hour each day and daily outdoor sports activities (football and basketball) for one hour. The academic curriculum focuses primarily on movement, music, drama and art, culminating in festival displays by the group. It is known that high levels of physical exercise can be beneficial in the autistic population, particularly in reducing levels of self-stimulation, and improving attention and learning potential (Watters and Watters 1980).

Parallels can be drawn between the active and verbally directive Higashi approach and the Peto method of Conductive Education for working with cerebral palsy (Cottam and Sutton, 1986; Hari and Akos, 1988; Trevarthen and Burford, 1995). Enthusiastic group participation, as well as frequent vigorous and sustained physical activity, is encouraged in both.

Cognitive Management and Life Skills Training: Treatment and Education of Autistic and Related Communication-Handicapped Children (TEACCH)

This unique state-wide public health and education programme, run from The School of Medicine, University of North Carolina at Chapel Hill, Chapel Hill, USA, has been in operation for over 30 years. Research at the university furthers development and evaluation of the programme. Highly effective materials have been developed to aid in the assessment and education of autistic children (Schopler and Reichler, 1979; Schopler, Reichler and Lansing, 1980). Currently there are approximately 130 classes for children, and several centres for adolescents and adults in North Carolina run on TEACCH principles. The method, which is an evolving technique of therapy and teaching, has been exported to several European countries by an active training programme. It is popular with informed parent action groups and National Societies oriented to the new cognitive and neuropsychological theories of autism. Workshops on TEACCH methods are frequently run in the UK and a number of other European countries, and it has been actively adopted in a number of centres for autistic children.

The focus of TEACCH is on the development of appropriate communication skills and personal autonomy, step by step, through structured instruction in predicting and controlling the environment, rather than on reducing problem behaviours by behavioural training, or promoting relationships and self-expression through identification with the child's emotional needs. Respect is given for the different way an autistic person perceives and responds to the environment and other persons, and teaching is evocative rather than didactic. Parents are associated closely with the implementation of the programme and selection of goals for their child. There is an emphasis on control of visual information, and photographs and pictures are used to help less able children organise their habits and learning. The approach is client-centred and an evolving supportive environment is structured around each individual's assessment protocol: the Psycho-Educational Profile or **PEP** (see Mesibov, Troxler and Boswell, 1988) for children, complemented by the Adolescent and Adult Psycho-Educational Profile or AAPEP, for adolescents and adults.

TEACCH integrates ideas from a wide variety of different methods in an attempt to provide a complete programme of service for the autistic individual and their family. Components of TEACCH are only adopted once there is research evidence for their efficacy. Furthermore, since no specified intervention may be necessary or can be sufficient with any particular individual, tailored solutions are adopted in every case. This is a well-researched and validated system designed to maximise quality of life for individuals with autism (Schopler, Mesibov, and Baker, 1982; Schopler et al., 1981; Schopler et al., 1984; Schopler and Olley, 1982; Schopler and Reichler, 1971).

Functional and vocational skills are taught as soon as the child can cope well with them, and mastery of effective work habits enables development of independence in an appropriately structured environment. Thus, older, more able autistic individuals are enabled to move from development of communication skills, group work and academic skills in school classroom instruction to vocational training. Adult services include the Carolina Living and Learning Farm where a small group gain confidence in self-care, cooking, cleaning and work practices. There is also employment for supervised mobile crews who do a variety of landscape gardening jobs for a wage that is adjusted to their efficiency, and less closely supervised jobs are supported by hotels and supermarkets who find that well-trained autistic employees are conscientious and reliable. Finally, there are placements where individuals are paid the normal going wage, with intermittent contact with a job coach and counselling in social skills and leisure activities when necessary. Thus, with a supportive community autistic adults can achieve a considerable independence and satisfaction in their daily work.

Meta cognitive or 'Theory of Mind' Training Approaches

A large body of data has been amassed by psychologists on the 'Theory of Mind' (TOM) deficits that can be demonstrated in pre-school children and older autistic children (Baron-Cohen, 1989b, 1990, 1991c; Baron-Cohen,

Leslie and Frith, 1985; Frith, 1989; Happé, 1994; Premack and Woodruff, 1978; Wimmer and Perner, 1983), and this has generated an explosion of the literature on 'mentalising' or 'thinking about thinking' in autism. Autistic children have a particular difficulty with both pretend play and interpersonal 'perspective taking' (Leslie, 1987), and it is proposed that this feature is specific to this disorder, that is, that it will not appear in children developmentally disabled by other conditions who are matched in mental age with the autistic subjects.

This claim that TOM deficits are characteristic of autism, and not found with other communicative disabilities or mental retardation, such as Down's syndrome (Baron-Cohen, 1989b, 1989c, 1991c), is attractive theoretically, but not supported by more recent studies. There is also evidence that older autistic children develop mentalising abilities as they gain in communicative competence. Children with Asperger's syndrome, while resembling autistic children in other respects, have higher verbal ability (Ehlers and Gillberg, 1993), and, compared to high functioning autistic children of the same age, they perform relatively well on both first and second order TOM tasks, the latter requiring imagination of other person's beliefs about still other person's mental states. Asperger's syndrome, at least, does not appear to have a TOM deficit as a fundamental or primary feature (Ozonoff, Rogers and Pennington, 1991). Finally, there are studies of autistic children that do not replicate the findings of Baron-Cohen and others (Dahlgren and Trillingsgaard, 1996; Prior, Dahlstrom and Squires, 1990).

It appears that an inability to conceive mental states is neither typical of autism nor a primary feature of the condition. A recent study compared children with autism, children with Asperger's syndrome, children with deficits in attention, motor control and perception (DAMP), and non-vocal children with cerebral palsy, and found that overall, group performance differences on TOM tasks disappeared when the children were matched for verbal competence and intelligence (Dahlgren et al., 1997). Evidently linguistic and communicative skills are significant precursors to development of representations of mentalising or theory of mind.

There is, to date, no published test of the efficacy of any intervention strategy directly based on the meta-cognitive or 'theory of mind' model of autism, though several unpublished studies are cited in Baron-Cohen and Howlin (1993). It appears that it is possible to train verbal autistic children to pass at least the 'first order' model of mind tasks, such as the 'Sally Anne' test of Baron-Cohen, Leslie and Frith (1986). However, the evidence to date seems to indicate that there is only limited generalisation of these abilities, and that the effect on everyday functioning is likely to be slight. Meltzoff and Gopnik (1993) propose that imitative communication is an important way in which infants learn how to understand persons and what they are thinking, and it is likely that it is faults in this more basic intersubjective function that determine why autistic children have such difficulty in comprehending other persons' thoughts and feelings.

In a more general way, the TOM conception of the autistic child's mind has, however, been influential in the development in the UK of a new 'cognitive' approach to education, as described below. It remains to be seen if this is a more effective way of perceiving the educational needs of all autistic children, including pre-school children and those with little language, than one which treats intuitive interpersonal awareness and emotional reactions as more fundamental.

Cognitive Education

On the belief that autism is fundamentally a disorder in the social and emotional reactions to persons that mediate communication, compounded with a variable and proportionately mild cognitive disability, Jordan and Powell (1991, 1995) advocate a programme of education that builds on the capacity the child retains for cognitive learning and reflective intelligence, while recognising the importance of interpersonal transactions at every stage.

Johnson and Powell emphasise that the driving force for learning, and a particular handicap of the autistic child, is the meta cognitive *understanding* that the child can muster to 'think about' the consequences that follow acting in a particular way. They compare their method with TEACCH, confirming the importance of regulating the environment so that is as stress-free as possible for the autistic child, and clearly structured in time and space according to the needs of each child at each developmental stage, to make it familiar and predictable or cognitively assimilable. They accept the need to compensate for the child's individual handicaps in awareness and comprehension, and the difficulties he or she has in responding to other people and performing useful tasks, so the child's autonomy can be progressively developed. But Jordan and Powell propose that cognitive instruction can profitably go further in giving the autistic child control over his or her learning, by directly addressing the behaviours and mentalising by which understanding is mediated and expressed.

As with all methods that focus on the problems autism causes in thinking or understanding, this kind of education accommodates best the needs of more able pupils, especially those who can be taught self-analysis and the skills of planning and monitoring that enable difficulties to be overcome, be they practical or social. Younger and less able autistic pupils will need practice in developing rudimentary processes of understanding step by step. Visual aids, including photographs of significant objects and activities, can be employed to aid the least able, as in the TEACCH method.

A key component of the Jordan and Powell method is guidance to understanding through practice in reflecting on reasons why people behave as they do, and on their feelings, so the child can gain at least some insight into other persons' minds. The child is also encouraged to reflect on their own experiences, actions and feelings – to develop a 'theory' of their own mind. Interpersonal and emotional processes that a teacher will need to engage with to accomplish this programme are left implicit, or are dealt with at a 'common sense' level, but attention is given to details of non-verbal and verbal communication, and Jordan (1993; Jordan and Powell, 1995) has examined the best methods for aiding communication and language development with autistic pupils. Davies (1997) discusses communication games and signals that can help autistic pre-school children in making the first steps towards effective communication.

Emotions are acknowledged to be important and necessary in any process enabling learning and development of communication and social skills by an autistic child. Thus the approach of Hobson (1993), with its acceptance of the fundamental role of problems in intersubjectivity in development of both self-image and thinking in the pathogenesis of autism, is incorporated. The autistic child should be encouraged to develop and communicate about personal experiences and memories of life events of importance to them. In this, and in the preparation of understanding for future events, re-presentation of significant objects and photographs of the child in the situation can be helpful. As in Gentle Teaching and the Option Method, an affectionate regard for the child and the development of consistent and supportive relationships to teachers and classmates are found to be key elements in a successful cognitive learning process. It is recommended that emotional involvement be rated and recorded, with the child involved in their own assessments.

Cognitive Education, and its foundation in various psychological studies of cognitive and emotional processes in autistic children, including the Theory of Mind and 'executive functioning' hypotheses (Baron-Cohen, 1995; Frith, 1989; Happé, 1994; Ozanoff, Pennington and Rogers, 1991) and Hobson's theory of emotional and self-concept problems in autism (Hobson, 1993a), are fully explained in a recent monograph on *Understanding and Teaching Children with Autism* (Jordan and Powell, 1995). It is not presented as a 'method' or 'package', but rather as a set of principles to apply in conjunction with, or to supplement, other successful procedures. It has been used and found effective in a number of schools and centres in the UK, but, as yet, no long-term or controlled evaluations are available.

Activating Intersubjective Behaviours to Enhance Communication

The preceding methods of helping autistic children develop in adaptation to society and in awareness of its meanings have not primarily addressed the question of how human beings are motivated to interact mentally with sympathy and purposeful cooperation – the aptitude which seems to us to be at the centre of what has failed to develop normally in autism. Behavioural learning, and cognition and meta cognition have been their main concern, though most have been pragmatic in accepting the need for skilled interpersonal communication if any teaching or therapy for autism is to be effective. Gains in scientific understanding of intermental processes, of their key part in child development, and of the brain mechanisms that may mediate them, give grounds for accepting complementary approaches to supporting development in autism – methods that, by varied means, consciously seek sympathy of motives with the affected child.

Infants are born capable of expressing rhythmic patterns of movement and various qualities of emotional state with all parts of the body. Postures, attitudes, gestures of the hands, movements of the face and vocalisations are coordinated, even in newborns. We have seen, in Chapter 6, that anatomists have found that the human brain is built around an Emotional Motor System, and that this includes nerve cell mechanisms that regulate awareness and learning in the cognitive mechanisms of the cerebral hemispheres. Children with profound disturbances of brain development possess at least some of the core motive mechanism, though its organisation and functions may be seriously disturbed, and at a very basic level in the worst affected individuals. Autism appears to be a more subtle developmental disorder, in which the fundamental core regulations are still intact, overlaid by confusing and anarchic processes in later developing components of the intrinsic systems of the brain.

Autistic children express themselves abnormally and fail to relate what they do to other persons, and their expressions, in the normal way. They appear inattentive or avoidant when approached by others seeking communication, and their vocalisations, gestures and general body movements are irregular or bizarre. An autistic child fails to develop easy coordination between expressions of feeling and orientations to events and objects around them, behaviours on which meaningful communication and intelligent cooperation with other persons depends. Thus, one of the earliest signs that a baby is becoming autistic is a loss of motivation to coordinate looking at others with focusing on objects, and the baby does not point to gain others' attention, respond to others' pointing, or integrate vocal expressions with orientation of gaze and gesture to a partner's attentions and actions. At the same time a young autistic child makes impulsive and aimless movements, becomes isolated in circular self-stimulatory rituals and periodically suffers emotional storms, the cause of which is hard for others to understand. Tantrums and screaming may signal pain or discomfort, or they may be caused by frustration in coping with experiences, or by failed attempts to approach the persons to whom the child is affectionately attached, persons who, in turn, are puzzled and hurt by the aimless force of the display. A smile that seems a clear sign of the autistic youngster's pleasure seems to have no relation to events that others can share – for example, it is not combined with a search for eye contact.

Despite these discouraging failures to communicate expressively in normally integrated ways, autistic children, if aided to overcome their perceptual confusion and distracting impulses, can become very responsive to gestural and emotional communication. Many can learn to react to and use conventions of vocalisation and gesture. Appropriately responsive teaching can lead some autistic children to speech and language, enriching their relationships with other children and with adults.

Efforts to enter into communication that are 'appropriately responsive' means that these are efforts that acknowledge, and sensitively adjust to, the weakened and disordered motives, reactions and understanding of an autistic child, due to the disturbed functions of the psychological system that recognises and reacts to other persons, their body movements, gestures, facial expressions and vocalisations. It is a case of compensating for mis-steps in the intricate dance of rhythms and sympathetic signs that constitutes human communication. Autistic children need support and augmentation of their intersubjective awareness and skills. They can be guided to pay more attention to eyes, to look at people they wish to address, or to point when they want to direct another person's attention; they can be drilled in the discrimination and interpretation of facial expressions or the postures and gestures of other people, and they can learn mnemonics to help them through awkward social situations that they do not easily understand. But general mastery of such skills requires consistent and attentive companionship from teachers, which is more than training of discrete behaviours.

A range of techniques have proved effective in strengthening communicative engagements and emotional self-regulation of autistic children. Those that work best do not attempt immediately to inculcate an interactive skill, a form of expressive behaviour that requires a high level of motor coordination, or a symbolic and grammatically constrained mode of communication. Nor do they concern themselves with the rational understanding that may underlie sympathetic communication. It is necessary to pass by way of a level of engagement with the child that activates and strengthens what the child can already do. This implies attention to the rhythmic and body-matching or imitative fundamentals of human intersubjectivity, of the kind that is evident in normal infancy and in the ways that toddlers acquire language through mimetic communication and cooperative play. Thus, for example, speech therapy or instruction in the use of language to communicate ideas and purposes, with correct identification of the persons who are the agents of psychological events, has to begin with support for the child's orientation to the teacher, and pleasurable awareness of the whole dynamic of the teacher's expressed interest. There has to be a reciprocity or turn-taking of expressions, and new skills must be built on whatever efforts the child makes to be received or comprehended by the teacher. The beginning may be little more than a game of repeated teasing gestures and interactive play with body movements and feelings that catches the child's curiosity, of which acceptance of eye contact is but one sign, and that elicits expressions of pleasure.

Educated and highly practised adult communication, and all artificial media, are stripped of much of the rhythmic and mimetic expressive accompaniments that are essential for shared comprehension with a very young or handicapped child. They short-circuit over these elementary levels, gaining speed, precision and complexity of referential content. But, speech and language are built out of infantile protoconversation, and reading is built upon speech. A baby can be trained by behavioural methods to read words before mastering speech, but the words read are no more than forms that have been associated with habits of acting. They are not part of a language. Similarly a child that has been taught by a speech therapist to articulate 'please', or 'hello' correctly may have no experience or understanding of a request or a greeting. The same imitation exists for artificial symbolic systems used with some handicapped populations to substitute communication by speech.

Since more than half of the autistic population will never develop spoken language, there is only a limited relevance for this group of formal, structural speech therapy that attempts to improve production skills of prosody, timbre, articulation, grammar, etc., or that seeks to increase awareness of speech and language. Autistic children who do not speak benefit most from programmes that emphasise pre-linguistic, interpersonal and cooperative aspects of communication (Davies, 1997; Hermelin and O'Connor, 1985; Howlin, 1989; von Tetzchner and Martinsen, 1992). Treatment of this kind may result in the child attempting to speak.

It is well recognised that high-functioning autistic children with good vocabularies and fluent speech exhibit marked abnormalities of language use, with semantic and pragmatic difficulties, and overly concrete interpretation of speech (Jordan, 1993). Such children would be the most likely to benefit from systematic speech therapy sessions to address their linguistic problems. However, it should be recognised that the proportion of children for which this should be a central aspect of their educational programme is small.

Dance and Drama, Intensive Movement Therapy, Basic Communication Therapy

Autistic children often have poor timing and coordination of movements, a need for human contact, but distress and panic with intrusive and unpredictable approaches of others, and discomfort with tactile and kinaesthetic stimuli that children normally find pleasurable or exciting. All these needs and problems can be addressed by a well-informed and sensitive course of physical expression and body movement in dance and drama (Lord, 1997). Autism is a disorder of body sense and moving as much as one of cognition and self–other awareness and communication (Donellan and Leary, 1995). Nind and Hewett (1988, 1994) have developed what they call 'intensive interaction' or Interactive Teaching, in which an attempt is made to engage with the child who has profound learning and communication problems like a mother does in play with an infant, to foster or relearn a feeling of mutual affection and the development of a satisfying interpersonal relationship or attachment. The teacher slows and emphasises responses and uses imitation to elicit a positive response and signs of pleasure. This may be seen to have much in common with Gentle Teaching, the Option Method or Interactive Music Therapy.

Work in Scotland shows that communication by non-verbal means through body contact and movement is highly successful in obtaining communication with mentally handicapped children, including those who are so profoundly affected as to have little learning or voluntary activity, and no symbolic communication (Burford, 1988, 1992; Latchford, 1989; Trevarthen and Burford, 1995). This highlights the power of intensive, direct interpersonal contact and transfer of motivation such as obtains naturally between carers and infants (Knight and Watson, 1990; Knight, 1991). Hogg (1991) reviews improvements in the care and education of handicapped adults by an approach that recognises the need for basic or direct communication in an integrated curriculum. The principles of this approach also apply to the improvement of interpersonal contact with autistic children.

Music-Assisted Learning

As we have mentioned, it is accepted that musical and rhythmic forms of play and interaction can be helpful in promoting the development of communication and relationships with autistic children, and music is used in various ways as a teaching aid (Christie et al., 1992; Wimpory et al., 1995; Jordan and Libby, 1997). Intensive music interaction therapy with a trained music therapist, as described in detail by Jacqueline Robarts in Chapter 11, can improve the emotional self-regulation and communicative readiness of autistic children, with benefits to relationships with parents and others, and to development and learning. This is a form of intervention that can incorporate both therapeutic and educational benefits to a disturbed autistic child.

Augmentative and Alternative Communication

As we saw in Chapter 3, although some children with autism or Asperger's syndrome may have additional problems that specifically affect their production and understanding of speech and language, their problems with learning and using language have to do with more fundamental aspects of intersubjective relating to other persons. Some autistic children are mute because they cannot pass the threshold of understanding with other people that allows entry to language of any kind. This, of course, is more likely when there are added learning disabilities as well as autism. Autism makes it difficult for a child to use any form of signalling to share experiences and intentions with other persons. This is not to say that the behaviour of an autistic child is inexpressive, however strange its form may be, or insensitive to other persons' reactions. Nor is it appropriate to assume, as the so-called Facilitated Communication method does, that all the child needs is support to the arms to overcome a motor coordination problem that frustrates efforts of the hands to signal purposes and thoughts (von Tetzchner, 1996). Training the child to perform partial acts of interpersonal contact, such as looking at the teacher's eyes, or pointing to what is wanted, may also not further communication outside the training situation. Help is needed in strengthening whatever expressive impulses there are, and to develop, by use of sympathetic physical, emotional and interpretative support, new skills in communicative expression, and new understanding of what other people mean when they offer talk. This may be thought of as 'alternative language' learning (Jordan, 1993; Jordan and Powell, 1995), but it rests upon pre-linguistic, or sublinguistic communications.

It is important for therapists and teachers not to give up the impulse to talk to a child who does not speak or who responds with apparent indifference, and one should act as if the child may speak, as a mother does with a young infant. Indeed, comprehension of the message may be made possible by eager and friendly speech, accompanied, as it is bound to be, by expressive gestures, prosodic vocal expressions and other animated activity that conveys the purpose of the message, and its interpersonal function, in non-verbal ways. After many years of not speaking, an autistic child may begin to use words. Speech may be brought forth from a child by animated sharing of activity, such as music therapy (Chapter 11).

It is important for any method that attempts to teach communication that, as far as possible, it should be part of a consistent relationship with the teacher, and shared by the family and school companions of the child. Thus instruction in a picture code or a sign language that only the teacher and the child can understand will not help the child communicate with others who cannot understand any messages the child attempts (Jordan and Powell, 1995). The bridge to shared experience has to be two-ended.

Peers and siblings can be of great assistance in breaking down barriers to learning of communicative conventions for an autistic child, and this is one strong argument for integrated education (Belchic and Harris, 1994; Jordan and Libby, 1997; Wooten and Mesibov, 1986). Indeed, young children acting without inhibitions or special conventional social skills, or handicapped non-autistic age-mates, may be specially helpful, if they imitate and provoke imitation in play (Nadel and Pézé, 1993; Roeyers, 1995). Group play gives a child opportunities to practise all the skills of communicative interaction, cooperative use of objects and shared imagination (Jordan and Libby, 1997).

Speech and Sign Training

Attempts to use a hand sign language to improve communication with autistic children, on the supposition that they have a specific defect in auditory comprehension and monitoring of speech (e.g. Konstantareas *et al.*, 1979), have not been successful. However, in an integrated programme in which the use of gestural communication is part of a plan to increase communication by all possible means, American Sign Language or Makaton (a system developed by simplification of the vocabulary of British Sign Language has proven of some use in establishing appropriate communicative vocalisation, with decrease in echolalia and other non-communicative utterances (Carr, 1979, 1982; Jordan, 1993). The performance of autistic children with signs matches their use of speech; in both there is a specific failure in using signs for gaining social contact and for sharing ideas. Teaching of signs should be integrated with practice to supporting all the other aspects of interpersonal communication, as well as efforts to overcome sensory or motor handicaps (von Tetzchner and Martinsen, 1992)

Interventions that Build on Interpersonal and Affective Engagements

The Option Method

The Option Method developed from one couple's determined efforts to help their autistic son (Kaufman and Kaufman 1976). Many of the ideas used in this approach can be seen to parallel principles which underlie the procedures of behavioural intervention, and particularly those used in 'Gentle Teaching'. Exaggerated responses and imitation are employed to engage the child in an interesting and interested social environment. Use of a therapy room is advocated, designed to offer as little distraction as possible – with diffusers on the windows, diffused artificial light source, and only one adult working with the child at any one time. Materials not in use are placed out of the child's reach, and these can only be obtained by the child through communication with the adult.

The strong emphasis on imitation in this approach is supported by research showing that imitation of the behaviour of the autistic child by the mother on a regular basis significantly increases gaze at mother's face and creative toy play (Dawson and Galpert, 1990), without relation to measures of social maturity (Vineland scale), IQ or severity of autistic symptomatology. This is a significant change because autistic children usually look significantly less than normal children do at others during interaction (Volkmar and Mayes, 1990), and they show clear evidence of joint attention deficits (Mundy and Sigman, 1989a, b). The work of Nadel (1992; Nadel and Pézé, 1993) supports the conclusion that an autistic child can use imitation, and especially being imitated by a partner, as a bridge to closer cooperation in communication.

To date, several books are available on the Option method of work with specific children (e. g. Kaufman, 1981). There has, however, been no systematic evaluation of this approach.

Low Intrusion or 'Gentle' Teaching

Many effective forms of teaching consciously adopt an approach that avoids intruding with strong stimulation or assertive efforts at communication that may provoke avoidance, which Tinbergen and Tinbergen (1983) proposed was an uncontrolled reaction of the autistic child. The aim is to give the child encouragement to take initiatives which are then supported or facilitated. This is a key feature of the 'child-centred' Option Method, and has been advocated by educators to increase the motivation of the child for enduring learning that is motivated by curiosity and positive feelings towards the teacher (McGee et al., 1987; Williams, 1990).

Family Education, Involvement of Parents

Home-Based Teaching

The Home Based Teaching Project (Howlin and Rutter 1987; Howlin and Yates, 1989) is a clinical programme, based in the Department of Child Psychiatry at the Maudsley Hospital in South London. It provides an outreach approach for young autistic children in families throughout the south of England. Treatment programmes are individually tailored to the needs of each child, with three main foci: fostering of language development; facilitation of social development; and treatment of behavioural problems that interfere with learning and development, such as obsessional and ritualistic behaviour.

This approach has been intensively investigated, comparing the progress of children in the programme against matched waiting-list controls. It has been shown to be highly successful in many instances.

An important conclusion is reported as follows:

> ...by focusing the analysis on the relationship between changes in children and parents, it became apparent that the association was bi-directional. Parental intervention can be successful in changing many different aspects of children's behaviour, but the extent to which this intervention is effective will depend very much on the abilities and handicaps of the individual child. The art of successful intervention would seem to lie in helping to encourage the most effective forms of parent–child interaction. (Howlin and Rutter, 1987, p.185)

Video Interaction Analysis and Video Hometraining

The technique of the Video Tape Recorded Playback (VTRP) is now widely used as an adjunct to behaviour therapy with emotionally disturbed patients and families in which there are difficulties of relating and communication. The client's or family's behaviour is videotaped and later played back for them to observe and appraise. Video Playback allows a person or each member of a family to experience and become aware of their actions and their effects on other persons (Berger, 1978). The use of this technique varies in: (1) the amount of the material replayed (the whole session or selected parts), (2) the conditions under which playback occurs, and (3) the timing of the playback (immediate or delayed (Hugh and Rosenthal, 1981).

> Video is a vehicle for discussion: it permits detailed observation; it records events that would otherwise go unseen; it has a distancing effect; it trains in observation and interpersonal skills. (Evans and Clifford, 1976, p.129).

Video Hometraining, developed by Harrie Biemans in the Netherlands, is a method of intensive help for families with disturbed children that uses guided viewing of video recordings of communication in the home. It is not a treatment focused on the child as a patient, but an intervention to aid communication and the development of good relationships in the whole family by self-education under the guidance of a 'home trainer'. The duration of the home training depends on the severity of the problem, on the level of the communication in the family and on the personal needs of the family. The aim is to teach the parents and the other members of the family, such as siblings and grandparents, how to achieve successful communication with a disturbed child. For this to be possible, it is important to know the characteristics of successful, mutually sympathetic, interaction, and how to identify elements of positive intersubjective contact. Microanalytic research on mother–infant interactions and the emergence of cooperative understanding in infants has been important in the development of effective video-analysis and feedback of information used in video hometraining.

Biemans and Van Rees began to use Video Hometraining at ORION, a day care centre in the South of Holland in 1982. Better results were obtained when help was provided in homes rather than at the institution. In 1987, the Netherlands Government approved the establishment of SPIN,[2] the Foundation for the Promotion of the Intensive Home-based Treatment in the Netherlands, which was established in 1988. Similar methods have been found appropriate for dealing with problems of severely disadvantaged children in many parts of the world (Hundeide, 1991).

Video home trainers help families where children are in trouble or causing concern: aggressive children, children with learning difficulties, neglected and sexually abused children, children with psychosomatic problems, children of

2 SPIN, Witte Vrouwensingel 27, 3581 GC Utrecht, The Netherlands.

neglected parents, parents that want to keep their child at home instead of sending him or her to a residential centre, and families who have problems in raising their children. Home training is not used when the child lives away from home, while other kinds of treatment are given to family members, while the parents continue to neglect, reject or abuse their children, when parents and children reject the home training, when unattended marital problems exist and when children suffer from severe personality disorders. It is integrated with the work of other services.

Home trainers are social workers, psychologists and family therapists who take extra training in the method. The home trainer has first to learn the principles of the contact scheme and to execute the patterns of the successful communication while reviewing the tape with the family. The principles are learned by discussion with those already experienced so the home trainer can teach them to the members of the family who are seeking assistance.

Once a film has been made of a representative family scene in the home, the home trainer views it frame by frame, determines which elements should be mentioned to the parents and discusses with his supervisor about how he should proceed. Having decided which items of the contact scheme should be increased, still video pictures are chosen to show these to the parents presenting some 'small' positive move as 'big' to persuade them that they are doing well and that they should work on that more in the future.

Van Rees and Biemans (1986) showed in a demonstration video summarising Video Hometraining that a child with primary autism can respond to, and benefit from, a carefully adjusted and sustained regime of communication and play in which the mother benefits by guided interpretation of her behaviours and the child's responses. Review of videos of interaction with an autistic child can help parents or teachers gain insight into the child's behaviour and the adequacy or efficacy of their own behaviours. The use of video-review has also been found highly effective to help parents of autistic children gain better awareness of the problems the child has in communicating feelings and needs by therapists and educators using interactive, 'child-centred' or 'gentle teaching' approaches, and it is a key element in the Option Method.

Although tending to withdraw from attempts of others to break into their separateness, autistic children can be attracted to gently regulated responses that are timed and measured to match any moves they themselves make in relation to others, and contact can be established and extended in this way (Nadel, 1992; Nadel and Pézé, 1993). Communication by rhythmic movements with gently exaggerated attunement of vocalisations and touching to the child's behaviour, by music, by imitation of the child's gestures or sounds, and reaction to the child imitating, can lead to periods of strong mutual engagement. All of these types of intervention can be made objective with the aid of video analysis, and video feedback can enhance their efficiency.

The Benefits of Early Intervention

Intervention by therapy, work with the family, or special education should be commenced at as early a stage as possible with autistic children. One of the best predictors of how well an autistic child will develop socially and learn is the level of functional language use at 30 months. Assessment before the third birthday gives a good indication of the level of assistance that will be needed. Early intervention will minimise behavioural difficulties that often arise from inappropriate obsessions and rituals of autistic children, behaviours that can interfere with learning. Early childhood is the time that parents have to come to terms with the discovery that their child is not developing normally, and that is when they most need help and advice, and information about the provisions that their child will need. Pre-school children with autism can, with responsive specialist help to aid them with communication difficulties, be attracted to form relationships and learn cooperative social behaviours by involving them in educational games similar to those used with their unaffected peers, and the company of other young children, with their direct approaches and enthusiasm, can help in this. Responses to play or music therapy, or intensive individual treatment of other kinds, may be rapid and have lasting benefits with the youngest autistic children. Special pre-school education in a structured situation specifically tailored to their needs can prepare the autistic child to gain later from integrated schooling, or give important assistance to establishment of special needs for more seriously affected children who are unlikely to adapt to a mainstream school.

Until recently, early diagnosis was difficult and many children were not identified until approaching school entry, when most of them have already acquired very deviant or unmanageable behaviours. New assessments, such as the CHAT and IBSE described in Chapter 2, promise to facilitate early identification by drawing the attention of doctors, health visitors and parents to the most reliable early signs of autistic withdrawal and disordered motives.

A wide range of early intervention methods is available, from those adapted specifically for the autistic pre-schooler (Davies, 1997; Jordan and Libby, 1997; Lord, 1997; Simmeonson, Olley and Rosenthal, 1987; Strain, Jamieson and Hoyson, 1986), to more general methods for helping developmentally disabled young children which can also be of use for autistic children (see Tingey, 1989, and Meisels and Shonkoff, 1990, for an excellent introduction to this literature). The many advantages of a policy of specialist pre-school provision are detailed by Jordan and Powell (1995, p.142).

Conclusions

The central abnormality in an autistic child's brain is one that interferes with awareness and thinking; but, above all, it is the awareness of others as persons who have their own consciousness that is affected. Autism prevents the normal motivation for learning and being taught through sharing attitudes, experiences and purposes with others. It follows that autistic children need types of intervention that systematically facilitate as much cooperative, negotiated and culturally relative learning to occur as possible – intervention that is deliberately monitored with attention to the autistic learner's moment-to-moment motivation for interpersonal response. In this effort a wide variety of techniques for increasing interpersonal sympathy, joint motivation and, in the end, cooperative awareness and skill in communicating, prove to be effective.

As with all young children, it is parents or their substitutes in intimate and consistently active relationships who have the key position in at least the early stages of an autistic child's learning. Any educational or therapeutic provision for autistic children, however expert, must be child-and-family based, involving the parents as collaborators with teachers or therapists as co-beneficiaries in a changed communicative relationship with their child. There is room for the specialist knowledge that therapists in the psychoanalytic tradition, and in music therapy, have acquired concerning the management of the more troubling emotional disturbances that often accompany autism. But there is no therapy that can cure autism – even if there are cases who appear to have recovered to the extent of passing through mainstream schooling with their peers and achieving normal adult family life and employment.

Behavioural, and skills training and cognitive enrichment techniques seeking to change the child will work only if the intersubjective, person-presenting aspect is adjusted to the child's special, reduced or deviant interpersonal needs. This requires careful and monitored management of relationships and routines in the group where the child is taught. As the autistic child becomes an adolescent and adult, a regular pattern of tasks and environmental situations, and consistent working relationships with others, can bring years of special education to fruition in useful paid employment with satisfying friendships.

Although there have been advances in drug treatment of autistic children over the past two decades, and there are now a range of beneficial interventions, no 'magic bullets' have been found. This should not be surprising, given the heterogeneous manifestations of the disorder and its undoubtedly complex underlying pathophysiology. It cannot be imagined that such fundamental ways of intervening with the brain activity actively will ever replace the need for psychological and empathic forms of treatment, and special educational methods.

The quest for improved interventions and advice to parents can be supported by research on the normal development of communication through infancy and pre-school stages to school, as discussed in Chapter 8. We would repeat that early intervention, as soon as possible after the autistic symptoms are recognised, is important, and communication in infancy and pre-school ages offers the best model for the kind of one-to-one or small-group teaching that autistic children respond to best. Information on these aspects is the best way to counteract the discouragement parents will feel on receiving the diagnosis of autism for their child (Eikeseth and Lovaas, 1992).

CHAPTER 11

Music Therapy for Children with Autism

Interactive music therapy is to be distinguished from stimulation with music, or the use of simple instrumental or singing patterns as an adjunct to moving the body, learning names or participating in a group. Music-supported communication, to encourage and accentuate body expression and gesture in interaction and with imitation, has been adopted as a method for increasing empathy, cooperation and learning with autistic children by the Sunderland House School in Nottingham, based on Newson's theory of intersubjective communication in infancy (Christie *et al.*, 1992; Newson, 1979; Prevezner, 1990). An evaluation of this approach to therapy indicated that it did, in one case, improve development (Wimpory *et al.*, 1995), and there are reports of other evaluations that support confidence in the method (Jordan and Libby, 1997).

In this chapter, the first concern is with music therapy directed to helping with emotional disturbance in autism. Many autistic children have, besides their handicaps in social relating and thinking, variable and sometimes severe emotional problems. These require methods and skilled interpretation that go beyond providing guidance with expressive movement and negotiating interactions. Therapeutic modification of a person's abnormal expressions and feelings does lead to improvements in learning, but is not skills training. It is an intensive process of two persons engaging with and transforming the source of motives distorted by trauma, disease or developmental disorder in one of them.

The aims of improvisation led by a trained musician include: freeing of positive motives for experience, and for pleasurable companionship; encouraging efforts at meaningful and mutually satisfying communication, including the responsive use of speech that is clearly articulated and appropriately oriented to a partner and expressed with appropriate prosody or intonation. There are cognitive spin-offs as well, that facilitate more coherent and flexible action, as well as exploration of body movement and of experiences with spaces and objects. But the essence of spontaneous musical expression is that it directly engages and activates the core of rhythmic and sympathetic impulses from which all human communication comes. Music therapists have, as

Jacqueline Robarts explains, many years of experience in helping very disturbed children and adults, including those diagnosed as autistic, to more equilibrated emotions in themselves and more satisfying relations with others. Their practice gives a valuable window onto the dynamic foundations of human relating.

Music therapy is now recognised as an appropriate and efficient way to help children with autism develop their capacities for emotional communication and social interaction (Aarons and Gittens, 1992; Baron-Cohen and Bolton, 1993). This chapter examines why and how improvisational music therapy, carried out by a trained practitioner, can help an autistic child. In response to the increasingly early identification of autism, and to the growing numbers of referrals of very young children with autism and other complex communication disorders now being reported in the UK (Aarons and Gittens, 1992), a case study of individual music therapy with a three-and-a-half-year-old boy with Kanner's autism is presented. The music therapy process with this child demonstrates the value of this medium as an early intervention, and it illustrates some of the commonly recurring features encountered in work with many, but far from all, autistic children. The therapy that lies in the experience of active and communicated 'musicality' that this child clearly came to enjoy can benefit the emotional well-being of autistic persons at different stages of life, and those who may have very different histories (Brown, 1994; Pedersen, 1992).

A comprehensive account of music therapy with autistic children and adolescents across the spectrum of the disorder is beyond the scope of this chapter. To give adequate description of music therapy with autistic children who have severe learning difficulties, autistic children from families who need additional support, autistic children who have suffered abuse (and abused children who present as autistic), 'atypical' autistic children, and children with Asperger's syndrome would comprise a book in itself.

Background Information on Music Therapy as a Profession[1]

The development of music therapy as a profession spans some 40 years. It is a State Registered profession in the UK health and social services. There are now six professional post-graduate courses for musicians to train as music therapists in the UK, including some which offer Masters degree courses. Various kinds of music therapy are practised in over 50 countries, with many different client groups and in a variety of settings (Maranto, 1993). Research in music therapy is developing to provide evidence of positive benefits and efficacy of different applications of music therapy techniques (Smeijsters et al., 1995; Wheeler, 1995). In special schools, child and family centres, child development and

1   Further information on music therapy can be obtained from the British Society for Music Therapy, Tel/Fax: +44 (0)181 368 8879.

assessment units, and other specialist teams, music therapists are increasingly contributing to the multidisciplinary assessment and treatment of children and young people with emotional or psychiatric problems, learning disabilities, and a wide range of complex communication difficulties (Bunt, 1994; Davis, Gfeller and Thaut, 1992; Heal and Wigram, 1993; Wigram, 1995). The relevance of music therapy as part of a child's developmental curriculum is, however, not yet fully understood or recognized within some sectors of the education service in the UK. Thus, in some areas, it may not be possible to have music therapy included on a child's statement of special educational needs. Warwick (1995), a leading British music therapist, presents a convincing argument for music therapy in special education: she makes clear distinctions between the contributions made respectively by music therapy and music education, and describes the role that the music therapist can play within the transdisciplinary team.

What is Music Therapy?

Music Therapy provides a framework in which a mutual relationship is set up between client and therapist. The growing relationship enables changes to occur, both in the condition of the client and in the form that the therapy takes. (Association of Professional Music Therapists, 1995)

Music Therapy is:

the use of sounds and music within an evolving relationship between client and therapist to support and encourage physical, mental, social and emotional well-being. (Bunt, 1994)

Improvisational music therapy (Bruscia, 1987, 1989, 1991), in which the therapist encourages spontaneous musical expression, is a mainstream practice, basic to all the UK post-graduate training courses in music therapy, and it is widely used in the treatment of autistic children (Alvin and Warwick, 1991; Bunt, 1994; Nordoff and Robbins, 1971a,b, 1977; Warwick, 1995; Wigram, 1995). There are two notable alternatives to the main practice of improvisational music therapy. First, the Argentinian psychiatrist and music therapist, Rolando Benenzon, has developed a 'didactic music therapy' for autistic children and their families, which has made an original contribution to the profession (Benenzon, 1997). Second, the work of American music therapist and researcher, Michael Thaut, who takes a more directive, 'behavioural' or educational approach, has significantly contributed to research and teaching of music therapy with autistic children, and other client groups (Thaut, 1980, 1983, 1987, 1988, 1992).

There are many theories to explain the motivating and therapeutic effects of music, but the main forms of practice use music to affect the emotions, and to offer stimulation and emotional communication. This can benefit clients of all ages with emotional, cognitive, physical and/or sensory difficulties, engaging in depth their awareness, motivation and feelings. The power of music to affect the emotions has been documented within many fields of knowledge, including aesthetics, philosophy, music psychology, and the neurosciences (e.g. Aiello, 1994; Buck, 1984; Critchley and Henson, 1977; Dewey, 1934; Evans and Clynes, 1986; Langer, 1953; Meyer, 1956, 1994; Radocy and Boyle, 1997; Wallin, 1991; Zuckerkandl, 1973, 1976). The interactive use of music as in improvisational music therapy using clinically conceived improvisation techniques to develop emotional communication, relationship or relatedness adds a new dimension to this literature.

How Does It Work?

The Essential Motivating Power of Improvisational Music Therapy

Used creatively, music improvised by a practitioner with clinical perception, can meet, engage, and support a child in spontaneously evolving interaction. As their experiences of sympathetic relating and of self-regulation in co-activity progress, autistic children appear to find both security and freedom in the music. Music therapy offers a context in which to build a sense of 'self-in-relationship'. In many cases, music therapy instigates and supports developments in communication (for example, joint attention, intentionality, initiation, imitation and variation, communication of feelings, and use of words). Within such a musically attuned relationship, shared meaning and symbolic (i.e. cultural) imagination can grow.

Nordoff and Robbins offer some of the most detailed descriptions of the process of clinical musical improvisation with autistic children:

> The flexibility of the therapist's playing searches out the region of contact for that child, creates the emotional substance of the contact and sets the musical ground for interactivity. The timing of his playing – the tempo, its rhythms and pauses – attentively follows, leads and follows the child's activity, supporting the experience it carries; his capacity for musical expressiveness in his playing and his singing is at the service of the child's involvement... His improvising is free of any restrictions of conventional musical form for it must constantly meet the changing forms of the child's response. (Nordoff and Robbins, 1971a, p.144)

Nordoff and Robbins describe the extensive range of emotional experience that music, spontaneously improvised in relationship to a child, can offer:

> ...in addition to the conventional range of emotions, all kind of moods and nuances of feeling can be realised, all subtleties and progression of change, all degrees of intensity. There are experiences of *form* and

order...and the forms that are creatively, expressively realised. There are the basic elements of *tempo* and *rhythm*, fundamental to music and fundamental to our extramusical organisation and life. The *melodic* element contains all the above as well as the evocative concurrences between speech and music – these also make directly possible in *song* the setting and expression of thought forms and ideas that have personal significance for a child. (Nordoff and Robbins, 1977, p.2)

Early publications by pioneer music therapists, Alvin (1968; revised edition, Alvin and Warwick, 1991), Gaston (1968), Sears (1968) and Nordoff and Robbins (1971a, 1977) emphasise the self-organising powers inherent in spontaneous musical engagement of the emotions, when this emotionality is directed to give both supportive structure and freedom in expression to the client or patient. Creating experiences of relationship in music, developing self-other expression through emotional involvement, and enhancing communication, have become primary goals in contemporary music therapy.

Music and Emotions: Dynamic Forms of Feeling
and the Music Therapy Process

At the root of musical responses is the power of music to express and to influence emotional states. This connection between music and emotion can be discussed only briefly here.

The impulses of walking, breathing, heartbeat, autonomic processes, and indeed all kinaesthetic or motion sensing aspects of expression through movement, with the tonal inflections of our voices (whether in laughing, crying, or speaking), form a musical hierarchy or orchestration of self-regulation and self-organisation, all directly linked to feeling states, and to their emotive transmission towards others. Tone and rhythm are intrinsic to our innate human functioning, and they are cultivated in music. The therapy that lies in music is thus directly connected to the inherent 'musicality' or innate responsiveness to music found universally in everyone, whether one is musically educated or not. This musicality is universal. It occurs cross-culturally and appears to survive considerable intellectual or neurological impairment (Nordoff and Robbins, 1971a, 1977), indicating music's deeply rooted biological origins (Dissanayake, 1992, 1997; Evans and Clynes, 1986; Wallin, 1991). Every individual, no matter how profoundly mentally handicapped or emotionally disturbed, can show some form of response to music.

The idea that musical expression functions in self-regulation of motive states and in the 'activation of basic integrative processes' has been captured in the infant developmental research of Papousek and Papousek (1979, 1981). This work testifies to the significance of certain fundamental processes found in music therapy, which appear homologous with features of maternal activity, sensitivity to which is present from birth. Human expression can be objectively perceived, and measured, as essentially musical. Musical 'data' display an individual 'blueprint' or dynamic 'gestalt' which transmits reliable information to other humans on essentially how we are at any moment, how we function and how we relate in the world (Aldridge, 1989; Brown, 1994; Nordoff and Robbins, 1971a, 1977).

Pavlicevic's Concept of Dynamic Expressive Form

Music therapist and researcher, Mercedes Pavlicevic (1995, 1997) has developed the concept of Dynamic Forms in expression of music and emotion. She has shown, with her Musical Improvisation Rating (MIR), how discrimination of these by a trained ear can make sensitive, objective, and replicable assessments of the degree of musical engagement between client and therapist (Pavlicevic and Trevarthen, 1989). This helps substantially an understanding of improvisational music therapy in both its theoretical and clinical aspects, giving proper emphasis to the functioning of the music as therapy in clinically conceived musical improvisation. Pavlicevic's paradigm shows how flexible musical relatedness (or communicativeness) achieves intimacy, requiring a balance to be sought and maintained between the extremes of rigidity and fragmentation of response (Pavlicevic, Trevarthen and Duncan, 1994). Without flexibility, a person's incapacity to empathise or adapt results in isolation.

An improvisational music therapist is trained to 'read' these dynamic forms (however idiosyncratic and fragmented they may be) as they unfold in the musical relationship, and respond to them instantly (Pavlicevic, 1990, 1995, 1997; Robarts, 1994). Music therapists are skilled musicians, who are trained to use music creatively with clinical objectives that are perceived within the musical and other dynamic forms of the therapeutic relationship. Musical dynamic forms may manifest across different modalities of expression, both 'sounded' in speech and singing (or on musical instruments) and silent in motor-kinaesthetic responses of gesture and dance. As they arise within the client, within the therapist, and between client and therapist, dynamic forms of personal and interpersonal expressions are objectified, enhanced and developed within the music.

Musical 'Shapes' as an Aid to Two-Way Communication

In work with autistic children, the dynamic musical processes in therapy bring valuable and fascinating glimpses of how a sense of self emerges and holds together a sense of self-and-other. The phenomena of musical entrainment indicate ways in which the sense of self, or, rather, self-in-relation-to-other, is maintained from moment to moment in a fullness and richness of being – and how the communicative bond characteristically 'collapses' when the sympathy breaks. Cohesion and entrainment of responses at a sensory-motor-affective-level frequently is difficult to bring about, but can often be drawn forth ('cathected') by music within a dynamic relational framework. This framework, in the hands of a skilled and creative music therapist, can incorporate familiar as well as novel forms of communication, encouraging creative reciprocity (Rider and Eagle, 1986). Musical inter-responsivity, carefully nurtured, can then stimulate the child to move away from habitual, perfunctory behaviour. Turn-taking, for instance, can be a meaningless compliance; however, by using creatively varied musical structures, moods, styles of approach, the autistic child may begin to discern (aurally) the varied temporal, musical 'shapes' that underpin and organise meaningful two-way communication. These 'shapes' correspond to the prosody that gives meaning to speech. Indeed, musical shapes were first described in psychotherapy with autistic children by Frances Tustin (1986). How music may engage motivational states and shape experiences of relationships has been elucidated by research on the responses of normal infants and the musical behaviours of mothers when they play with their infants (Beebe, 1982; Beebe *et al.*, 1979; Fernald, 1989, 1992; Papousek, 1992; Papousek and Papousek, 1981; Stern, 1974, 1985, 1994; Trehub and Chang, 1977; Trehub and Thorpe, 1989; Trevarthen, 1979, 1993a,b; Trevarthen, Kokkinaki and Fiamenghi, 1998), and, from a developmentally informed psychoanalytic perspective, by Alvarez (1992, 1997).

Sound and Silence

Dynamic forms of relationship in music comprise both sound and silence. Actively experienced silences can be provided in the improvisational music-making context as a 'space' in which self-awareness may begin to emerge (Nordoff and Robbins, 1971; Robarts, 1994). It is interesting to note in this context Beebe *et al.*'s (1985) research on interpersonal timing and the social development of the infant, which demonstrates the significance of the mother's matching the length of the *silences* in eliciting the infant's vocalisation. The therapist, too, needs 'to respect the child's silences and to give space, both physical and emotional, in which the relationship should develop' (Warwick, 1995, p.216). At first the music therapist sensitively supports and fosters the tiniest impulses, in order to find initial contact. Progressing from the first levels of response evoked or influenced by the music (but not yet engaging the child's intentionality), subsequent changes in feeling states may be nurtured through use of clinically directed musical techniques intended to heighten self-awareness and shared emotional communication. Such forms of self-experience and relatedness through the medium of music may help an evasive or remote child tolerate affective contact, whereupon two-way communication can be developed at the child's pace and in the child's own individual style.

Working with Avoidant, Habitual and Stereotypic Expression in Music Therapy

Habitual or stereotypic behaviour patterns may be the autistic child's way to regulate states of arousal and interest precipitated by the complex, often overwhelming, stimuli of social-emotional communication. As described above, avoidance or remoteness can be addressed musically and emotionally, by meeting the child's mood and mediating a carefully measured expression of feelings in communication. Through musical imitation or enhancement, through sound and silence, the therapist may support, heighten and bring out a new feeling-tone – may bring about a change in subjective experience, transforming the child's preoccupations, or those 'sensation-dominated states' or 'auto-sensuous barriers' described by Tustin (1986, 1994). Furthermore, musical improvisation can introduce a vital quality, which reflects the child's behaviour through matching tonal or rhythmic aspects of the child's expression, or offers a complementary or contrasting mood. This provides a relational context, a basis for musical-emotional interaction. Discovering security in predictable musical patterns as well as experiencing the tension of unresolved anticipation in musical interplay may help an autistic child deal with the variety and change in the routines and rituals of everyday life with other people. Maintaining a balance between the familiar and the novel is an important aspect of flexibility and adaptability of response, an aspect of freedom in self-expression and social interaction. In music therapy this can begin to be fostered to lead the child towards more creative and interactive forms of expression.

When spontaneity recedes into perseverative patterns of play, or when a lively sharing 'collapses' into habitual, stereotypic preoccupation, the dynamic musical contact must first return to a basic subjective (rather than intersubjective) experiencing – simply perceiving sound, silence, timbre, musical mood – enhancing the child's bodily sensing of self in 'lived' or 'experienced' time, as Langer (1953) described it. This is the basic ground of being or experiencing, to which musical relationship with an autistic child frequently needs to return, and from which motivational states may rise anew. The music therapist may then, again, proceed to offer various musical-emotional components (e.g. harmonic textures or sonorities). This process may involve sustaining of tones within melodic phrases (or contours), utilising subtle interpersonal temporal patterns, and being receptive clinically and musically (as one process) to the needs of the child. The therapist seeks to bring about moments of relatedness, however fleeting or fragmentary, and extend them creatively. It is through this cathexis of basic emotional communication in music that a sensation of 'I', 'You' and 'It' can begin to evolve and form as a relational entity (see Alvarez, 1992, p.154).

In the case of a child whose habitual or ritualistic behaviours are deeply entrenched, a more directive, intrusive intervention by the therapist can prove helpful. Such intervention, far from being insensitive or uncreative, requires very fine, careful perceptions by the therapist as to the child's inner capacities and strengths (or state of 'ego-development'). Intervention in therapy, whether behaviouristic or psychodynamic, tends to generate heated debate, and a directive approach by the therapist is not generally accepted. Tustin (1986) and Howlin and Rutter (1987), however, agree with the behaviour therapist Lovaas (1987) that autistic children often need active help to leave their habitual behaviour patterns. Autistic children often become 'wound up' in sensory, ritualistic, sometimes self-injurious actions and experiences and they need assistance to find different forms of self-experience, leading to a relatedness with others, which they usually cannot create for themselves. This perspective is expanded by the child psychotherapist Alvarez (1992, 1996) in her theory of ego deficit and reclamation. She describes the therapist's role of alerting and enlivening the autistic child, thus supporting the child's impoverished inner resources, or 'ego-deficit', in order to attain spontaneity and intentionality. A similar concept is exemplified in creative music therapy with autistic children developed in the 1960s and 1970s (Nordoff and Robbins, 1971, 1977). Autistic children frequently need help of this kind within a comprehensive educational or therapy programme.

Assessment

Music therapy offers a clinical context which can reveal useful information on a client's intersubjectivity or motivational states in relationship. There is no standardised music therapy assessment. Descriptive 'codings' of musical relationship, communicativeness, behaviours, and skills have been developed for music therapy with autistic children by Edgerton (1994), Nordoff and Robbins (1977, 1998), Wigram, 1995, and Robarts (1997). The procedures of Nordoff and Robbins, Wigram, and Robarts were devised for work in diagnostic and assessment units and are discussed briefly here.

Recording of Clinical Work

As music is a temporal art, many music therapists record their clinical work on audio or videotape for later analysis of the form and content of musical communicativeness and other behaviours.[2] This not only preserves the musical-dynamic data, but supports continuity and consistency of clinical direction in music therapy with each client. Whilst 'meeting', supporting and sometimes inviting, even challenging, the child in the music, the music therapist is gathering detailed information about the child's capacity for inter-

---

2   Audio and video recordings are kept as confidential clinical records, or as case studies for training purposes (with the signed consent of carers or clients).

responsiveness. The musical and emotional/behavioural features and the temporal (rhythmic) organisation of the interpersonal relationship provide vital information for the music therapist. From moment to moment, and from session to session, he or she can perceive how to further the child's development and how to address the child's individual strengths and needs.

Nordoff-Robbins Evaluation or Rating Scales

Evaluation or rating scales were developed by Nordoff and Robbins (1977, revised edition in press) from the Behaviour Rating Instrument for Autistic and Atypical Children (BRIAAC) (Ruttenberg et al., 1966) in research on music therapy with autistic and a range of emotionally disturbed children with learning disabilities. Therapists trained in Nordoff-Robbins techniques use (although not exclusively) these descriptive scales of evaluation to assess evolving clinical situations and to define clinical goals. Scale I (Child–Therapist Relationship) shows the hierarchical organisation (presented in two columns and ascending in seven parallel points) of both participatory and resistive responses in the child–therapist relationship; Scale II (Musical Comm-unicativeness) charts interpersonal musical communication across three modalities: vocal response, instrumental response, and body movements. The 'lower' levels of Scale II comprise 'evoked' responses, that is those that precede intentional communication, and that are of prime importance in the development of a musical relationship where the child's perceptual and/or motivational capacities are impaired. In Nordoff and Robbins' scheme, evoked levels bear many similarities to the interpersonal phenomena of Stern's 'emergent sense of self' (Stern, 1985), which continue within more highly developed, intentional forms and superstructures of communication. A third scale registers the structural-expressive elements of musical response.

Harper House Music Therapy Assessment

An extensive assessment of musical and non-musical behaviours has been developed by Wigram in his work at Harper House Children's Service in Hertfordshire (Wigram, 1995, 1998). This has practical uses in the context of trans-disciplinary assessment, where differential diagnosis is required for children presenting with a wide range of learning and communication difficulties. Several case studies illustrate Wigram's assessment procedures and make important distinctions between assessment and treatment in music therapy.

Profile of Empathic Musicality (POEM)

This profile was developed by the author (Jacqueline Robarts) as an aid to multidisciplinary assessment of young children with complex communication disorders, including autism and Asperger's syndrome. It is currently being modified for use with a wider range of people with mental health problems.

The term 'empathic musicality' implies, first, the innateness of basic elements of emotional communication (pitch, rhythm, phrasing, interpersonal training) and, therefore, its universal presence from earliest infancy; and, second, a direct link between the dynamic forms of musical expression and motive states (Trevarthen, 1993a,b). POEM focuses on the musical-dynamic components and the context of empathy. The form and context of musical support and musical interventions are defined, taking note of the idiosyncrasies and adaptations that are needed to obtain a cohesive and meaningful social interaction on a particular occasion. POEM identifies details of interpersonal timing in relation to the child's motive states, and defines his or her progress from sensory-motor-affective engagement to meaningful communication using language. Observations are made on: the use of pulse, the shared beat, timbre changes, and phrase structure, by means of which the child becomes engaged or disengaged; what initiatives and innovations the child offers; the contexts which lead to stronger symbolisation. The profile presents a musical-empathic 'blueprint' of the child or client, and charts the dynamic expressive relations, and the developmental level of the optimal communication sustained.

Research: Finding Appropriate Methods
The Phenomenological / Psychodynamic Debate

Two major philosophical and theoretical positions influence current music therapy practice: the phenomenological and the psychodynamic. On the one hand, the phenomenologists claim that the therapy lies 'in the music' and in the 'person' or 'musical being' of client and therapist (Aigen, 1995; Ansdell, 1995). They tend to regard psychodynamic conceptualisations as inappropriate, or merely adjunctive, to the creative-aesthetic and emotional-physiological phenomena at the core of the music therapy process. There are elements of 'absolute expressionism' in music therapy viewed from this perspective (Meyer, 1994). On the other hand, there are those music therapists whose understanding of the music therapy process is underpinned by a range of psychodynamic theories (Bruscia, in press; Dvorkin, 1994; Heal, 1994; Heal Hughes, 1995; Priestley, 1994; Rogers, 1994), or humanist and 'client-centred' theories (Bunt, 1994), which directly influence their clinical practice. Their various orientations seem to relate more closely to the position of 'referential expressionism' (Meyer, 1994). However, many useful correspondences exist between a phenomenological approach to music therapy and a psychodynamic perspective that encompasses the theories of 'self psychology', 'object relations', and that integrates these with the findings of the new infancy research (Robarts, 1994; Robarts and Sloboda, 1994). The paradigm shift in psychoanalytic and developmental perspectives which was heralded by Daniel Stern's book, *The*

Interpersonal World of the Infant (Stern, 1985), has particular relevance for music therapy and supports its increasing recognition within modern special education and healthcare services.

Documented Clinical Work

The claim that music therapy can help individuals with autism rests mainly on the profession's own substantial and rigorous clinical documentation, and on the recognition of its benefits by parents, carers and other professionals.

A common criticism by those without direct experience of the efficacy of music therapy is that the improvements reported to arise from improvisational music therapy and their generalisation to other settings have not been substantiated by controlled research studies. In response, experienced practitioners point out that while each client's individuality and the subtle aspects of emotional expression and creativity within the dynamics of relationship are paramount considerations in music therapy, these features do not lend themselves readily to measurement by research methods that are designed to compare treatment groups and to make 'blind' assessments of behaviours defined *a priori*.

In recent years, this problem of assessment has begun to be addressed: on the one hand, by psychological researchers such as Pavlicevic and Trevarthen (1989), and Aldridge (1991, 1993a,b, 1994), whose collaborations with music therapists (e.g. Aldridge, Gustorff and Neugebauer, 1995) have produced some convincing results within a quantitative perspective; and, on the other hand, by practitioner researchers, who have adopted qualitative methods to examine the music therapy process (Aigen, 1993, 1995; Forinash and Gonzalez, 1989; Lee, 1995; Payne, 1993; Rogers, 1995; Smeijsters and Van Den Hurk, 1993). Some of these studies have included quantitative measures (Rogers, 1993).

The move from old to new paradigm research models is demonstrated in Wheeler's text, *Music Therapy Research: Quantitative and Qualitative Perspectives* (Wheeler, 1995) and by recently documented music therapy research in Europe (Rogers, 1995; Smeijsters *et al.*, 1995). A potential for quantitative appraisal within an essentially qualitative design is suggested by such studies as Thaut's (1988),[3] which compared autistic, mentally retarded and normal children's spontaneous playing of a xylophone. However, this treatment did not employ the dynamic interpersonal interactions typical of improvisational music therapy.

One promising model for a research method to demonstrate the effects of improvisational music therapy may be offered by the recording and microanalytic techniques developed by infant developmental researchers,

---

3   Thaut (1988) concluded that: 'The low performance on complexity and rule adherence of such (autistic) children suggest an inability to organise and retain complex temporal sequences'.

whose interests in pre-verbal stages of communication and its emotional regulations have many parallels with those of music therapists. The precise measures and computerised technology developed by Beebe *et al.* (1985) and Burford (1988) for temporal analysis, and by Malloch *et al.* (1997) for comprehensive acoustic analysis, offer new levels of accuracy and validity for experimental and descriptive research in music therapy.

Two experimental studies in improvisational music therapy research with autistic children (Muller and Warwick, 1993; Edgerton, 1994) are discussed in the review of the literature below.

Early Communication and Music Therapy: Implications for Helping Autistic Children

For music therapists who are examining intersubjective aspects of their work, the microanalytic methodology and descriptive design of recent infant developmental research, especially that on the first communications of infants with other persons, holds much interest. Many of the basic principles of music therapy practice are represented in research studies that record and measure the musical elements of infant perception and expression (Papousek and Papousek, 1979, 1981; Trehub *et al.*, 1977, 1989, 1991) and the microanalytic descriptions of timing, phrasing and prosody in interaction between mother and infant (Stern, 1977, 1985; Trevarthen and Hubley, 1978; Trevarthen, 1979; Trevarthen and Marwick, 1986; Beebe *et al.*, 1985). The spontaneity, immediacy and adaptability of the dynamic and improvisatory relationship in music therapy seem closely related to the 'mutual influence structures' described by Beebe *et al.*, (1985), and to the 'dynamic interpersonal motives' of early communication (Trevarthen, 1993a, b). This concept of the infant's motivation, described by Stern (1985, p.67) as beginning in the 'domain of emergent relatedness...the coming-into-being of organization that is at the heart of creating and learning', is most pertinent to the music therapy process. Such immediate interpersonal experiences appear to be vital in the normal development of symbolisation and language, and they have special significance for autistic children. Research in adult attachment (Main, 1994) suggests that the principles of dynamic sympathy apply through adult life, giving meaning and coherence to relationships and the sense of self. This comparatively new focus on the developmental function of empathic modes of interaction (Alvarez, 1992, 1996, 1997; Emde, 1983, 1990; Schore, 1994; Tustin, 1986, 1994) has provided an impetus to a more informed understanding of music therapy as a medium for emotional communication with wide clinical application.

The similarities between the musical-emotional improvising in the music therapeutic relationship and mother and infant communication have been noted by many music therapists (Agrotou, 1988; Heal Hughes, 1995; Robarts, 1994; Pavlicevic, 1990, 1997). Infancy research, in its investigation of the beginnings of relationship, social interaction and communication, uncovers a spectrum of rhythmic phenomena and expressive tones that requires musical terminology to provide accurate and appropriate description. Microanalytic studies of mother and infant interaction demonstrate in detail the musical improvisatory features and phrased infra-structures of basic emotional communication, 'mother and infant both adjusting the timing, emotional form and energy of their expression to obtain intersynchrony, harmonious transitions and complementarity of feelings between them in an emotional partnership or "confluence"' (Trevarthen, 1993a, p.57). It is this very intersynchrony, flexibility and creative reciprocity that is absent in the autistic child, and which the music therapist seeks to help the child experience and assimilate to whatever extent she or he is able.

'Protoconversation' of mother and infant seems to invoke 'innate musicality', a rhythmic, phrased activity which provides, or *is*, the fundamental organisation of dynamic cerebral processes underlying perceptual, affective, motor and cognitive expression (Trevarthen, 1979, 1980, 1993b; Trevarthen, Kokkinaki and Fiamenghi, 1998). Infant and mother share a hierarchy of vocal elements in phrases and polyrhythmic gestures (Lynch *et al.*, 1995), exchanging their parts with split-second timing (Beebe, 1982). The sharing of affective states or moods that precedes development of higher, more cooperative levels of relatedness between mother and infant (Trevarthen and Hubley, 1978) can be very powerfully realised in music therapy. 'Vitality affects', 'affect attunement' and 'temporal feeling shapes' described by Daniel Stern (1977, 1985, 1994) are clinical realities in the musically empathic therapeutic relationship, as are the 'prosodic envelopes' in which the infant perceives and sympathises with the form of communicative exchanges (Papousek and Papousek, 1979, 1981). Such observations are particularly relevant to developmental objectives pursued in music therapy. They help explain the steps that therapy usually follows.

Dyadic, emotional and dynamic patterns of communication are shown by infancy research to form the foundations of psychological and cognitive development, social adaptation and personality integration (Beebe *et al.*, 1985; Brazelton *et al.*, 1974; Condon and Sander, 1974; Papousek and Papousek, 1981; Schore, 1994; Stern, 1977, 1985; Trevarthen, 1979, 1984a, 1993b; Trevarthen and Marwick, 1986):

> 'the motives and emotions excited between mother and baby, that live only in their communication have a primary directive and organizing role in cognitive and psychological growth.' (Trevarthen, 1993d)

Infancy research has also demonstrated the adverse impact on the child's development when this fundamental vitality of communication between infant and mother is disturbed or inhibited by innate or environmental factors (Murray and Trevarthen, 1985; Murray, 1992). In the case of the child with autism, the dynamic forms of the child's expressive-responsive behaviour are either imperceptible or idiosyncratic and therefore hard to 'read'. The emotional partnership of mother and infant becomes increasingly distorted; mutuality of emotional communication becomes difficult to engage and entrain. The lack of self-synchrony and inter-synchrony in the autistic child (Condon, 1975; Evans, 1986) has been described by Hobson (1989, p.42) as 'a biologically based impairment of affective-conative relatedness with the environment' and by Grotstein (1980) as the lack of a filter for incoming and outgoing stimuli. Secondary or acquired emotional and cognitive handicaps are likely to compound the almost inevitable dysfunctions in the primary relationship (Sinason, 1992).

In spite of the serious impairment of their intersynchrony of expression with other persons, autistic children's responsiveness to certain forms of music and musical stimuli (Rimland, 1964; Sherwin, 1953; Thaut, 1985) shows that some of the infantile foundations of their innate musicality remain unimpaired. It is not surprising then that such a deeply rooted biological response to music, when appropriately engaged, can begin to build new experiences of affective-conative relatedness for the children. In the education and treatment of children with autism, improvisational music therapy may assist the autistic child in many specific ways: entraining responses, giving a sense of temporal flow to develop a cohesive sense of self; expanding his/her capacities in social interaction; and helping assimilation of change and variation, while offering creative strategies instead of the autistic child's obsessive, fixated behaviours; helping to resolve problems of self-regulation, habituation and the modulation of states of arousal (Dawson and Lewy, 1989b; Frith, 1989). Above all, it is the emotional, aesthetic power of music that can offer a depth of shared emotions of the kind that brings people into spontaneous 'communion', regardless of their various abilities or disabilities.

Literature on Music Therapy for Children with Autism

Though more research is needed to understand the processes of music therapy, there is a significant body of clinical documentation showing how autistic children gain in communication and social interaction through the use of either structured or more freely creative techniques. Case studies give detailed evidence that music therapy can have highly beneficial effects on motivation. Some of the most substantial clinical documentations of the improvisational music therapy technique are those of Alvin and Warwick (1991), Warwick (1995) and Nordoff and Robbins (1971a, 1977).

The general principles of music therapy for children with autism are recorded by Alvin and Warwick (1991) who describe their experience of free improvisational music therapy in developing a trusting relationship, self-expression and social interaction. These authors emphasise the qualities of musical sound, and the therapeutically defined silence and space in which the autistic child may acquire new experiences of him or herself. The case material presents individual children across the autistic continuum, with varying degrees of learning difficulties, idiosyncratic and avoidant behaviour, and provides moment by moment accounts of the music therapy process in engaging these children in musical-emotional communication.

Warwick (1995) describes her innovative approach working with mothers and their autistic children in their homes. She gives a detailed account of how one mother gradually takes up some of the musical-relational and confrontational 'strategies' observed in the music therapy sessions, and, moreover, how she becomes more aware of her own feelings towards her son. Music therapy concluded when this mother was ready to assume the function of the music therapist. In this same paper, Warwick (1995) describes a research project (Muller and Warwick, 1993), which set out to measure the effects of mothers' involvement in music therapy. While results showed increases in turn-taking and in musical activity, as well as decreases in stereotypic behaviour in the children, the mothers' participation in the music therapy process was not shown to have any notable influence. Attempts to assess generalisation of communication and shared play outside the therapy setting were inconclusive in this study. The measured results of this study contrast with the descriptive evidence of the clinical case material.

A controlled research study by Edgerton (1994) supports the claim that improvisational music therapy can increase autistic children's communicative behaviours, and suggests that generalisation of skills to other settings does occur. Further research is required to confirm generalisation of communication skills, and to provide closer analysis of musical phenomena – their microstructures and dynamic forms – and to identify more precisely the intra- and interpersonal development in improvisational music therapy.

In the 1960s and 1970s, Nordoff and Robbins approached this level of microanalysis (although without the advantages of computer-driven technology) in their descriptive research on music therapy with autistic children. Combining their creative gifts and professional experiences, Paul Nordoff, as composer and pianist, and Clive Robbins, as an educator of children with learning difficulties, developed an original musical-therapeutic approach and began detailed empirical research into musical improvisation as therapy with autistic children and other children with a wide range of emotional and learning difficulties. They initiated several successive projects, the first being funded by the National Institute for Mental Health and carried out in association with Ruttenberg and his colleagues at the Daycare Center for Psychotic Children, University of Pennsylvania.[4] They examined and identified

4   It is perhaps of some interest to note that this early research in improvisational music therapy coincided with infant developmental researchers' identification of 'musical' improvisatory phenomena in mother–infant 'protoconversation' and games (Bateson, 1979; Beebe et al., 1979; Stern, 1974, 1977; Trevarthen, 1979, 1993a, b, 1998b).

the improvisational musical phenomena and how these influenced intra- and interpersonal development in these children. Nordoff and Robbins' many case studies, recorded on audio and later on videotape,[5] provide valuable documentation of the impact of their improvisational approach and techniques with autistic children. Their publications, *Therapy in Music for Handicapped Children* (1971a), *Music Therapy in Special Education* (1971b) and *Creative Music Therapy* (1977 – a new revised edition is in press), describe in detail the developmental and emotional growth of these children within and outside the music therapy setting.

In group music therapy, Nordoff and Robbins' use of creatively improvised as well as structured music making drew autistic children into a shared musical-emotional experience. Sometimes this was developed further in improvised or pre-composed musical plays or stories. In individual therapy, a very remote six-year-old autistic girl was gradually engaged by carefully improvised music that picked up her fleeting responses and met her mood. This mode of contact in music helped her overcome her tendency to avoid interpersonal communication. As a lively, rhythmic 'What's that?' song was improvised for her, exciting her participation, she began to use words more, including appropriate personal pronouns (Nordoff and Robbins, 1968).

A second case study demonstrates the progress in music therapy of a five-and-a-half-year-old emotionally and behaviourally disturbed autistic boy. Musically matching and meeting the emotional intensity of the boy's screaming heightened the child's awareness of himself, led to 'singing-crying' responses which began to show features of musical relatedness in pitch and in melodic and rhythmic patterns. Positive developments included spontaneous enjoyment, playful babbling conversational exchanges, development and appropriate use of words, improved emotional stability and adaptability to new situations, including improved response to speech and language therapy. The musical relationship was one of acceptance and careful nurturing, as well as challenge, expectation and confrontation, intended to support the child's potential abilities and thereby diminish pathological or habitual features of response. Nordoff and Robbins give eloquent accounts of the flowering of the children's individual personalities and their unique personal expression through this creative music therapy approach.

A further original aspect of Nordoff and Robbins' work was their conception that the resistive responses of the child were often 'a corollary to participation': 'Often, in a child's behaviour, resistiveness enfolds a developing response so closely as to require a most subtle transmission of musical experience' (Nordoff and Robbins, 1977, p.190). They observed that the

---

5   Archive material of The Nordoff-Robbins Music Therapy Center, New York
    University and of The Nordoff-Robbins Music Therapy Centre, London.

character of the child's 'resistiveness' changed with the level of participation. Within the musical relationship, working with 'resistiveness' was thus viewed positively as a means of meeting the child in the 'here and now' of relationship and seeking through this relationship to resolve and integrate the varied pathological aspects of the child's expression. A responsive 'self-structure' is implicit in Nordoff and Robbins' musical and relational perspective.

The case studies of other music therapists record results similar to those already cited. Stevens and Clark (1969) reported increases in 'pro-social behaviours' (adaptive, adjustive and socially acceptable behaviours); Saperston's (1973) study of an eight-year-old autistic boy demonstrated increases in awareness of and interaction with his environment, improved eye contact and increased vocalisation; Mahlberg's (1973) study of a seven-year-old boy in music therapy as part of a composite treatment programme, which included speech and occupational therapies, highlighted increased self–other awareness, showing affection and initiating 'caring acts'. Increases in attention span and development of vocal imitation were found by Saperston (1982). The episodic patterns of play of a ten-year-old girl with autistic features in music therapy was analysed by Agrotou (1988), drawing parallels between mother and infant communication and the music therapy process, and showing increases in communication and spontaneous shared play. A study of a small group of autistic adolescent boys and girls by Bryan (1989) illustrates the impact of a slow tempo in helping the group play together. A psychoanalytically oriented account by Levinge (1990) of a two-and-a-half-year-old girl traces the development of her sense of self and use of 'You' and 'I'. Howat (1995) provides a detailed session by session description of the ways in which music therapy helped a young autistic girl during significant changes in her life. The efficacy of music therapy for a young blind autistic girl, a possible case of 'acquired' autism, is described by Robbins (1993). This child's musical responsiveness in therapy brought joy, creative self-expression and emotional communication, as well as a more normal autonomy in relationships, normally hampered by her dependency on others for most needs. Robbins highlights the role of dance encouraged by music therapy in developing this child's spatial awareness and self-confidence. Toigo (1992) provides a comprehensive account of the many ways in which music therapy can address the problems of autism, referring to the experiences of Dr Temple Grandin (1984, 1995). In a philosophical and clinical paper, examining music therapy as a medium for change and emotional well-being, Brown (1994) discusses emotional-behavioural problems secondary to autism in five case studies.

Case Study of 'Colin', a Three-and-a-Half-Year-Old Boy with Autism

This account of music therapy with an autistic child is drawn from my work as music therapist from the early 1980s until 1994 in a music therapy department in Merton and Sutton Health Authority, Surrey.[6] Referrals came mainly from psychiatrists, paediatricians, clinical psychologists, psychotherapists, speech and language therapists, and general practitioners. In an NHS Music Therapy Department of four part-time music therapists, due to the rate of referrals and limited staffing, it became necessary to prioritise certain client groups: children with autism or complex communication disorders, and seriously emotionally disturbed children and adolescents. I have been fortunate to work with such a wide range of young people, parents and professionals over so many years. I thank them for their trust and commitment. Above all, 'Colin' and many other clients have taught me much about the fundamentals of relationship called forth and nurtured through music.

In the following case study of Colin we shall see how musical improvisation can develop social-emotional communication and imaginative representation.[7] In particular, musical improvisational processes which constitute 'temporal and emotional organisation' will be identified in their role of providing the autistic child with the kind of creative and self-regulating emotional experiences that can assist development of empathic communication and social interaction.

The dynamic forms of the musical improvisation were carefully and clinically adapted to meet and support the child's responses. In this way, emotional contact was made, sustained and developed through music. Change was instigated and supported by musical means that heightened Colin's self-awareness. The creative resources of the music therapy interaction helped him progress through early developmental patterns of spontaneous shared play. Patterns of more flexible inter-responsiveness were fostered musically, helping to diminish some of the restrictions imposed by his autism.

Colin's early history

Colin was a placid baby who was thought to be developing normally until the age of one and a half years, when his lack of progress in language and abnormalities in social development caused concern. He was then

---

6   In addition to autistic children, I have worked with children and adolescents referred for emotional and psychiatric problems (including eating disorders, sexual abuse and elective mutism), complex communication disorders, various syndromes, neurodisabilities, developmental delay, and other disabling conditions.

7   Colin's music therapy sessions were recorded on video (with the exception of the first two sessions) and audio tape. A colleague operated the video camera as unobtrusively as possible in the therapy room.

communicating by gesture only in a limited way, and did not babble, but rather screeched. He related to family members, but showed strong aversion to the voices of strangers. Colin had temper tantrums if his routines were upset, but, oddly, he did not cry if hurt or if toys were taken away from him. He showed no awareness of danger. He was physically energetic, often spinning himself around in circles, or jumping up and down, flapping his arms. He showed no 'symbolic' or imitative play, except with a telephone, with which he could echo speech-like sounds.

The diagnostic impression of Colin when he was three years old was given as 'autistic disorder with onset in childhood, accompanied by language delay and learning delay'. He was referred to music therapy for help with his emotional-behavioural and social communication difficulties.

Colin began individual music therapy when he was three and a half years old. He received 46 sessions of 30 minutes each over a period of 18 months. His mother played an important supportive role in his therapy sessions until the final months of treatment. The sessions took place at the same time and place each week, and he was carefully prepared for any holidays or other breaks in regularity of treatment.

At the age of four and a half, after a year of music therapy as his only formal therapeutic input, Colin was diagnosed by a leading authority as having autism in the classic form described by Kanner (1943). However, his imaginative play was described as being unusually advanced in view of the overall results of his specialist psychological-developmental assessment. The speech and language therapist who later treated Colin made a similar observation.

The music therapy room in which Colin was treated is a purpose-built, sound-attenuated room, dedicated to music therapy. It measures about six metres square and has no inessential equipment or other distractions.[8] An upright piano (well-maintained and in tune) stands in one corner of the room, and various large and small professional and percussion instruments are available, sometimes displayed on a low wooden bench. A lockable cabinet contains a collection of the smaller instruments, beaters, and the audio recording equipment.

Session 1: Working Musically with Rage: Making Contact Through Music[9]

Colin entered the therapy room, holding his mother's hand. The room contained a snare drum (with the snares removed to soften the sound), a cymbal

---

8 Individual music therapy with autistic children (or other children and adolescents with emotional and behavioural difficulties) is almost impossible to carry out in a large hall or playroom, where there is no properly contained or defined space, or in a room where there is the distraction of general play or physical education equipment.

9 The therapist continues the account, referring to herself as the first person.

(14 inches in diameter) on a stand, a pair of small beaters or drumsticks, a tambourine, two handchimes (on a wooden bench), and two small chairs, one larger chair, an upright piano and piano stool.

On seeing me, Colin threw himself onto the floor, where he lay prone and motionless. I remained where I was, by the bench. I tentatively tapped a few beats on the tambourine and paused. Colin showed no response or reaction. His mother sat down quietly on a chair some distance away from him. I began to sing softly, while trying to gauge his mood, and immediately Colin screamed and 'drummed' his feet on the floor, his rage soon escalating to a full-scale temper tantrum. To meet the intensity and match the tonal-rhythmic emotional characteristics of Colin's screaming and kicking, I began communicating with him from the piano, using intense, full-bodied and sometimes dissonant harmonies in a minor key. This seemed to resonate with and acknowledge some of the emotional tension and pathos in his sounds. After repeating this twice and pausing for about the same phrase-length between playing, I noticed that Colin's screaming was not only in the tonality of the music, but was showing more clearly defined tonal-rhythmic elements of the music with which I had matched his initial sounds. His 'drumming' feet had begun to acquire an emotionally expressive organisation in the music.

I lengthened my pauses between playing, whereupon Colin initiated a further 'drumming' of his feet as if requesting that the dialogue should continue. Soon his screaming became more clearly pitched, and showed a further communicative exchange of two notes possibly evoked or influenced by a quiet two-note motif I had played within the intensity of musical response to his rage. Through dynamic contrasts and temporal-emotional organisation of this kind which met Colin's mood and matched salient features of his emotional expression, a musical relationship began to form between us.[10]

In the increasing spontaneity and confidence of this exchange I sang 'hello'. From the comparative steadiness and regularity of our 'conversation', Colin's rage revived anew, his screams glissando-ing in an ascending scale to the tonic (high 'doh') of my/our music's tonality. Here we see the musical phenomenon of 'being in tune' with someone presenting at an evoked level (as opposed to a focused, intentionally aware response), assisting the child's self-organisation

10 Papousek and Papousek (1981, p.206) emphasise the *instructive* function of the parent's imitation of the infant's sounds, which, they claim, provide the infant, 'with a "biological mirror" or a "*biological echo*" allowing him or her to compare auditory products on both sides... This is an important condition for the development of the *infant's imitative capacity* and hence for the development of both language and self-concept'. Parents commonly imitate infants' expressions, and this is used conversationally to regulate the interpersonal contact, calming or exciting the infant and encouraging creative messages as seems appropriate to the infants' changing moods and interests (Trevarthen, 1979; Kugiumutzakis, 1993; Trevarthen, Kokkinaki and Fiamenghi, 1998).

and self-regulation, even when 'beside himself' with rage. As further episodes of conversational feet-drumming and vocalisation ensued, I began to overlap my responses with his, so that his responses would not be too exposed in the pauses and would be 'camouflaged' to avoid possibly overloading his newly heightened self-awareness. Later in the session Colin showed interest in spinning the cymbal. His emotional communication with me was replaced by the 'auto-sensuous' visual and tactile pleasure of this activity. At the end of the session he left the therapy room quietly with his mother.

INTERPRETATIONS

(1) This first session revealed Colin's capacity for two-way communication, not only imitating but initiating contact. This is not unusual in a first music therapy session with an autistic child, and the child's retreat into more perseverative and self-stimulatory behaviours in subsequent sessions is also a common clinical experience.

(2) Colin's mother was able to resist comforting her son in his rage and possible distress. When we spoke later, she said she had wanted to console him, but then had realised that 'something was going on in the music'. Her role in the early sessions was to support (and console) Colin when necessary, but to allow as much contact as possible to take place through the music. In this way communication could be developed within the musical-emotional framework. Regular contact between Colin's mother and myself was maintained away from the therapy room (and Colin) throughout his treatment, in order to discuss his progress and share information.

(3) Tonality, which forms a background for incipient (evoked) musical-emotional relatedness, is a musical phenomenon as influential as pulse in creating a basis for empathic relationship and entraining inter-responsiveness.

(4) The temporal structures using rhythmically placed rests or silences were particularly important in developing Colin's intentionality in musical-emotional dialogue and correspond to the 'burst-pause' neonatal patterns of interaction described by Brazelton and Cramer (1991) and the phrases identified in infant vocalisation by Lynch et al., (1995). The lengthening of the pause creates tension and anticipation for the child in interaction, very similar to the scaler timing process ('elastic band') described by Stern (1977, pp.91, 92). The tempi of intercommunication with Colin occurred within the range of timing in mother–infant interaction, at approximately 66–200 beats per minute (Beebe, 1982), which equals the range from *adagio* to *presto*.

Key aims of therapy were determined by these initial sessions, as follows:

(1) To help Colin increase his tolerance of dynamic forms of sensory-affective stimuli in communication.

(2) To develop his vocalisation and vocal dialogue.

(3) To increase his capacity for self-expression, and self and self–other awareness.

(4) To develop spontaneity and flexibility of his play in interaction.

(5) To find means whereby he could be more easily diverted from habitual, ritualistic, perseverative or obsessive behaviours.

Sessions 2–7: Transition to More Playful Vocal Communication

The second session was similar to the first, but there was a noticeable increase in stereotypic and avoidant behaviour, such as hand-flapping and cymbal-spinning, interspersed with fleeting moments of vocal communication within temper tantrums. His habit of lying on the floor seemed to 'ground' him emotionally as well as physically, and his responses were often similar to those of a baby. As he tended to roll away if I or his mother approached him in his withdrawn state, communication through music was essential as a medium for making emotional contact. Although it was hard to sustain any flow of vocal dialogue, my singing of two- and three-note tonal motifs elicited an almost gurgling-singing response from Colin. He now seemed to accept my voice, but otherwise seemed to be enjoying being quite calm in a world of his own.

INTERPRETATIONS

These sessions mark a settling-down period. The musical setting and myself, no longer novel, did not elicit the temper tantrums and rage reaction which had successfully transformed into carefully regulated dialogue. Colin may have experienced the improvised music and the therapist partly as 'intrusive', and partly as something about which he felt 'OK'. The balance between these two facets of response to music therapy interaction continued to be important for Colins's development, and the experience of negotiating with his feelings, from the extreme to the near imperceptible levels of expression, taught me a great deal about the role of more intrusive, yet creative musical intervention with autistic children. This less interactive period helped develop a sense of mutual acceptance and trust between Colin and myself.

Sessions 8–17: Increased Self-Expression, Initiative and Intention in Shared Musical-Emotional Play; Progressing Through Early Developmental Patterns

In Session 8 Colin showed intermittent interest in playing the cymbal, expressing himself, rather than just spinning it. My music playing in the wholetone scale enhanced the overtones of the cymbal, making as direct a connection as possible with Colin's auditory experience of his own actions. The 'on-goingness' of this scale (which has no harmonic cadences to bring a sense of closure) helped to sustain his playing for nearly four minutes in his characteristic 'action–pause' episodes. He would walk away after each period of six to eight seconds of engagement. This pattern of withdrawal seemed to be his way of modulating his excitement in the experience of shared play, which, while following and supporting him, was not solely on his terms. My use of 'active silences' (Nordoff and Robbins, 1977; Alvin and Warwick, 1991) offered a musically contrived encouragement for him to initiate a beat. This he did very tentatively on the drum, becoming rather excited and beating faster, accelerating until he could hardly maintain his rather immature grip on the beater. After a brief pause, I initiated (on the piano) a similar 'accelerando' within Colin's tempo range, which he spontaneously followed on the drum, looking directly across at me as he played, his excitement still evident.

Colin's obsessive play and prevaricating behaviour began to increase. His interests now included jumping from a low ledge that covered the heating system, lying on the floor and pushing or kicking away any musical instruments nearby, picking up and throwing beaters repeatedly, or lying on his back and kicking the door (which he did at home). He liked running and bumping himself against the wall, before running back to his mother and bumping into her in the same manner. In this particular young child, this behaviour seemed to represent a practising of early developmental phases of play. He seemed to be checking out physical boundaries and exploring the various basic self-experiences involved in losing and finding. At the same time, he was impervious to any alternative games or variations offered by myself or his mother.

Although I matched aspects of his activity in the music, or listened in silence to enable him to 'listen' to himself, he became increasingly caught up in the momentum of his own activity. In order to help him out of this vortex of separate activity, to re-enter shared play, I enhanced certain elements of his expression in such a way as to provide some shaping or modulation of his auto-sensory experience. I created sequential musical phrases on an ascending scale to form an external temporal-affective framework, into which Colin's repetitive activity might be drawn.[11]

Using a melodic phrase on the up-beat (known in musical terminology as the 'anacrusis') as a preparatory, tension/attention-creating device, I then resolved the tension on an accented beat. I sometimes shaped the 'anacrusis' both vocally

11 The research of Trehub and collaborators (1977, 1989, 1990) shows the early development of the infant's capacity to process rhythm and melody, particularly structural elements such as sequence, confirming that the 'global processing strategy' underlying language acquisition is already intact in infants. Infants enter language through rhythmic and prosodic communication (Bruner, 1983; Trevarthen, 1987a; Locke, 1993; Lynch *et al.* 1995).

(in a descending melodic phrase) and gesturally, raising my arms above my head before bringing them down in a slow arc onto the drum nearby, concluding the movement with a slight slowing (*rubato*) preceding a sudden louder (*sforzando*) beat to coincide exactly with his jump and landing on the floor. This device of anticipation and resolution-with-surprise was a temporal and emotionally/physically regulating, self-organising structure which caught his attention, especially when his mother matched her son's landing and my strong beat with a clap of her hands, so that all three of us finished 'together'. Colin now looked at his mother, then at me, prior to each jump – finally his activity became a shared experience, and for a time at least it seemed important to him that this was so.

His confidence seemed robust enough for me to assess his capacity for flexibility and adaptability by 'stretching' an interaction. I retained certain musical elements of the anacrusis by developing a hierarchy of sequential phrases, but shortened the final one to catch his attention. The first time the shortened phrase was used, Colin looked disconcerted and stared blankly past me for a moment, before he somehow accepted the 'new' shape of interaction, responding with a one-second time lag. Without this kind of shaping of inter-responsiveness, Colin would return to flapping his hands, throwing sticks, picking them up again and becoming 'stuck' in perseverative activity. I had to 'animate' the play in ways that did not overwhelm him, that struck a balance between structure (e.g. the temporal-affective organisation of the 'anacrusis') and freedom (e.g. periods of silence, or the introduction of variation, creative developments from familiar to unfamiliar elements of music). He seemed unable to discover and maintain a flexibility of motivation alone.

INTERPRETATIONS

(1) In these sessions, the 'temporal feeling shape', described by Stern (1994) as 'a temporal contour of feeling that unfolds during a moment in which a motive is in play', was useful in countering aspects of Colin's obsessive, habitual play. It embodied an emotional dynamic and a cohesiveness which could help Colin accommodate change and inter-responsiveness at his immature level of functioning.

'Temporal-affective contouring' proved to be a powerful 'self-regulator' for Colin, helping him accommodate and assimilate a variety of patterns of emotional and social interaction in this early play, and it laid the ground for more complex aesthetic forms of musical-emotional communication that were to develop later.

(2) Here the 'temporal feeling shape' is applied in therapy for a child who does *not* yet have a motive for play. The playful feeling, and especially its communicative aspects, has to be externally aroused and then regulated within the musical contour of 'feeling shape', giving form to his subjective and intersubjective (shared) experiences. Colin

began to laugh at our interactions. His mother commented that she had never seen him laugh so normally.

In music therapy this strategy can be particularly useful as a 'cueing' device to secure a dynamic structure for the child, whose attention needs to be focused or whose emotional awareness is being held or entrained. Where self-organisation is immature and poorly regulated, or the emotions labile – for example, in very young or developmentally delayed children, and in emotionally disturbed or traumatised children – the presentation of a musical 'anacrusis' or a feeling contour leading to a stressed beat can provide an invaluable (and infinitely variable) aid to regulation and a means to facilitate trust and emotional engagement in shared play.

Autistic children seem to derive particular benefit from such emotional regulation, and seem to require a much more carefully prepared and often more exaggeratedly intense expression of this than children with other learning and developmental difficulties. Maximum clarity of structure in the 'feeling shape' seems to be needed, often using more than one expressive modality.[12] Above all, timing and use of silences are critical factors in engaging and sustaining musical-emotional communication.

Session 18: Sustaining Self-Expressive Vocal and Cross-Modal Forms of Emotional Communication

This session marked an important shift in Colin's capacity to participate coactively. After several episodes of musical dialogue, which were entrained by the 'anacrusis' technique, Colin began to sustain the flow of the musical conversation with the support only of a steady andante accompaniment in a D major and minor tonality, which I played at the piano.

At first he was preoccupied in taking his shoes and socks off, but then Colin looked up at me as I sang about what he was doing: 'Colin's (pause) SOCK!' and 'taking it (pause) OFF!'. As usual Colin's attention was engaged and held by certain familiar aspects of the temporal-affective structure, and even more so when the resolution (or cadence) of the phrase was withheld, creating an increase of tension (and attention) that accompanies anticipation. This time I sang the 'anacrusis' allargando (i.e. at a much slower tempo), adding further tension by widening the melodic intervals within the contour or phrase. Colin's face and vocal sounds expressed heightened pleasure in his recognition and naming of 'sock' (at the phrasend), as he held it up in his right hand. Moments later, passing his sock to his left hand, he held it up with a deft movement, and

12 This concurs with the research study of Thaut (1988). See footnote 3, page 183.

echoed an approximation of the word 'off'. There followed several episodes of sustained pre-verbal musical communication, involving babble sounds and open vowel sounds in short rhythmic exchanges, as well as in intersynchronous cross-modal forms of communication.[13] The spontaneous vocalisations and variations in vocal exchange which Colin initiated were very encouraging developments. His facial expression and physical attitude registered occasional surges of pleasure and surprise (at himself and the musical dialogue, it seemed to me). His need to modulate the intensity of his new level of emotional communication manifested in periodic withdrawing – sometimes to the door (and its satisfyingly round handle), and sometimes to his mother, bumping up against her or almost throwing himself onto her lap.

The session ended with Colin sitting on his mother's lap beside me at the piano, and touching the keys with his bare feet. As one of his feet was about to strike a cluster of notes, I gently delayed its descent so that it then 'played' in time with the stressed beat of 'bye-bye'. Colin then played the two-beat motif with his hands, turn-taking within the 'bye-bye' song. Colin then sang bye-bye ('dye-dye') several times in turn with me, glancing at his mother and myself with pleasure and understanding.

After the session his mother and I discussed the use of short phrases and placing the 'key word' at the end of the phrase in helping Colin begin to develop more fluent interaction and to motivate him to use words.

INTERPRETATIONS

This session was significant for its development of vocalisation in prosodic, pre-speech forms of turn-taking. Rhythmic and melodic contouring were important factors in sustaining phrased vocal exchanges.

Session 21: Development of Variety and Flexibility in Interactive Play

Now Colin often became fractious and difficult to engage. However, when his tempestuous mood was met by my playing short 'volleys' of dissonant chord clusters (using a scale form with flattened second and sixth degrees) in an intense crescendo and in the tonality of his gurning sounds, he gave a half-smile. It seemed as if this music had 'struck the right note' for him. The intensity of the harmonies created a physical-emotional experience, involving cycles of successive tensions and resolutions. Having engaged Colin's interest, I offered a complete change of mood by introducing a playful *arpeggio* (an ascending/descending pattern of intervals) on the piano. Colin soon joined in, imitating my rather exaggerated prodding movements with his index finger – a

13 This sequence on video provides a fascinating record of Colin's processing across a spectrum of emotional and cognitive, pre-verbal and verbal communication. Similar sequences are described by Warwick (1995).

new experience for him. He then accepted successive variations in pattern and phrase length, which shortened or lengthened randomly and were too swift and spontaneous for him to echo or imitate exactly as the interaction gained momentum. This resulted in increased freedom from slavish copying and provided exposure to new musical experiences which he himself began initiating almost in spite of himself. Colin enjoyed this new game. It seemed to comprise the right balance of the expected and unexpected stimulating his emotional involvement from moment to moment, the structural elements giving him the means to contain his excitement.

Session 24: Developing Three-Way Communication

Colin had begun to 'jargon' communicatively – conversing in an invented speech-like way. At the beginning of this session he seemed to be trying to request his mother to play one of the reed horns. A three-way interaction with Colin, his mother and myself developed and continued in the subsequent months of therapy. His vocal range increased, particularly during his playing of the reed horns. His intentionality in vocal communication became much more consistent and playful in character, showing his desire to sustain the shared play with less reliance on adult support. He became able to communicate with more than one person at a time and this was noted outside of the music therapy sessions. It was possible to work more directly with any resistive or avoidant behaviour, for example, by offering 'yes no' games, which posed questions, and encouraged his close attention to the meaning of what his mother or I were asking him. Colin's use of words increased to short phrases, uttered somewhat stiltedly, as if he were retrieving newly acquired language and needing to concentrate while using it to communicate.

Session 40: Missing his Mummy; Expressing Sadness, Anger and Upset

Colin had begun to attend school and could separate easily from his mother, but he had become used to her being with him in the music therapy room and found it difficult to break this pattern. Both his mother and I felt it might a good time to try to effect this separation while encouraging more flexibility in the therapy sessions.

Colin entered the therapy room reluctantly, his lower lip quivering. As I sang to him, he responded: 'No want Jackie!', and proceeded to knock over the drum, the cymbal, and several small chairs in the room. Without reacting to this I responded to his mood, playing a slow pulse in a minor key in the mid to bass register of the piano. Reflecting his feelings musically and verbally, I sang about how he felt in the room without his mother. His pleased glances of recognition and understanding alternated with ambivalent angry and sad glowering expressions. Both the music's pulse, its sonorities and harmonies and my verbal reflecting of his feeling states seemed to contain his feelings. His increased emotional stability and ability to self-regulate his feelings also seemed to help him reflect on himself in this unhappy situation. He played and sang a tearful goodbye at the piano, becoming more lively in response to my offering our familiar arpeggio patterns of play.

INTERPRETATIONS

In music therapy with autistic children, phenomenological and psychodynamic ways of working are mutually enhancing and reciprocally informative. This session provides a clear illustration of how the perspectives can be combined.

I made use of the following psychodynamic ideas:

(1) Bion's (1959, 1962) concept of the 'alpha' function of the mother who contains and transforms the baby's emotions when they threaten to overwhelm him.

(2) Winnicott's concepts of the infant's 'going-on-being' as the mother provides 'holding', and of 'transitional objects' as phenomena that support creative ideas (Winnicott, 1960, 1965, 1971). I consider musical or sonorous phenomena as such 'objects' of emotional relationship.

On the other hand, the phenomenological, musically defined elements of the therapy included:

(1) Application of changes in tone, rhythm and tempo to match or enhance Colin's vocal sounds, movements or gestures ('attunement').

(2) A 'pedal-point' or steady pulse played on the tonic, dominant or flattened second, to give a sense of continuity and support, while meeting Colin's mood, and holding his attention.

(3) Use of marked silences to evoke Colin's creative potential for self-experience and reflection.

Session 43: Hide and Seek – Further Developments in Symbolisation

Colin began to say 'I' and 'You' in this session, and he spontaneously used my name and that of the video camera operator. He had begun to enjoy hiding behind either the curtains or the piano. This theme of losing and finding, of disappearing and re-appearing continued in different ways. Colin was greatly amused by the alterations in these tensions and resolutions, but gradually reverted to rather fixed temporal patterns in his play, the sense of shared experience receding. He needed constant musical intervention to maintain flexibility and a real sense of interaction.

Session 44: Colin's Capacity for Compromise Between Social and Auto-Sensuous Play

Colin now more frequently and spontaneously initiated communicative play with me – vocally, with the other instruments (particularly the reed horn), and at the piano. However, in recent sessions he had become interested in the piano pedals, enjoying their feel, shape and taste as much as their action. He kept ducking down under the keyboard to touch and taste the pedals, coming up just in time, or almost in time, to complete the phrase in the 'Goodbye' song I was singing.[14] This was a good example of Colin's increased flexibility and capacity for what I perceived as a reasonable compromise between his autistic, sensory enjoyments, self-regulatory devices, and his taking part in a social world, which held as many joys as complexities for him. Our final goodbye in this song expressed mutual enjoyment, affection and humorous exasperation – sentiments shared by the best of friends.

Colin's parents reported that he was now relating more spontaneously to his siblings, although at times was almost too attached to his older brother. His school, psychology and speech therapy reports were very encouraging, particularly in respect of:

(1) his increased use of spontaneous language rather than gesture to express his needs and feelings

(2) his social awareness and sense of being in a group with his peers

(3) his symbolic and imaginative play continuing to develop well and in advance of his overall level of development.

Conclusion

Music therapy played a significant role in developing this autistic child's emotional, integrative and self-organisational experiences. Colin's case illustrates how the spontaneously created, clinically oriented use of musical improvisation shares many of the dynamic (and musical-improvisatory) forms of mother and infant communication fundamental to psychological development and personality growth.

Concerning the sense of self and self-in-relationship, music therapy addresses the fundamentals of what it is to be a human being reacting to other human beings, and it offers a context in which the motives of the self can be

---

14 With Colin I tended to improvise such songs in response to him in the moment, to ensure as far as possible a really shared, spontaneous, alive experience rather than a conditioned memorised repetition. Other children, particularly those who are emotionally disturbed, may need the security offered by repeated presentation of a familiar song, which may then become a basis for developing emotional expression and communication in improvisation.

nurtured, and the emotions can be experienced, expressed and brought into play in communication. In work with autistic children, musical experiences of this kind can have a significant impact on the overall mental development of the child. We have described how the 'music' inherent in all our human functioning can be traced in the rhythms and sympathetic responses of infants. New infancy research findings integrated with clinical observations and research in improvisational music therapy contribute to a richer understanding of how taking part in musical interaction helps autistic children to gain a self-awareness and relatedness to others – an awareness and relatedness that is cohesive rather than fragmented, enabling them to respond more readily in everyday social interaction.

The power of music to reach into the emotional experience and inner being of the child is the essence of music as therapy. It has the power to change awareness, initiative and the capacity for learning and for communication.

CHAPTER 12

Psychoanalysis and the Management of Pervasive Developmental Disorders, Including Autism

Olga Maratos

The psychoanalytic approach to autism, dismissed by many seeking a more objective, simpler or 'biological' explanation of the disorder, encourages an openness to the autistic person's real subjective experience – of life, and of other persons, their speech, their actions and their expressions of emotion. For this reason it is accused of over-interpreting responses of the child, attributing psychological abilities that are difficult to substantiate. Psychoanalysts are also to be reproached for developing elaborate theoretical and verbal structures to explain their insights into hidden psychic events. They have created layers of interpretation that may obscure the phenomena on which their work is based, and many of the intellectual and verbal models and metaphors they use among themselves are very obscure to the uninitiated.

This is changing. In a form that recognises the inherent person-related motives of the human infant, and that acknowledges that autism is an intrinsic pathology of the mind of a child, not just an avoidant adaptation or an immature responsiveness, psychoanalytic theory, bringing nearly a century of experience of work with children with emotional disorders, is coming to terms with a developmental psychology that is itself trying to grasp the complexity of a young child's mental processes (Stern, 1985). A training in psychoanalysis can give a therapist a unique enhanced insight to a child's confusions and fears, and can give support to a constructive education to increase the child's awareness and his or her capacity to regulate feelings with other persons' participation. This is important information for developmental psychologists.

We are very fortunate to have the following very frank account from Olga Maratos, an experimental psychologist who made a path-finding study of neonatal imitation and a practising child psychoanalyst, of her work in a small therapeutic nursery school for emotionally disturbed children, including children with autism.

The Psychoanalytic Approach to Autism

Psycholanalysts began studying autism as a different condition with special features soon after Kanner's famous article was published. Until then autism was described under the broadly defined category of 'early childhood psychosis'. Most psychoanalysts do not enter into speculation about the aetiology of autism, although early articles on the subject, including some by Kanner (Kanner and Eisenberg, 1956; Kanner, 1973), hypothesised a probable relation between maternal depression, which may take the form of maternal withdrawal from caring and emotional involvement with the child, and a child's autism. The main psychoanalytic concern is the description of the child's mental functioning, affective states and the way he or she relates to people.

There are many different theoretical attempts to explain autism within the psychoanalytic school of thought. Margaret Mahler's theory, based on classical Freudian Ego Psychology and the school of Self Psychology, stressed the pathological way in which 'symbiotic' and autistic children interact with people and objects, and their inability to interact meaningfully (Mahler, 1968). She thought of autism as a subgroup of infantile psychoses, with symptoms that become apparent quite early and certainly during the first year of life. Mahler also stressed the fact that these children seem to receive many sensations, from the inside of the body and from the objects of the environment, through the senses separately. It appears that the autistic child cannot integrate such sensory impressions into a meaningful whole, or into coherently perceived objects.

Donald Meltzer, of the Kleinian school, described the autistic state of mind, which can be found in many children who suffer from early mental disturbances, as follows (Meltzer *et al.*, 1975). He thinks that most autistic children are more intelligent than appears in formal tests and that they have an abnormally acute perceptual sensitivity and emotional sensibility. Meltzer has hypothesised a process which he calls 'dismantling', brought about by the suspension of attention to the whole function of an object, and which allows the senses to wander each to the most attractive part of the object at any one moment. This scattering of awareness brings about a passive dismantling of the self, and the sense of wholeness and the continuity of being is thus destroyed. When this happens the child is dominated by primitive emotions, some of which may be painful. This is why Meltzer suggests that it is necessary for the therapist to try to mobilise the child's suspended attention in order to bring it back to a coherent relationship with objects, and with the child's own self.

Frances Tustin (1981) also stresses the predominance of disorderly sensations in the life of the autistic child, and she describes a number of distinct types of autistic state in autistic and psychotic children ('shell'-type, 'segmented', 'confusional', etc.). On the basis of her wide clinical experience with psychotherapy of autistic children, her descriptions of their behaviour, of the psychological defence mechanisms that these children use, as well as of the actual techniques she herself practised with them in therapy, have all been extremely useful to child therapists.

French psychoanalysts have also helped in our thinking about autism: (1) by stressing the organising effect that language can have on children who do not themselves speak (psychoanalysts following the Lacanian school), (2) stressing the importance in therapy of the use of specific words referring to the body, food, emotions, etc. (Geneviéve Haag), and (3) in the introduction into the psychoanalytic literature of the 'pictogramme' (Piera Aulagnier) which is a theoretical concept referring to the link between the first mental representations and the somatic areas or zones, a link that forms a complex qualified by psychic energy. Autistic children, Aulagnier believes, have severe difficulties in forming this iconic representation.[1]

Psychoanalytically oriented psychotherapies with autistic children use a variety of psychoanalytic concepts and adapt the technique to suit each child's needs. The main concept of 'transference' is explored in attempts to relate with the child. Transference is the process by which the unconscious desires of the patient towards the other person are actualised during the psychoanalytic procedure; the desires and conflicts are usually considered to be repetitions of infantile prototypes. As with all children, play material is used during the therapeutic session. It is believed that the stability of the setting (that is, fixed days and hours as well as fixed length of the therapeutic hour), neutrality of the therapist and stability of interventions, all help the child build a basic trust in the other person. Special modification of the classical psychoanalytic technique for children may also be required with some autistic children. For instance, some kinds of food (milk or biscuits) or use of a potty may be employed on the assumption that somatic sensations and needs are important to children who interact in a primitive and disturbed way.

Finally, it should be stated that psychoanalytically oriented therapy has considerable success with autistic children, usually after many long years of treatment. Some such children can and do get out of the autistic state of mind, as has been described in many reports on the outcome of individual psychotherapies published in the psychoanalytic journals. It appears that the

---

1   The views of leading French psychoanalysts – René Diatkin, Geneviéve Haag, Piera Aulagnier, Didier Houzel, etc. – are presented in the following journals: *Topique: Revue Freudienne*, 1985, Nos. 35–36, with the subtitle 'Voies d'Entree dans la Psychose' (Access to Psychosis) *Journal de la Psychanalyse de l'Enfant*, 1988, No. 5, subtitled 'Psychoanalyse des Psychoses de l'Enfant' (Psychoanalysis of Infantile Psychoses). Paris: Editions Paidos/Centurion.

Jacques Hochmann Professor of Child Psychiatry at the Université Claude-Bernard in Lyon and director of a treatment centre for emotionally disturbed children in Villeurbanne, France, presents an account of the development of psychoanalytic treatment of autistic children in France (Hochmann 1997).

psychoanalytic treatment has significantly facilitated improvement in these cases.

My Experience in a School for Autistic Children

Some 12 years ago, I and a few other professionals decided to do something to fill a big gap in the Greek mental health system: to start what we then thought was going to be a therapeutic nursery school for children with pervasive developmental disorders (autistic and psychotic children, without marked mental retardation). Our aims were to provide services for the children and their families, to promote research, to provide specialist training for professionals and to exert pressure on the state and the public so they would look on these early disturbances of mental development in a different way.

We worked for ten years with children from two to eight years of age, relying exclusively on donations from the private sector in addition to the fees the parents paid, which covered one quarter of the total cost of the unit. Half of the money paid by the parents was reimbursed by their social security funds. During the last two years our work has gained official recognition and we now obtain financial help from the Greek state and from European funds. I must stress that we first became known in Europe and the US, and only later in Greece.

The unit is called *Perivolaki*, which in Greek means 'Small Garden' and has now 25 children from 2 to 14 years old, and over 20 professional workers including part-time therapists. It is a day unit, with two 'classes'. Parents are seen weekly during the first two years of the child's stay at *Perivolaki* and every fortnight thereafter. The average length of stay of a child at *Perivolaki* is 4–5 years.

How We Manage Autistic Children

At *Perivolaki* we observe the children, think about them a lot, discuss their behaviour at staff meetings, along with our feelings, with a view to understanding whether their autistic behaviour is defensive, refusing interaction and relations because they don't make sense for them or because they are painful, or whether there is a pervasive lack of motivation for relating and communicating. We find both conditions present, at different times, in all our children.

Classroom activities are organised to provide many kinds of interactional situations with people and with objects. One teacher becomes, through mutual choice and effort, the preferred caretaker of each child. There are activities normally found in nursery schools, primary school classrooms, and in the home: drawing, painting, story telling, dressing-up, make believe activities, puppet playing, educational toys, shopping, cooking and setting out lunch, video, etc., plus music therapy – individual or in groups of two to three children – organised psychomotor activities, outdoor activities, and so on. For children who can cope we go on to activities preparing for reading and writing, even some arithmetic lessons, usually individually or with two or three children together.

Children also go out once a week to picnics, to the zoo, to other schools, the local library, children's museum, the airport, and every week two children with one teacher are responsible for purchasing, preparing and setting the meals out for all the others. Nothing is imposed on the children, so that at any one moment one can see children who are quite isolated in the classroom, but an adult is always nearby, occasionally talking to them and confirming that they are not alone and that they are wanted to join in with other children in whatever activity is going on at the time. During the month of June, the children go to the seaside for swimming three times a week with their teachers and this 'summer programme' is much loved by staff, parents and children.

Each child has individual psychotherapy two or three times per week. Obviously these children do not have psychoanalysis in the traditional sense of the word since they don't function at a symbolic or verbal level that is required for such therapeutic intervention. The classical technique is very much modified. In effect, it is really play therapy modified to suit the child's needs by a therapist who, working through this interaction with the child, uses his or her psychoanalytic training, empathy and compassion as aids. The main modification of technique that we have introduced has to do with what we call 'physical objects', such as milk, sweets and biscuits, a blanket and the potty. As mentioned, we find that these modifications are necessary because of the importance bodily functions have for these children. We also hold the child when that seems necessary, so there is some bodily interaction, which in the classic psychoanalytic approach would not be permitted. In spite of these innovations, we keep the main principles of set days and times, and length of sessions, which is called the 'setting' in psychoanalytic terms. The repetition of set days and times and length of sessions gives the children a sense of rhythm which seems to help. They very quickly recognise these aspects and ask for their therapy sessions in their own way. We give the children frequent verbal interpretations, and we use 'transference', the sympathetic identification with the child's motives and emotions as expressed, as our main tool for understanding the child. With children who can use drawing and symbolic play, we operate with a more traditional psychoanalytic technique.

Now about the parents. As I have already mentioned, cooperation of the parents is a necessary condition in order for a child to be accepted at *Perivolaki*, and it is clearly stated at the initial contract. At the beginning, work with parents is done separately from the child. The couple sees the social worker and most of the session is usually spent in talking about the child and themselves at home. Very often one of the parents may ask for more sessions and this is offered to him or her, but if there is a demand for therapy we recommend to the couple or the individual to have psychotherapy outside *Perivolaki*. This is done to avoid the 'institutionalisation' of cases. The parents also meet with the teachers of their children individually or in a group with all the parents, three to four times per year.

When we come to know the child and the parents better, usually after the first two years' stay of the child at Perivolaki, we organise sessions with the whole family, parents and child together or even brothers and sisters together, where our aim is to help them interact with the child in such activities that we have singled out as most successful in getting the child to communicate. This is actually a new development which seems to help a lot, but is still in an experimental stage.

Training of professionals at *Perivolaki* comprises the following: each year we accept five to six people, pre-school teachers, teachers or developmental psychologists, in the classrooms for training. We also accept one or two social workers who take up cases under supervision. Every psychotherapist that joins *Perivolaki* also has supervision during his/her first two years at the unit. Finally, there is a seminar every fortnight on autism and childhood psychoses which can be attended by the staff members and by professionals that are interested. This year 30 people are attending the seminar.

In the 12 years of the unit's existence, over 300 children have been referred to us for differential diagnosis, over half of them from other specialist centres, with various diagnoses. Fifty of the children have been accepted to enrol at *Perivolaki*. Twenty five children have left, some because they were too old to stay with us. We have follow-up data for these children. Three of them (12%) were later diagnosed to have mild mental retardation with specific language disorder, in addition to autism. Another three children (12%) still have what can be called nuclear autism of the Kanner type and they attend the only state school for autistic children that exists in the Athens area. Ten children (40%) go to special schools, but have developed useful speech and are educable in spite of psychotic disturbances, in some cases delusions and hallucinations, and behaviour disorders. Last, but not least, nine children (36%) go to normal school, and two of them are in secondary school. Most children continued their individual psychotherapy for many years with the same psychotherapist after leaving *Perivolaki*.

Out of the total of 50 children who were enrolled at *Perivolaki*, only four (8%) suffer from epileptic fits and are under a neurologist's control. In none of the children was a Fragile-X syndrome detected, and none of the children has any identified brain abnormality. One boy was diagnosed as having Asperger's syndrome.

Two Clinical Examples

The two cases that follow are chosen to illustrate the way we think about the peculiarities of behaviour and the personal symptoms that an individual child may present at any one moment during his or her stay at *Perivolaki*, and the way we try to cope with them, both in the classroom and at individual psychotherapy sessions. The first child, Marco, is still at the unit, and the incident described took place during his second year at *Perivolaki*. The second child, Diana, presented the behaviour described during the third year she was with us. She stayed at the unit for five years.

MARCO

Marco is classically autistic, at the age of six looks like a two-year-old, and has muscular hypotonia which is not identified with any known neurological disorder. He can say three to four words, all echolalic and out of context, except for the word 'hair', *mallia* in Greek, which he always says in an appropriate context.

Marco is obsessed with the hair of all adult women at *Perivolaki*, and with the hair of little girls in his classroom. He pulls hair, caresses it, touches it with his face and always prefers long hair. His obsession is such that he can stay immobile for a long time just looking at somebody's hair from a distance, and his perseverance with this interest is of such strength that when he is seated next to somebody, he takes great care to put himself in a position parallel to the other person so that he excludes any eye contact but remains close to them. The behaviour looks like a trick devised to prevent Marco from doing anything else but be near hair.

We discussed this peculiar behaviour many times at staff meetings, making different hypotheses about Marco's obsession and the pathological relation he has established with a 'part object', the hair but not the person. Sometimes Marco gets very excited when he pulls our hair and we have often thought of a Greek proverb 'The drowning man grabs at hair'. We had learned from his parents that Marco's mother had long hair which she cut when Marco was nine months old in order to avoid the annoyance Marco's behaviour was causing her at that early age. It is remarkable that Marco's obsession with his mother's hair developed from around six months. We thought that maybe Marco equated hair with his mother's body and when his mother cut her hair, he felt despair as if he had lost the whole mother.

Confirmation of this hypothesis came when his preferred teacher, who, by the way he calls *Malli*[2] though her actual name is Maggie, informed the children

---

2   *Mallia* is the plural for hair in Greek, and *malli* is the singular. Marco articulates the word *mallia* for many different objects, and also when he is alone without any apparent relation to a particular object or situation. He uses the word *Malli* only to name his preferred teacher.

in her classroom that she was going to have a baby and would be leaving for a few months. Marco went into real mourning, crying almost constantly or having extremely depressed moods which caused many of the staff to feel despair. Marco tried to hold on to his teacher, and for the first time he articulated a sentence 'mallia, to go in mallia!'. We think at last that we have a solution to our puzzle about Marco's problem. *Mallia* means mother's belly and Marco wants to be in her, maybe like a foetus. This led us to handle Marco's behaviour towards hair in a different way. We started talking to him more about his mother, and the pregnancy of his mother and of his teacher, we showed him carefully how hair is only a part of a body, we gave him material that looks and feels like hair, and we tried to have him play with bald dolls, dolls with hair, etc.

Marco stopped mourning but is still extremely interested in hair. The matter was, of course, taken up in his individual psychotherapy sessions. The parents were informed of our thoughts, and we discussed the whole issue in their meetings with the family therapist.

DIANA

The second example is of a six year-old girl during her third year at *Perivolaki*. I shall call her Diana. When she first came, at the age of three and a half, she was very isolated, showing all the typical autistic symptoms: avoidance of eye-to-eye contact, stereotyped repetitive movements, silence, etc. After two years at *Perivolaki*, Diana was still inaccessible for social contact. However, she managed to cooperate in some educationally oriented activities. We felt that she agreed to cooperate in these activities more to comply with her mother's wishes than to obey her own.

During that time Diana, under great stress as all of us asked her to do things, started coming to the unit carrying between her fingers hard plastic nails from an educational toy. She was picking them up and wearing them between her fingers in a very ritualistic way, as if the nails were extensions of her fingers, a habit which restricted the movements of her hands and made her impotent, putting at the same time a safe distance between herself and the external world. We thought of this peculiar behaviour as Diana's attempt to defend herself against the anxiety she felt when in contact with people, and that at the same time it was an attempt to show some of the aggression she felt and a wish to dominate others.

Psychotherapy was focused for some time on that particular problem and the therapist put into words her feelings of anxiety, pain and aggression. Diana's motivation for relating to others and her actual interaction were ameliorated in the following months through psychotherapy and with the help of her mother. Her parents were divorced and Diana lived with her mother.

Diana eventually restricted the hard plastic nails to one hand, and she started touching people and objects with her other hand. Still later the nails were replaced by soft tissue paper. The behaviour persisted for a little over one year.

Diana is now ten years old. She goes to a special school, speaks quite well and can read and write.

I would like to stress that these children have intense feelings which they express very well and which are immediately recognisable: joy, anger, anxiety, fear, panic, sadness, despair, depressive moods and frustration. Some of these expressions are clearly related to specific situations, but for others it is much more difficult to find an explanation.

Problems of Diagnosis: a Need to Treat the Whole Child

We find that the category 'childhood autism' is on the one hand too restrictive to contain all the variations of disorders that affect many aspects of development in a child, and on the other hand too broad and imprecise to support any intuition into the psychological aspects of the disorder. To give an example: ICD-10 includes 'infantile psychosis' under the category of 'childhood autism' (F: 84.0), which we believe is very misleading, because the differences between the conditions are very marked. Infantile psychosis is a very real category that can differ from autism in terms of course, prognosis and social adaptation. Another problem is the key statement that differentiates a diagnosis of autism from 'early childhood schizophrenia', that is, 'absence of delusions and hallucinations'. Children diagnosed as autistic, when older and when some of them are functioning in what we could call a post-autistic mental state, often have delusions and hallucinations. Considering even earlier stages, how can we know that those sudden laughs and panic-stricken reactions that many autistic children exhibit are not accompanied by hallucinations?

Because the category of 'childhood autism' in DSM-III-R and ICD-10, if compared to their earlier forms, includes many more children under the category of 'autism', both professionals and lay people have been led to regard the whole group of children so labelled as very severely and perhaps permanently handicapped, because of the connotations the term 'autism' carries.

In our experience autism falls into a category we could call 'affective or emotional communication disorders', or, following Gillberg (1991a), 'empathic disorders'. These disorders certainly have tremendous and lasting effects on the total mental functioning of the child. The problems we observe in cognitive, language, social and learning areas are, we believe, secondary to the emotional-affective or empathic disturbance, which may be congenital and which certainly becomes apparent in infancy.

A clear diagnosis is important because the therapeutic approach one chooses depends on the way one thinks about the disorder. However, modern therapeutic approaches tend to replicate what we see in autism itself; namely a propensity to conceive mental functioning cut into pieces. Problems are identified in 'cognitive functioning', 'attention deficits', 'language' and 'communication'; organic deficits are found in glutine metabolism, serotonin, Fragile-X chromosomes, etc. The therapeutic approaches tend to address one or the other aspect as if we do not have to deal with a single individual whose pathology may or may not include other unidentified aspects as well. We may fail to look at the child as a whole human being who cannot relate to other people and to inanimate objects in ways that are so natural for the normal child, or who has not the motivation to do so.

At *Perivolaki* all therapists and most of the permanent staff, special teachers and psychiatric social workers, are trained in psychodynamic psychotherapy, with adults or with children. We find that the psychodynamic-psychoanalytic approach matches best the way we wish to view and understand autism. I would like, at this point, to remind you that psychoanalysts were the first to try to do something constructive with autistic children, by which I mean taking them in to a psychotherapy that could last ten or more years, and with some positive results. Most of all, psychoanalysts are the therapists most inclined to consider autism as an emotional disorder, a subcategory of early psychotic disturbances.

I am of course aware and very critical of the view of Bettelheim (1967) and some other psychoanalysts that autism is an environmental disorder, and of the blame some put on mothers of autistic children. However, Bettelheim, the main advocate of such a view, has not received support from the majority of psychoanalysts. They were, in fact, the first to criticise his views. Kanner, on the other hand, involved the parents of autistic children only indirectly, by trying to describe their personality structure. As to Margaret Mahler's original claim that there is an autistic stage in normal child development (Mahler, 1952, 1968), I would, of course, as a developmental psychologist who has studied communication with newborns, be the first to dismiss it, as she did herself, because I know that babies are born with the motivation to communicate with others and are emotionally very well attuned to interactive situations from birth. The same criticism must be made of Melanie Klein who claimed that there is a schizoid-paranoid position in normal development (Klein, 1946, 1963). Hana Segal (1964) is also revising this description. I must, however, stress that many of Melanie Klein's descriptions are extremely helpful when one does psychotherapy with autistic children. Her concepts of 'early fantasies', 'part objects', 'defence mechanisms', and so on are genuine clinical insights based on much experience (Hinshelwood, 1989). I would also like to remind you that Esther Bick (1964) managed to get mother–baby observation in the curriculum for training in child psychotherapy, a practice that is now disseminated across Europe and which started at the Tavistock Clinic when John Bowlby was its director (see Shuttleworth, 1989).

At *Perivolaki*, we find that many new concepts advanced by psychoanalysts are very useful to our psychotherapeutic approach towards autism. Such concepts are Piera Aulagnier's 'pictogramme', Bion's (1962) concepts of 'beta-function' and 'maternal reverie', Winnicott's (1965, 1977) concepts of 'primary maternal preoccupation', 'false self' and 'transitional objects', as well as Meltzer's concept of 'dismantling' (Meltzer, 1975), Tustin's (1981) concepts of 'autistic shells' and 'autistic contours', etc.

Tustin, Meltzer and Winnicott, in the UK, and McDougall and Lebovici (1960), Diatkine and Haag, in France (see Footnote 1, p.205), have also something to say about autistic children. Some of them call autistic children 'psychotic', and maybe this is not an acceptable term for a very young child, because it has connotations that lead us to think of very disturbed adults, condemned in mental hospitals. But when we talk of an emotional – a social, or an empathic – motive disorder, aren't we really saying what has already been said about some psychotic behaviour of adults, or about psychotic personality structure?

Finally, I would add that while an emphasis on biological research is certainly scientifically necessary, I do not think that it will fundamentally alter the therapeutic approach that is based on analysis of mental processes. The belief that scientists are going to find a single biological or organic cause for autism may be convenient because it relieves us from worry about our inadequacy to understand autistic children and to offer them an efficient therapy. This belief, we should note, also allows parents to think that there is very little they themselves can do to help their children, and this, in our view, is a very unfortunate consequence that makes the child's situation more precarious. It is necessary for scientists and parents to cooperate in approaching the autistic child as a being with complex psychology.

I wish to repeat that in our therapeutic approach at *Perivolaki* we are not concerned primarily with aetiology. We follow medical doctors' orders if the child has epilepsy or if the parents choose to follow a specific dietary regime, but we strictly resist any practice of looking at the child's stools to see if they float or if they sink into the toilet! We also advise against taking the child around to various specialist places to run medical tests, or attempts to find new drugs to improve the child's availability to social contact.

To Sum Up

We think of autism as a state in which there is insufficient differentiation between stimuli coming from the inside of the body or from the environment. The child cannot construct representations of sensations. All stimulation is thus experienced as fragmented, as if it were coming from a part object, or as a sensation coming from a fragmented body. Thus any bonds or relations that are formed are also fragmented and with 'part objects'. Whenever the children develop some speech, this is also fragmented and may have delusional elements. These children's senses are very sensitive and fragile, so feelings coming from bodily sensations are often very strong.

While the child lives within this type of autistic state there is no possibility of forming a sensible, whole, continuous experience either when alone or when in the presence of others. If a child becomes motivated to relate or to understand the continuity of his existence, that is tries to integrate experiences into a meaningful whole, then we may see what Tustin has called 'confusional states', or what in traditional French child psychopathology is called 'symbiotic psychosis', or even the 'infantile psychosis' of ICD-9 which is lost in ICD-10. Asperger's syndrome or schizoid disorder of childhood might also be the same nosological entities.

If I were to make a comment about prognosis in one sentence, I would say that apart from early diagnosis and early intervention, the course of autistic disorder and the final outcome depend mostly on the way parents perceive and think of their child, on how much they are ready to cooperate with therapists and how much they can really offer mentally and emotionally.

CHAPTER 13

Education for Autistic Children
Concepts and Strategies for Maximising Inclusion

Expert information is now available on a wide variety of effective therapeutic and educational practices and special services for young people with autism and Asperger's syndrome (Attwood, 1997; Cohen and Volkmar, 1997; Gerlach, 1993; Harris *et al.*, 1994; Howlin, 1997; Jordan, 1990, 1991; Jordan and Powell, 1995; Kitihara, 1983, 1984a,b; Klin *et al.*, 1995; Knott, 1995; Koegel and Koegel, 1995; Lovaas, 1980, 1987; Morgan, 1996; National Autistic Society, 1993; Peeters, 1997; Powell and Jordan, 1997; Reynolds *et al.*, 1987; Gould, Rigg and Bignell, 1991; Schopler and Mesibov, 1988, 1992, 1995; Schopler and Reichler, 1983a,b; Smith *et al.*, 1994). Books by psychologists summarise research findings about the inner workings of the mind of a child with autism (Baron-Cohen, 1993; Baron-Cohen *et al.*, 1993; Dawson, 1988, 1989; Frith, 1989, 1991; Happé, 1994, 1995b; Hobson, 1993; Sigman and Capps, 1997). They demonstrate that the child has disturbances of awareness, intention and memory, inflexibility of thinking, emotional confusions in the face of novelty, and incomprehension of what other persons feel and mean. These effects of autism are measured against other conditions that cause children to have special educational needs. Epidemiological studies show that only autism has all these features (Wing, 1996).

The research findings help parents and teachers improve the world of the child or young adult with autism, indicating steps that can be taken to reduce confusion and stress and open ways to more independence in work and acceptance in society. Developmental comparisons reveal the potentials an autistic child or adolescent has for learning in the company of others. In the end, however, caring for and educating any child with special needs is bound to be a learning process itself, encountering far broader problems and opportunities than a specialist researcher can comprehend.

Extraordinary personal stories of authors who are autistic (Grandin and Scariano, 1986; Grandin, 1995; Williams, 1992, 1996), parents' accounts (Kaufman, 1976, 1994; Maurice, 1993; Miedzianik, 1986), and biographical stories by neuroscientists (Luria, 1969; Sacks, 1995) all give insights to what it is like to be autistic. Everyone with access to the needs of children with autistic disorders of awareness and leaning has something to offer. The theory of autism has to be a collaborative and evolving venture, in partnership with the affected children themselves.

There is a welcome shift from a focus on what the child with autism lacks in cognitive or socio-emotional processes compared to other children, what they cannot do, to a search for reliable information on the active motives and positive orientations towards people and objects that the child possesses, aptitudes on which good teaching practices can be built. Precise and accurate information is now easily obtained on the progress of autistic individuals with different needs and in different regimes of teaching, and on the effectiveness of therapies for emotional distress, distorted representations of experience, disorganised work habits and troubled relationships. This reveals that, while effective methods may have started from very different premises about autism and how to deal with it, they really have much in common. Involvement of parents in the evaluation of different kinds of provision, and dissemination of information through parent networks that compares different approaches, has stimulated improvements in services and teaching and animated researchers. Clear progress has been made in the last few decades.

Here we will not attempt to duplicate professional accounts of good educational practices adapted to the needs of children with autism, but will simply summarise our interpretation of the principles that link what is known of the autistic mind, especially of its early development, with the practical tasks facing parents and teachers. The evidence on which we base our view of the key factors in development of cooperative understanding is referred to in earlier chapters. Sigman and Capps (1997) present a similar developmental approach that recognises the importance of interpersonal factors at all stages, and age-related changes in these.

What Education Is, and How an Autistic Child May Fit In

Education is the formal application of teaching to instruct or guide children, through age-appropriate steps, towards levels of understanding, knowledge, forms of behaviour and habits of work that are deemed to be desirable and useful in adult society. In general, educational practices are driven, on the one hand, by notions of what the society desires or needs – assisting children to become socially-adapted and productive citizens according to the standards of the culture. On the other hand, there is the abiding conviction that educating must support the child's natural motives and satisfactions – their innate 'need' to learn a culture, a need they show from infancy (Trevarthen, 1995). Not all children have the same capacity for learning, and different interests drive different kinds of achievement. However, there is an idea of a minimal common curriculum that most children are expected to master.

Jerome Bruner (1996), in an inspiring essay on the nature and functions of education in relation to societies and their cultures, with the title 'Culture, Mind and Education', places the fostering of each child's 'identity and self esteem' as a fundamental tenet of a 'psycho-cultural' approach to education, one sometimes at odds with the institutional demands of the 'educational system'. The proportions of 'society-centred' or 'child-centred' components of educational practice differ at different times and in different places. The kinds of choice that experts on educational theory, psychology, and teacher training make will be affected by political considerations and by public opinion, and all these will constrain the teacher in his or her daily work with children.

Children who do not adapt readily to standard schooling, who will not apply themselves and who do not learn what is expected of them, who feel that they are judged to be failures, are unhappy and pose many problems. The more able ones may struggle for self-esteem by exaggerating their non-academic abilities, tempting fate, conforming to social norms outside school and outside the bounds of what their parents find as acceptable, rebelling against what is set for them to do. Those with handicaps, especially, swing the balance of need away from an ideal curriculum of tasks, facts or skills to be mastered at given ages, towards individual attention to what each child can do, and what feels good, in him or herself, about doing it. Bruner (1996) identifies the creation of a self-confident and cooperative self-with-others in a 'community of learners' as a most important achievement, for the child, in a good education. We now have much new research evidence for motives in all children, including those severely handicapped, mentally, physically or emotionally, for 'self–other' relating – their needs for generous companionship. These motives for learning in companionship begin at home with their parents and are evident from infancy (e.g. Aitken and Trevarthen, 1997; Reddy et al., 1997; Trevarthen and Burford, 1995).

Children with autism need and benefit from companionship. They can sense when they are sharing activities with others, and they need to form relationships of trust. But they cannot interact as normally developing children of their age do. What threatens the development of self-esteem for a child with autism? This must depend on the child's motives, which specify what is being sought, on the availability of what is being sought, and on the skill that the child has to make use of, deal with and remember objectives. If the human world is confusing, uncomprehending, and making negative judgements, any child's chances are weakened. All these problems are critical for children with autism. The weakest link in the functions of their brains is that which engages other persons in understanding.

The Key Deficits Indicate the Most Appropriate Approach

However varied its severity and whatever the precise forms of disability that may come with it in different children, autism is a disorder of relating. Whether they speak or make inarticulate sounds, all children with autism communicate in a way that makes sharing of experience, and especially teaching, difficult. This means that the fundamental task of anyone – parent, teacher, playmate or friend – who wants to help the child to communicate and learn better, is to find ways to be as accessible and comprehensible to the child as possible.

We have seen that there are many different techniques that are effective for opening communication with a child with autism. All adapt to what the child can perceive, understand and respond to. All rely upon sympathetic appreciation of what experiences cause confusion and anxiety for the child and impede learning and the desire to perform tasks effectively. The biggest problem is that the reciprocal, imitative, playful and cooperative contact that is perfectly simple and easy for a normally developing young child, even one who has severe sensory or motor handicap, is acutely difficult for a child who is autistic. The partner who tries to communicate may decide that the child does not want to communicate. A change of approach may reveal that this is certainly not the explanation. It is just that what we take for granted about persons' awareness of other persons, and how we intuitively, without any rational theory, negotiate and explore ideas, do not come naturally to the child with autism.

Finding the Right Balance of Educational Contact

There are two ways to misread autism. Both underestimate the child's need for responsive human companionship. One assumes that the avoiding child is better left alone to amuse him or herself with repetitive ritualised explorations of simple experiences, or more complex memory feats of an obsessional kind. The other tries to shape the child's behaviours by an imposed drill in desirable habits, according to a prescribed programme and with simple forms of coercion. Either of these approaches, by failing to accept a minimal awareness of other persons' feelings and purposes, and by failing to identify with the child's will to do things, can make the isolation of the child worse.

This is not to say that autistic children cannot respond to behavioural training that aims to teach a particular habit or skill. However, to transform the habits of a child with autism requires attention to what motivates the child to act and to repeat learned acts – what encourages perseverance and learning how to solve problems. The best rule is to try to find how to meet the child in a dialogue of action and attention that develops, and that leads the child away from avoidant or self-directed and repetitive behaviours. Such behaviours, including violent and self-injurious behaviours, may be the child's way of getting consolation for the confusion caused by other persons' impatient or unobservant efforts at contact, or they may be seeking reaction from others.

This dialogue-making by a parent or teacher is a difficult and delicate task, but surprisingly positive emotional and other-seeking responses, and pleasure in sharing tasks, can be elicited when the teacher has the right measure of the child with autism. These are both rewards for the teacher, and evidence of a constructive change in the motivation of the child. Autistic children that seemed completely cut off can be revealed to have playfulness and to be happy when an affectionate relationship is found. This opens the door to subsequent teaching or training, and to transferred motivation for learning to understand and think.

We have seen that simple descriptions of autism are misleading. It is not true that autistic children are unemotional, unaffectionate or incapable of forming attachments, even though they often seem to avoid direct or sustained recognition of other persons as persons, and they may treat someone to whom they obviously are attached, or parts of this person's body, as if they were just useful 'tools'. Children with autism are not unable to imitate, although the way they do so tends to be strange and rudimentary, or literal and uncreative, depending on how severely their motives for communicating, and intelligence, are affected. They tend to imitate immediately in an echoic way, or they repeat previously experienced actions or expressions of others like a tape recorder, triggered by the context or by an association with an emotion-generating event of the past in a way that makes no sense in the communication of the present. The speech of autistic children is often characterised by immediate or delayed echolalia, repeating the words of others with little sense, except by way of simple sensory association that only they may experience.

It is not true that children with autism never play or that they all lack symbolic play. However, it is true that their play tends to be repetitive and ritualised, lacking creativity or invention, and they tend to develop obsessive interests, of which some, indeed, may develop into phenomenal savant skills. The toddler with autism cannot join in that unique kind of fanciful guessing and inventing that makes pretend play of young children such an effective way of exploring playmates' imaginations and beliefs. And this fits with the most problematic characteristic of the autistic child for a teacher; learning of ordinary culturally significant roles and tasks is an immensely difficult task. The child neither has curiosity for new meanings in what people say or do, nor does he or she respond easily to the kind of drill that helps most of us develop flexible and refined skills of action and cognition under guidance from someone who knows better – a process that Barbara Rogoff (1990) calls 'apprenticeship in thinking'.

Before School: Infants and Toddlers with Autism

Autism, especially at its beginnings, is best understood in relation to the way cooperative awareness of meanings emerges in infancy, rather than from theories about how a mature, self-motivated adult communicates, thinks and learns. It is possible to see the change that causes a child to develop autism as a catastrophic disorganisation of an infant's innate abilities to find other people as teachers. Human beings are born with a mechanism for relating to other persons and for learning with them. If the contrary assumption is made, that the infant mind is only occupied with making up concepts from solitary sensory-motor or physical experiences, and that toddlers have egocentric minds, then, all two-year-olds would seem to be autistic – unable to react to persons as persons. Then the peculiar difficulties of a two-year-old with autism are quite incomprehensible. Clearly this idea of the infant as just a rudimentary cognitive, technical or scientific being is mistaken.

Infants make obvious signs of wanting to know the world as others know it. They express an eager sense of sharable meaning with 'protolanguage' expressions and gestures, about the end of the first year. They investigate things for themselves, but they are also becoming more and more interested in inviting other persons to join in their attention to activities and to objects. At the same time, they are developing both confident displays of personality, and clever responses to the playful and dramatic pleasures that are immediately a source of fun with other persons, especially family members, with whom the babies will normally have strong affectionate attachments. One-year-olds also become more aware of the risks of misunderstanding. Some are wary of persons they do not know, and unhappy at being separated from those they do know and love. Toward the end of the second year, around 18 to 20 months, while they are developing locomotor proficiency as toddlers, most children go through a restless and anxious time, just before they start to pick up words and start to talk. Sometimes they are very contrary with other persons, and preoccupied with details of the world that seem out of place or defects. At the same time as they can be sunny and delightful actors and actresses, the rebellious autonomy and emotional turbulence of two-year-olds is legendary.

Children who will later be diagnosed as having autism may pass through the first year much like other infants, but by the end of the second year their behaviour is almost always clearly not normal. The comprehension of shared interests and the self–other awareness that were developing seem to fall away, and interests become narrow and increasingly asocial. The child is unadventurous and behind in motor milestones. If first words had been learned, they are likely to be lost. Emotions, too, are stormy and often seem inconsolable. The day loses its satisfactions, and the night loses its sleep.

Peculiar behaviours, such as hand-flapping, spinning, babbling with stereotyped rhythms, staring and smiling enigmatically to nobody, may be reduced by offering engagement with any signs that the child notices another person, or what they are doing. Gently imitating the child often helps. Protest behaviours, including screaming, threshing about and throwing, will be reduced if the child can be made less anxious, and if responses of others are supportive or protective rather than challenging. It may be possible to change unwanted habits of a young autistic child by behavioural shaping, but it is better to change the motive state that is producing the behaviour, or to remove the stimulus that is triggering it.

Doctors, health visitors and playgroup leaders must know about autism to see these changes, and parents need help to cope with the child's distressing loss of coherence and the emotional storms, while keeping affectionate support. Given the extreme sensitivity of a child with autism to stimuli that another child would hardly notice, it is often necessary to comfort and shield from hurt and fear, which requires recognising often peculiar signs of need for protection from the environment. But there is still scope for joyful interactions, once the child's motives are brought to peace.

The child will need guiding to achieve companionship with family and peers. Body play, and moving to music, stimulating pleasurable use of the body, can aid emotional equilibrium and support a more flexible aim of attention on goals for action, and help learning of communication. It can also give the child enjoyment in participating in group activity with siblings or peers. Attracting the child's curiosity and freeing his or her voluntary application from obsessional repetition are both possible if the child's partner is watchful and trying to enter the child's world. Gradually the rewards that come from the excitement of repeating movements and self-stimulation of the senses can be redirected to more imaginative creation of meanings that others can share. The task is similar to accentuating the value of joint recognition of actions in the way parents do with all infants in the second year. Enthusiasm for this sharing has slipped from the grasp of a child with autism.

Autistic toddlers do play in simple ways with dolls and toys, and this offers moments to meet the child in forms of play that gently tease the imagination. One can even make tiny dramas, and open the way to narrative games that can be reinforced by sharing the emotions they generate, in companionship. An observant parent or teacher can find poetic wonder with the child in transitory effects – which have little conventional significance, but great importance, because, after all, they are the seeds of meaning – perceiving the magic in the world close to the child, and imitating reactions to it. The value of humour in play cannot be overestimated, but it must not be allowed to escalate out of control. As with a six-month-old, gentle teasing encourages learning about motives and emotions through game play, and the child can learn to repeat pleasurable routines such as rhythmic nursery chants and body games. Bruner (1983, 1990) has described such routines as evoking and practising the earliest foundations for linguistic structures. They certainly exercise narrative forms of emotion that can be shared through 'affect attunement' (Stern, 1985).

Accenting conversational gestures and signs helps keep the child who is showing autistic withdrawal in touch with others, but standard rituals or mimicry should not be reinforced as isolated responses. Actions identified as components of interpersonal relating (intersubjectivity) and joint attention – eye-regard, pointing, waving, the gesture of giving, emotional expressions –

should be encouraged or taught, not as mechanical habits, but as elements of mutually felt communication. They should be thought of as waiting to be elicited from the child, not completely absent tricks to be learned. Teaching 'social skills' is of less lasting value than sympathetic and encouraging attention to any spontaneous expressions of motives to communicate that the child may make.

While it is important for the child's partner to respect, and encourage, any impulse the child shows for private industry and investigation, the door should also be left invitingly open for sharing in this kind of investigative pleasure and concentration. Emotions need management, not by intellectual control, but by development of mutuality in which excitements produce predictable, reliable changes in relationships and experiences, and generate their own rewards. Fitting in with social conventions of expression is essential in society, and even a child with autism can become aware of this, but over-simplified drills or exaggerated responses by instructors are likely to produce artificial behaviours and reliance on prompts or cues that interfere with free communication in a variety of contexts. If acquired behaviours are too wooden they may increase the chances of oddness in behaviour later.

Teachers and parents may have to consciously 'understand', in order to adjust to the child's needs, until they are confident about the relationship and communication so it goes smoothly. The toddler with autism, however, need not understand, or have explained to it what to do. Doing in contexts of mutual collaboration and enjoyment of experience will naturally employ the behavioural 'devices' of interaction and self–other expression. When the young child wants to share, explanations are not needed.

Pre-school

From three to four toddlers normally add to their play many imaginary roles and imagined objects, building language on a foundation of active meanings that they happily create, on their own with 'imaginary friends', or shared eagerly with peers and playful adults. They take dolls and toy animals to be psychological beings like themselves, make them show intentions and feelings, talk, and follow the talk addressed to them. Objects are granted meaningful identity and uses as the children imitate domestic or community roles and purposeful, creative uses of things. Sometimes a young pre-school child, looking like a promising school pupil, is absorbed in private logical investigation of experiences, experimenting with the ways objects can be manipulated, sensed and combined, that is, problem solving. But, he or she will always be happy to cover abstract sensory-motor 'object concepts' with fanciful 'human' significance, and will enjoy showing others.

After four, the plots of imaginative play grow very elaborate, and the collaboration with peers requires more extended negotiations, more thinking about other points of view, more practical allowance for the differences between minds. Many of the games become clever character portrayals, with intricate and protracted plots. The child is developing a consciousness of the possibilities of fictional narrative, of the obligations of characters with different kinds of relationship and different tasks, and fluent language grows rapidly in this pragmatic context.

This development of narrative creation happens at the same time as the child develops a new kind of perseverance in solving manipulative problems requiring grouping and combination of objects. It is also a time of new readiness for absorbing mathematical notions of space, quantity, number and order.

In this period a child with autism is at great risk of being left behind in a solitary world that is losing meaning, that cannot be spoken about to others, that has no middle ground between the excitements of exploring titillating sensations and the comfort of affectionate contacts and soft toys ('transitional objects'). This is a time when understanding and dedicated help is greatly needed from parents and siblings close to the child, and from playgroup or nursery teachers who attempt to bring the child into awareness of the negotiated pleasures and adventures of shared play and learning.

Emotional confusion between panic and emptiness, struggle to balance the need for comforting contact, the experience of fear at others' closeness, and discomfort in the body when it is touched, have to be treated by caregivers as problems needing therapy rather than teaching. Especially therapy that will enter the child's world and find a way of meeting and encouraging every small sign of need for company and affection, healing anxiety and the impulse to pull away. Bewildering, fractured experiences, inability to think about tasks in an integrated, strategic way, and incomprehension of the purposes and messages of others, however well-meaning these may be, have to be treated as special educational problems. The daily environment and rituals, their spatial layout and timetables, have to be made simple, obvious and predictable, for autism is a confusion of consciousness that both limits the uptake of information from the world and interferes with the making of coherent memories from which new purposes and experiences can be generated. Teaching the rudiments of academic skills requires both sensitive and well-planned work with material that has obvious uses for the child.

Unaffected peers, with their natural enthusiasm and generous unwillingness to make critical judgements, need to be guided to approach the child with autism aware that this little girl or boy needs gentle partnership and patience. The experience of being a helpful friend who is kind and cheerful will be very valuable for them, building the sympathetic atmosphere or 'ethos' of the family or playgroup.

Obviously this is a time for maximum collaboration between all who feel they can give reliable information or help, with understanding on the part of professionals for parents who live the 24 hours of every day conscious of the child's plight. Therapists who find that play sessions and kind analytic talking, or improvising musical games, have good effects on the emotions of the child and his or her orientations towards other persons should include parents in the work, and involve their perceptions and feelings. Teachers need to hear from parents the child's likes and dislikes, preoccupations and self-comforting habits, or eccentric fears; and, in return, they should share any discoveries made at playgroup or school about how to change unwanted behaviours, or open out new interests and learning.

Young children can willingly play a part in regulated regimes, and this motivation to obey when strict conditions are imposed is exploited in Applied Behaviour Analysis programmes that claim important success in mainstreaming a high proportion of children with autism after they have completed their pre-school classes. With children of three to six or seven in Lovaas pre-school classes, basic skills (e.g. sitting, attending, looking at the teacher, responding to name, matching objects) are taught in intensive 1:1 contact with the teacher in specially structured work stations. Desired responses are prompted then rewarded systematically. The teaching depends on 'functional analysis', or observation of each child's skills. Undesirable habits are targeted with training in alternative, more acceptable behaviours. Conformity to some rules and standards will be important, and may require shaping of elementary behaviours by rigorous control of contingent reinforcements – immediate pleasures, rewarding experiences, or token inducements, combined with emphatic praise, all of which can be withheld to discourage non-compliance. But this is not a fully satisfactory method for learning mutual participation, even for a pre-schooler with autism. Behaviour shaping puts the child in a receiving position that may offer security, but may also establish rigidity, and close off interest in novelty or change. It offers limited scope for companionship and development of mutual respect. Successful behaviour therapy programmes for autistic children have adapted their methods to compensate for these disadvantages. Teachers work with two children together to guide them to more independent and social behaviours, and to shared problem solving and simple academic learning. Group activities lead to transitional integrated classes where the children with autism participate in organised school activity with unaffected children.

In the TEACCH programme the aim is less on training target behaviours, and more on achieving maximum autonomy for the child in an orderly social world and its work. It begins by introducing the pre-school child with autism to a completely structured environment where there are places for every activity and scholastic task, and objects are arranged to prompt involvement in learning. Visual distractions are limited and the architecture is arranged in every detail to have obvious relation to the activities in which the child is led to participate. Each child has a learning space for 1:1 instruction and, in a shared 'transition area', the daily schedule is displayed to which children refer to find what to do next. Photo and picture-holders illustrate the schedule, and these lead, with the older children, to a written schedule and diary. From the start TEACCH seeks to strengthen each child's emerging behaviours and skills identified by the Psycho-Educational Profile. The great strengths of this programme are the progression towards vocational training for adolescents and integration in a state-wide lifespan system of education and social services.

The Daily Life Therapy of the Higashi school imposes a regime based on Japanese values of conformity to family and community, so it believes in reducing autonomy or individual enterprise. It has success in stabilising the emotions and sense of bodily well-being of young children with autism by physical activity in a group – jogging, exercising to music, training in basic postures. Control of the body, combined with rituals of self-care, aids social interaction and self-esteem. Intellectual stimulation is provided by repetitious group instruction in academic tasks and social behaviours, with explicit transition between tasks by instructions spoken by the children in unison. The emphasis is clearly on communal participation.

In marked contrast, the Son-Rise programme of the Option Institute, puts each individual child in control and, in an intensive training, instructs parents in observation and self-analysis so that they can learn how to foster the child's pleasure in learning and every initiative to interact, by meeting the child's autism, imitating and modelling positive behaviours. Parents are advised to make a playroom in their home with an observation window, in which the pre-school child with autism spends almost all his or her waking hours, in the company of the parents or paid or volunteer helpers who have been trained in the ways to respond supportively to the child. This is continued for, on average, three years, before the child is expected to move into mainstream school.

It is fascinating that such diverse philosophies appear to lead to methods that all have beneficial effects on at least some pre-school children with autism. Evidently the motives of young children, even those with severe autism, are adapted to learn from a variety of human interventions. It also seems that the principles of good education for these young children resemble those that produce the most desirable results for children generally. They can be compared with the quality early childhood education methods that the Hi-Scope project have applied with such success to help children from socially disadvantaged families avoid the pitfalls of social failure throughout their subsequent lives (Weikert *et al.*, 1970, 1978; Schweinhart and Weikert, 1980; Berrueta-Clement *et al.*, 1984). They also recall the much admired methods of early education developed by Lorin Malaguzzi in Regio Emilia (Edwards *et al.*, 1993). In this prosperous Italian town young children demonstrate exuberant creativity and incidental learning in sustained relationships and in the community, identifying with its traditions and cultural celebrations. 'Good practice' rules even resemble closely the principles enunciated about 350 years ago by Jan Amos Comenius, who, in *The School of Infancy*, famously said, '...the roots of all sciences and arts in every instance arise as early as in the tender age, and that on these foundations it is neither impossible nor difficult for the whole superstructure to be laid; provided always that we act reasonably as with a reasonable creature' (Quick, 1910, pp.144–145). Evidently young children with autism have a degree of reasonableness, too. Adapting to the child means respect and interest for the child's experience.

Primary or Elementary School

The important changes described above in the communicative abilities of infants and young children at certain ages affect their understanding of the world and the sharing of meaning with other people. These developments are linked with changes of the children's personalities and self-confidence in relation to both peers and adults. There are 'critical periods' in which motives and emotions become more active and variable, and these seem, as a rule, to be followed by developmental advances, but also to be times of increased vulnerability for some children to illness or developmental problems. Less is known about such inner motivational changes of these kinds in school-age children, but it is clear that between five and puberty at 11 to 13, there are important differences.

Around eight, most children become rationally and practically 'responsible' or independent – anthropologists have reported that this is true in cultures with very different technologies and beliefs. In our world, the second half of primary school or elementary school is the time in which most children have settled into formal classroom instruction in academic subjects, and are acquiring many useful skills in language, especially reading and writing, and in mathematics and reasoning. In a mutually supportive community, they are also socially knowledgeable and enjoy a wide variety of environments and contacts with other people. Most are able to undertake many responsible jobs if they are required to do so. A curriculum of primary or elementary school in which learning flourishes is one fabricated around these potentialities for learning of the majority of children as they go through developmental changes. It is not that the children are moulded by an externally and arbitrarily determined schedule or curriculum.

School-age children with autism are both intellectually and, above all, socially at a disadvantage in their school work, as well as with other children outside school. They cannot meet the demands of a standard curriculum. The abnormal inner regulations of developments in their cognitive and communicative abilities mean that teachers and parents have to find both simpler arrangements for the children's environment and more stable routines, and special, more intimate and more reactive ways of eliciting their interest and cooperation in any tasks. Many children with autism do not master language, and most will require special placement in a regime that progressively builds ways to overcome their behavioural handicaps and their difficulties in relating to and communicating with other persons. As Marion Sigman and Lisa Capps emphasise, there is a need for research on the developmental changes of autistic children, on their relationship to normal developments, and on how they will affect responses to therapy and education at different ages (Sigman and Capps, 1997).

If a child with autism and his or her parents have been given intensive and responsive support over the time from the first signs of the condition at the end of infancy through pre-school, then there is a good chance that the child will be able to cooperate and learn in mainstream school with unaffected children, at least for some of the school day and with supervision and remedial instruction by a specialist teacher. Other autistic children will not progress as far and will need to be kept closely under a specially adapted tuition, continuing the behavioural training and the small group interactions with a therapist/teacher in the organised environment of a specialised unit, much as for the pre-school-aged child, with many aids to help communication. As was true then, the key to successful learning will reside in the teacher's ability to satisfy the child's motives for affectionate contacts and consistent relationships, first directly between teacher and child, then also by managing a good community among children with different abilities learning together. Academic learning is built within this interpersonal foundation.

We have seen that successful special therapies or educational practices developed in the US and Japan satisfy these needs by different routes – Lovaas emphasises behavioural shaping by regulating communication prompts and reinforcements that ideally meet the individual child's preferences, controlling the development of useful skills and communications and eliminating undesirable habits; the TEACCH method organises the environment so it becomes highly predictable and gives regulated visual and oral cues to daily routines in a programme matched to each child's needs and abilities, as determined by regular assessments of psychological functions and behavioural abilities; Higashi gives the child vigorous collective physical activity in a team, regulates behaviour and fosters cooperation in the group, inculcating habits identified with cultural norms; the Option Institute, having set up a foundation of positive behaviours by intensive education of the parents' understanding of the child's initiatives and expressions of emotion, and by strict limitation of environmental circumstances to give maximum opportunity for the child to orient towards and accept other persons' reactions, believes that in most cases integration will be possible in mainstream school.

A commendable trend in the US, in states where provision is well-supported, is for staff with different kinds of training to work as a team together, applying clinical knowledge, therapy and special educational practices cooperatively, adapting them to each child's assessed needs. But provision, the best of which is private and expensive, is usually segregated and varies greatly in availability and quality in different states. In the UK there is more provision for integration in mainstream schools, which are reliant on special assistance from personnel who have been trained in a variety of different professions to work separately on therapy or education with children with autism. The methods, often based on the idea of progressive 'developmental' teaching of basic skills, are less cooperative or integrated (Knott, 1995). In France, Italy and Spain there is a strong concentration of services for autistic children around medical assessment and treatment centres attached to hospitals, but in many places the American educational methods are being promoted; there are examples of excellent integration of clinical, educational and social services for children with autism, and for their families.

In attempting to fit the child with autism to the conventions of formal schooling, mistakes are made if the standard curriculum, planned for children with easy social and language skills, stable emotions and normal intellectual and motor abilities, is taken as a necessary goal, or if the child is measured against this impossible scholastic standard and identified as irredeemably handicapped by emotional and behaviour problems or lacking motivation. Nor is it possible by a strict behaviour-shaping regime to enforce any lasting change in learning and communication that the child will be able to adapt to different persons and situations. Each child's interpersonal and cognitive difficulties have to be engaged with, and a progressive line of experience established in a dependable environment with willing and sympathetic support from known social companions of all ages, all of whom attempt to know what the child understands and responds to. The question that has to be addressed is, 'What it is like to be that child with autism?'. Changes in cognitive and rational abilities and the development of practical skills will, in every case, depend upon success in overcoming the child's social confusion, misunderstandings in communication and the emotions of frustration and fear.

Given that mutual confidence has been gained, even a profoundly affected child with autism can learn by imitating and being imitated, and by experiences of objects and situations shared with a receptive but unintrusive teacher or friend. Children with autism do not need to be taught isolated pieces of communication behaviour, such as to seek eye contact, to imitate, or to perceive or express categories of emotion. However, as they grow up and appear more mature, it will become necessary for them to learn how to use prompts and routine responses so they can act appropriately in social interactions – so they will understand better what other people mean when they behave as they do, and so they themselves will not act in inappropriately intrusive or offensive ways. The important thing to remember is that for all children, including even those with developmental problems that affect their social awareness, all learning begins in spontaneous close interpersonal encounters. Even a child who is gifted for school learning needs to begin by sharing 'human sense' of the world – independence in learning is an achievement build on confidence in the social relevance of things (Donaldson, 1978). Children with autism need special help in keeping the bridge to others intact. Abilities that the child may have to observe and experiment with physical tasks will have to be guided from inflexible repetitive paths to those that are more constructive, goal-directed and useful.

In some UK schools, teaching children with autism puts emphasis on social skills training, and practice is given in recognising and understanding emotions and in making appropriate expressions of feeling. This teaching is aided, in the 'structured teaching' approach of the TEACCH institute, by use of photographs or videos that demonstrate clearly the forms and uses of different communicative behaviours. However, autism does not prevent a child from showing spontaneous awareness of emotions and positive expressions to other persons, provided interactions with the child are sensitive to his or her signs of consciousness of what a partner is feeling and doing (Jordan and Powell, 1995). It is perhaps helpful to view this sensitivity as comparable to that of a young infant responding in protoconversation or in a game. But a school-age child with autism is not an infant – and do we not all retain powerful intuitive reactions to other persons, however sophisticated our rational understanding of social roles has become? The autistic child will have learned tricks of communication and favourite activities that other persons have noticed and greeted with approval. The task of a teacher or parent is to keep these and the learning of new habits as open and cooperative as possible, and to make it unnecessary for the child to lapse into uncontrolled displays of annoyance, panic or confusion. Isolation from company is the main reason why children with autism or Asperger's syndrome develop self-stimulatory and avoidant mannerisms, or stereotyped motor displays that cut them off from the world of other persons.

Language is beyond very many children with autism, and the importance of speech and reading in school leads to this being treated as a matter of primary concern. Speech therapy has a significant place in special education for children with autism. However, direct attention to the skills of comprehending speech, speaking and reading may not be the most effective response (Jordan, 1993). The highest possible level of these skills is achieved through practice of non-verbal expressive behaviours and systematic encouragement of the child's responses to the whole of other persons' behaviour, to the motives behind them. This means that the social 'pragmatics', or interpersonal and situation-related uses of language, must be kept as clear to the child as possible, and every sign of willingness on the part of the child to cooperate in joint understanding of games, tasks, activities and situations must be encouraged with pleasure and appreciation. Other persons' messages, and the child's own purposes, can be communicated with the aid of pictures or photographs, by augmenting language with gestures or music, or offering training in alternative sign languages.

Children with autism often echo what they have heard, which may seem to make nonsense, as when they echo another's use of second person pronouns or repeat questions. They may give literal and uninformative answers to rhetorical questions. Their prosody or vocal inflections often betray their incomprehension of their role as an expressive speaker. But, odd and echolalic speech, and even bizarre gestures and actions, will usually have some communicative purpose for the child, which an observant parent or teacher can pick up and turn to good use in aiding or instructing. Some children learn grammar and the meanings of commands and questions with specially programmed computer games, and others read more easily than they speak. A different benefit is gained from use of music or poetic recitals to engage the child's pleasure in the rhythms and rhymes or repetitions and turn-taking cycles of assertion and acceptance that underlie all expressive communication. Shared interactive communication with a skilled music therapist can greatly aid a more handicapped child to speak more intelligibly and enjoy language in interaction.

In class, able children with autism, who speak and clearly do understand language, need care that they are not confused by more sophisticated metaphorical or ironic forms of speech, or courteous evasions, that normal children easily comprehend (Jordan and Powell, 1995). The teacher of autistic children must not talk 'over their heads', and should watch out for autistic imitation of didactic classroom talk or 'teacherese'. For the less able children speech will have to be kept simple and clear, with generous use of posture, gesture and expression to support its meanings. Review of video records of teacher–pupil interactions may be very useful in helping the teacher become aware of ways of communicating that gain positive responses from a child with autism, and how to avoid orienting, speaking and gesturing in ways that cause the child to avoid or lose touch. The Option trainers find that both observation of trained facilitators interacting with their child and review of videos can help parents.

The development of thinking, processing information and independent problem solving continue to be the focus of much attention in psychology, and they are naturally given great importance in educational theory. For children with autism the main problem is not just with cognitive mastery of reality, and learning how to resolve questions related to the behaviour of objects, or the rules of thinking embodied in mathematics. They are not just mentally handicapped by having reduced intelligence and cognition. However, they do fail to develop systematic problem-solving strategies, called executive functioning, and this impairs their ability to apply their sometimes relatively highly developed intuitive spatial and mathematical skills. They need special guidance in developing problem-solving habits, or 'tools' of reasoning, in thinking about the purpose of what they may be doing.

Nor are children with autism just lacking cognitive grasp of other persons' behaviour and a concept of themselves as like other persons. There is no evidence that the motivational problems of children with autism are *consequences* of failure to understand, rationally or verbally, how others feel and think. School children with autism are handicapped in the immediate or intuitive grasp of cooperative motives and conventions of communication between themselves and other persons, all of which we expect children of their age to know, and what is going on in the everyday world of work and news is beyond them. Their problem is at the core of motivation, where cognition, affect and social awareness meet.

Before school, infants and children with autism show a characteristic kind of detached fascination with items of their own experience. They often seem to prefer to amuse themselves in play with clothes, toys or household objects, especially electrical or electronic machines and tools that they can activate themselves, rather than join in interpersonal play, where they have to reciprocate the lively expressions and jokes of a partner. Some later turn a repeated private obsession into an astonishing special ability in one narrow area of rote memory and thinking or performance. But there are always difficulties in finding the right memory to fit the present situation, as is reported by both Donna Williams (1995, 1996) and Temple Grandin (1995, 1997). These two gifted individuals attest the need for artificial prompts to help them make useful sense of the vividly recalled but fragmentary images of their rich and specialised experiences, in language or methods in animal husbandry, respectively. This is why children with autism need exceptional consistency of situations and relationships to be able to function confidently and learn in school.

Because they experience the world and themselves in fragments and have difficulty connecting items and events into a continuous personal story or train of reasoning, children and adults with autism are said to have a specific loss in 'episodic autobiographical memory', as well as in 'executive functioning'. They are not unimaginative, but their imaginations tend to be focused, practical and 'short-term', with limited reflection on the purposes of activity, or on friendships and fun. A self-image and awareness of behavioural and social episodes requires both sensitivity for personal motives and a coherent memory record. The neurological disorder that causes autistic behaviour profoundly affects the inner creation and emotional regulation of purposes and their conscious control, the perception of and reaction to other persons' expressions of motives and emotions, and the remembering of what was done and by whom. Thus children with autism may recall things and incidents after a school or family outing, but not where and why they went and what happened (Jordan and Powell, 1995). These problems can be aided if they have reminders in the form of photographs, mementoes and discussions to make the story of the whole event more coherent. Again, a computer program can give practice in making sequences of ideas and memories, as well as providing relief from the incomprehension of an interrogator who has not perceived the child's difficulties. All isolating activities will need to be compensated by gentle intervention from adult helpers who can both facilitate independent initiatives, and keep the child in touch to communicate and cooperate about what he or she is doing so it makes more real-life sense.

Special needs of some primary school children with autism may include, besides specific problems with spoken language and/or reading, difficulties with hyperactivity, motor disorganisation and distracting motor automatisms. These can be brought under control by speech therapy, by music therapy, by alternative methods of movement therapy, by physical or occupational therapy, and by group physical exercise and rough-and-tumble games that help calm anxieties and build coordination. These therapy methods can be applied systematically, and in combination, to provide sensitive assessment of each child's strengths and weaknesses and special needs. It is important in relation to one-to-one teaching, and for parents, that the child's interactants learn to detect when odd movements are a form of communication that may signal pain, anxiety or frustration that will respond immediately to appropriate help. It is not always effective to attempt to change or eradicate such behaviours just by conditioning or aversive training.

Secondary or High School: Adolescence and Preparation for Adult Life

The age-related steps in socio-emotional development and cooperative cultural learning that can be seen to pattern educational needs in the pre-adolescent years are succeeded by a time when, in spite of physical development, much greater knowledge and wider social independence, children seem to return to motive states that, in some ways, resemble those of young children. These are not just changes in temperament and reactions to parents and friends. They also affect willingness and ability to learn. They have effects on the appropriate educational curriculum.

For example, second, non-maternal, languages are acquired from various sources, depending on feelings in new relationships, and also on developments in perception and learning. The ability to acquire fluency and accurate pronunciation in a second language and developments in recognition of individuals from their face or voice suggest that adolescence is a second period of enhanced brain plasticity, or of motivation for finding significant social partners and adaptation to new conventions of communication (Trevarthen, 1998c). Facial recognition, voice recognition and tonal memory mature about 7–9 years, then there is a dip in this ability at puberty, between 11–15, and a second period of enhanced ability for a few years after that. The distinctive intonation of a foreign language is learned best by a child between seven and eight and significantly worse at 11 to 12. The expressive arts, including music and dance, are also more easily learned before puberty. Differences in young people's aptitude for different crafts, professions and social roles become clear in secondary or high school.

Adolescents develop conceptual thinking, and grasp abstractions or principles of logic, in contrast to ordinary realistic sense, much more easily than younger children. They are open to learning the specialised symbolic and technical systems or 'toolkit' of thinking of their culture (Bruner, 1996). They also like to argue, often interminably, about possibilities and impossibilities, manners and beliefs, and they enjoy imagining quasi-impossible worlds inhabited by persons whose ideas and thoughts fascinate them. In learning tasks and practical skills they are aware of the meaning these have in relation to the way their community and its culture views work and play. They have become 'apprentices' in the conventional activities of their people (Rogoff, 1990), but they have to balance their wish to be independent and adventurous with increasing awareness of the need to conform to the roles and routines of society (Sigman and Capps, 1997).

Sexual maturity leads to a change in the motives for friendship and relationships, with curiosity about the opposite sex and concern for self-presentation and fashionable dress and behaviour. Many subtle skills are mastered to regulate the making and breaking of friendships, both with peers of the same sex and in romantic relationships with the other sex. Mixed groups of friends develop strong bonds and rivalries. Views of social roles are also moulded by identification with socially successful personalities, or persons famous for particular excellence in some cultural role. Failure in developing self-confidence in relation to these new challenges, or in reaching levels of attainment judged to be important by peers or elders, can lead either to depression or to angry rebellion.

These changes at adolescence generate a second crisis in development of young persons with autism. As with the changes that bring on autism in the pre-school period, there is an increase in confusion about how to relate with others and a decline in cognitive functions as well. Adolescents with autism suffer from bewildering disturbances in hormonal and neurochemical regulations as they become sexually mature, and these increase the problems they have in relating to their peers, and in learning conventional means of making and managing friendships. A further consequence is that the adolescent's sense of having an individual and confident personality, already weakened by impaired regulation of experience and recall of socially significant events, is threatened. He or she cannot define feelings in relation to the approval or disapproval of others, and may express a sense of naive and bewildered hurt when unable to act in ways expected by admired others.

Standard emotional reactions can be learned and their expressions recognised in formal learning situations using behavioural shaping methods or prompts in the form of picture cards, but these out-of-context experiences may not transfer spontaneously to everyday situations. A few children with autism or

Asperger's syndrome may show a special ability for learning the vocabulary of language, including foreign languages, but this will not be matched by comprehension of the social and idiomatic uses of speech and the sense of fictional socio-dramatic narratives. Their utterances are likely to be pedantic, monotonous or with unusual stress. Their spoken or written reasoning may be superficially brilliant, but lacking coherence and a clear practical conclusion. In the more gifted, this unusual way of thought may lead to original and challenging philosophical enquiry.

Children with Kanner's autism come to adolescence after many years of specialist care. If they were fortunate, their special needs were identified by the age of three, and provided for in pre-school. The problems of young persons with Asperger's syndrome, however, are very unlikely to have been identified in primary school, and the needs of many will never be recognised. They will become rather isolated, socially odd adults. Fortunate ones will have affectionate marriages with understanding partners. The focused intellectual and technical abilities of some may gain them respected and well-paid jobs.

'High-functioning' children with autism and those with Asperger's syndrome are characteristically awkward with their peers, because of their difficulties with emotional responses and social interactions. They will probably continue to be isolated as they were in the playground at primary school. They can be helped by teaching in social skills and general rules for how to join friends in a conversational group or a game, while avoiding too abrupt or too intimate approaches to others. If they can form relationships with understanding peers, this will help them gain independence from parental and teacher support, and open new chances for learning. Training that increases understanding of their own emotions, and those expressed by other people, will help them give evaluations to experiences and thinking, and emotional appraisals make the meanings of thoughts communicable, and connectable.

Inability to relate to others makes difficult the development of self-esteem and the experience of oneself as someone distinctive who experiences life as a coherent and purposeful existence of that person. An isolated person who does not have such an image of him or herself, who lacks confidence, is more likely to fall into bizarre behaviours that may cause others to keep away. The curriculum of special education for such a young person should include deliberate instruction in self-awareness and memory of the self as a purposeful actor – that is, in learning how to think with 'subjectivity' and an 'autobiographical memory' (Jordan and Powell, 1995). Volunteer peer companions who take adolescents with autism or Asperger's syndrome on outings and to play sports can help break the social barriers and give interest to new experiences and learning, and this can become a mutually rewarding experience.

Sigman and Capps (1997) review a number of revealing studies of the dilemmas and obstacles that adolescents with autism have in their social life, and their often desperate attempts to understand or to get help with situations they cannot grasp. Such young people are more likely to want to have social contacts than they were when younger, but they still lack understanding of how other people feel and cannot anticipate the effects of their own behaviour. They are consequently more dependent on persons in the family or residential school who know them well, and whom they can trust to provide compensatory understanding. Those adolescents and young adults with autism who do develop insight into why others find them odd have the best success in making adjustments.

The most highly developed programme for education of young adults with autism is that of TEACCH in North Carolina, which, in consultation with educational institutions and adult services, is aimed to confer independence of guidance from other persons within a structured situation. It relies on a comprehensive network of state-supported services. Older pupils are evaluated on the Adolescent and Adult Psycho-Educational Profile and trained in interpersonal and work skills in routines to be practised in the home or the community. An environment is created in which young people with autism and Asperger's syndrome can function through their life. The Institute runs a Living and Learning farm and manages competitive jobs, and local businesses cooperate in offering employment opportunities.

Institutions following the Lovaas method for autism include, in some cases, academic and pre-vocational training for young people from 11 to 21 leading to unpaid work in the community with supervision of trained staff. Many private institutions catering for children with autism and Asperger's syndrome offer consultation for parents needing help with older children. There is little provision for young adults with autism in the UK educational system, and this is a worrying situation for parents of children of secondary school age with autism, who may have nowhere to go but home after they are 16.

Autism has only been reliably classified in medical services in the past 20 years, and most cases are diagnosed in early childhood. Consequently, most individuals identified as autistic are now between around 18 months of age, the earliest at which reliable diagnosis is currently achieved, and 20 years. However, most children identified with autism are between 5 and 10 years of age. Asperger's syndrome is much more difficult to recognise in early childhood, and a majority with this condition will not have been identified before adolescence, and even then a large proportion will miss diagnosis completely. But, autism and Asperger's syndrome are, with possible rare exceptions, lifelong disorders. There will be many autistic individuals aged over 20 who are currently not appropriately diagnosed, and the more seriously affected of these are probably in the care of adult psychiatric and learning disability services, and not receiving the most appropriate care.

Now, however, recognition is being given to the fate of young people with autistic spectrum disorders as they pass from adolescence to adulthood (Attwood, 1997; Howlin, 1997; Sigman and Capps, 1997), and the specific needs of affected adults are also being addressed (Morgan, 1996). Appreciation of their experiences and beliefs, and how they perceive their difference from 'non-autistic' persons has been aided by the stimulating autobiographies of Williams (1992, 1996) and Grandin (1995). It can be hoped that as experience of how autism persists through to adulthood is shared, a change in mental health service provision, therapy and training will reflect our increasing ability to identify young children who have developed autism, and persuade governments of the human and economic advantages of early and sustained education that meets their needs.

Statutory Provision, and Access to Education

Policies for the education of children with severe mental handicaps, including autism, has been transformed over the past 25 years (Stow and Self, 1989). New laws code the belief that all children have a right to the kind of teaching that will enable them to attain their full potentiality for an autonomous life in society. Even the most handicapped are seen to have a right to free membership in the community, and the potential to gain from a place linked to the main stream of education, provided their special needs are understood and supported.

In the UK a fundamental change took place in 1970, from the idea that low intelligence rendered children ineducable so they had to be cared for by the local health authority, to a legally enforced provision for their needs by local educational authorities. At the same time, while it was realised that medical categories of handicap were not the best guide to appropriate education, fears grew that the resource demands of special segregated education were getting out of hand. The Warnock Report of 1978 abolished classification by handicapping condition and replaced this by a definition of Special Educational Needs that identified the strengths and weaknesses of a child in terms of 'mild', 'moderate' and 'severe learning difficulties' (DES, 1978). Statutory educational resources were to be targeted at the more numerous children with mild to moderate needs, especially in respect of language instruction. Before the Warnock Report, the emphasis was on diagnosis of the *cause* of the condition, rather than prescription of the *remedy*. Afterwards, as medical models were replaced by social models, the fault was perceived to be not in the child, but in the child's relation to the physical environment or other persons. At present it is increasingly recognised that perception of each child's needs must be based on reliable psychological, medical and educational research into the special problems that handicapped child has in responding to education. This is particularly important for a child with autism, or any related condition that impairs motivation for learning by communicating.

The 1981 Education Act defined a distinction between 'special educational needs' and 'learning difficulties'. Integration in mainstream schools was recommended, provided the child could receive the required special education that was compatible with the education of the other children and efficient in use of resources. Local Educational Authorities were empowered to initiate assessment or to respond to a request by parents. If a child is found to need special provision, a Statement of Needs, or a Record of Needs, is made. In 1987 a government Select Committee reported that, in addition to an insufficiency of resources, not all parents were receiving adequate information, and while integration was beneficial to many children, special schools were still necessary for the more severely handicapped. Moreover, it was felt that needs were being defined in too academic a manner, overlooking important emotional and social problems that required assistance from the social services. The Fish Report of 1985 recommended, once again, that handicaps should not be seen as permanent, and suggested that labelling handicaps, and assessment by a narrow range of standardised IQ tests had created problems. Curriculum-related assessment, establishing a criterion of reference, should enable setting of predetermined learning objectives, and 'ineducable' should no longer be accepted as a legal category.

In the US, over the same two decades, federal legislation has produced a series of Public Laws that require states to provide free public education for children with autism from pre-school ages. However, available services vary widely between states. The trend has been to provide individualised education based on multiprofessional assessment of each child's needs, which are to be met by appropriate teaching that will help the child up a 'learning ladder'.

The idea of 'normalisation' of the lives of handicapped persons by admitting them to life in the community, developed in Scandinavia in the post-war period, led in the US to the 1975 Integration Law and an attempt to 'mainstream' as many children as possible, on the understanding that all with disabilities have a right to a share in the life of the community. The effects of this concept were seen in the UK by 1980. It was recognised that children with autism or Asperger's syndrome benefit from mixing with other children, and teachers were encouraged to expect behaviour and attainment to be as normal as possible. Special schools should be retained as a resource for the more handicapped, but should not offer merely containment. In the 1980s in the UK it was found that off-loading disruptive adolescent pupils in special units could produce harmful effects and fail to benefit their education, and addressing this requires attention to the role of parents (Tattum, 1982; Topping, 1983, 1986).

For more severely handicapped children with autism and Asperger's syndrome, special schools for children with moderate to severe learning difficulties, which may offer 24-hour residential care, will be appropriate. Less affected children, and those with a better history of education and therapy, will be well taught in specialist units attached to mainstream schools, with opportunity for different degrees of access to mainstream classes. Integration by allowing children with autism to have some of their lessons and recreation with mainstream classes, and reverse integration where mainstream children come to the special unit, bring benefits of company and stimulation without loss of specialist support. All affected children will need introduction to formal learning of academic subjects alongside training in self-help, autonomous living and social skills. The child or adolescent with autism may require behavioural training to control inappropriate actions that may be an offence to others, and protection of themselves from hurt or abuse. Even the best conceived services will fail in their objectives to bring children to maximum realisation of their social and intellectual potentialities if all aspects of the condition of autism are not met within an integrated multidisciplinary programme. Achieving this is mainly a matter of providing adequate training to key staff who can establish a high level of understanding throughout the system.

Charting Individual Needs, Monitoring Progress

The questionnaires, observation instruments and tests we discuss in Chapter 2 and list in Appendix 2 are designed to identify specific psychological difficulties of children with autism, and to give a profile of strengths and weaknesses to guide therapy or education. In the UK results of such tests by a clinical or educational psychologist of the local authority, or professional assessment of the child in a specialist unit operated by a charity, form the basis for a statementing or recording that will require the local authority by law to offer appropriate special education. In the US private organisations offer multidisciplinary assessment, monitoring and counselling for those who can afford it, or who can gain financial aid from the state.

An accurate assessment will dispel uncertainty and give helpful encouragement to a caregiver or teacher. On the other hand, assessment and advice from an expert, or any system of therapy or training, even one known to be effective and based on scientifically established principles, should not be offered in such a way that it reduces the confidence or decreases the understanding of persons who will be responsible for day-to-day communication and care of the child, or for long-term teaching. Test performance scores are necessary for diagnosis and follow-up, but can be no substitute for the experiences of one-to-one interaction with the child. Expert awareness of autism must include knowledge of the ways different children adapt to regimes they have become used to. The contrasting views of medical, psychological and educational approaches to children with autism and Asperger's syndrome, and new advances in scientific understanding of the causes of their problems, need to be reconciled so that comprehensive and balanced advice is transmitted to those who need it. This is why a multi-specialist team is likely to give the best help.

Assessment of the precise ways that an autistic child moves, handles objects and accepts or rejects contact in a standard environment can help a caregiver or teacher know the kinds of joint activity that will be most acceptable and encouraging to the child. Record keeping and systematic reviews are essential in the training of parents and special education teachers in their efforts to find the supportive behaviour that works best with the individual child. Photos and review of video recordings can give valuable additional insight into the child's idiosyncrasies and psychological difficulties. Speech therapy and music therapy can also easily be made into audio records or written scores that can be analysed to obtain greater appreciation of an autistic child's specific preferences, emotional needs and difficulties with communication.

Teacher-Training and Educational Services

Children with autism need special care from pre-school ages. Diagnosis as early as possible is important to make sure that the most appropriate available therapy and teaching is given to the child when it will have the most benefit. Early intervention needs to be regular, in partnership with families, who have to be clear about its value, and continuous, acknowledging that the interruptions of the school year may limit the effects of treatment.

It is generally true that teachers of pre-school children need more, not less, awareness of the full range of factors and processes of child learning, in comparison with those who are responsible for older primary and secondary school children who learn in increasingly formal classroom settings. The peculiar characteristics of autistic children make understanding of the socio-emotional factors in early learning even more important, and this will continue to be the case for these individuals to adult life. Teachers of autistic children need, therefore, thorough training both in general principles of early child development, including the interpersonal aspects that recent research has brought to the fore, and in the special techniques for improving communication with autistic children. Autistic children cannot be adequately treated under non-specific Special Education for children of lower than normal intelligence. They are not simply mentally handicapped, and their learning difficulties are very different from, say, children with Down's syndrome. Persons responsible for teaching autistic children need training that pays special attention to the relationship between cognitive or intellectual development, skills learning and communication and the emotional regulation of personal relationships (Jordan and Powell, 1995; Sigman and Capps, 1997).

The most effective provision for children up to seven or eight years old is a broad specialist programme with input from professionals with a variety of expertise in a unit attached to a mainstream school, after which the child can be moved to another form of provision. In any transfer, the importance of continuity of relationships and environment for the maintenance of gains in learning for autistic children should be recognised. The most difficult problems concern the more than half of autistic children at the lower end of intellectual and linguistic ability, who will require long-term care in a special school.

It appears that little or no special training in care and teaching of autistic children is at present available for teachers in many areas of the UK. It would not be difficult, and would be economically sound, for modules on autism, and other developmental conditions affecting children's communication and learning, to be incorporated in general courses on child development for teachers, nursery nurses and auxiliary and volunteer workers. However, it will remain necessary to establish specialist posts to monitor services and teacher training as well as to aid parents through regular workshops. In the US, private organisations, including those using Lovaas' Applied Behaviour Analysis, Division TEACCH at the University of North Carolina, the Higashi School in Boston and the Option Institute, all maintain close links with parents, involving them in the recommended method. In the UK, the Home Based Teaching Project of the Maudsley Hospital in South London is an outreach service that guides parents and other family members in establishing conditions that are favourable for the autistic child, helping language learning and social development and reducing behavioural problems (Howlin and Rutter, 1987; Howlin and Yates, 1989). To improve services to parents in all communities, local authorities will need to take the lead in establishing effective lines of communication between various specialists in educational psychology, medical diagnosis and therapy, and making sure that parents are informed of how they may obtain appropriate help.

The situation of provision for children in Scotland with autism recently reported by Jordan and Jones (1997) is probably representative in main features for the UK in general. While some educational services were found to be well-informed about how to recognise autism and Asperger's syndrome, and the special needs of these children, parents felt that in many educational authorities and schools there was insufficient knowledge, often with a lack of realisation of the advantages of identification of autistic spectrum disorders as a particular group requiring specialist knowledge for determination of appropriate therapy and education. Many parents reported that the best assistance was coming from voluntary agencies. Cooperation between parents, schools and educational authorities varies. The authors of this report recommended: comprehensive, well-informed efforts at early diagnosis with admission to special units at pre-school level attached to mainstream nursery schools; a broad curriculum; professional development courses for specialist training; outreach support from specialist units placed to serve both centres of dense population and isolated rural areas; collaboration between schools run by voluntary agencies and mainstream schools to give the latter targeted training and support; and, above all, efficient dissemination of information to parents and services about the needs of children with autism and Asperger's syndrome. They recorded the advantages to both sides of inviting mainstream children into special schools or units for some activities, and the reciprocal benefits of having units attached to mainstream schools. Structural and administrative reorganisations were found to create uneven criteria for admission to specialist units and levels of care, and to be disruptive of teachers' efforts to set up the kind of services that they believed were desirable. There is concern for the relatively low numbers of adolescents receiving special education, and for the absence of provision for adults who still require protection, monitoring and supervised occupations.

Parental Action (see Appendix 3 for Internet sources)

Because an autistic child needs to be treated with carefully measured and conscious attention to their responses, which is a demanding and often frustrating task, parents, particularly, need both advice and forms of relief. It is important for them to have ready access to organisations to which they can turn to receive information and help, and that there is provision for care of the child outside the home by experienced persons from time to time. Parent self-help organisations which can disseminate knowledge, pool experiences and lobby for services are of great importance for such a difficult and rare problem of child care. They can also help parents deal with the clinical, social and educational authorities to obtain their legally established rights to state and local authority aid.

Parents of autistic children have, in the UK and overseas, set up mutual assistance and information-collecting groups or fora. Local and National Autistic Associations function in this way, and as effective pressure groups for promotion of the perceived needs of parents and their children with autism. It is also helpful if a similar coordination is organised among the professions who assume responsibility for different aspects of the care of autistic children. A regular Survey of Need is essential, to ascertain to what extent parents in different regions and in different socio-economic groups all have good access to the services and information that are available.

Autism is so rare that there will be few children with autism in any local community, unless they have been brought together in a special school from a large population. This means that most parents of an autistic child will probably, at first, never have seen one before and none of their family or friends are likely to have helpful experience. This argues for central integration of knowledge and skills specific to autism and Asperger's syndrome in centres of high population, and dissemination of information and assistance by an outreach service to those who need it. Teachers in small school districts, will require support from visiting specialist teachers, and children who are most affected may have to move to residential schools distant from their homes. On the other hand, the benefits of integration support the conclusion that for most children, the best solution will be a place in a specialist day unit linked to a mainstream school that offers periodic integration with other children, or reverse-integration visits to the specialist unit from mainstream classes. Parents can play an important part in less formal teaching in mixed groups of children, and can benefit emotionally from this and from sharing experiences and knowledge with other parents and with teachers.

Finding Appropriate Services (see Appendix 3 for Internet sources)

Children with autistic spectrum disorders occur in every country and cultural group which has been studied. Clinical, social and educational services addressing the needs of children with autism have developed in different countries with diverse policies of therapy, teaching, social support and respite care.

In the United Kingdom, available services vary widely. The lack of adequately coordinated services is being addressed as recommendations concerning the best evidence-based practice are being developed.

Resources are currently so varied, our advice to parents is simple and general:

- If you are worried that your child may be developing autism, obtain, as early as you can, a profile of your child's abilities and deficits, usually through the services of a child psychiatrist, or clinical or educational psychologist, and, if autism has been confirmed, try to have this updated on a regular basis, at least annually.

- Ensure that appropriate medical investigations of your child have been carried out, as outlined below. There are now a number of identifiable causes of autistic behaviour with implications for medical treatment and/or monitoring.

- Gather information on locally available resources, such as respite care facilities, outreach support services, specialised nurseries, after-school provisions, befriending services and parent support groups. Some of these may appear to be set up for other, more numerous, client populations, such as children with speech and language disorders, but they will usually have expertise in helping children with autism.

- Try to be constructively involved in as many as possible of the decisions which may concern the future development of your child, as in obtaining assistance from the Scottish system of Recording of Special Needs and the English Statementing process that are required to gain a child access to special education services.

- Make links with your National Autistic Society to keep informed about developments in resourcing and supports.

- Where possible, try to become involved in helping policy makers to recognise areas of unmet local need for yourselves and others who have children with autism in their care.

Liaison with Medical and Psychological Services

Because many medical problems are associated with autism, every toddler or pre-school child who is suspected to have autism should be given a detailed medical examination, with follow-up, to make sure of the following:

(1) that the child is not actually developing a different disorder (e.g. Rett's syndrome, Batten's syndrome or developmental dysphasia) that also emerges in a similar form before age three

(2) that any specific neurological disorders that are likely to lead to additional handicap, such as epilepsy or motor discoordination (ataxia), and that are commonly seen in children with autism have been checked for and accurately assessed

(3) that, when autism has been confidently diagnosed, sufficient evidence has been obtained to establish, as far as is possible, any identifiable organic basis to the condition – is there Fragile-X, tuberous sclerosis, etc.?

A thorough medical work-up helps identify medical needs that may respond to treatment, and can prevent inappropriate treatment. It may also be a guide to eventual special needs in education.

The following behavioural problems are common in children with autism, and will need special medical attention, therapy or specific behavioural training:

(1) Many children with autism fail to learn self-care skills beyond infancy. This often means that toilet training programmes will be required in nursery, pre-school, and primary school.

(2) If the child has epilepsy, staff will need to have been trained to recognise and treat fits. Children with autism require close monitoring if epileptic seizures are to be detected and appropriately treated.

(3) Motor and motor planning difficulties will respond to regular and sustained occupational therapy.

(4) Professional advice will be required for the assessment and treatment of behavioural management problems, such as excessive obsessional routines, extreme tantrums and self-injurious behaviours.

(5) Teenagers with autism will require carefully planned expert advice on sex education, pitched at their level of social understanding. In most cases this will focus on training in self-stimulatory means of gratification to discourage overtures to other children, in contrast to the more typical other-directed programmes for handicapped individuals of similar developmental level who do not suffer from autism. Mentally handicapped young adults are normally guided to

form stable relations and on how to manage intercourse. Teenagers with autism or Asperger's syndrome tend to make inappropriate sexual overtures and they fail to understand why these are rejected. This causes recurrent difficulties, especially in a residential home.

CHAPTER 14

Putting the Pieces Together

We see human nature with clearer eyes by observing and communicating with young children, sharing in the ways they play and learn. The strange detachment of children with autism teaches us something deeper. Autistic spectrum disorders, even by the widest definition, affect less than half a per cent of children, but these rare young people offer information of great value. They bring home to us in a unique way the vital importance of the human need for exchanging and negotiating feelings and ideas. They show, by their struggles to understand the world we take for granted, the contribution that intuitive sympathy makes to cultural learning.

Video programmes showing the same oddities of behaviour in children with autism and Asperger's syndrome from Greece, Japan, Africa, America, Europe and many other countries, and the results of psychological researches proving that such children have surprising similarities in intelligence and communication, cast a bright light on our common mental impulses. They help us perceive unconscious talents that we rely on for sharing thoughts and purposes. By showing that, in spite of their social handicaps, they have a capacity for guileless trust and for joining in affectionate attachments with those who care for them, children with autism underline the fundamental moral obligations of our most complex communities.

Adolescents with autism or Asperger's syndrome are sometimes described as 'lacking a conscience'. What is meant is that they are incapable of working out moral rules that depend upon a more philosophical and detached sense of justice – upon a rational analysis of the moral sense. The eighteenth-century philosopher of the Scottish Enlightenment, Adam Smith, gave a famous definition of the conscience. In his *Theory of Moral Sentiments*, he called this self-critical faculty a 'dispassionate observer' of one's behaviour and thoughts, a personality who resides within one (Smith, 1759). He founded this ability for self-criticism, not on reason, but on the innate sympathy that humans have for each other's expressive movements, as persons. It is clear that such an innate sympathy is not the product of any set of reasoned moral rules, nor of any meta cognitive theory of the workings of one's own mind, or the minds of others. By their affections and their emotional responses to the treatment they receive from others, individuals with autism certainly show this sympathy. Therefore, in spite of the difficulties they have in keeping up with the motives and purposes behind other persons' actions and expressions, people with autism are most certainly moral beings who call on our trust and sympathy. We can use our understanding to deal with their misbehaviours and shortcomings, assuming they would do differently if they could.

Different Kinds of Knowledge of Autism

At this point, we have many pieces of the puzzle of autism before us, but not the whole picture. There are many gaps. Nevertheless, we can compare and relate various explanations for the different forms of autistic disturbance in children's development, and the different ideas about how to help make autism less of a handicap for the child and for the family. This requires an attitude that tolerates the different insights of child psychiatrists, teachers, therapists, psychologists, brain scientists, geneticists and parents and other family members. Everyone who collects information on the features that define childhood autism, who follows how these features change with development of the child, and notices how they differ in different children, and especially everyone who has had success in communicating with, teaching or emotionally healing an autistic child, has something to offer. There is now so much experience from different viewpoints, and such good communication of findings, that what appeared to be rival and largely incompatible views begin to seem as if they each have part of the truth. They may have more value if brought together. The confrontations of the recent past among some psychologists, doctors, therapists, and teachers can be seen to be unproductive. At the same time, we can check out misinterpretations or fads that have not benefited autistic children, and that have led parents and teachers along fruitless paths, raising false hope of a cure, or undermining confidence in communication with an autistic child.

Research into the organic or biological causes of autism, and into its many effects on behaviour and psychological function, is revealing fascinating details about the mechanisms that give power to human emotions, and their communication. It focuses attention on how the brain normally coordinates the internal states and feelings, and how it aims movements of the body, directing consciousness here and there as we deal with the world and learn about it. We discover maps of the body in the brain that, by an imitative resonance, can recognise other persons and interpret their feelings and intentions from the ways their bodies move. Studies aimed to find which parts of the brain are defective in persons with autism locate tissues where there are abnormal nerve cell arrangements. Functional brain scans reveal abnormal concentrations of nerve net activity, or absences of activity in places that should be active.

Attention has been drawn by these findings to hitherto neglected centres in the brain where emotions and cognitions interact, confirming evidence from many other kinds of study that the core of the brain, in partnership with the endocrine mechanisms of the body, contains a crucial set of structures and chemical communications that is actively directing consciousness and purposeful actions. Created in a baby's brain before birth, these neural and hormonal systems continue, throughout life, to control our sleeping and waking, the shifting focus of attention, the unconscious automatic movements that support our wilful actions, as well as the expressions of our emotions, interests and purposes, upon which other persons rely to understand us. All these systems must be working together in dynamic balance for our own alert well-being, and also for our awareness of one another. If we are sick, depressed, tired or old there are problems in the brain/body regulators that affect consciousness and interpersonal life. If we are joyful and energetic, the whole system works in an integrated way, tackles the cognitive problems of relating with the world of objects and situations, and communicates with other people, enthusiastically and cooperatively. A boy or girl who is developing autism is losing some of this coherence. He or she is becoming confused about surrounding events, and especially about the intricate patterns of other persons' behaviour when they seek to interact and share what they are experiencing, doing and thinking.

There is tantalising information suggesting how genes may be involved in the generation of autism, producing the range of autistic spectrum conditions. Shared genes also set the conditions for emergence of related features in temperament and body chemistry, preferences for certain kinds of cognition, and difficulties in language and communication in some members of the families of individuals with autism or Asperger's syndrome. The fact that children with autism and Asperger's syndrome are more frequently boys leads to interest in evidence concerning abnormal gene activity on the X chromosomes, known as sex chromosomes, which play a part in determination of sex differences in the body and the brain. However, the story of how genes guide brain development is not at all simple, and there is little likelihood that a single gene will be found to determine autism. Nor will any combination of genes that regulate the deviant chemistry and anatomy of the brain and body in a person with autism act in development without response to the environment. It should also be pointed out that the abnormalities of psychology that characterise autism are very likely to be exaggerations of individual differences in consciousness, imagination, thinking and learning ability that have great value in the cooperative community that makes up a human culture.

All of this extraordinarily interesting information on human nature from scientific research on factors that may cause autism, when it is projected to real life situations, makes increasing sense. It fits intuition. But it has to be said that the most up-to-date knowledge of what is going wrong in the brain of a child with autism may add little to what an experienced and skilled parent, therapist or teacher has already perceived when observing the child and interacting with him or her from day to day. And this is the practical situation. Other persons and the feelings they express hold the key to a life that will be happier, less fraught with confusion and anxiety and richer in meaning for the child – provided that they have enough knowledge, experience and patience to identify with the strange changes of mood and awareness that an autistic child will present. In so far as information about what the brain is doing helps this task, well and good. Brain science is not very likely to give us a cure for autism. The best it will do is to lead to treatments that control some symptoms, in some cases.

Agreed Principles of Practice

Efforts to care for, comfort and teach children with autism come from a great variety of traditions and theories. These reflect the uncertainty we have about how to reason in a modern, scientific way about mental life, and the ways we ourselves experience other persons. It may be important to realise, when attempting to sort out what seem like conflicting approaches, that human beings naturally exhibit that variety of attitudes to reality and one another, which we mentioned above. Some of us are attracted to practical and technical solutions to problems. Some like to rationalise and verbally analyse experience. Others are more intuitive and directly emotional about life and other people. And it has to be said that some are more sympathetic to other persons, more involved with them, while others prefer to keep a formal distance, concentrating on their own affairs. It is not surprising that parents and professionals may have different preferences for interpreting a condition such as autism that opens questions about the inner motivations of all of us.

In spite of this confusion about our psychological natures, it is also true that the most effective methods for helping children with autism appear to come to similar conclusions, at least concerning fundamental needs of these children, and how they respond to regimes of intervention. The most coercive, externally and factually structured methods of teaching children with autism acknowledge the need to adjust to the individual child's motives and pace of learning, as well as the child's attachments and positive orientations to persons who give consistently sympathetic attentions. The methods that seek to enter as deeply as possible into these inner motivations and their disturbances, in a 'child-centred' way, discover that the child's motives cannot be disentangled and supported towards beneficial growth by elaborate verbal interpretations and by delving into supposed shortcomings of past relationships. There has to be a constructive and well-informed response to how the child is behaving and emotionally reacting, here and now. The educational and therapeutic methods that attempt to apply findings from diagnostic tests of intelligence or reasoning performed in the laboratory or clinic also discover that they must negotiate with the feelings the child expresses, even if these feelings cannot be explained by the clearest and most statistically significant of proofs that most autistic children have this or that abnormality in problem solving or thinking. That said, research has led to discoveries in the last 20 years concerning the strange confusions and odd understandings of children with autism, who, at first sight, seem well-coordinated and alert – especially as regards the difficulties they have in perceiving and reacting to expressions of states of mind in other persons. These discoveries concerning the effects of autism on a child's 'theory' of person's minds have helped parents and teachers match their more articulate understanding better to these children's problems in interpreting and remembering what goes on round them. Cognitive educational practice puts to good use this new insight into the errors of 'mentalising' that children with autism and Asperger's syndrome are prone to make (Jordan and Powell, 1995)

Many different ways of helping the development of young children with autism have proved successful. They reflect differences in culture and government provision of social services, as well as different traditions of medical or educational practice. There are ways to regulate over-taxed senses and uncomfortable feelings in the body, and to calm anxieties and symptoms of stress that arise from pain or sensory confusion. Physical group activity in the Higashi school promotes bodily well-being and strengthens cooperation. One-to-one behavioural shaping to target behaviours on a progressive schedule of tasks, as practised by Lovaas, can develop communication and learning while reducing undesirable activities, and has led some young children with autism into mainstream school classes. Individual or small group teaching in an environment with structured layout and visually sign-posted routines guiding towards autonomous self-care and supervised work, the method of TEACCH, has proved to bring great benefits for integration of children with autism in family and school routines, in the company of siblings and peers. It can be extended to life skills training for adolescents and adults until some, at least, achieve, with outreach support, a high degree of autonomy and regular waged work. The Option Method starts from boundless acceptance of the child's own motives and encourages identification with these motives and the child's experiences by familiar companions in a consistent environment. It gives a unique assistance for parents and other caregivers that enables them to adopt a 'child-centred' approach with confidence.

There are other kinds of method that seek to develop the learning abilities of children with autism and Asperger's syndrome by helping them with basic processes of interpersonal relating and communication. Shared enjoyment of self-expression in dance and drama, and interaction with a musician trained to support improvised creation of musical expressions and narratives in dialogue, or improvisational music therapy, can help with emotions and give a boost to learning of other ways of communicating, including language.

Every programme of intervention now recognises the great importance of beginning therapy and teaching as early as possible, preferably after expert diagnosis at the toddler stage. And all perceive the advantages of 24-hour programmes, and the obligation to inform and involve parents and other family members as closely as possible in every aspect of the work. It is clear that the full implementation of such procedures requires health, social and community organisations and services – to promote effective early diagnosis and regular assessment, and to regulate good practice in care, treatment and education.

Conflicts Still to be Resolved

Nevertheless, there remain divisive differences of opinion. These may be exploited by pressure groups, or by privately promoted methods of therapy or education, undermining parental confidence and weakening the professional strategies for meeting the needs of children with autism. There is a gap between the more therapy-oriented methods that seek sympathetic engagement with emotions first, and those with more of a teaching aim that believe in systematic behavioural therapy or cognitive interpretation of teaching needs. The former object to approaches that appear to treat the child as a mechanism or organism, and that see the problem as made up of various faults in parts of a child with autism. The latter are likely to dismiss intuition as a poor basis for practice, and to defer to findings of controlled laboratory-based research. There is another traditional schism between the professional educators who, while seeing little value in medical diagnoses or brain explanations, are also sceptical of the applications of laboratory measures and intelligence tests of what is wrong in the child. They seek causal explanations in the environment outside the child and each child's past knowledge, and try to make improvements in teaching practice, or in the behaviours of family and society. It would seem that the wise approach is to attempt to take the best of each and every kind of experience, and to see if observation of how the child with autism responds in the long term can help us see the common truth in good practices, and weed out unpromising 'fads' and 'side issues'.

Educationalists and psychoanalysts are alike in feeling suspicious of information about the brain obtained by research that they do not understand and that is very remote from what they do. They must deal with the disturbed and uncomprehending child in front of them. Brain scientists and medical experts who may have never had to pacify or try to teach an autistic child may, on their side, be sceptical about insights to motive processes and mental fabrications for which they have no conceivable explanation. They may refer derisively to psychoanalytic interpretations. They may dismiss claims of music therapists, who have no scientific training, that they can turn around the avoidant and protesting displays of a child with autism, facilitating more constructive curiosity and behaviour and an interest in learning how to communicate and share experiences with a parent or teacher. Speech therapists intent on improving the rudimentary linguistic skills of the child may not be open to evidence that their work might be facilitated by first eliciting the help of someone who is experienced in gaining the child's involvement at another, less demanding level of human interaction.

Psychoanalytic methods are still widely used in parts of continental Europe to assess and treat children with autism, but they have been rejected as ineffective in many places, particularly in the UK and US. This rejection, which is partly motivated by a pragmatic mistrust of all theories of inner mental events, is comparable to the disapproval shown by some teachers and therapists to behaviour-shaping methods, especially those that have employed aversive reinforcement. Child-centred and 'gentle teaching' methods present themselves as opposed to behavioural techniques. Now it seems that certain aspects of the development of interpersonal functioning that have been acknowledged and explored by analytically oriented clinicians for many decades, gain credibility in the light of evidence on the functions of the emotional systems in human attachment and mental development (MacLean, 1993; Schore, 1994). At the same time, there has also been a transformation of psychology, with the acceptance that complex cognitive processes are essential in perception, thinking and language, and this has led to a more sympathetic and imaginative approach to teaching for children with autism.

Problems of the Unconscious in Autism

The history of psychodynamic approaches to therapy for disturbances of reason and learning from unconscious, emotional processes is instructive. New awareness of the innate foundations of mental processes and their communication in infancy brings renewed interest to this saga. Freud intended psychoanalysis to be the science of the emotional processes of the mind that are active between persons in relationships. As a young neurologist who wanted to work in psychiatry, he cast aside his expert and up-to-date knowledge of the brain, and attempted to discover how people could generate feelings – sometimes overwhelmingly strong feelings – of love, hate, jealousy, or admiration for people close to them. He had a doctor's concern for motives that had become compounded and distorted in emotional illness, affecting the patient's reason.

In therapy the analyst attempts to evoke communication about a patient's emotional life, including the memories of past relationships, especially their present effects in relationships that have become unhappy and destructive. The clinical sharing or transfer of inner experience is possible because a human being can take up another person's imagined states of being and interpret their representations or images of these states, 'intersubjectively', reliving the other's emotional reality in its privately created form. Through analysis, it is believed, a patient's emotions can, in time, be made more coherent, more flexible and positive, and their images of themselves and other people happier and more constructive. In the therapeutic relationship, the analyst gives acceptance to evidence of painful feelings that would normally be hidden from consciousness, or denied. Over many sessions, in an intense and protected process, the analyst, who must be trained to explore strong interpersonal emotions without being himself or herself disturbed, gives the patient strength to overcome obsessions and to discover painful or revolting elements in unconscious memories, freeing a more spontaneous, creative and sociable consciousness of self and others.

Unfortunately, this pursuit of what is reasoned about the unreasonable can become a highly intellectual activity, and gain a spurious literary credibility. Psychoanalytic texts and 'meta-theory', interpretations of interpretations outside real live negotiations of mental life, become forbidding, and increasingly implausible, to the uninitiated. Complex as it is, the emotional mind needs demystifying. It requires observations to be made away from the verbal recollections of the psychoanalytic session.

We know much more than Freud could about the intricacy of the organs of emotion in the brain, even though he was one of the leading brain scientists of his day. We can perceive how imbalance in the dynamic regulations of awareness, of moving and of emotionally reacting to events or memories can be caused, not only by events remembered of interpersonal relationships, but also by failures developing from within the counterbalanced chemical machinery of the mind, some of which trace their cause back to abnormal genes affecting brain development. Of course, this knowledge does not invalidate the kind of exploration that Freud attempted. We still have to face the irrational states of mind as they directly affect interpersonal contacts and relationships. There is no hope of entirely translating these into brain chemistry or genetics. They affect a whole person and his or her relationships.

Can psychodynamic theory be put to use in helping children with autism? What of the idea that autism is an emotional illness reflecting an unresponsive human environment? This is the claim that, by setting ideas of organic and psychogenic causes in opposition, has done the cause of psychoanalysis the most damage. True, a neglected or abused child can acquire fearful, aggressive, passive or rigid reactions to other persons that make subsequent relationships fail. Hard experiences can affect a child's ability to adapt to new situations, and to learn. Psychoanalysts were right to identify conflicts in the unhappy child between desire for parental affection and the need for autonomy. In at least one subgroup of children with autism, it is likely that early trauma from failure of interpersonal support has played a part in precipitating the condition (Alvarez, 1996). However, analysts, and medical science generally, seriously misunderstood the potential for complex emotional pathology in the child. Melanie Klein and her followers partly corrected this error, insisting that even an infant can be locked with a caregiver in a struggle for understanding of feelings of incompatibility, need, loss and self-protection (Klein, 1963). But, the positive motives of the infant for joyful and creative engagement with companions were not explored by clinicians faced with the dissolutions of adult psychoses. This left them with a one-sided, and sad, model of the infant mind.

A correction to the inadequate psychoanalytic perspective on early childhood, and indeed to mainstream psychological theory of the natural origins of human feelings, has come from observations of the active and constructive contribution an infant normally makes to the building of communication and companionship with parents, siblings and an increasing circle of acquaintances (Stern, 1985; Beebe and Lachmann, 1988; Emde, 1988; Murray, 1991). In fact, systematic explorations of abnormal states of mind confirm that emotional regulation of relationships and the building of the self have very substantial foundations in the child. A baby is not born as an organism without psychology, a diffuse and fragile being that is easily deformed by imperfect support from a mother. On the contrary, infants have powerful evocative and regulatory effects on their caregivers. They act purposefully to stimulate positive and fully reciprocal communication and sharing of intentions, experiences and emotions, in companionship (Aitken and Trevarthen, 1997; Papousek and Papousek, 1987; Reddy et al., 1997; Stern, 1985, 1993; Trevarthen, 1993a; Weinberg and Tronick, 1997).

A Clear Way Ahead

This new perspective on infant mental life is of fundamental significance for the science of child and adult psychopathology. By demonstrating the efforts a baby normally makes to develop with the help of live company that is both comforting and exciting, identifying those who know more and who have much greater powers of understanding and action, it explains how relationships with the infant are affected when these innate motives fail to function in the normal way (Aitken and Trevarthen, 1997; Murray and Cooper, 1997; Papousek and Papousek, 1997; Schore, 1994; Stern, 1985; Tronick and Weinberg, 1997).

Recent writings show that psychodynamic theory and practice has opened itself to better knowledge of infant psychology, and that it is finding ways to use its rich heritage of experience in exploring the darker, self-defending processes of the human mind to help children who are emotionally disturbed and confused in their motives for relating to the world, so they can find joy in companionship with persons (Alvarez, 1992, 1996; Emde, 1990; Hobson, 1990d, 1997; Schore, 1994; Stern, 1990; Tustin, 1981, 1994; Urwin, 1989). The same new theory of the infant mind requires adjustment of rational cognitive models that have, so far, offered no explanation for the remarkable abilities that young children have for responding effectively in communication with adults who are behaving with intuitive affection towards them, skilfully supporting their child's efforts to make sense of the world (Papousek and

Papousek, 1987; Tronick and Weinberg, 1997). How childish behaviour, and intuitive parental support, facilitates human mental development has been left obscure by increasingly refined studies of parameters of perception, reasoning and memory in single individuals.

For the child with autism, too, the most effective way to meet his or her needs will be one that responds immediately and with intuitive sensitivity to the child's motives for taking interest in the world and in people (Hobson, 1993a, 1993b). It will be one that compares the development of communication and intelligence, at each age, to that in unaffected children, looking for the beginning and the evolution of the deviant changes, and identifying psychological strengths that remain (Sigman and Capps, 1997). In the development of any child's intelligence, the effects of the environment, including all forms of intervention, are conditioned by the state of motivating and self-regulating activity within the receiving mind. Effective response to the needs of children with autism or Asperger's syndrome – be it care in the home, therapy addressed to their emotional and bodily disorders, or education of their minds so they can take some part in a world with meaning and companionship – will need to be both eclectic and developmental. It will start where each child is, and try, by all available means, to support the functions and motives he or she possesses, protecting them from disorder, and supporting consistency and self-satisfaction. Child development research has proved the central importance for intellectual development of relationships and communication. The deviant responses of children with autism only add weight to this view. Brain research, showing how cognitive processes are inseparable from emotions and their communication, increasingly supports the same conclusion.

We hope this book has made an approach to interventions for children with autism through attention to their interpersonal communicative needs and their development seem both practical and right. We hope it will be a source of encouragement for the common aim of parents, therapists and teachers – to bring a richer, happier and stress-free life to these children, in affection and companionship.

Autism in Medical Diagnostic Systems

International Classification of Diseases: ICD-9 and ICD-10

The WHO International Classification of Diseases (ICD) has been widely adopted outside the USA. ICD-8 placed autism under 'schizophrenia'. The two most recent revisions of this system, ICD-9 and a draft of ICD-10, were published in 1980 and 1987 respectively, and the final form of ICD-10 appeared in 1993. Both categorise autism as 'psychoses with an origin in childhood'.

ICD-9 distinguishes among 'Psychoses with Origins Specific to Childhood' as follows:

(1) Typical autism, onset before 30 months (**Infantile Autism** – 299.0)

(2) Social impairment and stereotyped behaviour after a few years of normal development (**Disintegrative Psychosis** – 299.1)

(3) **Atypical Autism** (299.8)

(4) **Remainder** (299.9)

Four major criteria are specified for Infantile Autism:

(1) Onset before 30 months

(2) Deviant social development

(3) Abnormalities of language development

(4) Restricted and abnormal stereotyped patterns of behaviour.

Asperger's syndrome (or 'autistic psychopathy') is excluded.

ICD-10 defines a number of separable categories under the general heading of 'Pervasive Developmental Disorders':

Childhood Autism (F84.0): impaired or abnormal development must be present *before* three years of age, manifesting the *full triad* of impairments:

(1) in reciprocal social interaction

(2) in communication, and

(3) in restricted, stereotyped, repetitive behaviour.

Atypical Autism (F84.1): onset of impaired or abnormal is seen *after* three years of age, and is shown in *one or two* of the above triad of impairments.

Rett's Syndrome (F84.2) (see Chapter 3)

Other Childhood Disintegrative Disorder (F84.3) (see Chapter 3)

Overactive disorder associated with mental retardation and stereotyped movements (F84.4) 'An ill-defined disorder of uncertain nosological validity'. This diagnosis is used to identify individuals who show prepubertal hyperactivity, stereotyped movements and problems with attention in association with severe mental retardation.
Asperger's Syndrome (F84.5) (see Chapter 3)

Other pervasive developmental disorders (F84.8)

Pervasive developmental disorder, unspecified (F84.9)

Diagnostic and Statistical Manual: DSM-III, DSM-III-R and DSM-IV

The American Psychiatric Association Diagnostic and Statistical Manual (DSM) has been revised several times (APA, 1980, 1987, 1994). In the United States literature, four distinct periods may be distinguished: (1) pre DSM-III (up to 1980), when there was little consistency in criteria employed in different research centres, and autism was not included as a diagnostic category in DSM; (2) DSM-III (1980–1987), (3) DSM-III-R (1987–1994), and (4) DSM-IV (1994 to the present). The three more recent systems are summarised in TableVI.

In DSM-III-R, 'autistic disorder' was classified as a 'pervasive developmental disorder'. Diagnosis required the presence of at least eight items from three groups of criteria:

(1) Qualitative impairment in social interaction (five subsets, scoring on two of which was required for diagnosis)

(2) Qualitative impairments in verbal and non-verbal communication, and in imaginative activity (six subsets, scoring on one of which was required)

(3) Markedly restricted repertoire of activities and interests (five subsets, scoring on one of which was required).

Onset during infancy or childhood was to be noted, but this was not required as a diagnostic criterion, as it is in all other DSM systems.

With older and more able subjects it was possible, in most cases, to evaluate the full set of 16 features. However, the criteria were scored as 'present' only if developmentally inappropriate, which led to far greater difficulty in reaching a diagnosis if the child was very young, developmentally delayed or mute. For a positive diagnosis with young or delayed children, the eight criteria for diagnosis often had to be drawn from as few as nine possible features (Aitken, 1991b). This was a serious defect in DSM-III-R, given the importance of early diagnosis for effective intervention. Furthermore, the DSM-III-R was highly redundant, many of the items adding little to the diagnostic power of the system (Siegel, Vukicevic and Spitzer, 1990).

Table VI American Psychiatric Association DSM Systems
for Diagnosis of Autism

	DSM-III (1980)	DSM-III-R (1987)	DSM-IV (1994)
Name of Disorder	Infantile autism	Autistic disorder	Autistic disorder
Onset	Before 30 months.	During infancy or childhood.	Onset before 3 years of delayed or abnormal function in at least one of: social interaction, language for social communication, symbolic or imaginative play.
Social Behaviour	Pervasive lack of responses to other people.	Qualitative impairment in social interaction (5 mutually exclusive criteria).	Qualitative impairment in social interaction (at least 2 of 4 criteria).
Language and Communication	Gross deficits in language development. Speech, if present, has peculiar patterns.	Qualitative impairments in verbal and non-verbal communication and in imaginative activity.	Qualitative impairments in communication (at least 1 of 4 possible criteria).
Activities and Interests	Bizarre response to various aspects of the environment.	Markedly restricted repertoire of activities and interests.	Restricted repetitive and stereotyped patterns of behaviour, interests and activities (at least 1 of 4 possible criteria).
Exclusion Criteria	Absence of delusions, hallucinations, loosening of association and incoherence, as seen in schizophrenia.	None stated.	Rett's Disorder; Childhood Disintegrative Disorder; Asperger's Syndrome.

APPENDIX 2

Checklists and Questionnaires for Autism

The following instruments for identification and description of autism and its developmental features are here summarised, in alphabetic order, with notes on their principle applications:

- Autism Behaviour Checklist, ABC

- Autism Diagnostic Interview, ADI

- Autism Diagnostic Observation Schedule, ADOS

- Behaviour Observation Scale for Autism, BOS

- Behaviour Rating Instrument for Autistic and Atypical Children, BRIACC

- Behavioural Summarized Evaluation, BSE,

- Checklist for Autism in Toddlers, CHAT

- Childhood Autism Rating Scale, CARS

- Diagnostic Checklist for Behaviour-Disturbed Children, Forms E-1 and E-2

- Infant Behavioural Summarized Evaluation, IBSE

- Pre-Linguistic Autism Diagnostic Observation Schedule, PL-ADOS

The **Autism Behaviour Checklist, ABC,** (Krug, Arick and Almond, 1980) was developed to differentiate autistic children and young adults from severely mentally retarded, deaf-blind, severely emotionally disturbed individuals and people without disabilities. It is completed by professionals. It consists of 57 behaviour descriptors which have been distributed into five symptom areas: sensory, relating, body and object use, language and social. Weighting scores are assigned to each behaviour. The selection of descriptors was based on seven articles, including Kanner (1943), Form E-2 of Rimland (1964), Creak (1964) and BRIAAC (Ruttenberg *et al.*, 1966). The analysis pooled data from 1049 completed checklists concerning individuals ranging from 18 months to 35 years.

The **Autism Diagnostic Interview, ADI** (Rutter *et al.*, 1988; LeCouteur *et al.*, 1989) is an investigator-based interview which does not rely on forced choice responses. Successive probe questions build up a detailed picture of development in three key areas: language and communication; social development, and play.

The ADI was validated against ICD-10 criteria by psychiatrists' blind rating of 32 videotapes of unstructured interviews with mothers of autistic and non-autistic mentally handicapped children aged 7–19 years, matched for IQ. Inter-rater agreement was 81–89 per cent.

The **Autism Diagnostic Observation Schedule, ADOS** (Lord *et al.*, 1989) was created to standardise observations of communicative and social behaviours of individuals with autism and related disorders, and to form a diagnostic instrument for differentiation of autism from mentally handicapped and normally developing people. It is a developmental test rather than a diagnostic rating scale, and it focuses on the qualitative expression of subjects' communication and social behaviours. The examiner, whose behaviour has to be standardised during the administration of the test, interacts with the subjects using eight tasks to elicit certain behaviours. The test lasts 20–30 minutes. The behaviours are coded during the interview, and a score, from 'normal' to 'definitely abnormal' is assigned to each at the end of the interview.

The tasks and their corresponding target behaviours are:

Task	Target Behaviour
(1) a construction task	asking for help
(2) unstructured presentation of toys	symbolic or reciprocal play; giving help to the examiner
(3) drawing games	taking turns in a structured task
(4) demonstration of tasks	descriptive gesture and mime
(5) a poster task	description of agents and actions
(6) a book task	telling a sequential story
(7) conversation	reciprocal communication
(8) socio-emotional questions emotion.	the sophistication of language for

The ADOS was formed on a sample of 80 subjects from 6 to 18 years – 20 autistic children and adolescents with mild retardation, 20 mentally handicapped children and adolescents, 20 autistic without mental retardation and 20 normally developing individuals. It cannot be used for children having a MA of three years or lower. Although satisfactory inter-rater and test-retest reliability was found for some items, further validation is needed.

The **Behaviour Observation Scale for Autism, BOS,** (Freeman *et al.*, 1978; Freeman, Ritvo and Schroth, 1984) is intended to differentiate autistic from normal and mentally retarded pre-school children, to identify subgroups among autistic individuals and to develop an objective instrument for the description of autism in the fields of behavioural and biological research. It consists of 24 behaviours divided into four groups: solitary behaviour, relation to objects, relation to people and language. The child is filmed playing on his own with age-appropriate toys. The observer reviews the videotape and codes the occurrences of specific behaviours. The data are evaluated with a computer.

The BOS was tested on a sample of 137 children. They included both autistic children with IQ above 70 ('high autistic' or HA) matched with normal children, or autistic children with IQ below 70 ('low autistic' or LA) matched with mentally retarded children. The mean chronological age of the groups was between four and five years. Differences were found between both autistic groups and their controls. 'Repetitive solitary behaviours' and 'specific sensory use of objects' differentiated HA and LA from their controls, but they were more important for the HA group. All autistic children showed less 'purposeful use of objects' and more 'non-purposeful use of objects'. 'Relating to the examiner' was found to score higher for the LA group, but the HA group had more language.

The **Behaviour Rating Instrument for Autistic and Atypical Children, BRIAAC,** (Ruttenberg *et al.*, 1966; Ruttenberg *et al.*, 1977) was developed to complement a psychoanalytically oriented approach to intervention with behaviourally disturbed children. It is an observational measure derived from clinical practice and it consists of eight scales:

(1) relationship to an adult   (5) sound and speech reception

(2) communication   (6) social responsiveness

(3) drive for mastery   (7) body movement, and

(4) vocalisation and expressive speech (8) psychobiological development.

Each scale can be scored on ten developmental levels. Factor analysis yields a single main factor, 'resistance to realistic participation in various activities' (Wenar and Ruttenberg, 1976) and the individual scales correlate from 0.54 to 0.86. Cohen, Caparulo, Gold, Waldo, Shaywitz, Ruttenberg and Rimland (1978) also found one primary factor on principal components analysis which accounted for 69 per cent of the variance in the BRIACC. The BRIACC failed to discriminate among diagnostic groups when comparing primary and secondary autism, schizophrenia with onset in childhood, developmental aphasia and mental retardation without autism.

The **Behavioural Summarized Evaluation, BSE,** was developed by LeLord to evaluate the severity of behaviour problems in autistic children. It has been used for evaluations in educational contexts (Barthélémy, Hameury and LeLord, 1989) and in drug therapy (Martineau, Barthélémy, Cheliakine and LeLord, 1988), and has proved to be a sensitive clinical instrument that specifies autism well in relation to other disorders (Barthélémy *et al.*, 1992).

Schopler and his colleagues developed the **Childhood Autism Rating Scale, CARS,** (Schopler, Reichler, DeVillis and Kock, 1980), which was intended to broaden the classic conceptualisation of autism by including Kanner's criteria (1943), the nine diagnostic points of Creak (1964) and the National Autistic Society's definition. It consists of 15 scales, which are: impairment in human relationships, imitation, inappropriate affect, bizarre use of body movement and persistence of stereotypes, peculiarities in relating to non-human objects, resistance to environmental change, peculiarities of visual responsiveness, peculiarities of auditory responsiveness, near receptor responsiveness, anxiety reaction, verbal communication, non-verbal communication, activity level, intellectual functioning and general impressions. There is a continuum of seven scores for each of the above 15 scales, ranging from normal to severe abnormal behaviour. The rating depends on the child's age and the peculiarity, frequency and intensity of each behaviour.

The development of CARS is based on direct observations of the children's behaviour rather than on a theoretical baseline. The test was constructed on assessment of 537 children, who were distinguished into three categories: non autistic, mild to moderate autistic and severe autistic. The CARS is highly reliable and has good validity.

The **Checklist for Autism in Toddlers, CHAT,** (Baron-Cohen, Allen and Gillberg, 1992; Baron-Cohen *et al.*, 1996) is a scale of nine 'yes'/'no' questions to parents and five observation items to be completed by the health visitor or GP. It was used as a screening test at 18 months to assess 41 children at high genetic risk approximately 3 % risk of family recurrence of developing autism, and 50 randomly selected control toddlers. Over 80 % of controls passed on all items, none failing on more than one of the following:

- pretend play
- protodeclarative pointing
- joint-attention
- social interest
- social play.

Four of the high-risk children failed on two or more of these key items. On follow-up at 30 months, all of the children were developing normally with the exception of the four children who had failed two or more items, all of whom received a diagnosis of autism.

The **Diagnostic Checklist for Behaviour-Disturbed Children, Form E-1,** first developed in 1964 by Rimland, was answered by parents of children up to seven years old. It aimed to diagnose early infantile autism and to differentiate it from other childhood psychoses. It was based on Kanner's description (1943), on studies of childhood schizophrenia, and letters and reports from parents. It consisted of 76 questions about the child's birth history, symptoms, speech characteristics and age of onset.

The Form E-1 had to be revised because the parents reported that important changes occur at around the age of five-and-a-half years. The **Form E-2** (Rimland, 1971; 1984) was developed with an earlier cut-off age. It is a 109-item questionnaire completed by the parents of the index child that seeks information about the child's development from birth to the age of five.

Data are collected about social interaction and affect, speech, motor and manipulative skills, intelligence and reaction to sensory stimuli, characteristics of the family, development of any illness, physiological and biological history. A child is assigned plus points for indications of early infantile autism and minus points for non autistic behaviours. The major strength of the E-2 is that the results obtained are compared to a large continuously updated computerised database of over 16,000 cases. Systematic analysis of E-2 data has been instrumental in the assessment of a range of dietary and behavioural treatments. Thus, for example, the effects of supplementation of the diet with high dose vitamin B6 in combination with magnesium have been monitored (see under Treatments, Chapter 10).

The **Infant Behavioural Summarized Evaluation, IBSE** (Adrien *et al.*, 1992) is a recent adaptation of the BSE for younger children that has been used in a pilot version comprising 33 items for assessment of subjects from 6 to 48 months of age. Results with 89 developmentally disabled children, including 39 given a clinical diagnosis of autism, have been published. Statistical analysis demonstrated significant differences between the autistic children and the remainder in scores on a subset of 19 items.

The **Pre-Linguistic Autism Diagnostic Observation Schedule, PL-ADOS,** (DiLavore, Lord and Rutter, 1995) is a new scale based on a 30-minute semi-structured observation of the child engaging in 12 activities involving free play, imitation, joint attention, social routines, requests and responses, response to distress and separation from and reunion with the mother. It is designed for use with pre-verbal children, up to age six years, who are suspected of being autistic. It appears to have acceptable inter-rater reliability from blind rating of videotapes, and it correlated well with clinical judgement of diagnosis in the sample of 20 children, 12 autistic, upon which it is based.

Information on the Internet

http://web.syr.edu/~jmwobus/autism/ Probably the best link site to find information about papers on autism.

http://www.autism-uk.ed.ac.uk Contains information for parents and on UK support groups.

http://www.demon.co.uk/charities/AIA/aia.htm The Allergy Induced Autism. Good for up-to-date information on the medical basis for autism.

http://www.rmplc.co.uk/eduweb/sites/autism/ **SFTAH** is a very good site which contains lots of information on new treatments and therapies.

http://www.geocities.com/Athens/Acropolis/2408/SAS.html Strathclyde Autistic Society

http://www.lewisham.gov.uk/volorgs/alas/ All Lewisham Autism Support

http://www.ummed.edu/pub/u/ozabayrak/asperger.html Asperger's Disorder homepage with links.

http://www.info.med.yale.edu/childstdy/autism

http://www.udel.edu/bkirby/asperger

http://www.autism-society.org Autism Society of America

References

Aarons, M. and Gittens, T. (1992) *Autism: A Guide for Parents and Professionals*. London: Tavistock Routledge.

Abvitbol, M., Menini, C., Delezoide, A-L., Rhyner, T., Vekemans, M. and Mallet, J. (1993) 'Nucleus basalis magnocellularis and hippocampus are the major sites of FMR-1 expression in the human fetal brain.' *Nature Genetics 4*, 147–153.

Adamson, L. and Bakeman, R. (1985) 'Affect and attention: infants observed with mother and peers.' *Child Development 56*, 582–93.

Adrien, J.L. Barthélémy, C., Perrot, A., Roux, S., Lenoir, P., Haumery, L. and Sauvage, D. (1992) 'Validity and reliability of the Infant Behavioural Summarized Evaluation (IBSE): a rating scale for the assessment of young children with autism and developmental disorders.' *Journal of Autism and Developmental Disorders 22*, 375–394.

Adrien, J.L., Faure, M., Perrot, A., Hameury, L., Garreau, B., Barthélémy, C. and Sauvage, D. (1991a) 'Autism and family home movies: preliminary findings.' *Journal of Autism and Developmental Disorders 21*, 43–51.

Adrien, J.L., Lenoir, P., Martineau, J., Perrot, Haumery, L., Larmande, C. and Sauvage, D. (1993) 'Blind ratings of early symptoms of autism based upon family home movies.' *Journal of the American Academy of Child and Adolescent Psychiatry 32*, 3, 617–626.

Adrien, J.L., Perrot, A., Hameury, L., Martineau, J., Roux, S. and Sauvage, D. (1991b) 'Family home movies: identification of early autistic signs in infants later diagnosed as autistics.' *Brain Dysfunction 4*, 355–362.

Aggleton, J.P. (1992) *The Amygdala. Neurobiological Aspects of Emotion, Memory and Mental Dysfunction*. New York: Wiley-Liss.

Aggleton, J.P. (1993) 'The contribution of the amygdala to normal and abnormal emotional states.' *Trends in the Neurosciences 16*, 328–333.

Agrotou, A. (1988) 'A case study: Lara.' *Journal of British Music Therapy 2*, 1, 17–23.

Aiello, R. (ed) (1993) 'The music therapist as qualitative researcher.' *Music Therapy 12*, 1, 16–39.

Aiello, R. (ed) (1994) *Musical Perceptions*. New York and Oxford: Oxford University Press.

Aigen, K. (1995) 'Aesthetic foundations of clinical theory.' In C. Bereznak Kenny (ed) *Listening, Playing, Creating: Essays on the Power of Sound*. New York: State University of New York, 233–258.

Aitken, K.J. (1991a) 'Examining the evidence for a common structural basis to autism.' *Developmental Medicine and Child Neurology 33*, 933–938.

Aitken, K.J. (1991b) 'Diagnostic issues in autism: are we measuring the emperor for another suit of clothes?' *Developmental Medicine and Child Neurology 33*, 1015–1020.

Aitken, K.J. (1991c) *An Investigation into the Biological Perturbations of Prematurity.* PhD Thesis, University of Edinburgh.

Aitken, K.J. and Trevarthen, C. (1997) 'Self–other organization in human psychological development.' *Development and Psychopathology 9,* 651–675.

Akefeldt, A. and Gillberg, C. (1991) 'Hypomelanosis of Ito in three cases with autism and autistic-like conditions.' *Developmental Medicine and Child Neurology 33,* 737–743.

Aldridge, D. (1989) 'A phenomenological comparison of the organization of music and the self.' *Arts in Psychotherapy 16,* 91–97.

Aldridge, D. (1991) 'Physiological change, communication and the playing of improvised music: some proposals for research.' *The Arts in Psychotherapy 18,* 59–64.

Aldridge, D. (1993a) 'Music therapy research I: a review of the medical research literature with a general context of music therapy research.' *The Arts in Psychotherapy 20,* 1, 11–35.

Aldridge, D. (1993b) 'Music therapy research II: research methods suitable for music therapy.' *The Arts in Psychotherapy 20,* 2, 117–31.

Aldridge, D. (1994) 'Single-case research designs for the creative arts therapist.' *The Arts in Psychotherapy 21,* 5, 333–342.

Aldridge, D., Gustorrf, D. and Neugebauer, L. (1995) 'A preliminary study of creative music therapy in the treatment of children with developmental delay.' *The Arts in Psychotherapy 21,* 3, 189–205.

Allen, D.A. and Rapin, I. (1992) 'Autistic children are also dysphasic.' In H. Naruse and E.M. Ornitz (eds) *Neurobiology of Infantile Autism.* International Congress Series 965. Amsterdam: Excerpta Medica.

Alvarez, A. (1992) *Live Company: Psychoanalytic Psychotherapy with Autistic, Borderline, Deprived and Abused Children.* London: Routledge.

Alvarez, A. (1996) 'Addressing the element of deficit in children with autism: Psychotherapy which is both psychoanalytically and developmentally informed.' *Clinical Child Psychology and Psychiatry 1,* 4, 525–537.

Alvarez, A. (1997) 'Unconscious Phantasy, Thinking and Walking: some preliminary thoughts.' Paper given to the Westminster Pastoral Foundation, London, May.

Alvin, J. (1968) *Music Therapy for the Autistic Child.* Oxford: Oxford University Press.

Alvin, J. and Warwick, A. (1991) *Music Therapy for the Autistic Child.* Oxford: Oxford University Press.

American Psychiatric Association (1980) *Diagnostic and Statistical Manual of Mental Disorders, 3rd Edition. (DSM-III).* Washington, DC: American Psychiatric Association.

American Psychiatric Association (1987) *Diagnostic and Statistical Manual of Mental Disorders, 3rd Edition-Revised. (DSM-III-R).* Washington, DC: American Psychiatric Association.

American Psychiatric Association (1994) *Diagnostic and Statistical Manual of Mental Disorders, 4th Edition. (DSM-IV).* Washington, DC: American Psychiatric Association.

Ansdell, G. (1995) *Music for Life: Aspects of Creative Music Therapy with Adult Clients.* London: Jessica Kingsley.

Anthony, J. (1958) 'An experimental approach to the psychopathology of childhood autism.' *British Journal of Medical Psychology 31,* 211–225.

Armstrong, D. (1992) 'The neuropathology of Rett Syndrome.' *Brain and Development* *14*, (supplement), S89–S101.

Asperger, H. (1944) 'Die autistischen Psychopathen' in Kindersalter.' *Archiv. für Psyciatrie und Nervenkrankheiten 117*, 76–136. (English translation in Frith, 1991).

Association of Professional Music Therapists (1995) *A Career in Music Therapy.* London: APMT.

Attwood, A., Frith, U. and Hermelin, B. (1988) 'The understanding and use of interpersonal gestures by autistic and Down's syndrome children.' *Journal of Autism and Developmental Disorders 18*, 241–257.

Attwood, T. (1997) *Asperger's Syndrome: A Guide for Parents and Professionals.* London: Jessica Kingsley.

Austin, J.L. (1962) *How to Do Things with Words.* Oxford: Basil Blackwell.

Bailey, A., Phillips, W. and Rutter, M. (1996) 'Autism: towards an integration of clinical, genetic, neuropsychological and neurobiological perspectives.' *Journal of Child Psychology and Psychiatry 37*, 1, 89–126.

Bakeman, R. and Adamson, L. B. (1984) 'Coordinating attention to people and objects in mother–infant and peer–infant interaction.' *Child Development 55*, 1278–1289.

Ballotin, U., Bejor, M., Cecchini, A., Martelli, A., Palazzi, S. and Lanzi, G. (1989) 'Infantile autism and computerised tomography brain-scan findings: specific versus nonspecific abnormalities.' *Journal of Autism and Developmental Disorders 19*, 109–117.

Baltaxe, C.A.M. (1977) 'Pragmatic deficits in the language of autistic adolescents.' *Journal of Pediatric Psychology 2*, 176–180.

Barnard, P.J. and Teasdale, J.D. (1991) 'Interacting cognitive subsystems: a systematic approach to cognitive-affective interaction and change.' *Cognition and Emotion 5*, 1–39.

Barnes, C.D. and Pompeiano, O. (eds) (1991) *Neurobiology of the Locus Ceruleus.* (Progress in Brain Research, 88). Amsterdam: Elsevier.

Baron-Cohen, S. (1987) 'Autism and symbolic play.' *British Journal of Developmental Psychology 5*, 139–148.

Baron-Cohen, S. (1989a) 'Perceptual role taking and protodeclarative pointing in autism.' *British Journal of Developmental Psychology 7*, 113–127.

Baron-Cohen, S. (1989b) 'The autistic child's theory of mind: a case of specific developmental delay.' *Journal of Child Psychology and Psychiatry 30*, 285–297.

Baron-Cohen, S. (1989c) 'Are autistic children "behaviourists?" An examination of their mental-physical and appearance-reality distinctions.' *Journal of Autism and Developmental Disorders 19*, 579–600.

Baron-Cohen, S. (1990) 'Autism: a specific cognitive disorder of "mind-blindness".' *International Review of Psychiatry 2*, 81–90.

Baron-Cohen, S. (1991a) 'Precursors to a theory of mind: understanding attention in others.' In A. Whiten (ed) *Natural Theories of Mind: Evolution, Development and Simulation of Everyday Mindreading.* Oxford: Basil Blackwell.

Baron-Cohen, S. (1991b) 'Do people with autism understand what causes emotion?' *Child Development 62*, 385–395.

Baron-Cohen, S. (1991c) 'The theory of mind deficit in autism: how specific is it?' *British Journal of Developmental Psychology 9*, 301–314.

Baron-Cohen, S. (1992) 'Out of sight or out of mind? Another look at deception in autism.' *Journal of Child Psychology and Psychiatry 33*, 1141–1155.

Baron-Cohen, S. (1993) 'From attention-goal psychology to belief-desire psychology: the development of a theory of mind, and its dysfunction.' In S. Baron-Cohen, H. Tager-Flusberg and D. J. Cohen (eds.), *Understanding Other Minds: Perspectives from Autism.* London: Oxford University Press.

Baron-Cohen, S. (1995) *Mindblindness: An Essay on Autism and Theory of Mind.* Cambridge, MA: MIT Press.

Baron-Cohen, S., Allen, J. and Gillberg, C. (1992) 'Can autism be detected at 18 months? The needle, the haystack and the CHAT.' *British Journal of Psychiatry 161*, 839–843.

Baron-Cohen, S. and Bolton, P. (1993) *Autism – The Facts.* Oxford: Oxford University Press.

Baron-Cohen, S., Cox, A., Baird, G., Swettenham, J., Nightingale, N., Morgan, K., Drew, A. and Charman, T. (1996) 'Psychological markers in the detection of autism in infancy in a large population.' *British Journal of Psychiatry 168*, 158–163.

Baron-Cohen, S. and Hammer, J. (1997) 'Parents of children with Asperger Syndrome: what is the Cognitive Phenotype?' *Journal of Cognitive Neuroscience 9*, 548–554.

Baron-Cohen, S. and Howlin, P. (1993) 'The theory of mind deficit in autism: some questions for teaching and diagnosis.' In S. Baron-Cohen, H. Tager-Flusberg and D.J. Cohen (eds) *Understanding Other Minds: Perspectives from Autism.* London: Oxford University Press, 466–479.

Baron-Cohen, S., Leslie, A. and Frith, U. (1985) 'Does the autistic child have a theory of mind?' *Cognition 21*, 37–46.

Baron-Cohen, S., Leslie, A.M. and Frith, U. (1986) 'Mechanical, behavioural and intentional understanding of picture stories in autistic children.' *British Journal of Developmental Psychology 4*, 113–125.

Baron-Cohen, S., Tager-Flusberg, H. and Cohen, D. (eds) (1993) *Understanding Other Minds: Perspectives from Autism.* Oxford: Oxford University Press.

Barron, J. and Sandman, C. A. (1983) 'Relationship of sedative-hypnotic response to self-injurious behaviour and stereotypy by mentally retarded clients.' *American Journal of Mental Deficiency 88*, 177–186.

Bartak, L. and Rutter, M. (1976) 'Differences between mentally retarded and normally intelligent autistic children.' *Journal of Autism and Childhood Schizophrenia 6*, 109–120.

Bartak, L., Rutter, M. and Cox, A., (1975) 'A comparative study of infantile autism and specific developmental receptive language disorder. I. The children.' *British Journal of Psychiatry 126*, 127–145.

Barthélémy, C., Adrien, J.L., Roux, S., Garreau, B., Perrot, A. and LeLord, G. (1992) 'Sensitivity and specificity of the behavioural summarized evaluation (BSE) for the assessment of autistic behaviours.' *Journal of Autism and Developmental Disorders 22*, 23–31.

Barthélémy, C., Garreau, B., Bruneau, N., Martineau, J., Jouve, J., Roux, S. and Lelord, G. (1988) 'Biological and behavioural effects of magnesium + vitamin B6, folates and fenflouramine in autistic children.' In L. Wing (ed) *Aspects of Autism: Biological Research.* London: Gaskell, 59–73.

Barthélémy, C., Hameury, I. and LeLord, G. (1989) 'Exchange and Developmental Therapies (EDT) for children with autism: a treatment program from Tours, France.' In C. Gillberg (ed) *Autism: The State of Art.* New York: Elsevier, 263–284.

Bartlik, B. (1981) 'Monthly variation in births of autistic children in North Carolina.' *Journal of the American Medical Women's Association 36,* 363–368.

Bates, E. (1979) *The Emergence of Symbols: Cognition and Communication in Infancy.* New York: Academic Press.

Bateson M. C. (1979). 'The epigenesis of conversational interaction': a personal account of research and development. In Bullowa, M (Ed.) *Before Speech: The Beginnings of Human Communication.* London: Cambridge University Press.

Bauman, M.L. and Kemper, T.L. (1985) 'Histoanatomic observations of the brain in early infantile autism.' *Neurology 35,* 866–874.

Baumann, M.L. and Kemper, T.L. (1994) (eds.) *The Neurobiology of Autism.* Boston: John Hopkins University Press.

Beebe, B. (1982) 'Micro-timing in mother–infant communication.' In M.R. Key (ed) *Nonverbal Communication Today.* New York: Mouton.

Beebe, B., Jaffe, J., Feldstein, S., Mays, K. and Alson, D. (1985) 'Inter-personal timing: the application of an adult dialogue model to mother–infant vocal and kinesic interactions.' In F.M. Field and N. Fox (eds) *Social Perception in Infants.* Norwood, NJ: Ablex.

Beebe, B. and Lachmann, F.M. (1988) 'The contribution of mother–infant mutual influence to the origins of self- and object-representations.' *Psychoanalytic Psychology 5,* 4, 305–337.

Beebe, B., Stern, D. and Jaffe, J. (1979) 'The kinesic rhythm of mother–infant interactions.' In A.W. Siegman and S. Feldstein (eds) *Of Speech and Time: Temporal Speech Patterns in Interpersonal Contexts.* Hillsdale, NJ: Erlbaum.

Belchic, J.K. and Harris, S.L. (1994) 'The use of multiple peer exemplars to enhance the generalization of play skills to the siblings of children with autism.' *Child and Family Behaviour Therapy 16,* 1–25.

Bellugi, U., van Hoek, K., Lillo-Martin, D. and O'Grady, L. (1988) 'The acquisition of syntax and space in young deaf signers.' In D. Bishop and K. Mogford (eds) *Language Development in Exceptional Circumstances.* London: Churchill Livingstone.

Belmonte, M. and Carper, R. (1997) 'Neuroanatomical and neurophysiological clues to the nature of autism.' In B. Garreau (ed) *Neuroimaging in Childhood Developmental Disorders.* Berlin: Springer-Verlag.

Benenzon, R.O. (1997) *Music Therapy Theory and Manual: Contributions to the Knowledge of Nonverbal Contexts, Second Edition.* Springfield, Illinois: Charles C. Thomas.

Bérard, G. (1993) *Hearing Equals Behaviour.* New Caanan, CT: Keats.

Berger, J. (1990) 'Interactions between parents and their infants with Down Syndrome.' In D. Cicchetti and M. Beeghly (eds) *Children with Down Syndrome: A Developmental Perspective.* Cambridge: Cambridge University Press.

Berger, M.M. (1978) 'Video feedback confrontation review.' In M.M. Berger (ed) *Videotape Techniques in Psychiatric Training and Treatment.* New York: Bruner/Mazel.

Bernard-Opitz, V. (1982) 'Pragmatic analysis of the communicative behaviour of an autistic child.' *Journal of Speech and Hearing Disorders 47,* 99–109.

Berrueta-Clement, S., Barnett, W. S., Epstein, A. S. and Weikert, D. P. (1984) Changed lives: the effects of Perry Preschool Project on youths through age 19.

(Monograph No. 8 of the High/Scope Educational Research Foundation). Ypsilanti, MI: High/Scope Foundation.

Berthier, M.L., Starkstein, S.E. and Leiguarda, R. (1990) 'Developmental cortical anomalies in Asperger's Syndrome: neuroradiological findings in two patients.' *Journal of Neuropsychiatry and Clinical Neuroscience 2*, 197–201.

Bettelheim, B. (1967) *The Empty Fortess – Infantile Autism and the Birth of the Self.* New York: The Free Press.

Binet, A. and Simon, T. (1905) 'Sur la nécessite d'établir un diagnostique scientifique des états inférieur de l'intelligence.' *L'Année Psychologique, 11*, 162–336.

Bion, W. (1959) 'Attacks on linking.' *International Journal of Psycho-analysis 40*, 308–315.

Bion, W. (1962) 'Theory of thinking.' *International Journal of Psycho-analysis 43*, 306–310.

Bishop, D.V.M. (1989) 'Semantic pragmatic disorders and the autistic continuum.' *British Journal of Disorders of Communication 24*, 115–122.

Bishop, D.V.M. (1990) *Handedness and Developmental Disorder.* Clinics in Developmental Medicine, 110. London: Mackeith Press.

Bishop, D.V.M. (1992) 'The underlying nature of specific language impairment.' *Journal of Child Psychology and Psychiatry 33*, 3–66.

Bishop, D.V.M. (1993) 'Autism, executive functions and theory of mind: a neuropsychological perspective.' *Journal of Child Psychology and Psychiatry 34, 3*, 279–295.

Bleuler, E. (1913) 'Autistic thinking.' *American Journal of Insanity 69*, 873–886.

Blomquist, H. K., Bohman, M., Edvinson, S-O., Gillberg, C., Gustavson, K-H., Holmgren, G. and Wahlstrom, J. (1985) 'Frequency of the Fragile-X syndrome in infantile autism: A Swedish multicenter study.' *Clinical Genetics, 27*, 113–117.

Bohman, M., Bohman, I.L., Björck, P. O. and Sjöholm, E. (1983) 'Childhood psychosis in a northern Swedish county: some preliminary findings from an epidemiological survey.' In M.H. Schmidt and H. Remschmidt (eds) *Epidemiological Approaches in Child Psychiatry 2.* Stuttgart: Thieme, 164–173.

Bolton, P., Pickles, A., Harrington, R., Macdonald, H. and Rutter, M. (1992) 'Season of birth: issues, approaches and findings for autism.' *Journal of Child Psychology and Psychiatry 33*, 509–530.

Boucher J. (1977) 'Hand preference in autistic children and their parents.' *Journal of Autism and Childhood Schizophrenia 7*, 177–187.

Brask, B.H. (1970) A prevalence investigation of childhood psychosis. Presented paper, 16th Scandanavian Conference on Child Psychiatry.

Bråten, S. (1988) 'Dialogic mind: the infant and adult in protoconversation.' In M. Cavello (ed) *Nature, Cognition and System.* Dordrecht: Kluwer Academic Publications.

Bråten, S. (1998) 'Companion space theorems: imitational learning from (e)motional memory.' In S. Bråten (ed) *Intersubjective Communication and Emotion in Early Ontogeny.* Cambridge: Cambridge University Press.

Brazelton, T.B. and Cramer, B.G. (1991) *The Earliest Relationship: Parents, Infants, and the Drama of Early Attachment.* London: Karnac.

Brazelton, T.B., Koslowski, B. and Main, M. (1974) 'The origins of reciprocity: the early mother–infant interaction.' In M. Lewis and L.A. Roseblum (eds) *The Effect of the Infant on its Caregivers.* London: Wiley Interscience.

Bremner, G., Slater, A. and Butterworth, G. (1997) (eds) *Infant Development: Recent Advances*. Hove, East Sussex: Psychology Press.

Bretherton, I. and Bates, E. (1979) 'The emergence of intentional communication.' In I.C. Uzigiris (ed) *Social Interaction and Communication During Infancy, New Directions for Child Development*. Vol. 4, 81–100. San Francisco: Jossey-Bass.

Brodie, M.J. (1996) 'Antiepileptic drugs, clinical trials and the marketplace.' *Lancet 347*, 777–779.

Brodtkorb, E., Nilsen, G., Smevik, O. and Rinck, P. A. (1992) 'Epilepsy and anomalies of neuronal migration: MRI and clinical aspects.' *Acta Neurologica Scandinavica 86*, 24–32.

Brown, R. (1973) *A First Language: The Early Stages*. Cambridge: Harvard University Press.

Brown, S.M.K. (1994) 'Autism and music therapy – is change possible, and why music?' *Journal of British Music Therapy 8*, 1, 15–25.

Brown, W.T., Jenkins, E.C., Cohen, I.L., Fisch, G.S., Wolf-Schen, E.G., Gross, A., Waterhouse, L., Fein, D., Mason-Brothers, A., Ritvo, E., Ruttenberg, B.A., Bentley, W. and Castells, S. (1986) 'Fragile-X and autism: a multicenter survey.' *American Journal of Medical Genetics 23*, 341–352.

Brown, W. T., Jenkins, E. C., Fiedman, E. Brooks, J., Wisniewski, K., Raguthu, S. and French, J. (1982) 'Autism is associated with the Fragile X syndrome.' *Journal of Autism and Developmental Disorders, 12*, 303–308.

Bruner, J.S. (1975) 'The ontogenesis of speech acts.' *Journal of Child Language 2*, 1–19.

Bruner, J.S. (1983) *Child's Talk*. New York: Norton.

Bruner, J.S. (1990) *Acts of Meaning*. Cambridge, Mass.: Harvard University Press.

Bruner, J.S. (1996) *The Culture of Education*. Cambridge, MA.: Harvard University Press.

Bruner, J.S. and Feldman, C. (1993) 'Theories of mind and the problem of autism.' In. S. Baron-Cohen, H. Tager-Flusberg and D. Cohen (eds) *Understanding Other Minds: Perspectives from Autism*. Oxford: Oxford University Press.

Bruscia, K.E. (1987) *Improvisational Models of Music Therapy*. Springville, IL: Charles C. Thomas.

Bruscia, K.E. (1989) *Defining Music Therapy*. Phoenixville: Barcelona Publishers.

Bruscia, K.E. (1991) 'The fundamentals of music therapy practice.' In K.E. Bruscia (ed) *Case Studies in Music Therapy*, 3–13.

Bruscia, K.E. (ed) (in press) *The Dynamics of Music Psychotherapy*. Phoenixville, PA: Barcelona Publishers.

Bryan, A. (1989) 'Autistic group case study.' *Journal of British Music Therapy 3*, 1, 16–21.

Bryson, S. E., Clark, B. S. and Smith, I. M. (1988) 'First report of a Canadian epidemiological study of autistic syndromes.' *Journal of Child Psychology and Psychiatry, 29*, 433–445.

Buber, M. (1937) *I and Thou* (First English edition, translated by R. G. Smith). Edinburgh: T. and T. Clark Ltd.

Buck, R. (1984) *The Communication of Emotion*. New York: Guilford Press.

Buitelaar, J.K., Van Engeland, H., van Ree, J. and De Weid, D. (1990) 'Behavioural effects of ORG 2766, a synthetic analog of the adrenocorticotrophic hormone

(4–9) in 14 outpatient autistic children.' *Journal of Autism and Developmental Disorders 20*, 467–478.

Buitelaar, J. K., Van Engeland, H., De Koegel, K., De Vries, H., Van Hooff, J. and Van Ree, J. (1992) 'The adrenocorticotrophic hormone (4–9) Analog ORG 2766 benefits autistic children: Report on a second controlled clinical trial.' *Journal of the American Academy of Child and Adolescent Psychiatry, 31*, 1149–1156.

Bullowa, M. (ed) (1979) *Before Speech: The Beginnings of Human Communication.* London: Cambridge University Press.

Bunt, L. (1994) *Music Therapy: an Art Beyond Words.* London: Routledge.

Burford, B. (1988) 'Action cycles: rhythmic actions for engagement with children and young adults with profound mental handicap.' *European Journal of Special Educational Needs 3.*

Burford, B. (1992) 'Communicating through movement and posture.' In W. MacGillivray, W.I. Fraser and A. Green (eds) *Hallas' Caring for People with Mental Handicap.* London: Butterworth Heinemann.

Busch, F. (1977) 'Theme and variation in the development of first transitional objects.' *International Journal of Psychoanalysis 58*, 479–486.

Bushnell, I.W.R., Sai, F. and Mullin, J.T. (1989) 'Neonatal recognition of the mother's face.' *British Journal of Developmental Psychology 7*, 3–15.

Butterworth, G. (1991) 'The ontogeny and phylogeny of joint visual attention.' In A. Whiten (ed) *Natural Theories of Mind: Evolution, Development and Simulation of Everyday Mindreading.* Oxford: Blackwell.

Butterworth, G., and Grover, L. (1988) 'The origins of referential communication in human infancy.' In L. Weiskrantz (ed) *Thought Without Language.* Oxford: Clarendon.

Campbell, M. (1975) 'Pharmacotherapy in early infantile autism.' *Biological Psychiatry 10*, 399–423.

Campbell, M. (1988) 'Fenfluramine treatment of autism.' *Journal of Child Psychology and Psychiatry 29*, 1–10 (Annotation).

Campbell, M. (1989) 'Pharmacotherapy in autism: an overview.' In C. Gillberg (ed) *Diagnosis and Treatment of Autism.* New York: Plenum, 203–217.

Campbell, M., Adams, P., Small, A.M., Tesch, L. McV. and Curren, E.L. (1988) 'Naltrexone in infantile autism.' *Psychopharmacology Bulletin 24*, 135–139.

Campbell, M., Anderson, L.T., Meier, M., Cohen, I.L., Small, A.M., Samit, C. and Sachar, E.J. (1978) 'A comparison of haloperidol, behaviour therapy and their interaction in autistic children.' *Journal of the American Academy of Child Psychiatry 17*, 640–655.

Campbell, M., Rosenbloom, S., Perry, R., George, A.E., Kricheff, I.I., Anderson, L., Small, A.M. and Jennings, S.J. (1982) 'Computerised axial tomography in young autistic children.' *American Journal of Psychiatry 139*, 510–512.

Capps, L., Sigman, M. and Mundy, P. (1994) 'Attachment security in children with autism.' *Development and Psychopathology 6*, 2, 249–261.

Capps, L., Yirmiya, N. and Sigman, M. (1992) 'Understanding of simple and complex emotions in non-retarded children with autism.' *Journal of Child Psychology and Psychiatry 33*, 1169–1182.

Carr, E.G. (1979) 'Teaching autistic children to use sign language: some research issues.' *Journal of Autism and Developmental Disorders 9*, 4, 345–359.

Carr, E.G. (1982) 'Sign language.' In R.L. Koegel, A. Rincover and A.L. Egel (eds) *Educating and Understanding Autistic Children*. New York: College Hill Press.

Carr, E. G. and Durand, V. M. (1985) 'Reducing behaviour problems through functional communication training.' *Journal of Applied Behaviour Analysis, 18,* 111–126.

Carter, C.S., Lederhendler, I.I. and Kirkpatrick, B. (eds.) (1997) 'The Integrative Neurobiology of Affiliation.' *Annals of The New York Academy of Sciences, 807.* New York: The New York Academy of Sciences.

Changeux, J.-P. (1985) *Neuronal Man: The Biology of Mind.* New York: Pantheon.

Charlop, M.H. and Walsh, M.E. (1986) 'Increasing autistic children's spontaneous verbalisations of affection: an assessment of time delay and peer modelling procedures.' *Journal of Applied Behaviour Analysis 19,* 307–314.

Chess, S. (1977) 'Follow-up report on autism and congenital rubella.' *Journal of Autism and Childhood Schizophrenia 7,* 68–81.

Chess, S., Korn, S.J. and Fernandez, P.B. (1971) *Psychiatric Disorders of Children with Congenital Rubella.* New York: Brunner/Mazel.

Christie, P., Newson, E., Newson, J. and Preveser, W. (1992) 'An interactive approach to language and communication for nonspeaking children.' In D.A. Lane and A. Miller (eds) *Child and Adolescent Therapy: A Handbook.* Buckingham: Open University Press.

Chugani, D.C., Muzik, O., Rothermel, R., Behen, M., Chakraborty, P., Mangner, T., da Silva, E.A. and Chugani, H.T. (1997) 'Altered seotonin synthesis in the dentatothalamocortical pathway in autistic boys.' *Annals of Neurology 42,* 666–669.

Chugani, H.T. and Phelps, M.E. (1986) 'Maturational changes in cerebral function in infants determined by FDG position emission tomography.' *Science 231,* 840–843.

Cialdella, P. and Mamelle, N. (1989) 'An epidemiological study of infantile autism in a French Department (Rhaene): a research note.' *Journal of Child Psychology and Psychiatry 30,* 165–175.

Cicchetti, D. and Sroufe, L.A. (1978) 'An organizational view of affect: illustration from the study of Down's syndrome infants.' In M. Lewis and L.A. Rosenblum (eds) *The Development of Affect.* pp.309–350. New York: Plenum.

Cieleski, K. T., Harris, R. J., Hart, B. L. and Pabst, H. F. (1997) 'Cerebellar hypoplasia and frontal lobe cognitive deficits in disorders of early childhood.' *Neuropsychologia, 35,* 643–656.

Clark, P. and Rutter, M. (1981) 'Autistic children's responses to structure and to interpersonal demands.' *Journal of Autism and Developmental Disorders 11,* 201–217.

Claustrat, B., Brun, J., David, M., Sassolas, G. and Chazot, G. (1992) 'Melatonin and jet-lag: confirmatory result using a simplified protocol.' *Biological Psychiatry (USA), 32,* 8, 705–711.

Clements, J. (1987) *Severe Learning Disability and Psychological Handicap.* Chichester: John Wiley and Sons.

Coggins, T.E. and Frederickson, R. (1988) 'Brief report: the communicative role of a highly repeated utterance in the conversations of an autistic boy.' *Journal of Autism and Developmental Disorders 18,* 687–694.

Cohen, D.J., Carparulo, B.K., Gold, J.R., Waldo, M.C., Shaywitz, B.A., Ruttenberg, B.A. and Rimland, B. (1978) 'Agreement in diagnosis: clinical assessment and behaviour rating scales for pervasively disturbed children.' *Journal of the American Academy of Child Psychiatry, 17,* 589–603.

Cohen, D., Donnellan, A. and Paul, R. (eds) (1987) *The Handbook of Autism and Pervasive Developmental Disorders.* New York: Wiley.

Cohen, D.J. and Volkmar, F.R. (eds) (1997) *Handbook of Autism and Developmental Disorders, 2nd Edition.* New York: Wiley.

Cohen, I.L., Brown, W.T., Jenkins, E.C., Krawczun, M.S., French, J.H., Raguthu, S., Wolf-Schein, E.G., Sudhalter, V., Fisch, G. and Wisniewski, K. (1989) 'Fragile-X syndrome in females with autism.' *American Journal of Medical Genetics 34,* 302–303.

Cohen, I.L., Campbell, M., Posner, D., Small, A.M., Triebel, D. and Anderson, L.T. (1980) 'Behavioral effects of haloperidol in young autistic children.' *Journal of the American Academy of Child Psychiatry 19,* 655–677.

Cohn, J.F. and Tronick, E.Z. (1983) 'Three-month-old infants' reaction to simulated maternal depression.' *Child Development 54,* 185–193.

Comings, D.E. (1986) 'The genetics of Rett Syndrome: the consequences of a disorder where every case is a new mutation.' *American Journal of Medical Genetics 24,* 383–88.

Comings, D.E. (1990) *Tourette Syndrome and Human Behaviour.* Duarte: Hope Press.

Condon, W.S. (1975) 'Multiple response to sound in dysfunctional children.' *Journal of Autism and Childhood Schizophrenia 5,* 3–56.

Condon, W.S. and Sander, L. (1974) 'Neonate movement is synchronised in adult speech.' *Science 183,* 99–101.

Cook. E.H., Rowlett, R., Jaselskis, C. and Leventhal, B.L. (1992) 'Fluoxetine treatment of children and adults with Autistic Disorder and mental retardation.' *Journal of the American Academy of Child and Adolescent Psychiatry 31,* 739–745.

Cook, E.H. Jr., Courchesne, R., Lord, C., Cox, N.J., Yan, S., Lincoln, A., Haas, R., Courchesne, E. and Leventhal, B.L. (1997) 'Evidence of linkage between the serotonin transporter and autistic disorder.' *Molecular Psychiatry 2,* 247–250.

Cook, E.H. Jr. and Leventhal, B.L. (1996) 'The serotonin system in autism.' *Current Opinion in Pediatrics 8,* 348–354.

Corballis, M. (1991) *The Lopsided Ape: Evolution of the Generative Mind.* New York: Oxford University Press.

Cottam, J. and Sutton, A. (1986) *Conductive Education: A System for Overcoming Motor Disorder.* London: Croom Helm.

Courchesne, E. (1989) 'Neuroanatomical substems involved in infantile autism. The implications of cerebellar abnormalities.' In G. Dawson (ed) *Autism: Nature, Diagnosis and Treatment.* New York: Guilford Press.

Courchesne, E. (1995a) 'Infantile autism, part 1: MR imaging abnormalities and their neurobehavioral correlates.' *International Pediatrics 10,* 141–154.

Courchesne, E. (1995) 'Infantile autism, part 2: a new neurodevelopmental model.' *International Pediatrics 10,* 155–165.

Courchesne, E. (1997) 'Brainstem, cerebellar and limbic neuroanatomical abnormalities in autism.' *Current Opinion in Neurobiology 7,* 269–278.

Courchesne, E., Hesselink, J.R., Jernigan, T.L. and Yeung-Courchesne, R. (1987) 'Abnormal neuroanatomy in a non-retarded person with autism: unusual findings with magnetic resonance imaging.' *Archives of Neurology 44,* 335–341.

Courchesne, E., Yeung-Courchesne, R., Press, G.A., Hesselink, J.R. and Jernigan, T.L. (1988) 'Hypoplasia of cerebellar vermal lobules VI and VII in autism.' *New England Journal of Medicine 318*, 1349–1354.

Cowan, M.W., Fawcett, J.W., O'Leary, D.D.M. and Stanfield, B.B. (1984) 'Regressive events in neurogenesis.' *Science 225*, 1258–1265.

Creak, M. (1964) 'Schizophrenic syndrome in childhood: further progress report at a working party.' *Developmental Medicine and Child Neurology 6*, 530–535.

Critchley, M. and Henson, R.A. (eds) (1977) *Music and the Brain: Studies in the Neurology of Music*. London: Heinemann.

Cummins, R.A. (1988) *The Neurologically Impaired Child: Doman-Delacato Techniques Reappraised*. London: Croom Helm.

Cunningham, M.A. (1968) 'A comparison of the language of psychotic and non-psychotic children who are mentally retarded.' *Journal of Child Psychology and Psychiatry 9*, 229–244.

Curcio, F. (1978) 'Sensorimotor functioning and communication in mute autistic children.' *Journal of Autism and Childhood Schizophrenia 8*, 281–292.

Dahlgren, S.O. and Gillberg, C. (1989) 'Symptoms in the first two years of life: a preliminary population study of infantile autism.' *European Archives of Psychiatry and Neurological Sciences 238*, 169–174.

Dahlgren, S.-O., Sandberg, A., Helmqvist, E. and Trillingsgaard, A. (1997) 'The nonspecificity of theory of mind deficits. Evidence from children with communicative disabilities.' (in press).

Dahlgren, S.-O. and Trillingsgaard, A. (1996) 'Theory of mind in non-retarded children with autism and Asperger's syndrome. A research note.' *Journal of Child Psychology and Psychiatry 37*, 759–763.

Damasio, A. R. (1994). *Descartes' Error : Emotion, Reason and the Human Brain*. New York: Grosset/Putnam.

Damasio, H., Maurer, R.G., Damasio, A.R. and Chui, H.C. (1980) 'Computerised tomographic scan findings in patients with autistic behaviour.' *Archives of Neurology 37*, 504–510.

Davies, G. (1997) 'Communication.' In S. Powell and R. Jordan (eds) *Autism and Learning: A Guide to Good Practice*. London: David Fulton, 134–151.

Davis, W.B., Gfeller, K.E. and Thaut, M.H. (eds) (1992) *An Introduction to Music Therapy: Theory and Practice*. Dubuque, Indiana: William C. Brown Publishers.

Dawson, G. (1988) *Cerebral Lateralization in Autism: Its Role in Language and Affective Disorders*. New York: Guilford Press.

Dawson, G. (ed) (1989) *Autism: Nature, Diagnosis and Treatment*. New York: Guilford.

Dawson, G. (1994) 'Development of emotional expression and emotion regulation in infancy: contributions of the frontal lobe.' In G. Dawson and K. Fischer (eds) *Human Behavior and the Developing Brain*. New York: The Guilford Press, 346–379.

Dawson, G. and Adams, A. (1984) 'Imitation and social responsiveness in autistic children.' *Journal of Abnormal Child Psychology 12*, 209–226.

Dawson, G. and Fischer, K.W. (eds) (1994) *Human Behavior and the Developing Brain*. New York: The Guilford Press.

Dawson, G. and Galpert, L. (1990) 'Mothers' use of imitative play for facilitating social responsiveness and toy play in young autistic children.' *Development and Psychopathology 2*, 151–162.

Dawson, G., Hill, D., Spencer, A., Galpert, L. and Watson, L. (1990) 'Affective exchanges between young autistic children and their mothers.' *Journal of Abnormal Child Psychology 18*, 335–345.

Dawson, G. and Lewy, A. (1989) 'Reciprocal subcortical-cortical influences in autism: The role of attentional mechanisms.' In G. Dawson (ed) *Autism: Nature, Diagnosis, and Treatment.* New York: Guilford, 144–173.

Dawson, G. and McKissick, F.C. (1984) 'Self recognition in autistic children.' *Journal of Autism and Developmental Disorders 14*, 383–394.

DeCasper, A. and Fifer, W. (1980) 'Of human bonding: newborns prefer mother's voices.' *Science 208*, 1174.

Delacato, C.H. (1974) *The Ultimate Stranger: The Autistic Child.* New York: Doubleday and Co.

Demb, H.B. and Weintraub, A.G. (1989) 'A five year follow-up of preschool children diagnosed as having an atypical pervasive developmental disorder.' *Journal of Developmental and Behaviour Paediatrics 10*, 292–298.

DeMyer, M.K., Mann, N.A., Tilton, J.R. and Loew, L.H. (1967) 'Toy-play behaviour and use of body by autistic and normal children as reported by mothers.' *Psychological Reports 21*, 973–981.

DES (1978) *Special Educational Needs: Report of the Committee of Enquiry into the Education of Handicapped Children and Young People (Warnock Report).* London: Department of Education and Science.

Deutsch, S.I. (1986) 'Rationale for the administration of opiate antagonists in treating infantile autism.' *Journal of Mental Deficiency Research 90*, 631–635.

Dewey, J. (1934) *Art As Experience.* New edition, 1980. New York: Perigree.

DiLavore, P.C., Lord, C. and Rutter, M. (1995) 'The pre-linguistic autism diagnostic observation schedule.' *Journal of Autism and Developmental Disorders 25*, 4, 355–379.

Dissanayake, E. (1992) *Homo Aestheticus: Where Art Comes From and Why.* New York: Free Press.

Dissanayake, E. (1997) 'Antecedents of the temporal arts in early mother–infant interaction.' Paper presented at the Florentine Workshop in Biomusicology, May–June, 1997, Florence, Italy.

Donaldson, M. (1978) *Children's Minds.* London: Fontana/Collins.

Donaldson, M.L. (1995) *Children with Language Impairments: An Introduction.* London: Jessica Kingsley Publishers.

Donellan, A. and Leary, M. (1995) *Movement Differences and Diversity in Autism and Mental Retardation. Appreciating and Accommodating to People with Communication and Behaviour Challenges.* Newmarket, Ontario: DRI Press.

Dore, J. (1983) 'Feeling, form and intention in the baby's transition to language.' In R. Golnikoff (ed) *The Transition from Pre-Linguistic Communication.* Hillsdale, NJ: Lawrence Erlbaum Associates.

Duboule, D. (1994) *Guidebook to the Homeobox Genes.* New York: Oxford University Press.

Dunn, J. (1988) *The Beginnings of Social Understanding.* Oxford: Blackwell.

Durig, A. (1996) *Autism and the Crisis of Meaning.* Albany: State University of New York Press.

Dvorkin, J.M. (1994) 'Considerations of developmental issues in choosing interventions for resistance in music therapy.' *British Journal of Music Therapy 8*, 1, 5–6.

Echelard, Y., Epstein, D.J., St-Jaques, B., Shen, L., Mohler, J., McMahon, J.A. and McMahon, A.P. (1993) 'Sonic hedgehog, a member of a family of putative signaling molecules, is implicated in the regulation of CNS polarity.' *Cell 75*, 1417–1430.

Edgerton, C.-L. (1994) 'The effect of improvisational music therapy on the communicative behaviours of autistic children.' *Journal of Music Therapy 31*, 1, 31–62.

Edwards, C., Gandini, L. and Forman, G. (1993) *The Hundred Languages of Children: The Reggio Emilia Approach to Early Childhood Education.* Norwood, NJ: Ablex.

Ehlers, S. and Gillberg, C. (1993) 'The epidemiology of Asperger syndrome: A total population study.' *Journal of Child Psychology and Psychiatry, 34*, 1327–1350.

Eikeseth, S. and Lovaas, O.I. (1992) 'The autistic label and its potentially detrimental effect on the child's treatment.' *Journal of Behaviour Therapy and Experimental Psychiatry 23*, 151–157.

Eisenberg, L. and Kanner, L. (1956) 'Early infantile autism.' *American Journal of Orthopsychiatry 26*, 556–566.

Ellis, D. (ed) (1986) *Sensory Impairment in Mentally Handicapped People.* Beckenham: Croom Helm.

Emde, R.N. (1983) 'The prerepresentational self and its affective core.' *Psychoanalytic Study of the Child 38*, 165–192. New Haven, CT: Yale University Press.

Emde, R.N. (1988) 'Development terminable and interminable. I: Innate and motivational factors from infancy.' *International Journal of Psychoanalysis 69*, 23–42.

Emde, R.N. (1990) 'Mobilizing fundamental modes of development: empathic availability and therapeutic action.' *Journal of American Psychoanalytic Association 38*, 4, 880–913.

Eriksson, A. and DeChateau, P. (1992) 'Brief report: a girl aged two years and seven months with autistic disorder videotaped from birth.' *Journal of Autism and Developmental Disorders 22*, 127–129.

Evans, J.R. (1986) 'Dysrhythmia and disorders of learning and behaviour.' In J.R. Evans and M. Clynes (eds) *Rhythm in Psychological, Linguistic and Musical Processes.* Springfield, IL: Charles C. Thomas, 249–274.

Evans, J.R. and Clynes, M. (eds) (1986) *Rhythm in Psychological, Linguistic and Musical Processes.* Springfield, IL: Charles C. Thomas.

Evans, R. and Clifford, A. (1976) 'Captured for consideration – using videotape as an aid to the treatment of the disturbed child.' *Child: Care, Health and Development 2*, 129–137.

Fay, W.H. (1993) 'Infantile autism.' In D. Bishop and K. Mogford (eds) *Language Development in Exceptional Circumstances.* Hillsdale, NJ: Lawrence Erlbaum Associates.

Fein, D., Humes, M., Kaplan, E., Lucci, D. and Waterhouse, L. (1984) 'The question of left hemisphere dysfunction in infantile autism.' *Psychological Bulletin 95*, 258–281.

Fein, D., Pennington, B., Markowitz, P., Braverman, M. and Waterhouse, L. (1986) 'Toward a neuropsychological model of infantile autism: are the social defects primary?' *Journal of American Academy of Child Psychiatry 25*, 2, 198–212.

Fein, D., Pennington, B. and Waterhouse, L. (1987) 'Implications of social deficits in autism for neurological dfysfunction.' In E. Schopler and G.B. Mersibov (eds) *Neurobiological Issues in Autism.* New York: Plenum Press.

Fein, D., Waterhouse, L., Lucci, D., Pennington, B. and Humes, M. (1985) 'Handedness and cognitive functions in pervasive developmental disorders.' *Journal of Autism and Developmental Disorders 15,* 323–334.

Fein, D., Waterhouse, L., Lucci, D. and Snyder, D. (1985) 'Cognitive subtypes in developmentally disabled children: a pilot study.' *Journal of Autism and Developmental Disorders 15,* 77–95.

Fein, G.G. (1981) 'Pretend play: an integrative review.' *Child Development 52,* 1095–1118.

Feldstein, S., Konstantareas, M., Oxman, J. and Webster, C.D. (1982) 'The chronography of interactions with autistic speakers: an initial report.' *Journal of Communication Disorders 15,* 451–460.

Fernald, A. (1985) 'Four-month-old infants prefer to listen to motherese.' *Infant Behaviour and Development 8,* 181–195.

Fernald, A. (1989) 'Intonation and communicative interest in mother's speech to infants: Is the melody the message?' *Child Development, 60:* 1497–1510.

Fernald, A. (1992) 'Meaningful melodies in mothers' speech to infants.' In, Papousek, H., Jurgens, U. & Papousek, M. (eds.) *Nonverbal Vocal Communication: Comparative and Developmental Aspects.* Cambridge: Cambridge University Press/ Paris: Editions de la Maison des Sciences de l'Homme, 262–282.

Fiamenghi, G.A. (1997) 'Intersubjectivity and infant–infant interaction: imitation as a way of making contact.' Annual Report, Research and Clinical Center for Child Development, No. 19, 15–21. Hokkaido University, Sapporo, Japan.

Field, T., Healy, B., Goldstein, S., Perry, S., Bendell, D., Schanberg, S., Zimmerman, E.A. and Kuhn, C. (1988) 'Infants of depressed mothers show "depressed" behavior even with nondepressed adults.' *Child Development 59,* 1569–1579.

Field, T.M. and Fox, N. (eds) (1985) *Social Perception in Infants.* Norwood, NJ: Ablex.

Field, T.N., Woodson, R., Greenberg, R. and Cohen, D. (1982) 'Discrimination and imitation of facial expressions by neonates.' *Science 218,* 179–181.

First, M.B., Frances, A., Widiger, T.A., Pincus, H.A. and Davis, W.W. (1992) 'DSM-IV and behaviour assessment.' *Behavioural Assessment 14,* 297–306.

Fisch, G.S., Cohen, I.L., Wolf, E.G., Brown, W.T. and Jenkins, E.C. (1986) 'Autism and fragile-X syndrome.' *American Journal of Psychiatry 143,* 71–3.

Fish, B., Shapiro, T. and Campbell, M. (1966) 'Long term prognosis and the response of schizophrenic children to drug therapy: a controlled study of trifluoperazine.' *American Journal of Psychiatry 123,* 32–39.

Fish, J. (1985) *Special Education: The Way Ahead (The Fish Report).* Milton Keynes: The Open University.

Forinash, M. and Gonzalez, D. (1989) 'Phenomenology as research in music therapy.' *Music Therapy 8,* 1, 35–46.

Fraiberg, S. (1980) *Clinical Studies in Infant Mental Health: The First Year of Life.* London: Tavistock.

Franco, F. and Wishart, J.G. (1994) 'The use of pointing and other gestures by young children with Down syndrome.' *American Journal on Mental Retardation 100,* 160–182.

Freeman, B. J., Ritvo, E. R., Guthrie, D., Schroth, P. and Ball, J. (1978) 'The behaviour observation scale for autism: initial methodology, data analysis and preliminary findings on 89 children.' *Journal of the American Academy of Child Psychiatry, 17*, 576–588.

Freeman, B.J., Ritvo, E.R. and Schroth, P.C. (1984) 'Behaviour assessment of the syndrome of autism: behaviour observation system.' *Journal of the American Academy of Child Psychiatry 23*, 588–594.

Freitag, G. (1970) 'An experimental study of the social responsiveness of children with autistic behaviours.' *Journal of Experimental Child Psychology 9*, 436–453.

Friedman, E. (1969) 'The "Autistic Syndrome" and phenylketonuria.' *Schizophrenia 1*, 249–261.

Frith, U. (1989) *Autism: Explaining the Enigma.* Oxford: Basil Blackwell.

Frith, U. (1991) *Autism and Asperger Syndrome.* Cambridge: Cambridge University Press.

Frith, U. and Happé, F. (1994) 'Autism: beyond 'theory of mind'. *Cognition, 50*: 115–132.

Gaffney, G.R., Kuperman, S., Tsai, L. and Minchin, S. (1989) 'Forebrain structure in infantile autism.' *Journal of the American Academy of Child and Adolescent Psychiatry 28*, 534–537.

Garber, H.J. and Ritvo, E.R. (1992) 'Magnetic resonance imaging of the posterior fossa in autistic adults.' *American Journal of Psychiatry 149*, 245–247.

Gardner, R.L. and Stern, C.D. (1993) 'Integration in development.' In C.A.R. Boyd and D. Noble (eds) *The Logic of Life: The Challenge of Integrative Physiology.* Oxford: Oxford University Press.

Garfin, D.G. and Lord, K. (1986) 'Communication as a social problem in autism.' In E. Schopler and G. Mesibov (eds) *Social Behaviour in Autism.* New York: Plenum Press.

Garreau, B., Jouve, J., Bruneau, N., Muh, J.P. and LeLord, G. (1988) 'Urinary homovanillic acid levels of autistic children.' *Developmental Medicine and Child Neurology 30*, 93–98.

Gaston, E.T. (1968) 'Man and music.' In E.T. Gaston (ed) *Music in Therapy.* New York: Macmillan.

George, M.S., Costa, D.C., Kouris, K., Ring, H.A. and Ell, P.J. (1992) 'Cerebral blood flow abnormalities in adults with infantile autism.' *The Journal of Nervous and Mental Disease 180*, 413–417.

Gerlach, E. K. (1993) *Autism Treatment Guide.* Eugene, OR: Four Leaf Press.

Geschwind, N. and Galaburda, A. (1985) 'Cerebral lateralization: biological mechanisms, associations, and pathology: I, II, III: a hypothesis and program for research.' *Archives of Neurology 42*, 428–459, 521–552, 634–654.

Geschwind, N. and Galaburda, A. (eds) (1987) *Cerebral Lateralization: Biological Mechanisms, Associations, and Pathology.* Cambridge MA: The MIT Press.

Ghaziuddin, M., Tsai, L.Y. and Ghaziuddin, N. (1992) 'Brief report: a comparison of the diagnostic criteria for Asperger Syndrome.' *Journal of Autism and Developmental Disorders 22*, 643–649.

Gillberg, C. (1984) 'Infantile autism and other childhood psychoses in a Swedish urban region: epidemiological aspects.' *Journal of Child Psychology and Psychiatry 25*, 35–43.

Gillberg, C. (1988a) 'The neurobiology of infantile autism.' *Journal of the of Child Psychology and Psychiatry 29*, 257–266.

Gillberg, C. (1988b) 'The role of the endogenous opioids in autism and possible relationships to clinical features.' In L. Wing (ed) *Aspects of Autism: Biological Research*. London: Gaskell.

Gillberg, C. (1989) (ed) *Diagnosis and Treatment of Autism*. New York: Plenum Press.

Gillberg, C. (1990) 'Do children with autism have March birthdays?' *Acta Psychiatrica Scandinavica 82*, 152–156.

Gillberg, C. (1991a) 'The Emanuel Miller Memorial Lecture: autism and autistic-like conditions: subclasses among disorders of empathy.' *Journal of Child Psychology and Psychiatry 33*, 813–842.

Gillberg, C. (1991b) 'The treatment of epilepsy in autism.' *Journal of Autism and Developmental Disorders 21*, 61–77.

Gillberg, C. and Coleman, M. (1992) *The Biology of the Autistic Syndromes (2nd edn)*. Clinics in Developmental Medicine, 126. London: MacKeith Press.

Gillberg, C., Ehlers, S., Schaumann, H., Jakobsson, G., Dahlgren, S.O., Lindblom, R., Bågenholm, A., Tjuus, T. and Blinder, E. (1990) 'Autism under age 3 years: a clinical study of 28 cases referred for autistic symptoms in infancy.' *Journal of Child Psychology and Psychiatry 31*, 921–934.

Gillberg, C., Hagberg, B., Witt-Engerström, I. and Eriksson, I. (1990) 'CSF beta-endorphin in childhood neuropsychiatric disorders.' *Brain and Development, 12*, 88–92.

Gillberg, C., Persson, E. and Wahlström, J. (1986) 'The autism-fragile-X syndrome (AFRAX): a population-based study for ten boys.' *Journal of Mental Deficiency Research 30*, 27–39.

Gillberg, C. and Schaumann, H. (1982) 'Social slass and infantile autism.' *Journal of Autism and Developmental Disorders 12*, 223–228.

Gillberg, C. and Steffenburg, S. (1987) 'Outcome and prognostic factors in infantile autism and similar conditions: a population based study of 46 cases followed through puberty.' *Journal of Autism and Developmental Disorders 17*, 273–87.

Gillberg, C., Steffenburg, S. and Schaumann, H. (1991) 'Autism: epidemiology: is autism more common now than 10 years ago?' *British Journal of Psychiatry 158*, 403–409.

Gillberg, C., Terenius, L. and Lonnerholm, G. (1985) 'Endorphin activity in childhood psychosis.' *Archives of General Psychiatry 42*, 780–783.

Gillberg, I.C. and Gillberg, C. (1989) 'Asperger Syndrome – some epidemiological considerations: a research note.' *Journal of the of Child Psychology and Psychiatry 30*, 631–638.

Goldfarb, W. (1961) *Childhood Schizophrenia*. Cambridge, Mass.: Harvard University Press.

Goldman-Rakic, P.S. (1987) 'Development of cortical circuitry and cognitive function.' *Child Development 58*, 601–22.

Grafman, J., Litvan, I., Massaquoi, S., Stewart, M., Sirigu, A. and Hallett, M. (1992) 'Cognitive planning deficit in patients with cerebellar atrophy.' *Neurology 42*, 1493–1496.

Gram, L.F. and Rafaelsen, O.J. (1972) 'Lithium treatment of psychiatric children and adolescents: a controlled clinical trial.' *Acta Psychiatrica Scandinavica 48*, 253–260.

Grandin, T. (1984) 'My experiences as an autistic child and review of selected literature.' *Journal of Orthomolecular Psychiatry 13*, 144–174.

Grandin, T. (1992) 'Calming effects of deep touch pressure in patients with autistic disorder, college students, and animals.' *Journal of Adolescent and Child Pharmacology* 2, 63–72.

Grandin, T. (1995) *Thinking in Pictures.* New York: Doubleday.

Grandin, T. (1997) 'A personal perspective on autism.' In D.J. Cohen and F.R. Volkmar (eds) *Handbook of Autism and Developmental Disorders, 2nd Edition.* Wiley: New York, 1032–1042.

Grandin, T. and Scariano, M. (1986) *Emergence, Labelled Autistic.* London: Costello.

Gray, J.A. (1990) 'Brain systems that mediate both emotion and cognition.' In J.A. Gray (ed) *Psychobiological Aspects of Relationships between Emotion and Cognition.* Hove and London (UK)/Hillsdale (US): Erlbaum, 269–288.

Grieser, D.L. and Kuhl, P.K. (1988) 'Maternal speech to infants in a tonal language: support for universal prosodic features in motherese.' *Developmental Psychology 24*, 14–20.

Groden, G. and Baron, M.G. (eds) (1988) *Autism: Strategies for Change: A Comprehensive Approach to the Education and Treatment of Children with Autism and Related Disorders.* New York: Gardner Press.

Grotstein, J. (1980) 'Primitive mental states.' *Contemporary Psychoanalysis 16*, 479–546.

Haag, G. (1984) 'Autisme infantile precoce et phenomenes autistiques.' *Psychiatrie de l'Enfant, 27,* 2

Hagberg, B. (1989) 'Rett syndrome: clinical peculiarities, diagnostic approach, and possible cause.' *Pediatric Neurology 5*, 75–83.

Hagberg, B. (ed) (1993) *Rett Syndrome – Clinical and Biological Aspects.* London: Mac Keith Press (Clinics in Developmental Medicine, No. 127).

Hagberg, B., Aicardi, J., Dias, K. and Ramos, O. (1983) 'A progressive syndrome of autism, dementia, and loss of purposeful hand use in girls: Rett syndrome: a report of 35 cases.' *Annals of Neurology 14*, 471–479.

Hagberg, B. and Gillberg, C. (1993) 'Rett variants – Rettoid phenotypes.' In B. Hagberg (ed) *Rett Syndrome – Clinical and Biological Aspects.* (pp.40–60) London: Mac Keith Press (Clinics in Developmental Medicine, No. 127).

Hagberg, B., Naidu, S. and Percy, A.K. (1992) 'Tokyo Symposium on Rett Syndrome: neurobiological approach.' *Brain and Development 14* (supplement), S151–153.

Hagerman, R. J., Jackson, A. W., Levitas, A., Rimland, B. and Braden, M. (1986) 'An analysis of autism in fifty males with Fragile X syndrome.' *American Journal of Medical Genetics, 23,* 359–374.

Halliday, M.A.K. (1975) *Learning How to Mean.* London: Arnold.

Hammes, J.G.W. and Langdell, T. (1981) 'Precursors of symbol formation and childhood autism.' *Journal of Autism and Developmental Disorders 11*, 331–346.

Happé, F. (1994) *Autism: An Introduction to Psychological Theory.* London: UCL Press.

Happé, F.G.E. (1995a) *Autism: An Introduction to Psychological Theory.* Cambridge: Harvard University Press.

Happé, F.G.E. (1995b) 'The role of age and verbal ability in the theory of mind task performance of subjects with autism.' *Child Development 66*, 843–855.

Hardy, P. (1991) 'The efficacy of Daily Life Therapy at Boston Higashi School.' In *Therapeutic Approaches to Autism: Research and Practice.* Sunderland: Autism Research Unit, Sunderland Polytechnic, 115–127.

Hari, M. and Akos, K. (1988) *Conductive Education.* London: Routledge.

Harris, P. (1989) *Children and Emotion.* New York: Basil Blackwell.

Harris, S.L., Handleman, J.S., Gordon, R., Kristoff, B., and Fuentes, F. (1991) 'Changes in cognitive and language functioning of preschool children with autism.' *Journal of Autism and Developmental Disorders 21,* 3, 281–290.

Hauser, S., DeLong, G. and Rosman, N. (1975) 'Pneumographic findings in the infantile autism syndrome: a correlation with temporal lobe disease.' *Brain 98,* 667–688.

Heal, M. (1994) 'The development of symbolic function in a young woman with Down's syndrome.' In D. Dokter (ed) *Arts Therapies and Clients with Eating Disorders.* London: Jessica Kingsley Publishers.

Heal, M. and Wigram, T. (1993) *Music Therapy in Health and Education.* London: Jessica Kingsley Publishers.

Heal Hughes, M. (1995) 'A comparison of mother–infant interactions and the client–therapist relationship.' In T. Wigram, B. Saperston and R. West (eds) *The Art and Science of Music Therapy: A Handbook.* Chur, Switzerland: Harwood Academic Publishers, 296–308.

Hebb, D.O. (1949) *The Organization of Behaviour.* New York: Wiley.

Heilman, K.M. and Satz, P. (eds) (1983) *Neuropsychology of Human Emotion.* London: Guildford Press.

Heimann, M., Tjus, T., Nelson, K.E. and Gillberg, C. (1995) 'Increasing reading and communication skills in children with autism through an interactive multimedia computer program.' *Journal of Autism and Developmental Disorders 25,* 458–480.

Hermelin, B. and O'Connor, N. (1970) *Psychological Experiments with Autistic Children.* Oxford: Pergamon Press.

Hermelin, B. and O'Connor, N. (1985) 'Logico-affective states and non-verbal language.' In E. Schopler and G. Mesibov (eds) *Communication Problems in Autism.* New York: Plenum Press.

Herold, S., Frackowiak, R.S., Le Couteur, A., Rutter, M. and Howlin, P. (1988) 'Cerebral blood flow and metabolism of oxygen and glucose in young autistic adults.' *Psychological Medicine 18,* 823–831.

Hermann, B. and Seidenberg, M. (1995). 'Executive system dysfunction in temporal lobe epilepsy: Effects of nociferous cortex versus hippocampal pathology.' *Journal of Clinical & Experimental Neuropsychology, 17,* 809–819.

Hertzig, M.E., Snow, M.E., New, E. and Shapiro, T. (1990) 'DSM-III and DSM-III-R diagnosis of autism and pervasive developmental disorder in nursery school children.' *Journal of the American Academy of Child and Adolscent Psychiatry 29,* 123–126.

Hinshelwood, R. D. (1989) *A Dictionary of Kleinian Thought.* London: Free Association Books.

Hobson, R.P. (1983) 'The autistic child's recognition of age-related features of people, animals and things.' *British Journal of Developmental Psychology 1,* 343–352.

Hobson, R.P. (1984) 'Early childhood autism and the question of egocentrism.' *Journal of Autism and Developmental Disorders 14,* 85–104.

Hobson, R.P. (1986a) 'The autistic child's appraisal of expressions of emotion.' *Journal of Child Psychology and Psychiatry 27,* 321–342.

Hobson, R.P. (1986b) 'The autistic child's appraisal of expressions of emotion: a further study.' *Journal of Child Psychology and Psychiatry 27,* 671–680.

Hobson, R.P. (1987) 'Childhood autism: a once and future theory.' *Medical Research Council News*, 9–10.

Hobson, R.P. (1989) 'Beyond cognition: a theory of autism.' In G. Dawson (ed) *Autism: New Perspectives on Diagnosis, Nature and Treatment.* New York: Guilford, 22–48.

Hobson, R.P. (1990a) 'On the origins of self and the case of autism.' *Development and Psychopathology 2*, 163–182.

Hobson, R.P. (1990b) 'Concerning knowledge of mental states.' *British Journal of Medical Psychology 63*, 199–213.

Hobson, R.P. (1990c) 'On acquiring knowledge about people and the capacity to pretend: response to Leslie (1987).' *Psychological Review 97*, 114–121.

Hobson, R.P. (1990d) 'On psychoanalytic approaches to autism.' *American Journal of Orthopsychiatry 60*, 324–336.

Hobson, R.P. (1991) 'Against the theory of "theory of mind".' *British Journal of Developmental Psychology 9*, 33–51.

Hobson, R.P. (1993a) *Autism and the Development of Mind.* Hove/Hillsdale: Laurence Erlbaum Association.

Hobson, R.P. (1993b) 'Through feeling and sight to self and symbol.' In U. Neisser (ed) *The Perceived Self: Ecological and Interpersonal Sources of Self-Knowledge.* New York: Cambridge University Press, 254–279.

Hobson, R.P. (1997) 'Psychoanalysis and infancy.' In G. Bremner, A. Slater and G. Butterworth (eds) *Infant Development: Recent Advances.* Hove, East Sussex: Psychology Press. pp. 275–290.

Hobson, R.P., Ouston, J. and Lee, A. (1988a) 'What's in a face? The case of autism.' *British Journal of Psychology 79*, 411–453.

Hobson, R.P., Ouston, J. and Lee, A. (1988b) 'Emotion recognition in autism: co-ordinating faces and voices.' *Psychological Medicine 18*, 911–923.

Hochmann, J. (1997) *Pour Soigner l'Enfant Autiste: Des Contes à Rever Debut.* Paris: Odile Jacob.

Hogg, J. (1991) 'Developments in further education for adults with profound intellectual and multiple disabilities.' In J. Watson (ed) *Innovatory Practice and Severe Learning Difficulties.* (Meeting Educational Special Needs: A Scottish Perspective, Volume 1, Series Editors, G. Lloyd and J. Watson) Edinburgh: Moray House Publications.

Holroyd, S., Reiss, A.L. and Bryan, R.N. (1991) 'Autistic features in Joubert Syndrome: genetic disorder with agenesis of the cerebellar vermis.' *Biological Psychiatry 29*, 287–294.

Holstege, G., Bandler, R. and Saper, C.B. (eds) (1997) *The Emotional Motor System.* Amsterdam: Elsevier.

Horowitz, B., Rumsey, J.M., Grady, C.L. and Rapoport, S.I. (1988) 'The cerebral metabolic landscape in autism: intercorrelations of regional glucose utilization.' *Archives of Neurology 28*, 775–785.

Hoshino, Y., Kumashiro, H., Yashima, Y., Tashibana, R. and Watanabe, M. (1982) 'The epidemiological study of autism in Fukushima-Ken.' *Folia Psychiatrica Neurological Japan 36*, 115–124.

Howat, R.A. (1995) 'Elizabeth: a case study of an autistic child in individual music therapy.' In T. Wigram, B. Saperston and R. West (eds) *The Art and Science of Music Therapy: A Handbook.* Chur: Harwood Academic Publishers, 238–260.

Howlin, P. (1989) 'Changing approaches to communication and training with autistic children.' *British Journal for Disorders of Communication 24,* 151–168.

Howlin, P. (1997) *Autism: Preparing for Adulthood.* London: Routledge.

Howlin, P. and Rutter, M. (1987) *Treatment of Autistic Children.* Chichester: Wiley.

Howlin, P., Wing, L. and Gould, J. (1995) 'The recognition of autism in children with Down Syndrome: implications for intervention and some speculations concerning pathology.' *Developmental Medicine and Child Neurology 37,* 406–14.

Howlin, P. and Yates, P. (1989) 'Treating autistic children at home. A London based programme.' In C. Gillberg (ed) *Diagnosis and Treatment of Autism.* New York: Plenum, 307–322.

Howorth, C. (1997) QED Challenging Children: 'I want my little boy back.' 12 September, BBC1 WhiteCity, London: BBC Television.

Hubley, P. and Trevarthen, C. (1979) 'Sharing a task in infancy.' In I. Uzgiris (ed) *Social Interaction During Infancy, New Directions for Child Development.* San Francisco: Jossey-Bass, 4, 57–80.

Hugh, J.H. and Rosenthal, T.L. (1981) 'Therapeutic videotaped playback.' In J.L. Fryrear and B. Fleshman (eds) *Videotherapy in Mental Health.* Illinois: Charles C Thomas.

Hulse, W.C. (1954) 'Dementia infantilis.' *Journal of Nervous and Mental Disease 119,* 471–477.

Hundeide, K. (1991) *Helping Disadvantaged Children.* London: Jessica Kingsley Publishers.

Hurtig, R., Ensrud, S. and Tomblin, J.B. (1982) 'The communicative function of question production in autistic children.' *Journal of Autism and Developmental Disorders 12,* 57–69.

Hutt, C., Hutt, S.J., Lee, D. and Ounsted, C. (1964) 'Arousal and childhood autism.' *Nature 204,* 908–909.

Hutt, C. and Ounsted, C. (1966) 'The biological significance of gaze aversion with particular reference to the syndrome of infantile autism.' *Behavioural Science 11,* 346–356.

Imbert, M. (1985) 'Physiological underpinnings of perceptual development.' In J. Mehler and R. Fox (eds) *Neonate Cognition.* Hillsdale, NJ: Erlbaum.

Itard, J.M.G. (1801) *The Wild Boy of Aveyron.* Trans. G. and M. Humphrey (1932), New York: Appleton-Century-Crofts.

Izard, C.E. (1993) 'Four systems for emotion activation: cognitive and noncognitive processes.' *Psychological Review 100,* 68–90.

Jan, J.E., Espezel, H. and Appleton, R.E. (1994) 'The treatment of sleep disorders with melatonin.' *Developmental Medicine and Child Neurology 36,* 97–107.

Jan, J.E. and O'Donnell, M.E. (1996) 'Use of melatonin in the treatment of paediatric sleep disorders.' *Journal of Pineal Research 21,* 193–199.

Jarrold, C., Boucher, J. and Smith, P.K. (1994) 'Executive function deficits and the pretend play of children with autism: a research note.' *Journal of Child Psychology and Psychiatry 35,* 1473–1482.

Jarrold, C., Smith, P.K., Boucher, J. and Harris, P. (1994) 'Comprehension of pretense in children with autism.' *Journal of Autism and Developmental Disorders 24*, 433–455.

Jenson, W.R. and Young, K.R. (1985) 'Childhood autism: developmental considerations and behavioral interventions by professionals, families and peers.' In R.J. McMahon and R. DeV. Peters (eds) *Childhood Disorders: Behavioral and Developmental Approaches.* New York: Brunner/Mazel.

Johnson, M.H. (1993) *Brain Development and Cognition.* Oxford: Blackwell.

Johnson, M.H., Dziurawiec, S., Ellis, H.D. and Morton, J. (1991) 'Newborns preferential tracking of face-like stimuli and its subsequent decline.' *Cognition 40*, 1–21.

Johnson, M.H. and Morton, J. (1991) *Biology and Cognitive Development: The Case of Face Recognition.* Oxford: Basil Blackwell.

Johnson, M.H., Siddons, F., Frith, U. and Morton, J. (1992) 'Can autism be predicted on the basis of infant screening tests?' *Developmental Medicine and Child Neurology 34*, 316–320.

Jonsson, C.O., Reimbladh-Taube, G. and Sjöswärd, E. (1993) 'Forms, uses and functions of children's favourite objects.' *Scandanavian Journal of Psychology 34*, 86–93.

Jonsson, C.O. and Sjöswärd, E. (1993) 'Favourite objects of autistic children.' *Scandanavian Journal of Psychology 34*, 237–245.

Jordan, R. (1990) *The Option Approach to Autism: Observer Project Report.* Willesden: National Autistic Society.

Jordan, R. (1991) *The National Curriculum: Access for Pupils with Autism.* London: Inge Wakehurst Trust.

Jordan, R. (1993) 'The nature of linguistic and communication difficulties of children with autism.' In D.J. Messer and G.J. Turner (eds) *Critical Influences on Child Language Acquisition and Development.* New York: St. Martin's Press.

Jordan, R. and Libby, S. (1997) 'Developing and using play in the curriculum.' In S. Powell and R. Jordan (eds) *Autism and Learning: A Guide to Good Practice.* London: David Fulton, 28–45.

Jordan, R. and Powell, S. (1991) 'Teaching thinking – the case for principles.' *European Journal of Special Needs Education 6*, 112–123.

Jordan, R. and Powell, S. (1993a) 'Being subjective about autistic thinking and learning to learn.' *Educational Psychology 13*, 359–370.

Jordan, R. and Powell, S. (1993b) 'Diagnosis, intuition and autism.' *British Journal of Special Education 20*, 26–29.

Jordan, R. and Powell, S. (1995) *Understanding and Teaching Children with Autism.* Wiley: Chichester.

Jordan, R.R. (1989) 'An experimental comparison of the understanding and use of speaker–addressee personal pronouns in autistic children.' *British Journal of Disorders of Communication 24*, 169–179.

Junck, L., Gilman, S., Rothley, J.R., Betley, A.T., Koeppe, R.A. and Hichwa, R.D. (1988) 'A relationship between metabolism in frontal lobes and cerebellum in normal subjects studied with PET.' *Journal of Cerebral Blood Flow and Metabolism 8*, 774–782.

Kagan, J. (1982) 'The emergence of self.' *Journal of Child Psychology and Psychiatry 23*, 363–381.

Kanner, L. (1943) 'Autistic disturbances of affective contact.' *Nervous Child 2,* 217–250.

Kanner, L. (1946) 'Irrelevant and metaphorical language in early infantile autism.' *American Journal of Psychiatry 103,* 242–245.

Kanner, L. (1949) 'Problems of nosology and psychodynamics of early infantile autism.' *American Journal of Orthopsychiatry 19,* 416–426.

Kanner, L. (1973) *Childhood Psychosis: Initial Studies and New Insights.* Washington, DC: V.H. Winston and Sons.

Kanner, L. and Eisenberg, L. (1956) 'Early infantile autism, 1943–1955.' *American Journal of Orthopsychiatry 26,* 55–65.

Kasari, C., Sigman, M., Mundy, P. and Yirmiya, N. (1988) 'Caregiver interactions with autistic children.' *Journal of Abnormal Child Psychology 16,* 45–56,

Kasari, C., Sigman, M., Mundy, P. and Yirmiya, N. (1990) 'Affective sharing in the context of joint attention interactions of normal, autistic and mentally retarded children.' *Journal of Autism and Developmental Disorders 20,* 87–101.

Kaufman, B.N. (1976) *Son-rise.* New York: Harper and Row.

Kaufman, B.N. (1981) *A Miracle to Believe In.* New York: Ballantine Books.

Kaufman, B.N. (1994) *Son Rise: The Miracle Continues.* Tiberon, CA: H. J. Kramer Inc.

Kaufman, B.N. and Kaufman, S. (1976) *To Love is to be Happy With.* Human Horizons Series. London: Souvenir Press.

Kerr, A.M. (1995) 'Early clinical signs in the Rett disorder.' *Neuropediatrics 26,* 67–71.

Kitahara, K. (1983) *Daily Life Therapy: A Method for Educating Children with Autism., Volume I: Principles and Methods for Educating Autistic Children by Daily Life Therapy.* Tokyo: Musashino Higashi GakuenSchool/ Boston: Boston Higashi School.

Kitahara, K. (1984a) *Daily Life Therapy: A Method for Educating Children with Autism., Volume 2: Record of Actual Education of Autistic Children by Daily Life* Therapy,. Tokyo: Musashino Higashi Gakuen School/ Boston: Boston Higashi School.

Kitahara, K. (1984b) *Daily Life Therapy: A Method for Educating Children with Autism., Volume 3: Physical Education of Autistic Children by Daily Life Therapy.* Tokyo: Musashino Higashi Gakuen School/ Boston: Boston Higashi School.

Kleiman, M.D., Neff, S. and Rosman, N.P. (1990) 'The brain in infantile autism: is the cerebellum really abnormal?' *Annals of Neurology 28,* 422 (Abstract).

Klein M. (1946) 'Notes on some schizoid mechanisms.' *International Journal of Psycho-Analysis, 27,* 99–110.

Klein, M. (1963) *Our Adult World and its Roots in Infancy, and Other Essays.* London: Heinemann Medical.

Klin, A., Volkmar, F.R., Sparrow, S.S., Cicchetti, D.V. and Rourke, B.P. (1995) 'Validity and neuropsychological characterization of Asperger Syndrome: convergence with nonverbal learning disabilities syndrome.' *Journal of Child Psychology and Psychiatry 36,* 7, 1127–1140.

Klinnert, M.D., Campos, J.J., Sorce, J.F., Emde, R.N. and Svejda, M. (1983) 'Emotions as behavior regulators: social referencing in infancy.' In R. Plutchik and H. Kellerman (eds) *Emotion: Theory, Research and Experience, Volume Two.* New York: Academic Press.

Knight, C. (1991) 'Developing communication through interaction.' In J. Watson (ed) *Innovatory Practice and Severe Learning Difficulties.* (Meeting Educational Special

Needs: A Scottish Perspective, Volume 1, Series Editors, G. Lloyd and J. Watson) Edinburgh: Moray House Publications.

Knight, C. and Watson, J. (1990) *Intensive Interaction Teaching at Gogarburn School.* Edinburgh: Moray House College.

Knott, F. (1995) 'Approaches to Autism in the USA.' Report for the Winston Churchill Travelling Fellowship, 1995. (Obtainable from the author: Fiona Knott, Clinical Child Psychologist, Rainbow House, Ayeshire Central Hospital, Irvine KA12 8SS, Scotland, UK.)

Koegel, R.L. and Koegel, L.K. (1995) *Teaching Children with Autism.* London: Paul H. Brookes.

Konstantareas, M.M., Hauser, P., Lennox, C. and Homatidis, S. (1986) 'Season of birth in infantile autism.' *Child Psychiatry and Human Development 17*, 53–65.

Konstantareas, M.M., Webster, C.D. and Oxman, J. (1979) 'Manual language acquisition and its influence on other areas of functioning in four autistic and autistic-like children.' *Journal of Child Psychology and Psychiatry 20*, 337–350.

Konstantareas, M.M., Zajademan, H., Homatidis, S. and McCabe, A. (1988) 'Maternal speech to verbal and higher functioning versus nonverbal and lower functioning autistic children.' *Journal of Autism and Developmental Disorders 18*, 647–656.

Kraemer, G.W. (1992) 'A psychobiological theory of attachment.' *Behavioural and Brain Sciences 15*, 3, 493–541.

Krug, D.A., Arick, J. and Almond, P. (1980) 'Behaviour checklist for identifying severly handicapped individuals with high levels of autistic behaviour.' *Journal of Child Psychology and Psychiatry 21*, 221–229.

Kubicek, L.F. (1980) 'Organization in two mother–infant interactions involving a normal infant and his fraternal twin brother who was later diagnosed as autistic.' In T. Field, S. Goldberg, D. Stein and A. Sostek (eds) *High Risk Infants and Children: Adult and Peer Interactions.* New York: Academic Press.

Kugiumutzakis, J.E. (1993) 'Intersubjective vocal imitation in early mother–infant interaction.' In J. Nadel and L. Camaioni (eds) *New Perspectives in Early Communicative Development.* London: Routledge.

Landry, S.H. and Loveland, K.A. (1989) 'The effect of social context on the functional communication skills of autistic children.' *Journal of Autism and Developmental Disorders 19*, 283–299.

Langer, S. (1953) *Form and Feeling.* London: Routledge.

Latchford, G. (1989) *Towards an Understanding of Profound Mental Handicap.* Unpublished PhD Thesis, University of Edinburgh.

Lauder, J.M. and Krebs (1986) 'Do neurotransmitters, neurohumors, and hormones specify critical periods?' In W.T. Greenough and J.M. Juraska (eds) *Developmental Neuropsychobiology.* (pp.119–174) Orlando, FL: Academic Press.

Le Couteur, A., Bailey, A., Goode, S., Pickles, A., Robertson, S., Gottesman, I. and Rutter, M. (1996) 'A broader phenotype of autism: the clinical spectrum in twins.' *Journal of Child Psychology and Psychiatry 37*, 785–802.

Le Couteur, A., Rutter, M., Lord, C., Rios, P., Robertson, S., Holdgrafter, M. and McLennen, J.D. (1989) 'Autism diagnostic Interview: a standarised, investigator-based instrument.' *Journal of Autism and Developmental Disorders 19*, 363–387.

Lee, C. (1995) 'The analysis of therapeutic improvisatory music.' In A. Gilroy and C. Lee (eds) *Art and Music Therapy and Research.* London: Routledge.

Lees, A.J. (1985) *Tics and Related Disorders* (Clinical Neurology and Neurosurgery Monographs, 7) Edinburgh: Churchill Livingstone.

Leiner, H., Leiner, A.L. and Dow, R.S. (1993) 'Cognitive and language functions of the human cerebellum.' *Trends in Neurosciences 16,* 444–447.

LeLord, G., Muh, J.P., Barthélémy, C., Martineau, J., Garreau, B. and Callaway, E. (1981) 'Effects of pyridoxine and magnesium on autistic symptoms: initial observations.' *Journal of Autism and Developmental Disorders 11,* 219–230.

Lesch, M. and Nyhan, W.L. (1969) 'A familial disorder with uric acid metabolism and central nervous system function.' *American Journal of Medicine 36,* 561–570.

Leslie, A.M. (1987) 'Pretense and representation: the origins of "Theory of Mind".' *Psychological Review 94,* 412–426.

Leslie, A.M. (1991) 'The theory of mind impairment in autism: evidence for a modular mechanism of development?' In A. Whiten (ed) *Natural Theories of Mind: Evolution, Development and Simulation of Everyday Mindreading.* Oxford: Basil Blackwell.

Leslie, A.M. and Frith, U. (1988) 'Autistic children's understanding of seeing, knowing and believing.' *British Journal of Developmental Psychology 6,* 315–324.

Leslie, A.M. and Happé, F. (1989) 'Autism and ostensive communication: the relevance of metarepresentation.' *Development and Psychopathology 3,* 205–213.

Levinge, A. (1990) '"The use of I and me": music therapy with an autistic child.' *Journal of British Music Therapy 4,* 2, 15–18.

Lewis, V. and Boucher, J. (1988) 'Spontaneous, instructed and elicited play in relatively able autistic children.' *British Journal of Developmental Psychology 6,* 325–339.

Liddle, P.F. (1992) 'PET Scanning and schizophrenia: what progress?' *Psychological Medicine 22,* 557–560.

Liddle, P. F. and Morris, D. L. (1991). 'Schizophenic symptoms and frontal lobe performance.' *British Journal of Psychiatry, 158,* 340–345.

Lillard, A.S. (1993) 'Pretend play skills and the child's theory of mind.' *Child Development 64,* 348–371.

Locke, J.L. (1993) *The Child's Path to Spoken Language.* Cambridge MA: Harvard University Press.

Lord, C. (1997) 'Diagnostic instuments in autism spectrum disorders.' In D.J. Cohen and F.R. Volkmar (eds) *Handbook of Autism and Pervasive Disorders, 2nd Edition.* New York: John Wiley.

Lord, C., Rutter, M., Goode, S., Heemsbergen, J., Jordan, H., Mawhood, L. and Schopler, E. (1989) 'Autism diagnostic observation schedule: a standarized observation of communicative and social behaviour.' *Journal of Austim and Developmental Disorders 19,* 185–212.

Lotter (1967) *The Prevalence of the Autistic Syndrome in Children.* London: University of London Press.

Lotter, V. (1966) 'Epidemiology of autistic conditions in young children. I: Prevalence.' *Social Psychiatry 1,* 124–137.

Lovaas, O.I. (1978) 'Parents as therapists for autistic children.' In M. Rutter and E. Schopler (eds) *Autism: A Reappraisal of Concepts and Treatment.* New York: Plenum Press.

Lovaas, O.I. (1980) *Teaching Developmentally Disabled Children: The ME Book.* Austin, Texas: Pro-Ed Publishers.

Lovaas, O.I. (1987) 'Behavioural treatment and normal educational and intellectual functioning in young autistic children.' *Journal of Consulting and Clinical Pschology 55*, 1, 3–9.

Lovaas, O.I. and Smith, T. (1988) 'Intensive behavioral treatment for young autistic children.' In B.B. Lahey and A.E. Kazdin (eds) *Advances in Clinical Child Psychology, Volume II*, 285–324. New York: Plenum.

Loveland, K.A., Laundry, S.H., Hughes, S.O., Hall, S.K. and McEvoy, R.E. (1988) 'Speech acts and the pragmatic deficits of autism.' *Journal of Speech and Hearing Research 31*, 593–604.

Loveland, K. and Laundry, S. (1986) 'Joint attention in autistic and language delayed children.' *Journal of Autism and Developmental Disorders 16*, 335–350.

Lowe, M. (1975) 'Trends in the development of representational play in infants from one to three years – an observational study.' *Journal of Child Psychology and Psychiatry 16*, 33–47.

Luria, A.R. (1969) *The Mind of a Mnemonist.* (Trans. L. Solotaroff; Foreword by J. Bruner) London: Jonathan Cape.

Lynch, M.P., Oller, D.K., Steffens, M.L. and Buder, E.H. (1995) 'Phrasing in prelinguistic vocalizations.' *Developmental Psychobiology 28*, 3–25.

Lyon, G. and Gadisseux, J.-F. (1991) 'Structural abnormalities of the brain in developmental disorders.' In M. Rutter and P. Casaer (eds) *Biological Risk Factors for Psychosocial Disorders.* Cambridge: Cambridge University Press, 1–19.

Lyons, J. (1977) *Semantics.* Volume Two. London: Cambridge University Press.

Macdonald, H., Rutter, M., Howlin, P., Riss, P, Le Couteur, A., Evered, C. and Folstein, S. (1989) 'Recognition and expression of emotional cues by autistic and normal adults.' *Journal of Child Psychology and Psychiatry, 30*: 865–878.

MacKinnon, P.C.B. and Greenstein, B. (1985) 'Sexual differentiation of the brain.' In F. Falkner and J.M. Tanner (eds) *Human Growth. A Comprehensive Treatise.* Vol. 2, Postnatal Crowth; Neurobiology. (pp.437–468) New York: Plenum.

MacLean, P.D. (1992) *The Triune Brain in Evolution. Role in Paleocerebral Function.* New York: Plenum.

MacLean, P.D. (1993) 'Introduction: perspectives on cingulate cortex in the limbic system.' In B.A. Vogt and M. Gabriel (eds) *Neurobiology of Cingulate Cortex and Limbic Thalamus: A Comprehensive Handbook*, 1–19. Boston: Birkhauser.

Mahlberg, M. (1973) 'Music therapy in the treatment of an autistic child.' *Journal of Music Therapy 10*, 4, 189–193.

Mahler, M.S. (1952) 'On child psychosis and schizophrenia. Autistic and symbolic psychoses.' *Psychoanalytic Study of the Child, Vol. 7.* New York: International Universities Press, 286–305.

Mahler, M. (1968) *On Human Symbiosis and the Vicissitudes of Individuation. Volume I : Infantile Psychosis.* New York : International Universities Press.

Mahoney, G., Fors, S. and Wood, S. (1990) 'Maternal directive behavior revisited.' *American Journal of Mental Retardation 94*, 398–406.

Main, M. (1994) 'A move to the level of representation in the study of attachment organisation: implications for psychoanalysis.' Annual Research Lecture to the British Psychoanalytic Society, London.

Main, M. and Goldwyn, R. (1984) 'Predicting rejection of her infants from mother's representation of her own experience. Implications for the abused–abusing intergenerational cycle.' *International Journal of Child Abuse and Neglect 8*, 203–217.

Malloch, S., Sharp, D., Campbell, D.M., Campbell, A.M., & Trevarthen, C. (1997) 'Measuring the human voice: Analysing pitch, timing, loudness and voice quality in mother/infant communication.' *Proceedings of the Institute of Acoustics, 19 (5):* 495–500.

von der Malsberg, C. and Singer, W. (1988) 'Principles of cortical network organization.' In P. Rakic and W. Singer (eds) *Neurobiology of Neocortex.* New York: Wiley.

Maranto, C.D. (ed) (1993) *Music Therapy: International Perspectives.* Pipersville, Pennsylvania: Jeffrey Books.

Marchant, R., Howlin, P., Yule, W. and Rutter, M. (1974) 'Graded change in the treatment of the behaviour of autistic children.' *Journal of Child Psychology and Psychiatry 15*, 221–227.

Martineau, J., Barthélémy, C., Cheliakine, C. and LeLord, G. (1988) 'An open middle-term study of combined B6-Mg in a subgroup of autistic children selected on their sensitivity to this treatment.' *Journal of Autism and Developmental Disorders, 18*, 583–591.

Massie, H.N. (1978a) 'The early natural history of childhood psychosis.' *Journal of the American Academy of Child Psychiatry 17*, 29–45.

Massie, H.N. (1978b) 'Blind ratings of mother–infant interaction in home movies of pre-psychotic and normal infants.' *American Journal of Psychiatry 135*, 1371–1374.

Matthews, W.S. (1977) 'Modes of transformation in the initiation of fantasy play.' *Developmental Psychology 13*, 212–216.

Maurice, C. (1993) *Let Me Hear Your Voice: A Family Trimph over Autism.* New York: Knopf.

McDougall, J. and Lebovici, S. (1960) 'Un cas de psychose infantile.' Paris, Presses Universitaires de France. (English translations: *Dialogue with Sammy: A Psychoanalytical Contribution to the Understanding of Child Psychosis.* London: Hogarth Press, 1969; and, London: Free Association Books, 1989, with a preface by D. W. Winnicott.)

McDougle, C. J. (1997) 'Psychopharmacology.' In D. J. Cohen and F. R. Volkmar (eds.) *The Handbook of Autism and Pervasive Developmental Disorders, Second Edition.* New York: Wiley, 707–729. Meltzer, D.(1975) Explorations in Autism. London : The Roland Harris Educational Trust.

McDougle, C.J., Naylor, S.T., Cohen, D.J., Volkmar, F.R., Heninger, G.R. and Price, L.H. (1996) 'A double-blind placebo controlled study of fluvoxamine in adults with autistic disorder.' *Archives of General Psychiatry 53*, 1001–1008.

McEachin, S.J., Smith, T. and Lovaas, I.O. (1993) 'Long-term outcome for children with autism who receive early intensive behavioural treatment.' *American Journal of Mental Retardation 97*, 4, 359–372, discussion 373–391.

McGee, J.J., Menolascino, F.J., Hobbs, D.C. and Menousek, P.E. (1987) *Gentle Teaching: A Non-Aversive Approach for Helping Persons with Mild Retardation.* Human Sciences Press.

McHale, S.M. (1983) 'Social interactions of autistic and non-handicapped children during free play.' *American Journal of Orthopsychiatry 53*, 81–91.

McHale, S.M., Simeonson, R.J., Marcus, L.M. and Olley, G.J. (1980) 'The social and symbolic quality of autistic children's communication.' *Journal of Autism and Developmental Disorders 10*, 299–310.

McNeill, D. (1992) *Hand and Mind: What Gestures Reveal About Thought.* Chicago: University of Chicago Press.

Mehler, J. and Fox, R. (1985) *Neonate Cognition: Beyond the Blooming Buzzing Confusion.* Hillsdale, NJ: Erlbaum.

Meisels, S.J. and Shonkoff, J.P. (eds) (1990) *Handbook of Early Childhood Intervention.* Cambridge: Cambridge University Press.

Meltzer, D. (1975) 'The psychology of autistic states and of post-autistic mentality.' In D. Meltzer, J. Bremner, S. Hoxter, D. Weddell, and I. Wittenberg (eds.) *Explorations in Autism.* London: Clunie Press.

Meltzer, D., Bremer, J., Hoxter, S., Weddell, D. and Wittenberg, I. (1975) *Explorations in Autism. A Psycho-Analytical Study.* Strath Thay: Clunie Press.

Meltzoff, A.N. (1985) 'The roots of social and cognitive development: models of man's original nature.' In T.M. Field and N.A. Fox (eds) *Social Perception in Infants.* Norwood, NJ: Ablex, 1–30.

Meltzoff, A.N. and Gopnik, A. (1993) *The Role of Imitation in Understanding Persons and Developing a Theory of Mind.* Oxford: Oxford University Press.

Merzenich, M.M. *et al.,* (1996) 'Temporal processing deficits of language-learning impaired children ameliorated by training.' *Science 271*, 77–81.

Mesibov, G.B., Troxler, M. and Boswell, S. (1988) 'Assessment in the classroom.' In E. Schopler and G.B. Mesibov (eds) *Diagnosis and Assessment in Autism.* New York: Plenum, 261–270.

Meyer, L. (1956) *Emotions and Meaning in Music.* Chicago: Chicago University Press.

Meyer, L. (1994) 'Emotions and meaning in music.' In R. Aiello (ed) *Musical Perceptions.* Oxford: Oxford University Press.

Miedzianik, D. C. (1986) *My Autobiography.* Nottingham: Nottingham Child Development Research Unit, University of Nottingham.

Miller, M.T. and Strömland, K. (1993) 'Thalidomide embryopathy: an insight into autism?' *Teratology 47*, 387–388.

Mishkin, M. and Appenzeller, T. (1987) 'The anatomy of memory.' *Scientific American 256*, 80–9.

Mittler, P. (1966) 'Psychological assessment of autistic children.' In J.K. Wing (ed) *Early Childhood Autism: Clinical, Educational and Social Aspects.* Oxford: Pergamon Press.

Morgan, H. (1996) *Adults with Autism: A Guide to Theory and Practice.* Cambridge: Cambridge University Press.

Morgane, P.J. and Panksepp, J. (eds) (1981) *Handbook of the Hypothalamus.* New York/Basel: Marcel Dekker.

Muller, P. and Warwick, A. (1993) 'The effects of maternal involvement in therapy.' In M. Heal and A. Wigram (eds) *Music Therapy in Health and Education.* London and Philadelphia: Jessica Kingsley Publishers.

Mundy, P., Kasari, C. and Sigman, M. (1992) 'Nonverbal communication, affect sharing and intersubjectivity.' *Infant Behaviour and Development 15*, 377–81.

Mundy, P. and Sigman, M. (1989a) 'The theoretical implications of joint attention deficits in autism.' *Development and Psychopathology, 1*, 173–183.

Mundy, P. and Sigman, M. (1989b) 'Specifying the nature of the social impairment in autism.' In: G. Dawson (ed.), *Autism: New Perspectives on Diagnosis, Nature and Treatment.* New York: Guilford, 3–21.

Mundy, P., Sigman, M. and Kasari, C. (1990) 'A longitudinal study of joint attention and language development in autistic children.' *Journal of Autism and Developmental Disorders 20*, 115–129.

Mundy, P., Sigman, M. and Kasari, C. (1994) 'Joint attention, developmental level and symptom presentation in autism.' *Development and Psychopathology 6*, 3, 389–401.

Mundy, P., Sigman, M., Ungerer, J. and Sherman, T. (1986) 'Defining the social deficits of autism. The contribution of non-verbal communication measures.' *Journal of Child Psychology and Psychiatry 27*, 657–669.

Mundy, P., Sigman, M., Ungerer, J., and Sherman, T. (1987) 'Non-verbal communication and play correlates of language development in autistic children.' *Journal of Autism and Developmental Disorders 17*, 3, 349–364.

Murakami, J.W., Courchesne, E., Press, G., Yeung-Courchesne, R. and Hesselink, J.R. (1989) 'Reduced cerebellar hemisphere size and its relationship to vermal hypoplasia in autism.' *Archives of Neurology 46*, 689–694.

Murphy, G. and Wilson, B. (eds) (1985) *Self-Injurious Behaviour.* London: British Institute for Mental Handicap.

Murray, D.K.C. (1997) 'Autism and information technology: therapy with computers.' In S. Powell and R. Jordan (eds) *Autism and Learning: A Guide to Good Practice.* London: David Fulton, 100–117.

Murray, L. (1988) 'Effects of post-natal depression on infant development: direct studies of early mother–infant interactions.' In I. Brockington and R. Kumar (eds) *Motherhood and Mental Illness, Vol. 2.* Bristol: John Wright.

Murray, L. (1992) 'The impact of postnatal depression on infant development.' *Journal of Child Psychology and Psychiatry 33*, 3, 543–561.

Murray, L. and Cooper, P.J. (eds) (1997) *Postpartum Depression and Child Development.* New York: Guilford Press.

Murray, L. and Trevarthen, C. (1985) 'Emotional regulation of interactions between two-month-olds and their mothers.' In T. Field and N. Fox (eds) *Social Perception in Infants.* Norwood, NJ: Ablex.

Nadel, J. (1986) *Imitation et Communication entre Jeunes Enfants.* Paris: PUF.

Nadel, J. (1992) 'Imitation et communication chez l'enfant autiste et le jeune enfant pr,langagier.' In J. Hochman and P. Ferrari (eds) *Imitation et Identification chez l'Enfant Autiste.* Paris: Bayard.

Nadel, J. and Fontaine, A. M. (1989) 'Communicating by imitation: a developmental and comparative approach to transitory social competence.' In B. Schneider, G. Attili, J. Nadel and R. Weissberg (eds) *Social Competence in Developmental Perspective.* Dordrecht: Kluwer.

Nadel, J. and Pezé, A. (1993) 'Immediate imitation as a basis for primary communication in toddlers and autistic children.' In J. Nadel and L. Camioni (eds) *New Perspectives in Early Communicative Development.* London: Routledge.

Nadel-Brulfert, J. and Baudonnière, P.M. (1982) 'The social function of reciprocal imitation in 2-year-old peers.' *International Journal of Behavioral Development 5*, 95–109.

Nagy, E. and Molnár, P. (1994) 'Homo imitans or Homo provocans?' *Abstract, International Journal of Psychophysiology 18*, 2, 128.

National Autistic Society (1993) *Approaches to Autism, 2nd Edition.* London: National Autistic Society.

Nauta, W.J.H. and Feirtag, M. (1979) 'The organization of the brain.' *Scientific American 241*, 78–100.

Newport, E.L. and Meier, R.P. (1985) 'The acquisition of American Sign Language.' In D.E. Slobin (ed) *The Crosslinguistic Study of Language Acquisition. Vol. I: The Data.* Hillsdale, NJ: Erlbaum.

Newson, J. (1979) 'The growth of shared understandings between infant and caregiver.' In M. Bullowa (ed) *Before Speech: The Beginnings of Human Communication.* Cambridge: Cambridge University Press.

Nicholich, L. (1977) 'Beyond sensor motor intelligence: assessment of symbolic maturity through analysis of pretend play.' *Merrill-Palmer Quarterly 23*, 89–99.

Nielsen, J.B., Friberg, L., Lou, H., Lassen, N.A.S. and Sam, I.L. (1990) 'Immature pattern of brain activity in Rett syndrome.' *Archives of Neurology 47*, 98–986.

Nind, M. and Hewett, D. (1988) 'Interaction as curriculum.' *British Journal of Special Education 15*, 55–57.

Nind, M. and Hewett, D. (1994) *Access to Communication: Developing the Basics of Communication with People with Severe Learning Difficulties through Intensive Interaction.* London: David Fulton.

Nir, I, Meir, D., Zilber, N., Knobler, H., Hhadjez, J. and Lerner, Y. (1995) 'Brief report: circadian melatonin, thyroid stimulating hormone, prolactin and cortisol levels in serum of young adults with autism.' *Journal of Autism and Developmental Disorders 25*, 641–654.

Nomura, Y., Segawa, M. and Higurashi, M. (1985) 'Rett syndrome – an early catecholamine and indolamine deficient disorder?' *Brain and Development 7*, 3, 334–341.

Nordoff, P. and Robbins, C. (1968) *The Second Book of Play-Songs.* Bryn Mawr, Pennsylvania: Theodore Presser Co.

Nordoff, P. and Robbins, C. (1971a) *Therapy in Music for Handicapped Children.* London: Gollancz.

Nordoff, P. and Robbins, C. (1971b) *Music Therapy in Special Education.* New York: John Day Company.

Nordoff, P. and Robbins, C. (1977) *Creative Music Therapy.* (Including case studies on audio cassette.) New York: John Day Company. (Out of print. Available from The Nordoff-Robbins Music Therapy Centre, London.)

Nordoff, P. and Robbins, C. (1998) *Creative Music Therapy, Second Edition.* St Louis, MO: MMB.

Nowell, M.A., Hackney, D.B., Muraki, A.S. and Coleman, M. (1990) 'Varied MR appearance of autism: fifty-three paediatric patients have the full autistic syndrome.' *Magnetic Resonance Imaging 8*, 811–816.

O'Rahilly, R. and Müller, F. (1994) *The Embryonic Human Brain: An Atlas of Developmental Stages.* New York: Wiley-Liss.

Ohta, M. (1987) 'Cognitive disorders of infantile autism: a study of employing the WISC, spatial relationship conceptualization and gesture imitations.' *Journal of Autism and Developmental Disorders 17*, 45–62.

Oppenheim, R.W. (1984) 'Cellular interactions and the survival and maintenance of neurons during development.' In S.C. Sharma (ed) *Organizing Principles of Neural Development.* (pp.49–80) New York: Plenum.

Ornitz, E.M., Guthrie, D. and Farley, A.H. (1977) 'The early development of autistic children.' *Journal of Autism and Child Schizophrenia 7,* 207–229.

Ornitz, E.M. and Ritvo, E.R. (1968) 'Perceptual inconstancy in early infantile autism: the syndrome of early infant autism and its variants including certain cases of childhood schizophrenia.' *Archives of General Psychiatry 18,* 76–98.

Ozonoff, A., Pennington, B.F. and Rogers, S. (1991) 'Executive function deficits in high-functioning autistic individuals: relationship to a theory of mind.' *Journal of Child Psychology and Psychiatry 32,* 1081–1105.

Ozonoff, S., Rogers, S.J. and Pennington, B.F. (1991) 'Asperger's syndrome: evidence of an empirical distinction from high-functioning autism.' *Journal of Child Psychology and Psychiatry 32,* 1107–1122.

Panksepp, J. (1979) 'A neurochemical theory of autism.' *Trends in the Neurosciences 2,* 174–177.

Panksepp, J. (1990) 'Gray zones at the emotion/cognition interface.' In J.A. Gray (ed) *Psychobiological Aspects of Relationships between Emotion and Cognition.* Hove and London (UK)/Hillsdale (US): Erlbaum, 289–304.

Panksepp, J., Nelson, E. and Sivy, S. (1994) 'Brain opioids and mother–infant social motivation.' *Acta Paediatrica Supplement 397,* 40–46.

Panksepp, J. and Sahley, T.L. (1987) 'Possible brain opioid involvement in disrupted social intent and language development in autism.' In E. Schopler and E.B. Mesibov (eds) *Neurobiological Issues in Autism.* New York: Plenum Press, 357–372.

Papoudi, D.I. (1993) *Interpersonal Play and Communication between Young Autistic Children and their Mothers.* PhD Thesis, The University of Edinburgh.

Papousek, H. (1967) 'Experimental studies of appetitional behaviour in human newborns and infants.' In H.W. Stevenson, E.H. Hess and H.L. Rhinegold (eds) *Early Behaviour, Comparative and Developmental Approaches.* New York: Wiley.

Papousek, H. and Papousek, M. (1979) 'The infant's fundamental adaptive response system in social interaction.' In E.B. Thoman (ed) *Origins of the Infant's Social Responsiveness.* Hillsdale, NJ: Lawrence Erlbaum.

Papousek, H. and Papousek, M. (1987) 'Intuitive parenting: A dialectic counterpart to the infant's integrative competence.' In Osofsky, J. D. (ed.) *Handbook of Infant Development: Second Edition.* New York: Wiley.

Papousek, M. (1992) 'Early ontogeny of vocal communication in parent-infant interactions.' In, Papousek, H., Jurgens, U. and Papousek, M. (eds.) *Nonverbal Vocal Communication: Comparative and Developmental Aspects.* Cambridge: Cambridge University Press/ Paris: Editions de la Maison des Sciences de l'Homme, 230–261.

Papousek, M. and Papousek, H. (1981) 'Musical elements in infants' vocalization: their significant for communication, cognition and creativity.' In L.P. Lipsitt (ed) *Advances in Infancy Research, Vol. 1.* Norwood, NJ: Ablex.

Papousek, M., Papousek, H. and Bornstein, M.H. (1985) 'The naturalistic vocal environment of young infants: on the significance of homogeneity and variability in parental speech.' In T.M. Field and N. Fox (eds) *Social Perception in Infants.* Norwood, NJ: Ablex.

Parks, S.L. (1983) 'The assessment of autistic children: a selective review of available instruments.' *Journal of Autism and Developmental Disorders 13*, 255–267.

Parnas, J. and Bovet, P. (1991) 'Autism in schizophrenia revisited.' *Comprehensive Psychiatry 32*, 1, 7–21.

Paulesu, E., Frith, U., Snowling, M., Gallagher, A., Morton, J., Frackowiak, S.J. and Frith, C.D. (1996) 'Is developmental dyslexia a disconnection syndrome? Evidence from PET scanning.' *Brain 119*, 114–157.

Pavlicevic, M. (1990) 'Dynamic interplay in clinical improvisation.' *Journal of British Music Therapy 4*, 2, 5–9.

Pavlicevic, M. (1995) 'Interpersonal processes in clinical improvisation: towards a subjectively objective systematic definition.' In T. Wigram, B. Saperston and R. West (eds) *The Art and Science of Music Therapy: A Handbook.* Chur, Switzerland: Harwood Academic Publishers, 167–178.

Pavlicevic, M. (1997) *Music Therapy in Context: Music, Meaning and Relationship.* London: Jessica Kingsley Publishers.

Pavlicevic, M. and Trevarthen, C. (1989) 'A musical assessment of psychiatric states in adults.' *Psychopathology 22*, 6, 325–334.

Pavlicevic, M., Trevarthen, C. and Duncan, J. (1994) 'Improvisational music therapy and the rehabilitation of persons suffering from chronic schizophrenia.' *Journal of Music Therapy 31*, 2, 86–104.

Payne, H. (1993) 'Directory of arts therapies research.' In H. Payne (ed) *Handbook of Inquiry in the Arts Therapies: One River, Many Currents.* London and Philadelphia: Jessica Kingsley Publishers.

Peace, K. A., Orme, S. M., Thompson, A. R., Padayatty, S., Ellis, A. W. & Belchetz, P. E. (1997). 'Cognitive dysfunction in patients treated for pituitary tumours.' *Journal of Clinical & Experimental Neuropsychology, 19*, 1–6.

Pedersen, I.N. (1992) 'Music therapy with autistic clients.' In Proceedings of the British Society for Music Therapy/Association of Professional Music Therapists Conference, 'Music Therapy in Health and Education'. London: British Society for Music Therapy.

Peeters, T. (1997) *Working with Autism: Theory into Practice.* Whurr Publications: London.

Pennington, B. F. and Ozonoff, S. (1996). 'Executive functions and developmental psychopathology.' *Journal of Child Psychology & Psychiatry, 37*, 51–88.

Perner, J., Frith, U., Leslie, A.M. and Leekam, S.R. (1989) 'Exploration of the autistic child's theory of mind: knowledge, belief, and communication.' *Child Development 60*, 689–700.

Philippart, M. (1990) 'The Rett syndrome in males.' *Brain and Development 122*, 33–36.

Piaget, J. (1954) *The Construction of Reality by the Child.* New York: Basic Books.

Piaget, J. (1962) *Play, Dreams, and Imitation in Childhood.* New York: Norton.

Piven, J., Berthier, M., Starkstein, S., Nehme, E., Pearlson, G. and Folstein, S. (1990) 'Magnetic resonance imaging evidence for a defect of cerebral cortical development in autism.' *American Journal of Psychiatry 147*, 734–739.

Piven, J., Tsai, G., Nehme, E., Coyle, J.T., Chase, G.A. and Folstein, S.E. (1991) 'Platelet serotonin, a possible marker for familial autism.' *Journal of Autism and Developmental Disorders 21*, 51–60.

Plomin, R. DeFries, J.C., McClearn, G.E. and Rutter, M. (1997) *Behavior Genetics, 3rd edition*. New York: W.H. Freeman and Company.

Porges, S.W. (1995) 'Orienting in a defensive world: mammalian modifications of our evolutionary heritage. A polivagal theory.' *Psychophysiology 32*, 301–18.

Porges, S.W. (1997) 'Emotion: an evolutionary by-product of the neural regulation of the autonomic nervous system.' In C.S. Carter, B. Kilpatrick and I.I. Lederhendler (eds) *The Integrative Neurobiology of Affiliation. Annals of the New York Academy of Science 807*, 62–77.

Porges, S.W. (1998) 'Love and the Evolution of the Autonomic Nervous System: The Polyvagal Theory of Intimacy.' *Psychoneuroendocrinology.*

Powell, S. and Jordan, R. (eds) (1997) *Autism and Learning: A Guide to Good Practice.* London: David Fulton.

Premack, D. and Woodruff, G. (1978) '"Does the chimpanzee have a theory of mind?"' *Behavioural and Brain Sciences 4*, 515–526.

Prevezner, W. (1990) 'Strategies for tuning in to autism.' *Therapy Weekly 18*, October, 4.

Priestley, M. (1994) *Essays on Analytical Music Therapy*. Phoenixville, PA: Barcelona Publishers.

Prior, M. and Cummins, R. (1992) 'Questions about facilitated communication and autism.' *Journal of Autism and Developmental Disorders 22*, 331–337.

Prior, M., Dahlstrom, B. and Squires, T. (1990) ~'Autistic children's knowledge of thinking and feeling states in other people.' *Journal of Child Psychology and Psychiatry 31*, 587–601.

Prior, M.R., Tress, B., Hoffman, W.L. and Boldt, D. (1984) 'Computed tomography study of children with classic autism.' *Archives of Neurology 431*, 482–484.

Prizant, B.M. and Schuler, A.L. (1987) 'Facilitating communication: Language approaches.' In D.J. Cohen and A.M. Donnellan (eds) *Handbook of Autism and Pervasive Developmental Disorders.* New York: Wiley.

Quick, R. H. (1910) *Essays on Educational Reformers.* London: Longmans, Green, and Co.

Quill, K., Gurry, S. and Larkin, A. (1989) 'Daily Life Therapy: a Japanese model for educating children with autism.' *Journal of Autism and Developmental Disorders 19*, 625–635.

Radocy, R.E. and Boyle, J.D. (1997) *Psychological Foundations of Musical Behaviour (Third Edition).* Springfield, Illinois: Charles C. Thomas.

Rakic, P. (1991) 'Development of the primate cerebral cortex.' In M. Lewis (ed) *Child and Adolescent Psychiatry: A Comprehensive Textbook.* (pp. 11–28) Baltimore: Williams and Wilkins.

Rakic, P. (1995) 'A small step for the cell, a giant leap for mankind: a hypothesis of neocortical expansion during evolution.' *Trends in Neuroscience 18*, 383–388.

Rapin, I. and Allen, A. (1983) 'Developmental language disorders; nosological considerations.' In U. Kirk (ed) *Neuropsychology of Language, Reading and Spelling.* London: Academic Press.

Reber, S.A. (1985) *The Penguin Dictionary of Psychology*. London: Penguin.

Reddy, V. (1991) 'Playing with others' expectations; teasing and mucking about in the first year.' In A. Whiten (ed) *Natural Theories of Mind: Evolution, Development and Simulation of Everyday Mindreading*. Oxford: Blackwell, 143–158.

Reddy, V., Hay, D., Murray, L. and Trevarthen, C. (1997) 'Communication in infancy: mutual regulation of affect and attention.' In G. Bremner, A. Slater and G. Butterworth (eds) *Infant Development: Recent Advances.* (pp. 247–273). Hillsdale, NJ: Erlbaum.

Reiss, A.L. (1988) 'Carbellar hypoplasia and autism.' *New England Journal of Medicine 319,* 1152–1153, (Letter).

Reiss, A.L., Aylward, E., Freund, L., Joshi, P. and Bryan, R.N. (1991) 'Neuroanatomy of fragile X sysndrome: the posterior fossa.' *Annals of Neurology 29,* 26–32.

Relelle, W. and Loftus, D.A. (1990) 'Individual differences and arousal: implications for the study of mood and memory.' In J.A. Gray (ed) *Psychobiological Aspects of Relationships between Emotion and Cognition.* Hove and London (UK)/Hillsdale (US): Erlbaum. 209–238.

Repp, A.S. (1983) *Teaching the Mentally Retarded.* Englewood Cliffs NJ: Prentice-Hall.

Rett, A. (1966) 'Über ein eigenartiges ?hirnatrophiches Syndrom bei Hyperammonmie im Kindersalter.' *Weiner Medizinsche Wochenschrift 116,* 723–726.

Reynolds, D., Sullivan, M. and Murgatroyd, S. (1987) *The Comprehensive Experiment.* Brighton: Falmer.

Rheingold, H., Hay, D. and West, M. (1976) 'Sharing in the second year of life.' *Child Development 83,* 898–913.

Richardson, J.S. and Zaleske, W.A. (1983) 'Naloxone and self-mutilation.' *Biological Psychiatry 18,* 99–101.

Richdale, A.L. and Pryor, M.R. (1995) 'The sleep/wake rhythm in children with autism.' *European Journal of Child and Adolescent Psychiatry 4,* 175–186.

Richer, J.M. (1976) 'The social avoidance behaviour of autistic children.' *Animal Behaviour 24,* 898–906.

Richer, J.M. (1978) 'The partial communication of culture to autistic children: an application of human ethology.' In M. Rutter and E. Schopler (eds) *A Reappraisal of Concepts and Treatment.* New York: Plenum Press.

Richer, J.M. (1983) 'Development of social avoidance in autistic children.' In A. Oliverio and M. Zappella (eds) *The Behaviour of Human Infants.* London and New York: Plenum.

Richer, J. M. and Nicol, S. (1971) 'A playroom for autistic children and its companion therapy project.' *British Journal of Mental Subnormality, 17,* 132–143.

Ricks, D.M. (1975) 'Vocal communication in pre-verbal normal and autistic children.' In N. O'Connor (ed) *Language, Cognitive Deficits and Retardation.* London: Butterworth.

Ricks, D.M. (1979) 'Making sense of experience to make sensible sounds: experimental investigations of early vocal communication in pre-verbal autistic and normal children.' In M. Bullowa (ed) *Before Speech. The Beginning of Interpersonal Communication.* Cambridge: Cambridge University Press.

Ricks, D.M. and Wing, L. (1975) 'Language, communication and the use of symbols in normal and autistic children.' *Journal of Autism and Childhood Schizophrenia 5,* 191–221.

Rider, M.S. and Eagle, C.T. Jnr. (1986) 'Rhythmic entrainment as a mechanism for learning in music therapy.' In J.R. Evans and M. Clynes (eds) *Rhythm in Psychological, Linguistic and Musical Processes.* Springfield, Illinois: Charles C. Thomas, 225–248.

Rigg, M., Gould, G.A.. and Bignell, L. (1991) *The Higashi Experience. The Report of a Visit to the Boston Higashi School.* London: National Autistic Society.

Riguet, C.B., Taylor, N.D., Benaroya, S. and Klein, L.S. (1981) 'Symbolic play in autistic, Down's, and normal children of equivalent mental age.' *Journal of Autism and Developmental Disorders 11,* 439–448.

Rimland, B. (1964) *Infantile Autism.* New York: Appleton-Century-Crofts.

Rimland, B. (1971) 'The differentiation of childhood psychoses: an analysis of checklists for 2,218 psychotic children.' *Journal of Autism and Childhood Schizophrenia 1,* 161–174.

Rimland, B. (1994) 'The modern history of autism: A personal perspective.' In J. L. Matson (ed.) *Autism in Children and Adults: Etiology, Assessment, and Intervention.* Pacific Grove, CA: Brooks-Cole.

Rimland, B. and Edelson, S.M. (1995) 'Brief report: a pilot study of Auditory Integration Training in autism.' *Journal of Autism and Developmental Disorders 25,* 61–70.

Ritvo, E. R., Freeman, B. J., Pingree, C., Mason-Brothers, A., Jorde, L. B., Jensen, W. R., McMahon, W. M., Petersen, P. B., Mo, A., and Ritvo, A. (1990) 'The UCLA-University of Utah epidemiologic survey of autism: prevalence.' *American Journal of Psychiatry, 146,* 194–199.

Ritvo, E.R., Freeman, B.J., Scheibel, A.B., Duong, T., Robinson, H., Guthrie, D. and Ritvo, A. (1986) 'Lower Purkinje cell counts in the cerebella of four autistic subjects: initial findings of the UCLA-NSAC autopsy research report.' *American Journal of Psychiatry 143,* 862–866.

Ritvo, E.R., Ritvo, R., Yuweiler, A., Brothers, A., Freeman, B.J. and Plotkin, S. (1993) 'Elevated daytime melatonin concentrations in autism: A pilot study.' *European Journal of Child and Adolescent Psychiatry, 2,* (2): 75–78.

Robarts, J.Z. (1994) 'Towards autonomy and a sense of self: the individuation process in music therapy in relation to children and adolescents suffering from early onset anorexia nervosa.' In D. Dokter (ed) *Arts Therapies and Clients with Eating Disorders.* London: Jessica Kingsley Publishers, 229–246.

Robarts, J.Z. and Sloboda, A. (1994) 'Perspectives on music therapy with people suffering from anorexia nervosa.' *Journal of British Music Therapy 8,* 1, 7–14.

Robbins, C. (1993) 'The creative processes are universal.' In M. Heal and T. Wigram (ed) *Music Therapy in Health and Education.* London and Philadelphia: Jessica Kingsley Publishers, 7–25.

Rodier, P.M. (1996) 'Animal model of autism based on developmental data.' *Mental Retardation and Developmental Disabilities Research Reviews 2,* 249–256.

Rodier, P.M., Ingram, J.L., Tisdale, B., Nelson, S. and Romano, J. (1996) 'Embryological origin for autism: developmental anomalies of the cranial nerve motor nuclei.' *Journal of Comparative Neurology 370,* 247–261.

Roeyers, H. (1995) 'Peer-mediated interventions to facilitate the social interactions of children with pervasive developmental disorder.' *British Journal of Special Education 22,* 161–164.

Rogers, P.J. (1993) 'Research in music therapy with sexually abused clients.' In H. Payne (ed) *Handbook of Inquiry in the Arts Therapies: One River, Many Currents.* London and Philadelphia: Jessica Kingsley Publishers, 196–217.

Rogers, P.J. (1994) 'Sexual abuse and eating disorders: a possible connection indicated through music therapy?' In D. Dokter (ed) *Arts Therapies with Clients with Eating Disorders*. London: Jessica Kingsley Publishers, 262–278.

Rogers, P.J. (1995) 'Music therapy research: a European perspective.' *British Journal of Music Therapy 10*, 2.

Rogers, S.J. and Pennington, B.F. (1991) 'A theoretical approach to the deficits in infantile autism.' *Development and Psychopathology 3*, 137–162.

Rogoff, B. (1990) *Apprenticeship in Thinking*. New York: Oxford University Press.

Rönnqvist, L. and von Hofsten, C. (1992) 'Varieties and determinants of finger movements in neonates.' Poster, fifth European Conference on Developmental Psychology. Seville, Spain.

Rosenblatt, D. (1977) 'Developmental trends in infant play.' In B. Tizard and D. Harvey (eds) *Biology of Play*. London: Heineman, 34–44.

Rubin, Z. (1980) *Children's Friendships*. Cambrigde: Harvard University Press.

Rumsey, J.M., Duara, R., Grady, C., Rapoport, J.L., Margolin, R.A., Rapoport, S.I. and Cutler, N.R. (1985) 'Brain metabolism in autism: resting cerebral glucose utilization rates as measured with positron emission tomography.' *Annals of Neurology 28*, 775–785.

Ruttenberg, B.A., Dratman, M.L., Fraknoi, J. and Wenar, C. (1966) 'An instrument for evaluating autistic children.' *Journal of the American Academy of Child Psychiatry 5*, 453–478.

Ruttenberg, B.A., Kalish, B.I., Wenar, C. and Wolf, E.G. (1977) *Behaviour Rating Instrument for Autistic and Other Atypical Children (Revised Edition)*. Philadelphia: Developmental Center for Autistic Children.

Rutter, M. (1966) 'Behavioural and cognitive characteristics of a series of psychotic children.' In J.K. Wing (ed) *Early Childhood Autism*, 51–81.

Rutter, M. (1968) 'Concepts of autism. A review of research.' *Journal of Child Psychology and Psychiatry 9*, 1–25.

Rutter, M. (1978) 'Diagnosis and definition of childhood autism.' *Journal of Autism and Childhood Schizophrenia 8*, 139–161.

Rutter, M. (1983) 'Cognitive deficits in the pathogenesis of autism.' *Journal of Child Psychology and Psychiatry 24*, 513–531.

Rutter, M. (1985) 'Infantile autism and other pervasive developmental disorders.' In M. Rutter and L. Hersov (eds) *Child and Adolescent Psychiatry: Modern Approaches*. Oxford: Blackwell Scientific, 545–566.

Rutter, M. (1991) 'Autism as a genetic disorder.' In P. McGuffin and R. Murray (eds) *The New Genetics of Mental Illness*. (pp.225–244) Oxford: Butterworth-Heinemann.

Rutter, M., Bartak, L. and Newman, S. (1971) 'Autism – a central disorder of cognition and language?' In M. Rutter (ed) *Infantile Autism: Concepts, Characteristics and Treatment*. London: Churchill Livingstone.

Rutter, M., Le Couteur, A., Lord, C., MacDonald, H., Rios, P. and Folstein, S. (1988) 'Diagnosis and subclassification of autism: Concepts and instrument development.' In E. Schopler and G. B. Mesibov (eds.), *Diagnosis and Assessment in Autism*. New York: Plenum, 239–259.

Rutter, M. and Schopler, E. (1987) 'Autism and pervasive developmental disorders: concepts and diagnostic issues.' *Journal of Autism and Developmental Disorders 17*, 159–186.

Rutter, M. and Schopler, E. (eds) (1978) *Autism: A Reappraisal of Concepts and Treatment.* New York: Plenum Press.

Sacks, O. (1995) *An Anthropologist on Mars.* New York: Knopf.

Sandman, C.A., Datta, P.C., Barron, J., Hoehler, F.K., Williams, C. and Swanson, J.M. (1983) 'Naloxone attenuates self-injurious behaviour in developmentally disabled clients.' *Applied Research in Mental Retardation 4,* 5–12.

Saperston, B. (1973) 'The use of music in establishing communication with an autistic mentally retarded child.' *Journal of Music Therapy 10,* 184–188.

Saperston, B. (1982) 'Case study: Timmy.' In D.W. Paul (ed) *Music Therapy for Handicapped Children: Emotionally Disturbed.* Washington DC: Office of Special Education and the National Association for Music Therapy, 42–57.

Scaife, M. and Bruner, J.S. (1975) 'The capacity for joint visual attention in the infant.' *Nature 253,* 265–6.

Schaefer, G.B., Thompson, J.N., Bodensteiner, J.B., McConnell, J.M., Kimberling, W.J., Gay, C.T., Dutton, W.D., Hutchings, D.C. and Gray, S.B. (1996) 'Hypoplasia of the cerebellar vermis in neurogenetic syndromes.' *Annals of Neurology 39,* 3, 382–385.

Schain, R.J. and Freedman, D.X. (1961) 'Studies on 5-hydroxyindole metabolism in autistic and other mentally retarded children.' *Journal of Pediatrics 58,* 315–320.

Schonfelder, T. (1964) 'Uber fruhkindlische antriebsstrorungen.' *Acta Paedopsychiatrica 31,* 112–129.

Schopler, E. (1983) 'New developments in the definition and diagnosis of autism.' In B.B. Lahey and A.E. Kazdin (eds) *Advances in Clinical Child Psychology, Vol. 6.* New York: Plenum Press.

Schopler, E. (1992) 'Editorial comment on Prior and Cummins.' *Journal of Autism and Developmental Disorders 22,* 337.

Schopler, E. and Mesibov, G.B. (eds) (1987) *Neurobiological Issues in Autism.* New York: Plenum.

Schopler, E. and Mesibov, G.B. (eds) (1988) *Diagnosis and Assessment in Autism.* New York: Plenum.

Schopler, E. and Mesibov, G.B. (eds) (1992) *High Functioning Individuals with Autism.* New York: Plenum.

Schopler, E. and Mesibov, G.B. (eds) (1995) *Learning adn Cognition in Autism.* New York: Plenum Press.

Schopler, E., Mesibov, G.B. and Baker, A. (1982) 'Evaluation of treatment for autistic children and their parents.' *Journal of the American Academy of Child Psychiatry 21,* 262–267.

Schopler, E., Mesibov, G.B., DeVellis, R. and Short, A. (1981) 'Treatment outcome for autistic children and their families.' In P. Mittler (ed) *Frontiers of Knowledge in Mental Retardation. Volume 1. Special Educational and Behavioral Aspects.* Baltimore: University Park Press, 293–301.

Schopler, E., Mesibov, G.B., Shigley, R.H. and Bashford, A. (1984) 'Helping autistic children through their parents: the TEACCH model.' In E. Schopler and G.B. Mesibov (eds) *The Effects of Autism on the Family.* New York: Plenum Press, 65–81.

Schopler, E. and Olley, J.G. (1982) 'Comprehensive educational services for autistic children: the TEACCH model.' In C.R Reynolds and T.R Gutkin (eds) *Handbook of School Psychology.* New York: Wiley, 629–643.

Schopler, E. and Reichler, R.J. (1971) 'Developmental therapy by parents with their autistic child.' In M. Rutter (ed) *Infantile Autism: Concepts, Characteristics, Treatment.* London: Churchill-Livingstone, 206–227.

Schopler, E. and Reichler, R.J. (1979) *Individualized Assessment and Treatment of Autistic and Developmentally Disabled Children, Vol. 1, Psychoeducational Profile, (2nd Edition).* Austin, Texas: Pro-Ed.

Schopler, E. and Reichler, R.J. (1983a) *Individualized Assessment and Treatment for Autistic and Developmentally Disabled Children. Volume I, Psychoeducational Profiles.* Baltimore: University Park Press.

Schopler, E. and Reichler, R.J. (1983b) *Individualized Assessment and Treatment for Autistic and Developmentally Disabled Children. Volume II, Teaching Activities for Autistic Children.* Baltimore: University Park Press.

Schopler, E., Reichler, R.J., DeVellis, R.F. and Kock, K. (1980) 'Toward objective classification of childhood autism: Childhood Autism Rating Scale (CARS).' *Journal of Autism and Developmental Disorders 10*, 91–103.

Schopler, E., Reichler, R.J. and Lansing, M. (1980) *Individualized Assessment and Treatment of Autistic and Developmentally Disabled Children, Vol. 2, Teaching Strategies for Parents and Professionals.* Dallas, Texas: Pro-Ed.

Schore, A.N. (1994) *Affect Regulation and the Origin of the Self: The Neurobiology of Emotional Development.* Hillsdale, NJ: Erlbaum.

Schreibman, L. (1988) *Autism, Developmental Clinical Psychology and Psychiatry, 15.* Sage Publications, Newbury Park.

Schweinhart, L.J. and Weikert, D.P. (1980) 'Young children grow up: the effects of the Perry Preschool Project on youths through wage 15.' (Monograph No. 7 of the High/Scope Educational Research Foundation) Ypsilanti, MI: High/Scope Foundation.

Sears, W. (1968) 'Processes in music therapy.' In E.T. Gaston (ed) *Music in Therapy.* New York: Macmillan.

Segal H. (1964) *Introduction to the Work of Melanie Klein.* London: Hogarth Press.

Segawa, M. (1992) 'Possible lesions of the Rett syndrome: opinions of contributors.' *Brain and Development 14*, (Supplement), S149–S150.

Seguin, É. (1846) *Traitement Moral des Idiots.* Paris: Baillière.

Seibert, J.M. and Hogan, A.E. (1982) *Procedures Manual for Early Social Communication Scales (ESCS).* Miami: Mailman Centre for Child Development.

Selfe, L. (1978) *Nadia: A Case of Extraordinary Drawing Ability in an Autistic Child.* London: Academic Press.

Selfe, L. (1983) *Normal and Anomalous Representational Drawing in Children.* London: Academic Press.

Shah, A. and Frith, U. (1993) 'Why do autistic individuals show superior perfomance on the block design task?' *Journal of Child Psychology and Psychiatry 34*, 8, 1351–1365.

Shapiro, T., Frosch, E. and Arnold, S. (1987) 'Communicative interaction between mothers and their autistic children: application for a new instrument and changes after treatment.' *Journal of the American Academy of Child and Adolescent Psychiatry 26*, 485–490.

Shapiro, T., Sherman, M., Calamari, G. and Kock, D. (1987) 'Attachment in autism and other developmental disorders.' *Journal of the American Academy of Child and Adolescent Psychiatry 26*, 480–484.

Sherwin, A.C. (1953) 'Reactions to music of autistic (schizophrenic) children.' *American Journal of Psychiatry 109*, 823–831.

Shields, J., Varley, R., Broks, P. and Simpson, A. (1996) 'Social cognition in developmental language disorders and high level autism.' *Developmental Medicine and Child Neurology, 38*, 487–495.

Shuttleworth, J. (1989) 'Psychoanalytic theory and infant development.' In L. Miller, M. Rustin, M. Rustin and J. Shuttleworth (eds) *Closely Observed Infants.* London: Duckworth., 22–51.

Siegel, B., Vukivec, J. and Spitzer, R.L. (1990) 'Using signal detection methodology to revise DSM-III-R: Reanalysis of the DSM-III-R National Field Trials for autistic disorder.' *Journal of Psychiatric Research, 24*, 293–311.

Sigman, M. (1989) 'The application of developmental knowledge to a clinical problem: The study of childhood autism.' In D. Cicchetti (ed) *Rochester Symposium on Developmental Psychopathology, Vol.1: The emergence of a discipline.* Hillsdale, NJ: Erlbaum, 165–187.

Sigman, M. and Capps, L. (1997) *Children with Autism: A Developmental Perspective.* Cambridge MA: Harvard University Press.

Sigman, M. and Mundy, P. (1989) 'Social attachments in autistic children.' *Journal of the American Academy of Child and Adolescent Psychiatry 28*, 74–81.

Sigman, M., Mundy, P., Sherman, T. and Ungerer, J. (1986) 'Social interactions of autistic, mentally retarded and normal children and their caregivers.' *Journal of Child Psychology and Psychiatry 27*, 647–656.

Sigman, M. and Ungerer, J. (1981) 'Sensorimotor skills and language comprehension in autistic children.' *Journal of Abnormal Child Psychology 9*, 149–165.

Sigman, M. and Ungerer, J. A. (1984a) 'Cognitive and language skills in autistic, mentally retarded and normal children.' *Developmental Psychology 20*, 293–302.

Sigman, M. and Ungerer, J.A. (1984b) 'Attachment behaviours in autistic children.' *Journal of Autism and Developmental Disorders 14*, 231–244.

Simmeonson, R.J., Olley, G.J. and Rosenthal, S.L. (1987) 'Early intervention for children with autism.' In M.J. Guralnick and F.C. Bennett (eds) *The Effectiveness of Early Intervention for At-Risk and Handicapped Children.* New York: Academic Press.

Sinason, V. (1992) *Mental Handicap and the Human Condition: New Approaches from the Tavistock.* London: Free Association Books.

Skuse, D.,H., James, R.S., Bishop, D.V.M., Coppin, B., Dalton, P., Aamodt-Leeper, G., Bacarese-Hamilton, M., Creswell, C., McGurk, R. and Jacobs, P.A. (1997) 'Evidence from Turner's syndrome of an imprinted X-linked locus affecting cognitive function.' *Nature 387*, 390–402.

Sloman, L. (1991) 'Use of medication in pervasive developmental disorder.' *Pediatric Clinics of North America 14*, 165–182.

Smalley, S.L., Tanguay, P.E., Smith, M. and Guitierrez, G. (1992) 'Autism and Tuberous Sclerosis.' *Journal of Autism and Developmental Disorders 22*, 339–355.

Smeijsters, H. and Hurk, P. van den (1993) 'Research and practice in the music therapeutic treatment of a client with symptoms of anorexia nervosa.' In M. Heal and A. Wigram (eds) *Music Therapy in Health and Education*. London and Philadelphia: Jessica Kingsley Publishers, 255–263.

Smeijsters, H., Rogers, P., Kortegaard, H-M., Lehtonen, K. and Scanlon, P. (eds) (1995) *The European Music Therapy Research Register Vol. II*. The Netherlands: The Stichting Muziektherapie Foundation.

Smith, A. (1759) *Theory of Moral Sentiments*. Edinburgh (Modern Edition: D. D. Raphael and A.L. Macfie, General Editors, Glasgow Edition. Oxford: Clarendon, 1976. Reprint, Indianapolis: Liberty Fund, 1984).

Smith, M.D., Beicher, R.G. and Juhrs, P.D. (1994) *A Guide to Successful Employment for People with Autism*. London: Paul H. Brookes.

Snow, M.E., Hertzig, M.E. and Shapiro, T. (1987) 'Expression of emotion in young autistic children.' *Journal of the American Academy of Child and Adolescent Psychiatry 26*, 836–838.

Söderbergh, R. (1986) 'Acquisition of spoken and written language in early childhood.' In I. Kuroz, G.W. Shugar and J.H. Danks (eds) *Knowledge and Language*. Amsterdam: North Holland.

Sparling, J.W. (1991) 'Brief report: a prospective case report of infantile autism from pregnancy to four years.' *Journal of Autism and Developmental Disorders 21*, 229–236.

Sperry, R.W. (1963) 'Chemoaffinity in the orderly growth of nerve fiber patterns and connections.' *Proceedings of the National Academy of Sciences, USA, 50*, 703–710.

Squire, L.R. (1986) 'Mechanisms of memory.' *Science 232*, 1612–19.

Sroufe, A. (1996) *Emotional Development: The Organization of Emotional Life in Early Years*. Cambridge: Cambridge University Press.

Statistical Yearbook, (39th edn) (1994) UN, New York.

Steffenberg, S. (1991) 'Neuropsychiatric assessment of children with autism: a population-based study.' *Developmental Medicine and Child Neurology 33*, 495–511.

Steffenberg, S. and Gillberg, C. (1986) 'Autism and Autistic-like Conditions in Swedish Rural and Urban Areas: A Population Study.' *British Journal of Psychiatry, 149*, 81–87.

Stehli, A. (1991) *The Sound of A Miracle: A Child's Triumph over Autism*. Doubleday: New York.

Stern, D. N. (1974) 'The goal and structure of mother-infant play.' *Journal of the American Academy of Child Psychiatry, 13*, 402–421.

Stern, D.N. (1977) *The First Relationship: Infant and Mother*. Cambridge MA: Harvard University Press.

Stern, D.N. (1985) *The Interpersonal World of the Infant*. New York: Basic Books.

Stern, D.N. (1990) 'Joy and satisfaction in infancy.' In R.A. Glick and S. Bone (eds) *Pleasure Beyond the Pleasure Principle*. (pp. 13–25) Newhaven, CT: Yale University Press.

Stern, D, N. (1993) 'The role of feelings for an interpersonal self.' In U. Neisser (Ed.) *The Perceived Self: Ecological and Interpersonal Sources of Self-Knowledge*. New York: Cambridge University Press, 205–215.

Stern, D.N. (1994) 'One way to build a clinically relevant baby.' *Infant Mental Health Journal 15*, 1, Spring.

Stern, D.N. and Gibbon, J. (1980) 'Temporal expectancies of social behaviors in mother–infant play.' In E. Thoman (ed) *Origins of Infant Social Responsiveness*. New York: Erlbaum.

Stern, D.N., Hofer, L., Haft, W. and Dore, J. (1985) 'Affect attunement: the sharing of feeling states between mother and infant by means of inter-modal fluency.' In T.M. Field and N.A. Fox (eds) *Social Perception in Infants.* pp.249–268. Norwood, NJ: Ablex.

Stern, D.N., Spieker, S. and MacKain, K. (1982) 'Intonation contours as signals in maternal speech to prelinguistic infants.' *Developmental Psychology 18,* 727–735.

Stevens, E. and Clark, F. (1969) 'Music therapy in the treatment of autistic children.' *Journal of Music Therapy 6,* 93–104.

Stewart-Clarke, A. and Hevey, C. (1981) 'Longitudinal relations in repeated observations of mother–child interaction from one to two-and-a-half years.' *Developmental Psychology 97,* 127–145.

Sticker, T., Martin, E. and Boesh, C. (1990) 'Development of the human cerebellum observed with high-field strength MR imaging.' *Radiology 177,* 430–435.

Stone, W.L., Hoffman, E.L., Lewis, S.E. and Ousley, O.Y. (1994) 'Early recognition of autism: parental reports vs. clinical observation.' *Archives of Pediatric and Adolescent Medicine 148,* 174–179.

Stone, W.L., Lemanek, K.L., Fishel, P.T., Fernandez, M.C. and Altemeier, W.A. (1990) 'Play and imitation skills in the diagnosis of autism in young children.' *Pediatrics 86,* 267–72.

Stow, L. and Self, L. (1989) *Understanding Children with Special Needs.* London: Unwin Hyman.

Strain, P.S. (1987) 'Comprehensive evaluation of interventions for young autistic children.' *Topics in Early Childhood Education 7,* 97–110.

Strain, P.S., Jamieson, B. and Hoyson, M. (1986) 'Learning experiences. An alternative program for preschoolers and parents. A comprehensive service system for the mainstreaming of autistic-like preschoolers.' In C.J. Meisel (ed) *Mainstreaming Handicapped Children: Outcomes, Controversies and New Directions.* Hillsdale, NJ: Erlbaum.

Sugiyama, T. and Abe, T. (1989) 'The prevalence of autism in Nagoya, Japan: A Total Population Study.' *Journal of Autism and Developmental Disorders, 19,* 87–96.

Sutton-Smith, B. (1986) *Toys as Culture.* New York: Gardner Press.

Szatmari, P., Bertolucci, G. and Bremner, R. (1989) 'Asperger's Syndrome and autism: comparisons on early history and outcome.' *Developmental Medicine and Child Neurology, 31,* 130–136.

Szatmari, P., Tuff, L., Finlayson, M.A.J. and Bartolucci, G. (1990) 'Asperger's syndrome and autism: neurocognitive aspects.' *Journal of the American Academy of Child and Adolescent Psychiatry 29,* 130–136.

Tager-Flusberg, H. (1981) 'On the nature of linguistic functioning in early infantile autism.' *Journal of Autism and Developmental Disorders 11,* 45–56.

Tager-Flusberg, H. (1989) 'A psycholinguistic perspective on language development in the autistic child.' In G. Dawson (ed.) *Autism: Nature, Diagnosis and Treatment.* New York: Guilford Press, 92–115.

Tanoue, Y., Oda, S., Asano, F. and Kawashima, K. (1988) 'Epidemiology of infantile autism in Southern Ibaraki, Japan: difference in prevalence in birth cohorts.' *Journal of Autism and Developmental Disorders 18,* 155–166.

Tantam, D. (1988) 'Lifelong eccentricity and social isolation. I. Psychiatric, social and forensic aspects.' *British Journal of Psychiatry 153,* 777–782.

Tantam, D. (1991) 'Asperger Syndrome in adulthood.' In U. Frith (ed) *Autism and Asperger Syndrome.* Cambridge: Cambridge University Press.

Tattum, D. (1982) *Disruptive Pupils in Schools and Units.* Chichester: Wiley.

von Tetzchner, S. (1996) 'Facilitated, automatic and false communication: current issues in the use of facilitating techniques.' *European Journal of Special Needs Education 11,* 1, 151–166.

von Tetzchner, S. and Martinsen, H. (1981) 'Autism and receptive dysphasia: evaluation of comparative studies.' *Scandanavian Journal of Psychology 22,* 283–296.

von Tetzchner, S. and Martinsen, H. (1992) *Introduction to Sign Teaching and the Use of Communication Aids.* London: Whurr/San Diego, CA: Singular Press.

Thatcher, R.W. (1994) 'Psychopathology of early frontal lobe damage: dependence on cycles of development.' *Development and Psychopathology 6,* 565–596.

Thatcher, R.W, Lyon, G.R., Rumsey, J. and Krasnegor, M. (1996) *Developmental Neuroimaging: Mapping the Development of Brain and Behaviour.* San Diego: Academic Press.

Thatcher, R.W., Walker, R.A. and Giudice, S. (1987) 'Human cerebral hemispheres develop at different rates and ages.' *Science 236,* 1110–1113.

Thaut, M.H. (1980) *Music Therapy as a Treatment Tool for Autistic Children.* Unpublished Masters thesis. Michigan State University.

Thaut, M.H. (1983) 'A music therapy treatment model for autistic children.' *Music Therapy Perspectives 1,* 7–13.

Thaut, M. (1985) 'The use of auditory rhythm and rhythmic speech to aid temporal muscular control in children with gross motor dysfunction.' *Journal of Music Therapy 22,* 129–145.

Thaut, M.H. (1987) 'Visual versus auditory (musical) stimulus preferences in autistic children: a pilot study.' *Journal of Autism and Developmental Disorders 17,* 425–432.

Thaut, M.H. (1988) 'Measuring musical responsiveness in autistic children: a comparative analysis of improvised musical tone sequences of autistic, normal and mentally retarded individuals.' *Journal of Autism and Developmental Disorders 18,* 561–571.

Thaut, M.H. (1992) 'Music therapy with autistic children.' In W.B. Davis, K.E. Gfeller and M.H. Thaut (eds) *An Introduction to Music Therapy: Theory and Practice.* Dubuque, Indiana: William C. Brown Publishers, 180–196.

Thesleff, S. (1987) 'Denervation sensitivity.' In G. Adelman (ed.) *Encyclopedia of Neuroscience, Volume I.* Boston: Birkhäuser, 322–323.

Tiergerman, E. and Primavera, L. (1981) 'Object manipulation: an interactional strategy with autistic children.' *Journal of Autism and Developmental Disorders 11,* 427–438.

Tiergerman, E. and Primavera, L. (1984) 'Imitating the autistic child: facilitating communicative gaze behaviour.' *Journal of Autism and Developmental Disorders 14,* 27–38.

Tilton, J.R. and Ottinger, D.R. (1964) 'Comparison of the toy play behaviour of autistic, retarded and normal children.' *Psychological Reports 15,* 967–975.

Tinbergen, N. and Tinbergen, E.A. (1983) *'Autistic' Children: New Hope for a Cure.* London: Allen and Unwin.

Tingey, C. (1989) *Implementing Early Intervention.* Baltimore: Paul Brookes Publishing.

Toigo, D.A. (1992) 'Autism: integrating a personal perspective in music therapy practice.' *Music Therapy Perspectives 10*, 13–20.

Tomasello, M. (1993) 'On the interpersonal origins of self-concept.' In U. Neisser (ed) *The Perceived Self: Ecological and Interpersonal Sources of Self-Knowledge.* (pp. 174–184) New York: Cambridge University Press.

Tomasello, M. and Farrar, M.J. (1986) 'Joint attention and early language.' *Child Development 57*, 1454–1463.

Tomasello, M., Kruger, A.C. and Ratner, H.H. (1993) 'Cultural learning.' *Behavioral and Brain Sciences 16*, 3, 495–552.

Topping, K. (1983) *Educational Systems for Disruptive Adolescents.* London: Croom Helm.

Topping, K. (1986) *Parents as Educators.* London: Croom Helm.

Tredgold, R.F. and Soddy, K. (1956) *A Textbook of Mental Deficiency.* London: Balliere, Tindal and Cox.

Treffert, D.A. (1989) *Extraordinary People: An Exploration of the Savant Syndrome.* London: Bantam.

Trehub, S. E. (1990) 'The perception of musical patterns by human infants: The provision of similar patterns by their parents.' In: M. A. Berkley and W. C. Stebbins (eds.) *Comparative Perception; Vol. 1, Mechanisms.* New York: Wiley. 429–459.

Trehub, S.E. and Chang, Hsing-Wu (1977) 'Infants' perception of temporal grouping in auditory patterns.' *Child Development 48*, 1666–1670.

Trehub, S.E., Schneider, B.A., Thorpe, L.A. and Judge, P. (1991) 'Observational measures of auditory sensitivity in early infancy.' *Developmental Psychology 27*, 1, 40–49.

Trehub, S.E. and Thorpe, L.A. (1989) 'Infants' perception of rhythm: categorization of auditory sequences by temporal structure.' *Canadian Journal of Psychology 43*, 2, 217–229.

Trevarthen, C. (1974) 'Conversation with a two-month-old.' *New Scientist,* 2nd May, 230–235.

Trevarthen, C. (1979) 'Communication and cooperation in early infancy. A description of primary intersubjectivity.' In M. Bullowa (ed) *Before Speech: The Beginnings of Human Communication.* London: Cambridge University Press, 321–347.

Trevarthen, C. (1980) 'The foundations of intersubjectivity: development of interpersonal and cooperative understanding of infants.' In D. Olson (ed) *The Social Foundations of Language and Thought: Essays in Honor of J.S. Bruner.* New York: W.W. Norton, 316–342.

Trevarthen, C. (1984a) 'Emotions in infancy: regulators of contacts and relationships with persons.' In K. Scherer and P. Ekman (eds) *Approaches to Emotion.* Hillsdale, NJ: Erlbaum, 129–157.

Trevarthen, C. (1984b) 'How control of movements develops.' In H.T.A. Whiting (ed) *Human Motor Actions: Bernstein Reassessed.* Amsterdam: Elsevier (North Holland), 223–261.

Trevarthen, C. (1985a) 'Neuroembryology and the development of perceptual mechanisms.' In F. Falkner and J.M. Tanner (eds) *Human Growth (Second Edition).* New York: Plenum, 301–383.

Trevarthen, C. (1985b) 'Facial expressions of emotion in mother–infant interaction.' *Human Neurobiology 4*, 21–32.

Trevarthen, C. (1986) 'Form, significance and psychological potential of hand gestures of infants.' In J.L. Nespoulos, P. Perron and A. Roch Lecours (eds) *The Biological Foundation of Gestures: Motor and Semiotic Aspects.* Cambridge, MA: MIT Press, 149–202.

Trevarthen, C. (1987a) 'Sharing makes sense: intersubjectivity and the making of an infant's meaning.' In R. Steele and T. Threadgold (eds) *Language Topics: Essays in Honour of Michael Halliday, Volume I.* Amsterdam and Philadelphia: John Benjamins, 177–99.

Trevarthen, C. (1987b) 'Brain development.' In R.L. Gregory and O.L. Zangwill (eds) *Oxford Companion to the Mind.* Oxford, New York: Oxford University Press, 101–110.

Trevarthen, C. (1989) 'Development of early social interactions and the affective regulation of brain growth.' In C. von Euler, H. Forssberg and H. Lagercrantz (eds) *Neurobiology of Early Infant Behaviour.* (Wenner-Gren Center International Symposium Series, Vol 55) Basingstoke: Macmillan/New York: Stockton Press, 191–216.

Trevarthen, C. (1990a) 'Growth and education of the hemispheres.' In C. Trevarthen (ed) *Brain Circuits and Functions of the Mind: Essays in Honour of Roger W. Sperry* (pp.334–363). New York: Cambridge University Press.

Trevarthen, C. (1990b) 'Signs before speech.' In T.A. Sebeok and J. Umiker-Sebeok (eds) *The Semiotic Web,* 1989. Berlin, New York, Amsterdam: Mouton de Gruyter, 689–755.

Trevarthen, C. (1992) 'An infant's motives for speaking and thinking in the culture.' In A.H. Wold (ed) *The Dialogical Alternative* (Festschrift for Ragnar Rommetveit) Oslo/Oxford: Scandanavian University Press/Oxford University Press, 99–137.

Trevarthen, C. (1993a) 'The self born in intersubjectivity: an infant communicating.' In U. Neisser (ed) *Ecological and Interpersonal Knowledge of the Self.* New York: Cambridge University Press, 121–173.

Trevarthen, C. (1993b) 'The function of emotions in early infant communication and development.' In J. Nadel and L. Camaioni (eds) *New Perspectives in Early Communicative Development.* London: Routledge, 48–81.

Trevarthen, C. (1993c) 'Human Emotions and Why We Need Them.' Lecture to The Squiggle Foundation, London, 14 February.

Trevarthen, C. (1994) 'Infant semiosis.' In W. Nöth (ed) *Origins of Semiosis.* Berlin: Mouton de Gruyter, 219–252.

Trevarthen, C. (1995) 'The child's need to learn a culture.' *Children and Society 9,* 1, 5–19.

Trevarthen, C. (1996) 'Lateral asymmetries in infancy: implications for the development of the hemispheres.' *Neuroscience and Biobehavioral Reviews 20,* 571–586.

Trevarthen, C. (1997a) 'Language development: mechanisms in the brain.' In G. Adelman and B.H. Smith (eds) *Encyclopedia of Neuroscience, 2nd Edition, on CD-ROM.* Amsterdam: Elsevier Science.

Trevarthen, C. (1997b) 'Foetal and neonatal psychology: intrinsic motives and learning behaviour.' In F. Cockburn (ed) *Advances in Perinatal Medicine.* (Proceedings of the XVth European Congress of Perinatal Medicine, Glasgow 10–13 September, 1996) 282–291.

Trevarthen, C. (1998a) 'The nature of motives for human consciousness.' *Psychology: The Journal of the Hellenic Psychological Society 4*, 3, 187–221 (Special Issue, Part 2, December, 1997, 'The Place of Psychology in Modern Science'. Ed. T. Velli).

Trevarthen, C. (1998b) 'The concept and foundations of infant intersubjectivity.' In S. Bråten (ed) *Intersubjective Communication and Emotion in Early Ontogeny*. Cambridge: Cambridge University Press. (in press)

Trevarthen, C. (1998c) 'Language development: mechanisms in the brain.' In G. Adelman and B.H. Smith (eds) *Encyclopedia of Neuroscience, 2nd Edition, on CD-ROM*. Amsterdam: Elsevier Science.

Trevarthen, C. and Aitken, K.J. (1994) 'Brain development, infant communication, and empathy disorders: intrinsic factors in child mental health.' *Development and Psychopathology 6*, 599–635.

Trevarthen, C. and Burford, B. (1995) 'The central role of parents: how they can give power to a motor impaired child's acting, experiencing and sharing.' *European Journal of Special Needs Education 10*, 2, 138–148.

Trevarthen, C. and Hubley, P. (1978) 'Secondary intersubjectivity: confidence, confiding and acts of meaning in the first year.' In A. Lock (ed) *Action, Gesture and Symbol*. London: Academic Press.

Trevarthen, C., Kokkinaki, T. and Fiamenghi, G.A. Jr. (1998) 'What infants' imitations communicate: with mothers, with fathers and with peers.' In J. Nadel and G. Butterworth (eds) *Imitation in Infancy*. Cambridge: Cambridge University Press. (in press)

Trevarthen, C. and Logotheti, K. (1987) 'First symbols and the nature of human knowledge.' In J. Montangero, A. Tryphon and S. Dionnet (eds) *Symbolism and Knowledge*. Cahier No. 8. Geneva: Jean Piaget Archives Foundation, 65–92.

Trevarthen, C. and Marwick, H. (1986) 'Signs of motivation for speech in infants, and the nature of a mother's support for development of language.' In B. Lindblom and R. Zetterstrom (eds) *Precursors of Early Speech*. Basingstoke, Hampshire: Macmillan, 279–308.

Trevarthen, C., Murray, L. and Hubley, P.A. (1981) 'Psychology of infants.' In J. Davis and J. Dobbing (eds) *Scientific Foundations of Clinical Paediatrics, 2nd Edition*. London: Heinemann Medical, 211–274.

Tronick, E.Z., Als, H., Adamson, L., Wise, S. and Brazelton, T.B. (1978) 'The infant's response to entrapment between contradictory messages in face-to-face interaction.' *Journal of the American Academy of Child Psychiatry 17*, 1–13.

Tronick, E.Z. and Field, T. (eds) (1986) *Maternal Depression and Infant Disturbance*. New Directions for Child Development, No. 34. San Francisco: Jossey Bass.

Tronick, E. Z. & Weinberg, M. K. (1997) 'Depressed mothers and infants: Failure to form dyadic states of consciousness.' In: Murray, L. and Cooper, P. J. (Eds.) (1997) *Postpartum Depression and Child Development*. New York: Guilford Press, 54–81.

Tsai, L.Y. (1982) 'Handedness in autistic children and their families.' *Journal of Autism and Developmental Disorders 12*, 421–423.

Tsai, L.Y., Jacoby, C.G., Stewart, M.A. and Beisler, J.M. (1982) 'Unfavorable left–right asymmetries of the brain and autism: a question of methodology.' *British Journal of Psychiatry 140*, 312–319.

Tustin, F. (1980) Autistic objects. International Review of Psychoanalysis, 7, 27–40.

Tustin, F. (1981) *Autistic States in Children.* London: Routledge and Kegan Paul.

Tustin, F. (1986) *Autistic Barriers in Neurotic Patients.* London: Karnac.

Tustin, F. (1991) 'Revised understanding of psychogenic autism.' *International Journal of Psychoanalysis, 72, 4, 585–592.*

Tustin, F. (1994) 'Autistic children assessed as not brain-damaged.' *Journal of Child Psychotherapy 20,* 10, 209–225.

Tustin, F. (1994a) 'The perpetuation of an error.' *Journal of child Psychotherapy, 20(1):* 3–23.

Ungerer, J.A. and Sigman, M. (1981) 'Symbolic play and language comprehension in autistic children.' *Journal of the American Academy of Child Psychiatry 20,* 318–337.

Urwin, C. (1989) 'Linking emotion and thinking in infant development: a psychoanalytic perspective.' In A. Slater and Bremner, G. (eds) *Infant Development.* Hillsdale, NJ: Lawrence Erlbaum Associates, Inc., 273–300.

Van Rees, S. and Biemans, H. (1986) *Open–closed–open: An Autistic Girl at Home.* Video by Stichting Lichaamstaal, Scheyvenhofweg 12, 6093 PR Heythuysen, The Netherlands.

Varley, C., Kolff, C., Trupin, E. and Reichler, R.J. (1980) 'Hemodialysis as a treatment for infantile autism.' *Journal of Autism and Developmental Disorders 10,* 399–404.

Vogt, B.A. and Gabriel, M. (eds) (1993) *Neurobiology of Cingulate Cortex and Limbic Thalamus: A Comprehensive Handbook.* Boston: Birkhauser.

Volkmar, F.R. (1992) 'Child Disintegrative Disorder: Issues for DSM-IV.' *Journal of Autism and Developmental Disorders 22,* 625–642.

Volkmar, F. R. and Cohen, D. J. (1991) 'Comorbid association of autism and schizophrenia.' *American Journal of Psychiatry, 148,* 1705–1707.

Volkmar, F. R. and Cohen, D.J. (1989) 'Disintegrative disorder or 'late onset' autism?' *Journal of Child Psychology and Psychiatry, 30:* 717–724.

Volkmar, F.R., Klin, A., Seigel, B. Szatmari, P., Lord, C., Campbell, M., Freeman, B.J., Cicchetti, D.V., Rutter, M., Kline, W., Buitelaar, J., Hattab, Y., Fombonne, E., Fuentes, J., Werry, J., Stone, W., Kerbeshian, J., Hoshino, Y., Bregman, J., Loveland, K., Szymanski, L. and Towbin, K. (1994) 'Field trial for autistic disorders in DSM-IV.' *American Journal of Psychiatry 151,* 9, 1361–1367.

Volkmar, F.R. and Mayes, L. (1990) 'Gaze behaviour in autism.' *Development and Psychopathology 2,* 61–69.

Volkmar, F.R. and Nelson D.S. (1990) 'Seizure disorders in autism.' *Journal of the American Academy of Child and Adolescent Psychiatry 29,* 127–129.

Volterra, V. (1981) 'Gestures, signs and words at two years: when does communication become language?' *Sign Language Studies 33,* 351–362.

Walker, E.F., Grimes, K.E., Davis, D.M. and Smith, A.J. (1993) 'Childhood precursors of schizophrenia: facial expressions of emotion.' *Americal Journal of Psychiatry 150,* 1654–60.

Wallin, N.L. (1991) *Biomusicology: Neurophysiological, Neuropsychological and Evolutionary Perspectives on the Origins and Purposes of Music.* Stuyvesant, New York: Pendragon Press.

Wang, P.P. and Bellugi, U. (1993) 'Williams syndrome, Down syndrome, and cognitive neuroscience.' *American Journal of Diseases of Children 147,* 1246–1251.

Warwick, A. (1995) 'Music therapy in the education service: research with autistic children and their mothers.' In T. Wigram, B. Saperston and R. West (eds) *The Art and Science of Music Therapy: A Handbook.* 209–225.

Watters, R.G. and Watters, W.E. (1980) 'Decreasing self-stimulatory behaviour with physical exercise in a group of autistic boys.' *Journal of Autism and Childhood Schizophrenia 6,* 175–191.

Weikert, D.P., Deloria, D.J., Lawser, S.A. and Wiegerink, R. (1970) 'Longitudinal results of the Ypsilanti Perry Preschool Project.' (Monograph No. 1 of the High/Scope Educational Research Foundation) Ypsilanti, MI: High/Scope Foundation.

Weikert, D.P., Epstein, A.S., Schweinhart, L.J. and Bond, J.T. (1978) 'The Ypsilanti Preschool curriculum demonstration project: preschool years and longitudinal results.' (Monograph No. 4 of the High/Scope Educational Research Foundation) Ypsilanti, MI: High/Scope Foundation.

Weinberg, M.K. and Tronick, E.Z. (1994) 'Beyond the face: an empirical study of infant affective configurations of facial, vocal, gestural, and regulatory behaviors.' *Child Development 65,* 1503–1515.

Welch, M.G. (1983) 'Retrieval from autism through mother–child holding therapy.' In N. Tinbergen and E. A. Tinbergen (eds) *'Autistic' Children: New Hope for a Cure.* London: Allen and Unwin.

Wenar, C. and Ruttenberg, B.A. (1976) 'The use of BRIACC for evaluating therapeutic effectiveness.' *Journal of Autism and Developmental Disorders 10,* 379–387.

Wetherby, A.M. (1986) 'Ontogeny of communicative functions in autism.' *Journal of Autism and Developmental Disorders 16,* 295–316.

Wetherby, A.M. and Prutting, C.A. (1984) 'Profiles of communicative and cognitive social abnormalities in autistic children.' *Journal of Speech and Hearing Research 27,* 364–377.

Wheeler, B. (ed) (1995) *Music Therapy Research: Quantitative and Qualitative Perspectives.* Phoenixville, PA: Barcelona Publishers.

Wigram, T. (1995) 'A model of assessment and differential diagnosis of handicapped children through the medium of music.' In T. Wigram, B. Saperston, and R. West (eds) *The Art and Science of Music Therapy: A Handbook.* Chur, Switzerland: Harwood Academic Publishers, 181–193.

Williams, D. (1992) *Nobody Nowhere: The Remarkable Autobiography of an Autistic Girl.* London: Doubleday.

Williams, D. (1995) *Inside Out.* (TV self-portrait) London: Channel Four.

Williams, D. (1996) *Autism: An Inside-Out Approach.* London: Jessica Kingsley Publishers.

Williams, T. (1990) 'Low intrusion teaching.' In *Psychological Perspectives in Autism.* Sunderland: Autism Research Unit/ National Autistic Society, University of Sunderland.

Wiltshire, S. (1987) *Drawings.* (Foreword by Lorraine Cole) London: Dent.

Wiltshire, S. (1989) *Cities.* (Foreword by Oliver Sacks; Introduction by Anthony Clare) London: Dent.

Wimmer, H. and Perner, J. (1983) '"Beliefs about beliefs": representation and the constaining function of wrong beliefs in young children's understanding of deception.' *Cognition 13,* 103–128.

Wimpory, D., Chadwick, P. and Nash, S. (1995) 'Musical interaction therapy for children with autism: an evaluation case study with two-year follow up.' *Journal of Autism and Developmental Disorders 25*, 541–552D.

Wing, J.K. (ed) (1966) *Early Childhood Autism: Clinical, Educational and Social Aspects.* Oxford: Pergamon Press.

Wing, L. (1969) 'The handicaps of autistic children – a comparative study.' *Journal of Child Psychology and Psychiatry 10*, 1–40.

Wing, L. (1976) 'Diagnosis, clinical description and prognosis.' In L. Wing (ed) *Early Childhood Autism: Clinical, Educational and Social Aspects.* New York: Pergamon Press.

Wing, L. (1980a) 'Childhood autism and social class: a question of selection.' *British Journal of Psychiatry 137*, 410–417.

Wing, L. (1980b) 'Sex ratios in early childhood autism and related conditions.' *Psychiatry Research 5*, 129–137.

Wing, L. (1981) 'Asperger's Syndrome: A clinical account.' *Psychological Medicine, 11*, 115–130.

Wing, L. (1996) *The Autistic Spectrum.* London: Constable.

Wing, L. and Gould, J. (1979) 'Severe impairments of social interaction and associated abnormalities in children: epidemiology and classification.' *Journal of Autism and Developmental Disorders 9*, 11–29.

Wing, L., Gould, J., Yeates, S. and Brierly, L. (1977) 'Symbolic play in severely mentally retarded and in autistic children.' *Journal of Child Psychology and Psychiatry 18*, 167–178.

Wing, L., Yeates, S., Brierly, L. and Gould, J. (1976) 'The prevalence of early childhood autism: comparison of administrative and epidemiological studies.' *Psychological Medicine 6*, 89–100.

Winnicott, D.W. (1953) 'Transitional objects and transitional phenomena.' *International Journal of Psychoanalysis 34*, 89–97.

Winnicott, D. W. (1960) 'The theory of the parent-infant relationship.' *International Journal of Psychoanalysis, 41*, 585–595. (Republished in Winnicott, D. W., *The Maturational Process and the Facilitating Environment* London: The Institute of Psychoanalysis/ Karnak Books, 1990)

Winnicott, D.W. (1965) 'The theory of the parent–infant relationship.' In *The Maturational Processes and the Facilitating Environment.* London: Karnac.

Winnicott, D.W. (1971) *Playing and Reality.* New York: Penguin.

Winnicott D.W. (1977) *The Piggle: An Account of the Psychoanalytic Treatment of a Little Girl.* London: Hogarth Press.

Wishart, J.G. (1991) 'Taking the intiative in learning: a developmental investigation of children with Down Syndrome.' *International Journal of Disability, Development and Education 38*, 27–44.

Wishart, J.G. and Bower, T.G.R. (1984) 'Spatial relations and object concept: a normative study.' In L.P. Lipsitt and C. Rovee-Collier (eds) *Advances in Infancy Research, Vol. 3.* Norwood, NJ: Ablex.

Witt-Engerström, I (1990) 'Rett syndrome in Sweden: Neurodevelopment, disability, pathophysiology.' *Acta Paediatrica Scandinavica, Supplement 369.* Stockholm: Almqvist and Wiksell.

Wolff, P.H., Garner J., Paccia J. and Lappen J. (1989) 'The Greeting behaviour of Fragile-X males.' *American Journal of Mental Retardation 93*, 406–411.

Wolff, S. and Chess, S. (1964) 'A behavioural study of schizophrenic children.' *Acta Psychiatrica Scandinavica 40*, 438–466.

Wooten, M. and Mesibov, G. B. (1986) 'Social skills training for elementary school autistic children with normal peers.' In E. Schopler and G. Mesibov. (eds.) *Social Behavior in Autism.* New York: Plenum.

World Health Organisation (1978) *International Classification of Diseases, Ninth Revision (ICD-9): Mental Disorders: Glossary and Guide to their Classification.* Geneva: World Health Organization.

World Health Organisation (1987) *International Classification of Diseases, Tenth Revision (ICD-10): Draft of Chapter V: Mental and Behavioural Disorders.* Geneva: World Health Organization.

World Health Organisation (1993) *International Classification of Diseases, Tenth Revision (ICD-10): Chapter V: Mental and Behavioural Disorders.* Geneva: World Health Organisation.

Wulff, S.B. (1985) 'The symbolic and object play of children with autism: a review.' *Journal of Autism and Developmental Disorders 15*, 139–148.

Yirmiya, N., Kasari, C., Sigman, M. and Mundy, P. (1989) 'Facial expressions of affect in autistic, mentally retarded and normal children.' *Journal of Child Psychology and Psychiatry 30*, 725–735.

Zappella, M. (1992) 'Hypomelanosis of Ito is common in autistic syndromes.' *European Child and Adolescent Psychiatry 1*, 170–177.

Zappella, M., Chiarucci, P., Pinassi, D., Fidanzi, P. and Messeri, P. (1991) 'Parental bonding in the treatment of autistic behaviour.' *Ethology and Sociobiology 12*, 1–11.

Zelazo, P. D., Burack, J. A., Benedett, E. and Frye, D. (1996) 'Theory of mind and rule use in individuals with Down's syndrome: a test of the uniqueness and specificity claims.' *Journal of Child Psychology and Psychiatry, 37,* 479–485.

Zilbovicius, M., Garreau, B., Tzourio, N., Mazoyer, B., Bruck, B., Martinot, J-L., Raynaud, C., Samson, Y., Syrota, A. and Lelord, G. (1992) 'Regional cerebral blood flow in childhood autism: a SPECT study.' *American Journal of Psychiatry 149*, 924–930.

Zuckerkandl, V. (1973) *Sound and Symbol: Music and the External World.* Princeton, NJ: Princeton University/Bollingen Press.

Zuckerkandl, V. (1976) *Man the Musician.* Princeton: Princeton University/Bollingen Press.

Glossary

5-Hydroxyindoleacetic Acid (5-HIAA): A substance which is the end product of the breakdown of the transmitter serotonin in the brain.

ABC: The Autism Behaviour Checklist (see Appendix 2).

Acetylcholine (ACh): A major chemical transmitter of nervous systems. Cholinergic (ACh-releasing) nerves are found exciting the muscles of the body and in the sympathetic nervous system (regulating visceral muscles and glands) and parts of the central nervous system.

Action Potentials: Electrical pulses that transmit activity along nerve fibres.

AD/HD; Attention Deficit Hyperactivity Disorder: A developmental disorder of early childhood causing problems with attention, activity level and impulsivity.

ADI: The Autism Diagnostic Inventory (see Appendix 2).

ADOS: The Autism Diagnostic Observation Schedule (see Appendix 2).

Adrenals: The adrenal glands, next to the kidneys (see Epinephrine)

Adreno-Cortico-Trophic Hormone (ACTH): A hormone produced in the anterior pituitary gland of the brain that stimulates the adrenal gland with a range of effects, including release of sex hormone.

Affect Attunement: The term introduced by Daniel Stern to describe the sympathetic reflection and elaboration of infants' expressive vocalisations and gestures by mothers. The rhythms and dynamic forms expressed are often imitated with translation between senses; e. g. of what is heard to what can be seen, or felt in the body. This is called 'intermodal fluency'. Infants also attune to mothers' expressions sympathetically (see Intersubjectivity).

Affective: Related to emotions or feelings.

Afferent: Leading from the brain, or from a nucleus in the brain.

AFRAX (Autism with Fragile-X Syndrome): The combination of the chromosome fault Fragile-X syndrome with a behavioural profile sufficient for a diagnosis of autism.

Agenesis: Absence, failure of formation or lack of development of a particular structure in the body.

Ainsworth Strange Situation: A test of an infant's emotional relation with a mother or main caregiver developed by Mary Ainsworth. A one-year-old is left in a strange room through a sequence of situations – with the mother, alone, with a stranger, alone and then with the mother – and the reactions of the infant are observed, especially when the mother returns after the infant has been with the stranger. An estimation of the infant's security of attachment to the mother is made.

ALL; Acute Lymphoblastic Leukaemia: a cancer of the blood affecting circulating cells called lymphoblasts.

Alter-centred: Centred in the mental processes of another, 'other-centred'.

Alternative Communication: Communication other than by language with spoken or written words, especially communication that employs expressive movements of the body, hands and eyes, or non-verbal vocalisations, as in infancy. Communication can be mediated by pictures or signs that are pointed to, or placed on objects to label them. Symbol systems can be transmitted by hand movements, as in hand sign languages.

American Sign Language (ASL): A system of hand signs that has been devised in the United States for communication by and with the deaf. Deaf societies have developed many hand sign languages independently.

Aminergic: Neural systems that carry information in the Central Nervous System (CNS) by means of the amino acid excitatory transmitters, principally L-glutamate and L-aspartate.

Amygdala: A pair of almond-shaped nuclei, one near the tip of each temporal lobe of the brain. They are part of the limbic system and a key component in emotional regulation in learning and communication. (see Figure 3)

Anomalous Hand Dominance: Geschwind and Galaburda use this term for any handedness pattern other than strong right-handedness.

Antagonist: A substance which blocks or reduces the activity of another substance, such as a drug or a natural neurotransmitter or hormone.

Anterior: Towards the front of the body.

Aphasia: Impairment or absence of language.

Apraxia: A failure of voluntary movement in the absence of paralysis or a other sensory or motor impairment, due to a defect in the central motor coordinating systems of the brain.

Arnold-Chiari I: A congenital abnormality resulting in the cerebellum and caudate developing with extension down into the region of the upper spinal column.

Asperger's syndrome: A condition, similar to high functioning autism, characterised by marked social impairments and extremely circumscribed interests; clumsiness; performance difficulties on cognitive testing, and executive function problems, but no simple 'metacognitive', or 'model-of-mind', problems (see Theory of Mind).

Ataxia: Failure or irregularity in muscle activity, producing erratic movements

Athetoid Movements: Ceaseless rhythmic slow involuntary (automatic) movements, mainly of the hands.

Atrophy: Physical wasting of a tissue or organ.

Attunement: See Affect Attunement.

Augmentative Communication: Any assisted form of communication that incorporates a communication aid, such as a computer interface, or a signing system such as Bliss.

Automatic Movements: Uncontrolled, involuntary, movements of the body, limbs, hands, or face (See Athetoid Movements).

Autonomic: Self-regulating. Applied to the component of the nervous system that regulates the internal functions of the body.

Axon: A nerve fibre; the extension of the nerve cell that conducts impulses away from the cell body.

Basal Ganglia: A group of structures in the forebrain, including the caudate, putamen and globus pallidus. They are important in regulation of movement patterns (see Figure 3).

Batten's Syndrome (Infantile Neural Seroid Lipofuscinosis): A genetic disorder which can now be identified antenatally by a genetic marker. Up to the third year, it can be confused with autism or Rett's syndrome. Loss of head control and abnormal postures make differential diagnosis easier in older children.

Brard Auditory Training: A practical behavioural approach that attempts to reduce distress caused by hearing certain noises or loud noises in general, a common problem for children and adults with autism.

Bipolar Affective Disorder: A term used interchangeably with manic-depressive psychosis to indicate a specific psychiatric disorder with characteristic swings of mood.

Body-to-Body Mapping: The capacity of one person's brain to regulate mimicry of the form and movement of a part of another individual's body, making the same body parts correspond, as in imitation of hand gestures or facial expressions. A fundamental requirement for non-symbolic communication of motives and ideas (see Intersubjectivity).

BOS: The Behaviour Observation Scale for Autism (see Appendix 2).

Brain Imaging: Use of physical instruments to obtain pictures of the anatomy and function of living brains from outside the head.

Brain Stem: The part of the brain in the midline of the head beneath the cerebral hemispheres and cerebellum that connects these structures with the spinal cord. The brain stem contains the core systems that transmit information to and from the cerebral and cerebellar cortices, and that regulate their activities. It includes major components of the Emotional Motor System.

BRIAAC: The Behaviour Rating Instrument for Autistic and Atypical Children (see Appendix 2).

BSE: The Behavioural Summarised Evaluation (see Appendix 2).

British Sign Language (BSL): See American Sign Language.

CARS: The Childhood Autism Rating Scale (see Appendix 2).

Caudate: A pair of tadpole-shaped structures which make up part of the basal ganglia (see Figure 3).

Central Nervous System (CNS): The brain, brain stem and spinal cord, where integrative psychological functions of motivation, cognition and learning direct behaviour in relation to the perceived environment. Connected with the sense organs, muscles and vital organs by the Peripheral Nervous System.

Cerebellum: A large hindbrain structure situated under the rear portion of the cerebral cortex at the back of the head. It is important in motor control and planning, and in simple learning. It consists of two large hemispheres on left and right and a narrow middle region, the vermis (see Figure 3).

Cerebral Cortex: The grey, cell-rich layer, approximately three millimetres thick, which covers the entire surface of the cerebral hemispheres.

Cerebral Palsy: Non-progressive and lasting motor impairments of varying severity, appearing before the age of three years; caused by perinatal damage to the developing brain.

CGG Repeat: Abnormal reduplication of a sequence of three nucleic acids in the gene code, Cytosine, Guanine and Guanine; a characteristic of Fragile-X syndrome.

CHAT: The Checklist for Autism in Toddlers; an 18 month screening test for detection of precursor behaviours for autism (see Appendix 2).

Childhood Disintegrative Disorder (Heller's syndrome): Originally called 'dementia infantilis'. A condition, resembling autism, with normal development until the second year, followed by loss in language and cognitive skills.

Chromosome: One of the bodies in the nucleus of every cell that contain the gene material. They appear at the time of cell division, when genetic material is replicated.

Chromosomes: Structures in the cell nucleus containing DNA (deoxyribose nucleic acid), the physical genetic code which determines the inherited biochemical makeup of the individual and directs development of the body and all its components.

Chronological Age (CA): Age since birth.

Cingulate Cortex: Part of the limbic cortex, above the corpus callosum on the midline surface of each cerebral hemisphere (See Figures 3 and 6).

Cochlea: The part of the inner ear like a curled shell that is the receptor organ of hearing. It carries sense cells that are stimulated by sound to send sensory messages to the brain.

Cognition: The psychological process that generates perception, problem-solving and memory, and that sustains conscious knowing and thinking.

Co-morbidity: The term used to describe the possibility that two or more different medical conditions may exist in one person at the same time.

Companion-Space: The mutual awareness between two persons where their behaviours and consciousness may be regulated in communication.

Computerised Axial Tomography (CAT): An X-ray procedure which allows pictures to be made of deep brain structures from outside the head. The technique shows up denser structures; it is less effective in imaging deeper parts of the midbrain and the cerebellum than it is in revealing tissues of the cerebral hemispheres.

Conditioning: The learning process by which behaviours are modified by the stimuli that occur with them.

Congenital: Present at birth, thus reflecting the influence of genetic factors, conception, pregnancy or labour and delivery.

Context: The situation in which experiences or utterances occur. Surrounding effects that may influence perception or action.

Cooperative awareness: The mental ability, requiring joint attention, by which persons share what they are experiencing, and doing.

Corpus Callosum: The principal fibre bridge over the midline of the brain. It links equivalent areas of the cortex of the two cerebral hemispheres (see Figure 3).

Cranial Nerves: Nerves leading from the brain stem to the olfactory receptors, eyes, face, head, neck, mouth and tongue and the heart, gut and muscles of respiration. They have a central role in physiological changes associated with emotions, and in the communication of emotion (see Figures 4 and 5).

Cultural Learning: Learning, characteristic of humans, that requires cooperative awareness and interest in the understanding of companions. It is the generator of arbitrary or conventional meanings, symbols, languages, rituals, techniques, institutions, etc.

DAMP; Disorders of Attention, Motor Control and Perception: A recently recognised condition affecting coordination of awareness and movements. It overlaps with AD/HD and Asperger's syndrome, but also includes a large group of children who do not fit in either of these other groups.

Dandy-Walker: A condition in which the child has hydrocephalus (accumulation of fluid in the cavities of the brain), enlargement of the brain and abnormalities in the formation of the cerebellum.

Declive: Part of the central vermis of the cerebellum.

Dendrites: Relatively short branches of nerve cells that receive input of information-carrying impulses from other neurons at contact points called synapses (see Axons)

Denervation Supersensitivity: Abnormally high sensitivity to stimuli in a nerve centre after loss of part of the normal input, due to an imbalance of processing of the input.

Desensitisation: Repeated use of stimulation to reduce an abnormal sensitivity to that particular form of stimulus by a simple form of automatic learning called 'habituation'.

Diagnosis: Distinguishing one disease from another.

Diencephalon: The part of the brain between the cerebral hemispheres that includes the thalamus and hypothalamus (see Figure 3).

DNA: The molecule of the genetic code, 'desoxyribose nucleic acid'.

Dopamine: A neurotransmitter from cells found principally in the caudate and putamen of the basal ganglia and in the substantia nigra nucleus of the brainstem.

Down's Syndrome: A genetic developmental disorder which results from the presence of an extra copy of chromosome 21. It affects development of body and brain, and leads to mental handicap.

DSM-III-R: the classification system for behavioural and emotional disorders used by the American Psychiatric Association between 1987 and 1994.

DSM-IV: The most recent classification system for behavioural and emotional disorders used by the American Psychiatric Association introduced at the beginning of 1995.

Dyskinesias: Difficulty in performance of voluntary movements.

Dyslexia: A significant difficulty with or impairment in reading ability compared to other aspects of psychological functioning. Dylsexia can be of various types and have a variety of causes.

Dysphasia: Difficulty with the production of comprehensible speech.

Echolalia: Copying or repeating the content and/or intonation patterns of another person's speech.

Ego: The self, with coherent psychological representation of its separateness from the surrounding world. Freud thought that the newborn infant cannot conceive this separation, and therefore does not have an ego.

Egocentrism: Being unable to think of situations from any perspective other than one's own.

Embedded Figures Task: A test of awareness that confronts a subject with drawings or pictures of objects that have to be visually separated from a confusing context.

Embryo: The stage of development in which the basic form of the body and the central nervous system are laid down while the organism is inactive. The human embryo develops from a fertilised egg for eight weeks before, then becomes a Foetus. In the embryo the cerebral cortex and cerebellum are not yet formed (see Figure 5).

Emotional Motor System (EMS): The system of nerve cell groups and nerve fibre pathways that regulates emotional states, affecting all other functions of the Central Nervous System. The EMS generates expressions of emotion by which feelings about contacts and relationships between persons are communicated (see Figures 3, 4 and 5).

Emotional Referencing: Orientation of attention to other persons to evaluate their expressions of feeling about objects and events. Describes the way infants, when encountering a novel situation, check back to a evaluate a parent's expressions of emotion.

Emotions: Evaluative states of motivation, or feelings, communicated by expressive movements of the body, especially of the face, vocal apparatus and hands. Charles Darwin wrote a famous book showing that humans and animals share many principles of emotional expression.

Empathy Disorder: One of the variety of disorders that children develop which affect their communicative and emotional responses to other persons.

Endocrine System: The mechanisms of 'internal secretion' of the body. They produce chemical messengers or hormones that are distributed by the bloodstream round the body to organs performing a great variety of vital functions.

Endorphins and Encephalins: A range of naturally produced opium-like substances found in the brain that act as neurotransmitters and affect natural pain control.

Entorhinal Cortex: Part of the limbic cortex on the underside of the inner surface of the temporal lobe playing a part in emotions and memory processes.

Epilepsy: A range of chronic disorders that cause excessive neural discharge, either in restricted areas or more extensively in the brain, resulting in impairment in the functioning of those structures which are affected. Manifested as 'fits', which can affect emotions, consciousness, movement or perception in different combinations.

Epinephrine or Adrenaline: A substance produced by the adrenal gland next to the kidneys. It stimulates blood circulation in anticipation of vigorous activity.

ESCS (Early Social Communication Scales): A series of rated structured situations which are used with young infants (developmental level 8 to 24 months) to investigate early social interaction.

Ethology: The science of animal behaviour and communication observed in the natural environment.

Executive Function: The ability to plan complex cognitive tasks (such as the 'Wisconsin Card Sorting Test' or the 'Tower of Hanoi'). This ability is interfered with by dysfunction in the frontal lobes of the brain.

Eye Pointing: Looking to objects, pictures or symbols used to indicate a subject's interest or intention. Developed as a means of enhancing communication with persons who are incapable of verbal communication, especially the profoundly and multiply handicapped who have no alternative way of expressing their purposes or needs.

Familial: Present in several members of the same family group.

Fenfluramine: A medication used as an antagonist to the neurotransmitter serotonin to reduce the concentration of serotonin in the fluids of the central nervous system, blood and urine.

Field Trials: Application, to a large population, of diagnostic criteria for a putative illness, before these criteria are formally adopted for routine clinical use.

Foetus: The stage of development before birth, after the Embryo stage; that is, in weeks 9 to 40 of gestation, in which the cerebral hemispheres and cerebellum undergo their first phase of development.

Folium: A portion of the cerebellar vermis.

Forebrain: Cerebral hemispheres and Diencephalon of the brain.

Form E1/2: The standardised scale developed by Rimland in San Diego for characterisation of the typical developmental patterns seen in autism (see Appendix 2).

Fragile-X Syndrome: A genetic disorder frequently resulting in developmental delay and autism, in which there is an over-replication (repetition) of a small section of genetic substance near the tip of the X-chromosome. The cause and the mode of action are uncertain.

Frontal Lobe: Anterior part of the cerebral hemispheres (see Figure 2).

Gene: Unit of inheritance; part of the molecular genetic code or DNA.

Gene Locus: The place of a Gene on a Chromosome.

Genotype: See Phenotype.

Germinal: Generating growth by cell multiplication.

Gestalt: German word for 'form', used to describe the whole of a thing, unifying its parts.

Glia: 'Glue-like' support tissue of the Central Nervous System. Glia cells are more numerous than Neurons and are important environment for them, but are not capable of transmitting impulses.

Globus Pallidus: One of the Basal Ganglia.

Gonads: The ovaries and testes, glands that produce sex-cells.

Grey Matter: Tissue of the brain in which nerve cells are concentrated; White Matter is made up of nerve fibres, white because they are sheathed in Myelin.

Gustatory: Related to the sense of taste.

Habituation: A simple learning process that leads to the reduction in intensity or frequency of responses to a repeated stimulus.

Haemodialysis: Removal of water and soluble substances from the blood by diffusion through a semipermeable membrane in a dialysis machine.

Haloperidol: A medication which acts as a virtually pure antagonist or blocking agent for the D2 dopamine receptor.

Heller's Syndrome: See Childhood Disintegrative Psychosis.

Hemispheres: The two halves of the Forebrain.

Hindbrain: The lower or posterior part of the brain stem that carries the Cerebellum (see Figure 3).

Hippocampus: A paired structure in the temporal lobe of the brain forming part of the limbic system. It is involved in emotion and is essential for the laying down of short-term memories (see Figure 3).

Histo-Anatomic: Related to the anatomical organisation of tissues.

Homeotic genes, Hedgehog and Homeobox sequences: Regulator genes that govern the patterning and symmetry of the body, and the maps of the body in the Central Nervous System. They are important in the evolution of new processes and life functions by changing the proportions of the component parts of the body and brain.

Homovanillic Acid (HVA): A substance, the end product of chemical treatment of the transmitter dopamine in the body, which can be detected in brain fluids and urine.

Hormones: A chemical messenger that transmits effect between organs in the body; e.g. Endocrine secretions. Neurohormones are produced in the brain.

Hydrocephalus: An increase of fluid pressure in the brain which can result from a number of factors, such as increased production of fluid, decreased absorption of fluid, or some blockage within the ventricular system, the fluid-filled cavities inside the brain.

Hyper-acusis: Abnormally high sensitivity to sounds.

Hyperactive: Abnormally high levels of moving, unable to settle into inactivity.

Hypersensitivity: Abnormally high sensitivity.

Hypo-acusis: Abnormally low sensitivity to sounds.

Hypomelanosis of Ito: A condition of unknown cause which results in depigmented spots or pale streaks on the skin, best seen under ultraviolet light. This skin condition is often associated with skeletal and eye abnormalities, and there are central nervous system defects in approximately 50 per cent of cases.

Hypoplasia: Underdevelopment of a structure, normally due to a decrease in the number of cells.

Hypothalamus: Part of the brain, in the Diencephalon, in which there are many nerve centres that are responsible for regulating vital functions, such as hunger, thirst, sex. The hypothalamus is part of the Emotional Motor System (See Figure 3).

Hypotonia: Lowered muscle strength or weakness.

Hypotonia: Significantly reduced muscle tone or resting muscle tension.

IBSE: The Infant Behavioural Summarised Evaluation (see Appendix 2).

ICD-9: The World Health Organisation classification system for diseases in use between 1980 and 1994.

ICD-10: The World Health Organisation classification system for diseases in use from 1995 (a draft version of part of the psychiatric systems was introduced in 1987).

Iconic: Representing by a picture or sign that resembles the thing referred to, as in a religious icon showing a figure of Christ or a saint.

Immune Function: The process of protection against infection or disease, by natural response of the body or by inoculation. Antibodies are produced in response to the infectious material.

In utero: During foetal development inside the womb.

Inner Ear: The hidden organs of the ear, including the Cochlea, which responds to sound, and the semicircular canals, which are the sense organs of balance responding to gravitational force.

Insula: An oval region of the cerebral cortex covering the lenticular nucleus of the basal ganglia.

Inter-Rater Reliability: A measure of the extent of agreement between independent observers who are rating the same phenomenon using an agreed rating system.

Intermental: Psychological processes that enable persons to transmit their motives, intentions, ideas and feelings to one another.

Interneurons: Generally small nerve cells that interconnect locally the larger nerve cells, regulating their activities. The large cells take in information from many sources and transmit activity from place to place in the CNS or in the body.

Intersubjective: Mental activity that links the feelings, conscious purposes and thoughts of one person with those of another by means of expressive behaviours of all kinds..

Intersynchrony: The rhythmic synchronisation of expressive movements between persons who are communicating.

Intramuscular: Within a muscle.

Intrinsic Motive Formation (IMF): The organised mechanism in the CNS that coordinates all acting and perceiving within the individual. Its normal functioning is essential for communication of mental states or Intersubjectivity. Its disorders conspicuously affect functions of Empathy.

Intuitive Motherese: The instinctive pattern of talking that an affectionate mother uses when she speaks to her infant or young child.

IQ: Intelligence Quotient, a measure of understanding or thinking (or potential capacity to deal with the environment) that depends on comparison of a person's score on an intelligence test with the average score obtained by a large number of subjects of the same age who are taken to represent a normal population (standardised group). IQ = Mental Age/Chronological Age x 100.

Joint Attention; Joint Awareness; Joint Perspective Taking: Behaviours or abilities that attend to the orientations of other persons, to determine what is interesting them, or what they are intending to do. A necessary ability for a child to begin learning the meanings of words.

Joubert's Syndrome: A recessive genetic disorder resulting in Hypoplasia or Agenesis of the Cerebellar Vermis, and leading to Mental Retardation, Ataxia, Hypotonia and abnormal breathing and eye movements.

Kinaesthetic: The sense of movement in the body. Responds to stimulation from joints, muscles and skin indicating displacements or distortions of body parts.

Kleinian School: The psychoanalytic group who base their ideas on the work of the analyst Melanie Klein (see Chapter 12).

Lacanian School: The Psychoanalytic group who base their ideas on the work of the French analyst Lacan (see Chapter 12).

Landau-Kleffner Syndrome: A form of epilepsy that affects language centres of the brain and causes communication problems.

Lenticular Nucleus: A paired nucleus of the basal ganglia situated between the Caudate and the Thalamus.

Limbic System: A group of brain tissues between the Brain Stem and the Neocortex. The principal components of this system include hippocampus, mammillary bodies, septum, olfactory bulbs, fornix and cingulate gyrus. They are important in emotions and in regulation of consciousness and learning (see Figure 3).

Lithium: An alkali metal chemical element, used in the stabilisation of manic-depressive patients.

Locus Ceruleus: A centre in the Reticular Formation that has important influence over the function of other reticular nuclei (see Figure 5).

Lovaas Method: An intensive behaviourally based or training approach to working with young autistic children, based on the theories of Ivor Lovaas of the University of California, Los Angeles.

Magnetic Resonance Imaging (MRI): A brain imaging technique that images structures with high water content, enabling clear identification of faults in cerebellar and midbrain structures.

Mammillary Bodies: A pair of structures in the posterior part of the limbic system.

Melanin: A black pigment, found in the nerve cells of the substantia nigra of the brain stem, and in skin, hair and the retina of the eye. It is not present in the newborn but appears towards the end of the first year and increases steadily until puberty.

Melatonin: A chronobiotic or time regulating hormone, produced by the pineal gland, with a critical role in controlling the sleep–wake cycle. Oral melatonin can be used in treatment of sleep disorders.

Mental Age (MA): The age corresponding to the level of performance of a person in an intelligence test in relation to the level attained by a standard group of persons of different ages.

Mentalising: The process by which persons are said to 'represent' mental activities, of other persons and of themselves.

Mesofrontal: Referring to the area of each Frontal Lobe facing the midplane of the head.

Meta cognitive: Thinking about thinking.

Metabolism: All the processes of movement and change of material by which an organism maintains its living functions. The chemistry and physics of life.

Midbrain: The part of the Brainstem between the Diencephalon and the Hindbrain.

Middle Ear: The space behind the ear drum that contains the small auditory bones. These transmit sound through the middle ear to the Cochlea. Middle ear muscles stiffen the links between the auditory bones, and are important in tuning out disturbing frequencies of sounds, making speech easier to hear.

Mimetic: Imitating by movement and postures of the body.

Morphogenesis: The development of form in the body and organs of an organism.

Motives: The impulses of the mind that generate action and direct awareness.

Motor Stereotypies: Constant, involuntary repetition of meaningless gestures or movements.

Myelin, Myelinate: Myelin is a fat-like substance that is wrapped around the Axons of Neurons, acting as an insulator and facilitating rapid transmission of nerve impulses. Myelination is the process by which myelin is laid down in development of different nerve Tracts.

Naloxone: A short-acting, intramuscularly injected substance that blocks endorphin receptor binding sites (i.e. it is an endorphin 'antagonist').

Naltrexone: A long-acting, orally administered blocker of endorphin receptor binding sites.

Neocerebellar Cortex: The folded surface layer of the most advanced portions of the Cerebellum.

Neocortex: The grey matter layer covering the surface of the cerebral hemispheres, not including the 'older' limbic cortex.

Nerve Tracts: Bundles of nerve fibres.

Neuroendocrine System: The nerve systems that work with the Endocrine System in regulation of Hormones in the bloodstream and Neurotransmitters in the brain.

Neurofibromatosis (von Recklinghausen's Disease): A genetic (autosomal dominant) disorder of skin and nerve tissue with small pigmented skin lesions (often called cafe-au-lait spots) which may develop into abnormal tissue masses along the course of peripheral nerves.

Neurohormone: A Hormone stimulating the nervous system.

Neuron: A nerve cell.

Neurophysiology: The science of physiology or life processes in the nervous system, especially the transmission and processing of nerve impulses.

Neuropsychology: The clinical discipline that employs psychological concepts and tests to understand the functions of the brain and the effect of injury and disease in the brain.

Neurotransmitter: A chemical messenger in the nervous system, communicating impulses between nerve cells.

Non-Invasive: A medical intervention that does not involve opening the body.

Non-Mendelian Gene Fault: A genetic disorder, such as Fragile-X or other triple repeat condition, not inherited in an 'all or nothing' fashion, and capable of showing varying patterns of expression.

Norepinephrine (NE): See Epinephrine

Nosological: Related to the science of classification of diseases.

Nuclei: Clusters of nerve cells in the brain that are interconnected locally to facilitate performance of an integrative function. Nuclei are interconnected by Nerve Tracts.

Nucleic Acid: The chemical substance of the gene code.

Object Concept: A mental representation or memory of an object as separate thing to which the mind can direct actions of the body.

Object Permanence: The concept of an object that represents it as continuing to exist when it has ceased to stimulate the senses.

Object Relation: A psychoanalytic concept to define the separateness and relationship between a subject and the representation of another person.

Observational Learning: Learning by watching some other person do something.

Obsessional, Ritualistic: Forced repetition of a form of activity in a purposeless way. Activity with very restricted interest or usefulness.

Olfactory: Related to the sense of smell.

Olivary Nucleus: A paired structure in the brainstem with ascending connections into the cerebellum.

Olivo-Ponto-Cerebellar Degeneration: A progressive disorder of movement control with onset in adult life. Accompanied by degeneration of the cerebellum, olivary nuclei and pons.

Ontogeny: The process of development in the lifetime of an organism. Contrasted with Phylogeny, the development of the race, species, or other group of organisms by evolution.

Opiate; Opioid: Related to opium, a substance that has a sedative and pain reducing effect on the CNS. See Endorphins.

Option Approach: An intensive early intervention approach based on the work of Alan and Suzie Kaufmann. Parents and volunteer careers are trained to give total acceptance to the child with autism, and encouraged to use imitation and exaggerated social responses.

Orbito-Frontal: Referring to the part of the frontal lobe adjacent to the eye cavity or orbit (see Figures 3 and 6)

Para-Verbal: Expressions of communication that may accompany speech but that do not need words to have their communicative effect.

Paraldehyde: A medication sometimes used to control severe epileptic seizures, normally given by intramuscular injection.

Parietal Cortex: A region of the cerebral cortex which lies beneath the parietal bone of the skull at the back and side of the head (see Figure 2).

Part Objects: Representations in the mind that fail to appreciate the whole of an object.

Pathogenesis: The process causing disease.

Performative Aphasia: Deficiency in the act of speaking.

Peri-Aqueductal Grey: Grey Matter around the cavity in the centre of the Midbrain.

Peripheral Nerves: Nerves passing between the central nervous system (brain and spinal cord) and the sense organs, glands and muscles of the body (see Cranial Nerves).

Pertubation: Interference with the normal progress of a function.

Pharmacological Activation: Induction by medication of a physiological or psychological function under study.

Pharmacotherapies: Treatment by means of drugs.

Phenothiazines: A group of medications used primarily in the treatment of schizophrenia.

Phenotype: The adaptive form of an organism, a product of development or 'epigenesis'. Distinguished from the Genotype, or complement of genes.

Phenylketonuria (PKU): A genetic disorder resulting from lack of a single gene that normally codes for the enzyme required for the body to process phenylalanine, an amino acid present in most foodstuffs. Affected individuals, unless they are given a special diet with low levels of phenylalanine, show developmental delay, often with autism. Routine neonatal screening with the Guthrie Test has virtually eliminated this as a cause of autism in the UK.

Phonology: The study of systems of sound in a language, and their changes.

Phylogeny: See Ontogeny.

Picture Code: See Iconic.

Placebo-Controlled Trial: Test of medications in which one group of individuals is given an inactive agent (a placebo), while another group is administered the drug which it is hoped will produce improvement. A procedure to control for non-drug factors, such as a patient's expectation of improvement.

PL-ADOS: The Preschool Autism Diagnostic Observations Schedule (see Appendix 2).

Positron Emission Tomography (PET): A method for imaging blood flow through the brain. It allows the investigator to identify structures in which there is an increase or decrease of blood flow during particular psychological activities. It is also used to locate parts of the brain with abnormal (raised or lowered) levels of cell activity.

Post Synaptic: The surface of a nerve cell beyond a connection, or synapse, with another cell.

Posterior: Towards, or facing, the back or rear of the body.

Pragmatic: In language science, the use of language to have certain effects, taking account of the social circumstances.

Pre-Verbal: Before the development of speech.

Prefrontal Cortices: Anterior parts of the frontal lobes (see Figures 3 and 6).

Primary Maternal Preoccupation: Winnicott's term for the mother's state of mental orientation towards the emotional life with her expected or newborn baby.

Prognosis: A forecast of the probable course or result of a disease.

Pronominal Reversal: Misuse of the words to indicate first and second person in conversation, substituting 'me' for 'you' and vice versa.

Prosody: The musicality or tonal variation of speech.

Proto-conversation: Pre-verbal communicative interactions between infants and their caregivers which exhibit many of the rhythmic, affective, prosodic and intentional components observed in verbal conversations between adults.

Proto declarative Pointing: Pointing to make a communicative statement to another person before the age at which words are used.

Proto language: The form of pre-verbal communication in which infants around one year of age combine vocalisations and gestures to express themselves to others in 'acts of meaning'.

Psychoactive Drugs: Drugs that have effects in perception, memory and imagination, and that change psychological motives.

Purine Autism: Autism consequent on abnormalities in the processing of toxic substances called purines, which are related to uric acid.

Purkinje Cells: Large cells found in a single layer in the cerebellum. They are the source of the fibres leading from the cerebellum to other parts of the brain.

Receptive Aphasia: Failure of understanding of other persons' speech.

Receptive: Concerned with comprehension of the communicative messages of others. Also applied to cells or membrane structures that are affected by messenger substances released by other cells.

Record of Needs/Statement of Needs: A formal document, in the Scottish and English education systems, respectively, that specifies any additional input or support required to best meet the learning needs of an individual child.

Referential Eye Contact: Looking to another person's eyes to perceive their feelings or orientations of interest.

Reflexes: Automatic responses to stimuli that involve little or no consciousness or cognitive activity.

Refrigerator Parenting: The term used by Kanner, during the period when he felt autism to be psychogenic, or environmentally caused. He intended to describe cold, emotionless patterns of behaviour shown by parents, which he felt had led their children to develop autism. Kanner later gave up this explanation.

Reinforcement; Positive and Negative: Stimulation that increases or decreases pleasure and the likelihood that the behaviour causing those experiences will be repeated. Controlled in behavioural methods of therapy (see Lovaas Method).

Reticular Formation/System: The complex and widespread mechanisms of the brain core that regulate the activation or inhibition of processes in other systems of the brain (see Emotional Motor System and Intrinsic Motive Formation).

Rett's Syndrome: A condition, presumed to be genetic, which is found only in females. It is characterised by slow head growth, loss of speech and loss of functional hand use after normal progress in early infancy. Girls with Rett's syndrome suffer progressive muscle wasting and abnormal breathing. Electrical activity of the brain (EEG) is abnormal, and there is frequently late-onset epilepsy.

RNA: Ribose nucleic acid, a type of molecule in cells that serves in the storage and translation of gene information. Messenger RNA transfers information from the gene code (DNA) to the protein-forming system of the cell.

Rubella: The virus of German measles. There is a high incidence of developmental abnormalities in children born to women who contract the virus in the early months of pregnancy.

Schemas: Representations in the mind of objects, of actions that can be performed on objects, and of thoughts about objects and actions. Cognitive images.

Second-Order Representations: Mental images that represent mental processes themselves – thoughts about thoughts.

Secondary Intersubjectivity: The stage of development when an infant, over nine months of age, is motivated to take interest in the orientations and actions of other persons in such a way as to permit cooperation in object recognition and task performance. The beginning of 'person–person–object' awareness, and an essential step in the development of 'acts of meaning' and language.

Self–Other Differentiation: The supposed first requirement of the development of an Ego, or Representation of Self.

Self-Synchrony: Coordination of the rhythms of moving and attending between body parts of a single subject (See Intersynchrony)

Semantic Elements: Parts of language that carry defined meanings referring to objects and events in the world.

Septum: Part of the Limbic System, important in emotions and motivation (see Figure 3)

Serotonin (5-HT): A neurotransmitter, found in high levels in the hypothalamus, midbrain and caudate nucleus.

Sex Chromosome: The two Chromosomes, X and Y, that determine the sex of an individual. Normal females are XX, and normal males are XY.

Shaping: A training procedure that aims to achieve a learned performance by successive approximation.

Shared Focus: The object of Joint Attention between two persons who are seeking Cooperative Awareness.

Somesthetic: Pertaining to the sense of touch; tactile feeling in the body surface.

Speech Act Theory: The theory that language is concerned with the transmission of messages about the intentions of speakers, and the intended effects of messages on listeners.

Stereotypic Behaviour: Repetitive actions lacking curiosity and creativity. (see Athetoid Movements, Automatic Movements).

Sub-Cortical: Parts of the brain beneath the Cerebral Cortex.

Substantia Nigra: A nucleus in the Brain Stem that plays a key role in the regulation of motives and movements.

Sylvian Sulcus: The deep fold of the Cerebral Cortex that separates the Temporal Lobe of each hemisphere from the Parietal and Frontal Lobes (see Figure 2).

Synapses: Junction points between nerve cells at which nerve impulses are transmitted from Axon tips in chemical form across an intercellular gap to the post-synaptic cell surface (see Transmitter)

Tactile: Pertaining to the sense of touch.

TEACCH (Treatment and Education of Autistic and Related Communication-Handicapped Children): A 'whole-life' approach to helping people with autism, developed as a state-wide program in North Carolina by Eric Schopler and his associates. The aim is to maximise self-reliance and autonomy, with the assistance of work-place support services.

Tegmentum: The roof of the Midbrain.

Temporal Lobe: The lobe of the Cerebral Hemisphere against the temple or cheek, at the side of the head (see Figure 2).

Testosterone: The male sex hormone.

Thalamus: A group of nuclei in the diencephalon inside the cerebral hemispheres the cells of which transmit impulses to and from the cerebral cortex. Contains nuclei that convey information from the sensory receptors to the cortex (see Figure 3).

Theory of Mind: A philosophical concept of the understanding one has that another person can experience an individual perspective on states of affairs, and that this consciousness of theirs depends in part on information that is not available to oneself. Belief about beliefs.

Thymus: A gland in the chest important in the regulation of development.

Tourette's Syndrome (Gilles de la Tourette's syndrome): A disease of motivation, motor coordination and self-perception, in which many bizarre involuntary gestures and noises are made and speech becomes automatic and echoic, and may be charged with offensive emotion. The condition has a significant degree of overlap with other neurodevelopmental disorders, such as autism and AD/HD.

Tract: Bundle of parallel nerve fibres.

Transitional Object: Winnicott's term for an object to which an infant becomes attached and which serves as a comforting substitute for the mother when she is absent. A step in the development of a clearly defined Self–Other Differentiation.

Transmitter: A chemical agent that passes between cells in the nervous system, transmitting effects of nerve impulses (see Synapses).

Trimester: A period of three months.

Trisomy; Triplication of Chromosome 21: An abnormal condition in which there are three of the Chromosome 21, which causes Down's syndrome.

Tryptophan: An amino acid in proteins which is essential for optimal growth in infants. It is a precursor to serotonin, one of the main chemical messengers in the brain.

Tuber: A portion of the central vermis of the cerebellum.

Tuberous Sclerosis: Potato-like tissue masses in the brain caused by abnormal cell migration and clustering in development.

Turner's Syndrome: The abnormal condition of females who have only one X Chromosome..

Vagus: The tenth Cranial Nerve.

Ventricle: A fluid-filled cavity in the brain

Ventricular Dilatation: Expansion of the ventricular system, or cavities of the brain, commonly caused by raised pressure of brain fluids (see Hydrocephalus).

Vermis: The midline portion of the cerebellum, between the two cerebellar hemispheres (see Figure 3).

Vestibular Organs: The organs of balance in the Inner Ear.

Virtual Other: Brten's term for the representation in each person of a potential companion in communication.

Visceral: Related to the internal organs: the heart, lungs, digestive organs, etc.

Visuo-Spatial Skills: Mental abilities that represent the arrangements of surfaces and objects in the world seen around the body, and that thereby determine the forms of adaptive actions directed by vision. Intelligence that perceives the geometric organisation of visual stimuli.

Vitality Affects: Dynamic or active expressions of feelings that are changing in time. Ways of expressing feeling, contrasted with Categorical Affects, or named states of emotion, such as 'sadness', 'happiness', 'anger', etc.

William's Syndrome: A condition involving hypocalcaemia (low calcium levels) with characteristic physical and behavioural features, including an enlarged cerebellum, extreme sensitivity to certain noises (hyperacusis), learning disability, spatial problems and relatively good verbal ability.

Working Model: Bowlby's term for the memory image of the mother or other 'attachment object' that develops in the mind of a child.

X chromosome: The larger of the Sex Chromosomes, duplicated in females, and paired with a Y Chromosome in males

Y chromosome: The male Sex Chromosome.

Author index

Bion, W. 200, 212
Bishop, D.V.M. 15, 30, 38, 47, 55, 132
Bleuler, E. 6
Blomquist, H.K. et al. 79
Bohman, M., Bohman, J.L., Bjrck, P.O. and Sjholm, E. 41
Bolton, P., Pickles, A., Harrington, R., Macdonald, H. and Rutter, M. 47
Boucher, J. 47
Brask, B.H. 41
Bråten, S. 59, 60
Brazelton, T.B. and Cramer, B.G. 193
Brazelton, T.B., Koslowski, B. and Main, M. 185
Bremner, G., Slater, A. and Butterworth, G. 93, 98
Bretherton, I. and Bates, E. 101
Brodie, M.J. 146
Brodtkorb, E., Nilsen, G., Smevik, O. and Rinck, P.A. 92
Brown, S.M.K. 107, 173, 177, 189
Brown, W.T. et al. 79, 107
Brown, W.T., Jenkins, E.C., Cohen, I.L., Fisch, G.S., Wolf-Schen, E.G., Gross, A., Waterhouse, L., Fein, D., Mason-Brothers, A., Ritvo, E., Ruttenberg, B.A., Bentley, W. and Castells, S. 79
Bruner, J.S. 9, 35, 93, 100, 101, 103, 107, 124, 126, 195, 217, 221, 233
Bruner, J.S. and Feldman, C. 124
Bruscia, K.E. 174, 182
Bryan, A. 189
Bryson, S.E. et al. 41
Buck, R. 175
Buitelaar, J.K., Engeland, H. van, Ree, J. van, and De Weid, D. 88

Buitelaar, J.K. et al. 88
Bullowa, M. 93
Bunt, L. 174, 182
Burford, B. 35, 163, 184
Busch, F. 129
Bushnell, I.W.R., Sai, F. and Mullin, J.T. 67
Butterworth, G. 100
Butterworth, G. and Grover, L. 100, 101
Campbell, M. 143, 145
Campbell, M., Adams, P., Small, A.M., Tesch, L. McV. and Curren, E.L. 145
Campbell, M., Anderson L.T., Meier, M., Cohen, I.L., Small, A.M., Samit, C. and Sachar, E.J. 146
Campbell, M., Rosenbloom, S., Perry, R., George, A.E., Kricheff, I.I., Anderson, L., Small, A.M. and Jennings, S.J. 83
Capps, L., Sigman, M. and Mundy, P. 25
Capps, L., Yirmiya, N. and Sigman, M. 33, 52
Carr, E.G. 151, 165
Carr, E.G. and Durand, V.M. 151, 154
Carter, C.S., Lederhender, I.I. and Kirkpatrick, B. 71
Changeux, J.P. 77
Charlop, M.H. and Walsh, M.E. 152
Chess, S. 91
Chess, S., Korn, S.J. and Fernandez, P.B. 91
Christie, P., Newson, E., Newson, J. and Preveser, W. 163, 172
Chugani, D.C., Muzik, O., Rothermel, R., Behen, M., Chakraborty, P., Mangner, T., Silva, E.A. da and Chugani, H.T. 80, 145
Chugani, H.T. and Phelps, M.E. 85

Cialdella, P. and Mamelle, N. 41, 46
Cicchetti, D. and Sroufe, L.A. 34
Cieselski, K.T. et al. 57
Clark, P. and Rutter, M. 125
Claustrat, B., Brun, J., David, M., Sassolas, G. and Chazot, G. 146
Clements, J. 151
Coggins, T.E. and Frederickson, R. 123
Cohen, D., Donnellan, A. and Paul, R. 89
Cohen, D.J. and Volkmar, F.R. 14, 19, 215
Cohen, I.L., Brown, W.T., Jenkins, E.C., Krawczun, M.S., French, J.H., Raguthu, S., Wolf-Schein, E.G., Sudhalter, V., Fisch, G. and Wisniewski, K. 90
Cohen, I.L., Campbell, M., Posner, D., Small, A.M., Triebel, D. and Anderson, L.T. 146, 261
Cohn, J.F. and Tronick, E.Z. 117
Comings, D.E. 26, 36
Condon, W.S. 110, 186
Condon, W.S. and Sander, L. 67, 185
Cook, E.H., Rowlett, R., Jaselskis, C. and Leventhal, B.L. 145
Cook, E.H. Jr., Courchesne, R., Lord, C., Cox, N.J., Yan, S., Lincoln, A., Haas, R., Courchesne, E. and Leventhal, B.L. 80, 89, 145
Cook, E.H. Jr. and Leventhal, B.L. 143
Corballis, M. 104
Cottam, J. and Sutton, A. 155
Courchesne, E. 83, 84
Courchesne, E., Hesselink, J.R., Jernigan, T.L. and Yeung-Courchesne, R. 84, 87

Subject Index